D0978906

THE BEST
NEWS
EVER

Other books by H.M.S. Richards, Jr.:

Faith and Prayer (Pacific Press)
Making Marriage Work
New Ways to Tell the Old, Old Story (Pacific Press)
Through the Bible in 55 Minutes (Pacific Press)

To order, call 1-800-765-6955.

Visit us at www.reviewandherald.com for information on other Review and Herald products.

Dear Bev ~

You are one of our all-time dearest friends and we love you much. Keep looking to Jesus — and we'll see you again soon never to part again,

Yours in Him,

Lance + Jeannie

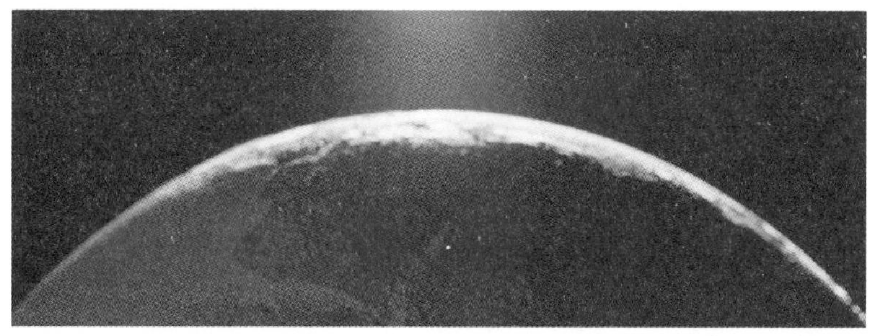

THE BEST NEWS EVER

Daniel R. Guild
H.M.S Richards, Jr.

REVIEW AND HERALD® PUBLISHING ASSOCIATION
HAGERSTOWN, MD 21740

The authors assume full responsibility for the accuracy of all facts and quotations as cited in this book.

This book was
Edited by Gerald Wheeler
Copyedited by Jocelyn Fay and Lori Halvorsen
Designed by Toya Koch
Cover art by Bill Tymeson
Typeset: 11/13 Times

PRINTED IN U.S.A.

05 04 03 02 01 5 4 3 2 1

R&H Cataloging Service
Guild, Daniel R., 1923-
The Best News Ever, by Daniel R. Guild and H.M.S. Richards, Jr.

1. Devotional calendars—Seventh-day Adventists. 2. Devotional literature. 3. Jesus Christ—Devotional works. I. Richards, Harold Marshall Sylvester, 1929-2000.

ISBN 0-8280-1099-4

DEDICATION

To our wives,
Mary Richards and Lillian Guild,
who have stood by us faithfully and participated with us
as we have shared the good news about Jesus through our ministry.

FOREWORD

Longfellow in his *Psalm of Life* wrote:
"Lives of great men all remind us
We can make our lives sublime,
And departing leave behind us
Footprints in the sands of time."

I realize the publishers have already chosen a title for this book. And it is a good one. But if I had opportunity to suggest an alternate one it would be *He's on His Way!* You see, this book features the writings of Harold Richards, Jr., together with my other good friend and colleague Dan Guild. But this title would have been an especially poignant tribute. A perfect salute to my radio friend who fell asleep in Jesus in April 2000.

"He's on His Way!" is the title of the sermon Harold never got to preach. Harold had hoped to preach again, just one more time. Quite frankly, however, he endured a very real time of trouble during his final years. He was only 61 years old but already quite ill when I came to his side in 1991 as colleague and associate on the Voice of Prophecy radio broadcast. We traveled to Brazil together in 1993 on the occasion of our Portuguese broadcast's fiftieth anniversary, where Harold encountered typhoid fever. Twice he landed in the hospital and almost died both times. As soon as he was able to get back on his feet, he was at my side preaching, once to a crowded soccer stadium with nearly 65,000 people present.

Upon returning home, however, a litany of life-threatening diseases and maladies hammered him without mercy. Typhoid was followed by a leaky heart valve, then shingles. Half his body was paralyzed. Next came the dreaded news of Parkinson's Disease. Then kidney failure and amyloid deposits of protein on his kidneys. Even cancer. Finally after encountering complications too great to combat, my friend Harold died of heart failure on April 11, 2000. He had barely reached the young age of "threescore and ten."

We fumble to find appropriate words to express our feelings for giants in the land who walk among us and who mean so much to so many. Harold Richards literally was a giant. Huge hands. Huge heart. Huge love for preaching and making altar calls. And a *passion* for lifting up Jesus.

With health failing, however, Harold spent more and more time at home and in the hospital, less and less in our broadcast studios. During the last few years he was too weak to come in to work at the office, let alone speak on the program or make public appearances. Every time we talked, he spoke of his dream to get back on his feet and preach. Then things began to shut down for him, and we began to suspect time was growing short. He never complained, though. Rather, he still spoke of getting back on the "sawdust trail" and doing evangelism for the Voice of Prophecy.

One day a serendipitous moment occurred—one I shall never forget. Shortly after I assisted in a private anointing service for Harold at the emergency room of Glendale Adventist Medical Center, he hoarsely whispered for me to approach his hospital bed so he could tell me something. He motioned for me to lean in close because he was getting so weak he could barely whisper. But he was eager to tell me something. Something important.

"Lon, you're God's man!" His hand took mine and squeezed it. "God brought you to my side to preach God's Word." His breathing came in short spurts. Heavy and laborious. Still, he spoke with determination.

"I personally prayed for you to come. I chose you to be speaker-director for this radio ministry." We were both weeping now. I sensed this might be Harold's final statement to me. And it was. But his gaze was steady, eyes focused on mine. Riveted on me.

"Listen, Lon. If God raises me up, I want to preach again! I've even got a sermon in mind. Got a title for it, too."

"Really, Harold? What is it?" I asked.

Brightening right up, he spoke out loud, " 'He's on His Way!' That's the title. Not 'He Might Be Coming' or 'He's Coming Soon,' but *'He's on His Way!'* And Lon, I've even got some of the thoughts together. Wanna' hear them?"

"Yes, Harold! Go ahead. Tell me." Tears streamed unashamedly down my cheeks as he held me close.

Harold was well-read and deeply impressed with world headlines. Also he was an expert in astronomy and physics. Every day he read the Los Angeles *Times* and kept up with current events as well as theological issues. Thus he was well aware that on May 5, 2000, all the planets were lining up in what astronomers call a conjunction. We had talked about it several times on previous visits, when he had told me how scientists can tell when something is out there—something big—that something of cosmic import is about to take place.

Harold began, with some difficulty at first, clearly enunciating phrases like: "Far out in space, light years behind the Great Nebula and the Pleiades, there's a great stirring and rush of excitement beyond human description. One can hear the chariots rumble. Thunder rolls like kettle drums, and lightning shakes its fiery white lances. The trumpets sound! *He's on His Way!* Past unnumbered universe systems. Down through the corridor of the Orion. Down, down, down toward a blue planet hanging out there in space. See it there? That lonely one. One that spat on Him and crucified Him. But one that He couldn't forget. *He's on His Way!"*

He laid back in his bed. With a twinkle in his eye he heaved a sigh of satisfaction. "What do you think, Lon?"

"It's your finest hour, Harold. Fantastic!"

"I think I might be getting a little sleepy now," he said.

I leaned in and prayed briefly. "Dear God, please hold Your servant Harold close!" Then I slipped out of the room with my wife, Jeannie. We were hardly in the hallway before we held each other and wept like babies.

Said the prophet: "At eventide it shall be light" (Zech. 14:7). There is always light and joy and life in the dwellings of God's saints. No matter how black or stormy the night, there is always light. Harold and I never spent more than one minute at his hospital bedside focusing on his troubles—and there were plenty of woes to focus on. Whenever I inquired about his pain he preferred to concentrate on Jesus and His soon return. "Lon," he would say, "I can't wait to see my daddy again!"

Harold Richards believed in the soon return of Jesus. It filled him with zest for life and a love for our message to such an extent that it defined him. But it manifested itself in a wonderful sense of humor about the crazy inequities of life. He believed with a passion in the Blessed Hope. In the soon coming of Jesus Christ. The Jesus who, more than anything else in the world, Harold wishes were your friend, too.

As you read this book, remember the life of this godly man, one of God's saints. For 70 years an evening star pushed back the dark world of night with light and joy and radiance. Evening stars are not always with us, but we love it when they are. For now, this evening star has set. But soon in the order of things, it will rise again with the Bright and Morning Star, this time never to fade. Never again to set. To shine for eternity!

Because . . . *He's on His Way!*

E. Lonnie Melashenko
Speaker-director, Voice of Prophecy
Moorpark, California

JANUARY 1

NEW EVERY MORNING

It is of the Lord's mercies that we are not consumed, because his compassions fail not. They are new every morning: great is thy faithfulness. . . . It is good that a man should both hope and quietly wait for the salvation of the Lord.
LAM. 3:22-26.

Diane, a perfectionist and a teacher pleaser, stood before her teacher, crying as if her heart would break. Why? Because she had completely spoiled the paper she was to write her assignment on. "Teacher, may I have a new page?" she wailed. Her compassionate teacher comforted her and gave her a new sheet. A happy smile now lit up Diane's face.

Every day our compassionate Saviour gives us a new page. "His compassions fail not. They are new every morning." So daily we can "both hope and quietly wait for the salvation of the Lord." Although we should constantly be growing in our relationship with Christ and should not fall into sin again and again, nearly every day in our Christian walk we consciously or unconsciously fail in some way. How thankful we can be for the good news that Jesus gives us not only one new page, but a new page and a new opportunity every day.

A woman came to me in deep distress. She felt she had committed a sin so terrible that God could not forgive her. I assured her that her concern itself clearly indicated that she had not committed the unpardonable sin. We read some of the wonderful promises of Scripture and prayed together. The Saviour gave her a new page. She left our home with a new hope and a realization that her salvation rested in the hands of a compassionate and loving Saviour.

Paul reminds us: "If a man is in Christ he becomes a new person altogether" (2 Cor. 5:17, Phillips). As long as a person remains "in Christ"—in close touch with Jesus—this promise is renewed every day. United with Jesus through faith each day of this new year, you can claim the promise that "the past is finished and gone, everything has become fresh and new" (verse 17, Phillips). Each day Jesus will give you a new page.

DRG

THE GOOD NEWS ABOUT JESUS

> ***The eunuch asked Philip, "Tell me, please, who is the prophet talking about, himself or someone else?" Then Philip began with that very passage of Scripture and told him the good news about Jesus.***
> *Acts 8:34, 35, NIV.*

Lillian and I were holding evangelistic meetings in the multiethnic city of San Pedro, California. It was only our second evangelistic series, and we had not yet seen many instant conversions. After only a few meetings, Marie, one of those attending, asked me if I would talk to her husband and explain some of the prophecies I'd been preaching about. After cautioning me that her husband, Reuben, was Jewish and did not believe in Jesus, she agreed to bring him to our home one evening that week.

Together we analyzed the remarkable prophecy in Daniel 9 in which Daniel predicted hundreds of years before Jesus' birth the very year and day He would die on the cross. I drove home the central point of the prophecy: Jesus, the coming Messiah, was "cut off, but not for himself" (Dan. 9:26, NIV, margin). Jesus never did a single thing for which He deserved to die. Yet He was "cut off [died], but not for himself."

"Reuben," I explained, "Jesus died not for Himself, but for your sins and my sins." Instantly that thought took hold of him. "The good news about Jesus" hit home, and there in our living room Reuben surrendered his heart to his Saviour. Through Daniel's prophecy Jesus changed Reuben's life. He was baptized, and we rejoiced with him and Marie.

When the Spirit of God directed Philip to go and sit in the chariot with the Ethiopian eunuch, he found him reading a prophecy from Isaiah. Through Isaiah's prophecy the "good news about Jesus" dying for our sins made an instant impact on the eunuch. It changed his life. As Philip and the eunuch "traveled along the road, they came to some water and the eunuch said, 'Look, here is water. Why shouldn't I be baptized?' " Philip baptized the eunuch on the spot, and he "went on his way rejoicing" (Acts 8:36, 39, NIV). As a result the eunuch carried the gospel to Ethiopia.

DRG

JANUARY 3

THE GOOD NEWS ANNOUNCED

> ***I will put enmity between you [Satan] and the woman [Eve], and between your offspring and hers [Christ]; he [Christ] will crush your head, and you will strike his heel.***
>
> *Gen. 3:15, NIV.*

When we lived in Singapore, our cat sometimes brought home baby cobras crushed between its teeth and deposited them on the walk near our back door. One day the cat came home with a fever and a paralyzed back leg. She hovered between life and death for weeks. When she recovered, she dragged her back leg around the rest of her life. We speculated that a young cobra may have bitten her.

God's sentence on Satan in Genesis 3:15 contains a bright message of hope for the human race. One of Eve's descendants, the "offspring" of the woman, would one day "crush" the "head" of Satan, the serpent. Jesus came to our world and fulfilled God's promise, but in so doing Calvary's cross bruised Christ's "heel." Sin cripples for many reasons.

It hurts God. When Adam and Eve sinned, Christ's death became a certainty. Satan would "strike his heel."

Sin injures other people. As a result of Adam and Eve's sin, one of their sons became a murderer, and the entire human race found itself involved in sin and suffering.

Yes, sin damages us. Adam and Eve and all other sinners since have experienced torturing guilt, sweat and tears, violence and bloodshed, depression and loneliness.

Thus sin cripples and led to the cross. But today's Bible text does not just simply symbolize what sin cost God, the human race, and each of us personally. It also contains the glowing promise of a coming Redeemer who would die to deliver us from sin. The good news of the cross radiates a bright hope for you, me, the world, and the entire universe—for the cross puts in focus a God of love who forgives us and gives us eternal life.

DRG

JESUS BRIDGES THE CHASM OF SIN AND DEATH

For God so loved the world that he gave his one and only Son, that whoever believes in him shall not perish but have eternal life.
John 3:16, NIV.

M*ass-produced, custom-made,* and *one of a kind* are terms that characterize items of increasing value. A one-of-a-kind oil painting by a master artist sells for millions. Jesus is God's "one and only Son," His "only begotten Son" (KJV). *The Amplified Bible* translates "only begotten" as "unique." Jesus is truly unique—He is one of a kind!

What is unique about Jesus? He is the essence of love, God's love distilled in a person. Something I once read about God's love so impressed me that I summarized it in my Bible next to John 3:16: "People can neglect, reject, ignore, beat, wound, and crucify Christ; and His only response is more love. God's bottom line is always red—outgo always exceeds income."

A terrible chasm of sin and death separates us from God (Isa. 59:2, 3). Because our sinfulness and rebellion condemned us to eternal death, His love for us led Christ to come to our world, and "whoever believes in him shall not perish but have eternal life." God did more than look sympathetically across the chasm of sin and death—He bridged the ever-widening gulf. Jesus came to our world to reveal what God is really like, cross the chasm, and restore our relationship with God. He reconnected saved sinners to their God, reestablishing a love relationship between Himself and the people He created.

Jesus is the bridge that takes us from a life of wasted living, over the fearful chasm of sin and death, to eternal happiness and eternal life. It is only when the precipice of sin and death has been bridged, and we walk over into the presence of God, that we can at last attain true satisfaction in life. Jesus laid bare God's aching heart of eternal love, as He grieves over our sorrows and our problems. He wants to satisfy our hidden longings, to heal every bruised and bleeding heart.

During the next two weeks we will look at 14 great truths that set Jesus apart as "unique," because they are not true of any other being in the universe. On these 14 pillars Jesus made a bridge with His own body that takes us from the realm of eternal death to both a new life now and eternal life in the future.

DRG

JANUARY 5

PILLAR 1—JESUS OUR ETERNAL GOD

By [Christ] all things were created: things in heaven and on earth, visible and invisible . . . ; all things were created by him and for him. He is before all things, and in him all things hold together.

Col. 1:16, 17, NIV.

In 1991 my wife and I arrived in St. Petersburg, Russia, one week after the coup that brought Boris Yeltsin into national prominence. We were there to participate in an evangelistic meeting with Bruce Johnston as speaker that resulted in 335 people confessing their faith in Jesus. Most of them had been atheists. Sixty percent of them were university graduates.

One of those baptized in our meetings was a university professor who taught astronomy. After accepting Christ as her Saviour she gave this testimony: "I have searched for a meaning to life in my scientific research, but found nothing to have confidence in. The scientists around me feel the same vacuum. As I looked at the vastness of the universe in my study of astronomy, and the emptiness of my soul, I felt there must be some meaning. Then I received the Bible you gave me and began reading it, and the vacuum in my life was filled. I have accepted Jesus as my Saviour and have found true peace, comfort, and satisfaction in life."

Would Jesus have caught her attention if He were just another person? Probably not. She accepted Jesus as her Saviour because He is the eternally existing One who has the power to forgive our sins and who meets the needs of the human heart.

Jesus not only created everything in the universe, He existed "before all things." In fact, He has always existed. He is "I am," the eternally existing God (John 8:58, NIV). What difference does that make to an atheist, to you, or to me? Innate within every human heart is a longing for God. The Communist countries tried to obliterate God from human existence. But He has remained in the hearts of millions of former Communists and millions of others around the world. Jesus, our eternal God, meets every human need and longing.

DRG

PILLAR 2—JESUS OUR LOVING CREATOR

> *In the beginning the Word already existed. He was with God, and he was God. He was in the beginning with God. He created everything there is. Nothing existed that he did not make. . . . The Word became human and lived here on earth among us. He was full of unfailing love and faithfulness.*
>
> JOHN 1:1-14, NLT.

He spoke, and galaxies whirled into place, stars burned the heavens, and planets began orbiting their suns—words of awesome, unlimited, unleashed power. He spoke again, and the waters and lands were filled with plants and creatures, running, swimming, growing, and multiplying—words of animating, breathing, pulsing life. Again he spoke, and man and woman were formed, thinking, speaking, and loving—words of personal creative glory. Eternal, infinite, unlimited—He was, is, and always will be the Maker and Lord of all that exists.

"And then he came in the flesh to a speck in the universe called planet Earth. The mighty Creator became a part of the creation, limited by time and space and susceptible to aging, sickness and death. But love propelled him, and so he came to rescue and save those who were lost and to give them the gift of eternity. He is the Word; he is Jesus" (*Life Application Study Bible,* p. 1614).

When I first looked at photos of what the Hubble telescope saw, I felt moved with awe and wonder at the vastness of the universe in contrast to our tiny speck of a world. After examining the photographs, astronomers concluded that the universe has at least 125 billion galaxies. We live in the Milky Way Galaxy, which contains 50 to 100 billion stars. Then multiply 125 billion galaxies times at least 50 billion stars! I can't even begin to comprehend the total sum. And wonder of wonders, the Creator of them all "became human and lived here on earth among us."

Our Creator takes a personal interest in each of us—you and me! He knows all about us, even how many hairs we have on our head. Jesus came to save us from sin and suffering and give us eternal life, because He is "full of unfailing love and faithfulness." Do you feel emotionally drained from pressure at work? From too much month left at the end of your money? Jesus cares enough that He wants to help you solve your problems now, but far more important, He wants to give you eternal life.

DRG

PILLAR 3—JESUS OUR DIVINE-HUMAN SAVIOUR

Therefore the Lord Himself will give you a sign: Behold, the virgin shall conceive and bear a Son, and shall call His name Immanuel [God-With-Us, margin].
Isa. 7:14, NKJV.

Many years ago a missionary went to the West Indies to preach to the slaves there. Seven days a week they toiled all day in the fields from sunup to sunset. Dead tired at night, they returned home and dropped onto their sleeping mats. So the missionary could not get near them. He did the only thing he could do to bring them the message of eternal hope—he had himself sold as a slave and toiled in the fields with them so he could tell them the story of God's love. That is what Jesus did. He was born into human life so He could become our Saviour—God revealing Himself in the flesh, so He could communicate His love to us in Christ's life.

The Old Testament records four major predictions of His birth on earth: (1) the promise of His coming made to Adam and Eve at the time of their expulsion from Eden (Gen. 3:15); (2) the promise in today's text declares that He would be born of a virgin; (3) the prediction of the exact year and day of His coming (Dan. 9:25); (4) Micah's promise that Jesus' birthplace would be Bethlehem (Micah 5:2). Such Messianic prophecies gave hope to God's people. It must have been a wonderful night in Bethlehem when the virgin Mary gave birth to Jesus. As the holy Babe rested in the manger, angels announced His birth to shepherds in a field outside Bethlehem (Luke 2:8-16).

I have been to Bethlehem and have seen the fields where some believe the shepherds kept their sheep. There I walked through the area where the glory of God may have suddenly appeared and heavenly voices spoke about the holy Baby Jesus to the ears of those simple shepherds. They were receptive enough to believe and to receive the blessing. Yes, it actually happened. God came to our world and lived among us. What if He hadn't come? How different our world would be! Let us never forget that Christ was born into the human family, making it possible for us to know the fullness of God's love through the life and death of Jesus. How different my life and your life would be if Jesus had not been born!

HMSR

PILLAR 4—JESUS OUR SINLESS LIFE-GIVER

> *Arise, shine, for your light has come, and the glory of the Lord rises upon you. . . . I, the Lord, am your Savior, your Redeemer. . . . The Lord will be your everlasting light.*
>
> *Isa. 60:1-20, NIV*

Several missionaries penetrated the very heart of old China. They arrived at an isolated village where they supposed the gospel had never reached, and asked the people, "Have you ever heard of Jesus Christ?" Describing Jesus to them, they told about His love, sympathy, and kindness, about His unwearied labors for other people, and about how everybody loved Him and how He loved them.

"Oh, yes," the peasants replied, "we've heard of Him. We knew Him well. He lived right here in our village."

"No, he didn't," said the missionary. "He lived far off in another land long ago."

"No, no, He lived here. We can show you His grave. Come with us."

You can imagine how startled the missionaries were when these people in the heart of China were sure they had known Jesus, and that He was now buried in their village. The missionaries followed them to the burial plot. They saw the simple headstone and the name of the missionary who had lived and died among them—a true servant of Christ.

Many have found themselves attracted to Jesus through the wonderful lives of God's children. The true Christian life is the greatest evidence and proof of the Christian faith. We do not win people to Christ when we talk straight and walk crooked. The way we live speaks louder than what we say.

"The Lord will be your everlasting light," and because He is, you can "arise, shine." You reflect the light, because you are plugged in to Him and "the glory," or character, "of the Lord rises upon you."

When Adoniram Judson went on his missionary journeys through the jungle villages of the Karens in northern Burma, the people called him "Jesus Christ's man." Would you like to have that said about you? Wouldn't it be wonderful? It would be for me. Let us seek such an experience today—to be Jesus Christ's person.

HMSR

JANUARY 9

PILLAR 5—JESUS OUR DYING SUBSTITUTE

God made him who had no sin to be sin for us, so that in him we might become the righteousness of God.
2 Cor. 5:21, NIV.

Some time ago I read a moving story in a San Francisco newspaper about a truck driver who gave his life to save the lives of several children. As the man's truck started down a steep San Francisco hill, the brakes failed. Feverishly the driver weaved about through the downhill traffic. At the bottom of the hill he realized that the only way to avoid hitting several children was to swerve into a bank to stop the truck. In doing so, the driver probably knew that he would die. Giving his life to save those of the children, he died in their place.

We admire the truck driver for what he did, but he could not give the children eternal life by dying for them. Able only to allow them a little longer to live, he couldn't even guarantee them happiness during their extra years.

We are all in imminent danger of death—eternal death. But Jesus died so He could substitute the death penalty we are under with the promise of eternal life (Rom. 6:23). Substitution includes even more than eternal life. God made Jesus, the only person who has never sinned, "to be sin for us." Why? "So that in him we might become the righteousness of God." It is a fantastic exchange—our life of sin for Jesus' one of righteousness. He overcame temptation and lived a sinless life with the express objective of passing His sinless life on to us in exchange for our old life of sin.

At the cross "the people stood watching, and the rulers even sneered at him. They said, 'He saved others; let him save himself if he is the Christ' " (Luke 23:35, NIV). The soldiers shouted, "If you are the king of the Jews, save yourself" (verse 37, NIV). One of the two thieves hanging on a cross next to Jesus echoed the same thought: "Aren't you the Christ? Save yourself and us!" (verse 39, NIV). Since Jesus never committed a single sin, why didn't He come down from the cross? Because He could not have saved Himself and saved us, too! Like the truck driver, Jesus made a calculated decision to die in our place. How thankful we should be for Jesus!

DRG

PILLAR 6—JESUS OUR FORGIVING LORD

God demonstrates his own love for us in this: While we were still sinners, Christ died for us.
Rom. 5:8, NIV.

On Father's Day someone stalked Shannon Bigger in Takoma Park, Maryland, tied her to her bed, and raped and ruthlessly murdered her. And she was only 25. Anthony, her assailant, when caught, confessed, and was sentenced to prison for life without parole.

Imagine the agony of Shannon's parents and her sister, who lived 3,000 miles away in Walla Walla, Washington. Her father, Darold Bigger, a religion teacher at Walla Walla College, first reacted with shock and disbelief. He later wrote: "I've always dreaded what I would do if someone hurt my girls. A man of ample temper and dogged determination, I've hoped strong friends would surround me at such a time to prevent me from doing something I would long regret. But those feelings didn't come. There was no clenched-teeth rage at Anthony, Shannon's killer; no seething passion for revenge. This wasn't my choice, mind you. It was a gift! . . .

"My real faith crisis came months later. As Anthony's sentencing approached, a deep unsettledness boiled up in me. No matter how much I wished to be charitable, no matter how many times I reminded myself that hating the sin allows loving the sinner, . . . the knots stayed in my stomach. Seeing him for the first time did not help. Not being able to detect any hint of sorrow or regret hardened me. . . . When he appealed his guilty pleas and wished to have his sentences reduced, trying to get out of what he had confessed to doing, it was too much for me. This journey has shown me how deeply sinful I am. . . . At the core I am an angry, resentful, selfish, unforgiving man! *I am a sinner! I cannot yet love my enemy as my Lord commands me to do!*" (*Ministry,* November 1997). (Bigger's resentment later healed.)

His feeling at the sentencing was a father's normal reaction to a person who had brutally killed his daughter. But it was a marked contrast to Jesus' response to those who inflicted suffering and death on Him. For the angry crowd who demanded His death, for Pilate and the priests who sentenced Jesus, and yes, even for Anthony and sinners like you and me—"While we were still sinners, Christ died for us." Jesus' lack of vengeance and His gracious response to His persecutors is a gift. What matchless love!

DRG

PILLAR 7—JESUS OUR RISEN SAVIOUR

I am the resurrection and the life. He who believes in me will live, even though he dies; and whoever lives and believes in me will never die. Do you believe this?
John 11:25, 26, NIV.

During a visit to Jerusalem we were greatly inspired when we entered the empty garden tomb. It's probably not the actual tomb where Jesus was buried, but to me it was the most inspiring place in old Jerusalem. My last day in Jerusalem I went a third time to the quiet garden near the Damascus Gate. As I meditated there, an old man wandered into the garden.

"Can you tell me what this place is?" the wiry old fellow shouted. Since he was deaf, I explained the best I could.

He disappeared into the empty tomb. A few minutes later he was by my side again. Now speaking in a subdued voice, he said, "So this is the place where our Lord lay! So this is the place where our Lord lay! It does a fellow good to come to a place like this; yes, it does a fellow good!" The man had experienced the meaning of the empty tomb.

We do not serve a dead Saviour in a musty grave, because His tomb is empty! Jesus lives! Our living Saviour declares, "I am the resurrection and the life. He who believes in me will live, even though he dies." Thank God for a living Saviour!

The old man and I walked to a viewing point in the garden and looked across to Gordon's Calvary, a skull-shaped hill where some believe Jesus died on the cross. Seeing it from the quietness of the garden, it seemed to be as hallowed ground.

Being in the presence of these reminders of the cross and the empty tomb was a sobering but exhilarating experience. Jesus died for me—yet He is alive! He "is the resurrection and the life." Christ will call believers from their graves at His coming. and those who are alive when He comes "will never die."

Our living Saviour promised, "I am with you always, to the very end of the age" (Matt. 28:20, NIV). Christ is with you at your work, with your children at play, with your mother on her hospital bed, with your daughter at college. He is as real as if you could feel Him reach His arm around you, squeeze your shoulder, and say, "I love you."

DRG

PILLAR 8—JESUS OUR ASCENDED LORD

You will receive power when the Holy Spirit comes on you; and you will be my witnesses . . . to the ends of the earth. After he said this, he was taken up before their very eyes, and a cloud hid him from their sight.

Acts 1:8, 9, NIV.

The account of the 40 days following Jesus' resurrection reads like a mystery. Two days after His crucifixion Peter and John came to His tomb and found it empty. That same morning as Mary wept in the garden near the empty tomb Jesus spoke to her, then disappeared as suddenly as he had appeared. Later that same day Jesus unexpectedly met two disciples on their way to Emmaus. Again He mysteriously vanished.

That evening the excited but still unbelieving disciples assembled in the upper room to discuss their unexpected encounters with Jesus. Suddenly Jesus stood with them. In spite of the testimony of Mary, Peter, and John they still thought they were seeing a ghost. But He held out His nail-scarred hands and said, "It is I myself! Touch me and see" (Luke 24:39, NIV).

A few days later the disciples had fished all night but caught nothing. A figure appeared and told them to cast their net on the other side of the boat. They did, and pulled in a net loaded with fish. When they reached shore with the boatload of fish, the same person had a fire going and fish frying, ready for them to eat. Then "they knew it was the Lord" (John 21:12, NIV).

Often during the days following His resurrection Jesus "showed himself to" his followers and "gave many convincing proofs that he was alive" (Acts 1:3, NIV). The mystery surrounding the appearances of Jesus convinced the disciples of His constant presence with them, and they began to expect to see Him around almost any corner.

The last time Jesus appeared to them, He promised His continuous presence with them and with us through His Holy Spirit. "You will receive power when the Holy Spirit comes on you; and you will be my witnesses . . . to the ends of the earth. After he said this, he was taken up before their very eyes." What a comfort to know that Jesus is near us, His modern-day disciples, in every activity we engage in today!

DRG

JANUARY 13

PILLAR 9—JESUS OUR SYMPATHETIC INTERCESSOR

We have a great high priest who has passed through the heavens, Jesus, the Son of God. . . . Let us then with confidence draw near to the throne of grace, that we may receive mercy and find grace to help in time of need.

Heb. 4:14-16, RSV.

On April 5, 1963, the Soviet Union officially agreed to the United States' proposal to set up a hot line between Moscow and Washington. The object was to lessen the risk of an accidental outbreak of World War III. It proved to be successful. Before the collapse of the Soviet Union several serious crises arose that made it imperative for the two governments to converse and resolve their problems before they reached the fighting stage.

We are all aware of the mental, spiritual, and physical catastrophes that threaten our personal lives. Often we need to talk directly and instantaneously with Someone who can help save the situation. The book of Hebrews speaks of a "hot line" to heaven, one from our inmost souls to the very heart of God through Jesus our High Priest.

Through prayer we have access to heaven at any time, no matter where we may be—in our homes, at work, on the freeway, or in a plane. Communication is instantaneous, with no need for anyone to unscramble or decode our message, because the Holy Spirit intercedes for us. It is private and easy. We can use our hot line to heaven "with confidence" as we "draw near to the throne of grace." And it is rewarding: "We may receive mercy and find grace to help in time of need."

Billy Graham says that "prayer is the most important spiritual exercise that a Christian can have. If you wish to live a happy, yielded, and victorious Christian life, a daily prayer is absolutely essential." Communication between you and your heavenly Father through Jesus is essential to receiving "help in time of need." If we are to live so that people take knowledge of us that we have been with Jesus, we must be in constant contact with heaven through Jesus, our priestly Intercessor.

Jesus represents us in heaven before His Father, and He is also ministering to us on earth, just as He promised His followers: "Lo, I am with you always, to the close of the age" (Matt. 28:20, RSV). He is with me to guide my every step, and He is with you every moment of every day.

HMSR

PILLAR 10—JESUS OUR EVER-PRESENT SAVIOUR

Lo, I am with you alway, even unto the end of the world.

Matt. 28:20.

The testimony of a close friend who sat with us in our living room deeply moved my wife, Lillian, and me. Because of a blood transfusion contaminated with hepatitis B, the woman's husband suffered liver failure. After various treatments, he finally had a liver transplant. Following surgery, he found himself at death's door. Then miraculously he recovered. But because of the heavy medical expenses, they lost their home. During his absence from work his employer filled his position with someone else. In spite of all this, his wife told us that their faith was stronger than it had ever been because Jesus had sustained them.

She told us a dream she was certain Jesus gave her near the beginning of their two-year ordeal. In it she saw a high mountain, and she and her husband were at the foot of the mountain, he in a wheelchair. Friendly well-known faces surrounded them. Someone instructed her to push her husband up a tortuous path to the top of the mountain. Along the way she met obstacle after obstacle. One was a rough railroad track she had to get the wheelchair over. It seemed impossible. As she shoved the chair, it bounced up and down over the tracks. Just as they reached the other side, a train came whizzing by. They felt the swish of the air as it passed. When they neared the top of the mountain, a solid masonry wall blocked the path. Then, miraculously, a hole opened, and they passed through.

During his lengthy illness, every time they faced a setback that seemed impossible to endure, they reminded each other of the dream and the assurance that Jesus would sustain them.

When David Livingstone returned to England after spending 15 years in Africa, experiencing 27 fevers and being mauled by a lion, he asked the students at Glasgow University, "Shall I tell you what sustained me amidst the toil, and hardship, and loneliness of my exiled life? It was Jesus' promise, 'Lo, I am with you alway, even unto the end.' "

You too may be going through an experience that seems impossible for you to face. Listen as Jesus whispers in your ear, "Lo, I am with you alway, even unto the end of the world." Thank God for a Saviour like that!

DRG

JANUARY 15

AMAZING GRACE

For by grace you have been saved, through faith, and that not of yourselves; it is the gift of God, not of works, lest anyone should boast.
Eph. 2:8, 9, NKJV.

Philip Yancey relates this incident in one of his books: "During a British conference on comparative religions, experts from around the world debated what, if any, belief was unique to the Christian faith. They began eliminating possibilities. Incarnation? Other religions had different versions of gods appearing in human form. Resurrection? Again, other religions had accounts of return from death. The debate went on for some time until C. S. Lewis wandered into the room. 'What's the rumpus about?' he asked, and heard in reply that his colleagues were discussing Christianity's unique contribution among the world religions. Lewis responded, 'Oh, that's easy. It's grace.'

"After some discussion, the conferees had to agree. The notion of God's love coming to us free of charge, no strings attached, seems to go against every instinct of humanity. The Buddhist eightfold path, the Hindu doctrine of karma, the Jewish covenant, and the Muslim code of law—each of these offers a way to earn approval. Only Christianity dares to make God's love unconditional" *(What's So Amazing About Grace?* p. 45).

The amazing quality of God's grace is that He gives us salvation as an absolutely free gift. Nothing we can do will earn or deserve salvation. How then do we receive it? "For by grace you have been saved through faith." And what is faith? A simple definition appears in Hebrews 12:2: "Looking unto Jesus, the author and finisher of our faith" (NKJV). Faith is "looking unto Jesus." It is "my total response to the activity of God in my behalf."

For the past few days we have looked at Jesus' activity in our behalf—at Jesus, the eternal Creator becoming our incarnate Saviour, our sinless Life-giver, dying Substitute, risen and ascended Conqueror, sympathetic Intercessor, coming Redeemer, and eternal King. By faith—simply "looking unto Jesus" and seeing revealed His amazing panorama of grace in our behalf—He becomes our salvation, "the author and finisher of our faith."

DRG

PILLAR 11—JESUS OUR CONSTANT GUIDE

> ***Your hand will guide me, your right hand will hold me fast.***
>
> *Ps. 139:10, NIV.*

In a borrowed pickup with a camper, my wife and I, along with son John and daughter Mary, headed for Mexico. Our destination was Guaymas, which we had heard was a picturesque little town. As we headed south into Mexico we had a large stretch of desert to cross. We were not in the desert long when our borrowed pickup went *chug, chug, chu, ch . . .* Rolling to the side of the road, we stopped. John and I got out and looked under the hood. The plugs sparked. The carburetor was getting fuel. Puzzled, we sat a while and waited, then turned on the key and the car started. To play it safe, we turned around to go for help. But as we headed back, the motor didn't miss a lick. So we reversed direction and continued down into Mexico.

We hadn't gone far when the pickup died again, and we coasted to the side of the road. A Mexican driver stopped to help us, but he could find nothing wrong. We decided to turn around again and get the car fixed. With the motor purring, my daughter Mary said, "Dad, maybe the Lord doesn't want us to go down to Guaymas today. Would you turn around just one more time?" The car immediately died. "Lord, wherever You want us to go we will go, but we'd sure like to stay in Mexico," I prayed.

As we retraced our route back to California we saw a sign pointing left to San Felipe, a town 90 miles away. We made a left turn, and the car ran beautifully all the way. After getting our camp ready for the night, we headed for the little town. It is on the ocean and has large sand dunes. I heard a dune buggy roar onto the main street. The vehicle stopped, and a voice said, "Richards, what are you doing here? Are you preaching these days? Meet my friend; he's an agnostic." I hadn't seen Duke since college days. He was there with a group of dune buggy friends and invited us to their campfire that night.

Our conversation at the campfire turned toward world conditions, God, life, and Jesus. I realized then why the pickup didn't work. We were now where God wanted us. He had fulfilled His promise: "Your hand will guide me, your right hand will hold me fast." Jesus had let me know, "You're still My man. I'm still guiding you, holding you fast."

HMSR

PILLAR 12—JESUS OUR COMING REDEEMER

Let not your heart be troubled; you believe in God, believe also in Me. In My Father's house are many mansions; if it were not so, I would have told you. I go to prepare a place for you. And if I go and prepare a place for you, I will come again and receive you to Myself; that where I am, there you may be also.

John 14:1-3, NKJV.

A confused and bewildered woman, after reading about some present-day developments, said excitedly to her husband, "Why, they will blow the world to bits!"

He calmly replied, "Never mind, dear. We would be better off without it."

Wouldn't we be better off without a world that is full of trouble and stained with lust and cruelty? The news repeatedly reports typhoons, earthquakes, air crashes, train wrecks, floods, suicides. What does it all mean?

Jesus knew of the perplexity that would fill people's hearts in today's chaotic world and in their lives. So He comforted His followers and us by saying, "Let not your heart be troubled." He assures us that He is aware of what we face and promises us: "I will come again and receive you to Myself; that where I am, there you may be also." Jesus is coming back. He is returning soon! And He said that He would, and His Word cannot fail. You can depend on it. The same real Jesus who was born as a babe in Bethlehem, who grew up as a man among the human race, who healed the sick, who died on Calvary, who rose the third day, and who ascended into heaven *will* return (Acts 1:11).

If you are discouraged or afraid because of conditions in the world or in your life, take heart. Jesus' comforting words are for you: "Let not your heart be troubled." Are you concerned about your sick child? Does one of your immediate family or one of your friends have some incurable disease? Is your spouse out of work? Is your family without real satisfaction or security in life? Have you kissed for the last time a loved one who then slipped into the grasp of death? Listen! Jesus promised, "I will come again." Jesus is coming! Life is coming!

HMSR

PILLAR 13—JESUS OUR LIBERATOR

If the Son liberates you [makes you free men], then you are really and unquestionably free.
JOHN 8:36, AMPLIFIED.

"You haven't seen Japan if you haven't seen the cormorant fishing," a friend told us. Because of his enthusiasm, we put a visit to Gifu on our "must" list. Quaint Japanese inns, crowded between shops and houses, overlook the river. With mat floors to sit on, low tables to eat at, down mattresses piled three high on the floor to sleep on, we found ourselves in a strangely fascinating environment. The inn where we stayed had tiny gardens with waterfalls, fishponds, and miniature pagodas tucked into every nook and corner.

Garbed in Japanese dress, we made our way to the dock and took our place on the mat floor of a long slender boat. Expert boaters poled our craft upstream, there to await the cormorant fishing. At dusk the fishing boats came down the river, each with a charcoal burner in front to attract the fish. Fishers standing in the boats held a handful of fishing lines above the water. But instead of hooks at the end of the lines were cormorants, each with a ring fastened around its neck. As the fishing boats headed downstream into a school of fish, the birds dived for the fish. Since the rings around their necks prevented them from swallowing the fish, the cormorants obediently coughed them up into the hands of the fishers. All the cormorant gets is the smell of the fish and the feel of it in its throat. When the fishing is over, the humans reward the bird with a few small fish.

Cormorant fishing is novel and entertaining, but it's also a grim reminder of the devil's deceits. He has millions shackled around their necks. Promising to fill all of our physical and emotional needs and give us freedom, he sets before us a whole banquet that he knows will bring us no lasting satisfaction. Instead we wind up with a ring around our necks that chokes off real happiness, and for all our frenzied efforts he offers us only a pittance of the catch in return.

In striking contrast, Jesus offers to all who link up with Him copious rewards in this existence and in the one to come. We enjoy not only unfettered freedom but fullness of life. "If the Son liberates you, . . . then you are really and unquestionably free." Who else but Jesus can promise us such good news?

DRG

JANUARY 19

PILLAR 14—JESUS OUR ETERNAL KING

> *Then I saw heaven opened, and behold, a white horse. And He who sat on him was called Faithful and True. . . . He was clothed with a robe dipped in blood. . . . And He has on His robe and on His thigh a name written: KING OF KINGS AND LORD OF LORDS.*
> *Rev. 19:11-16, NKJV.*

Crowds of eager watchers filled the streets. The air was tense with excitement. For days the entire city had been making preparations for the sultan of Malaya. Suddenly in one mighty wave a hush swept over the crowd as someone whispered, "Here comes the sultan." As the royal party came into view, a cheer roared from the crowd. Tears streamed down the cheeks of a mother with an infant in her arms. A crumpled old man buried his dark face in a handkerchief. Rapturous emotion surged through the crowd as their sultan approached.

When I witnessed this scene, I thought to myself, *A greater leader is coming. Not the head of state of one of earth's nations, but the King of kings.* Every line of prophecy in the book of Revelation builds to a grand and glorious climax—Christ riding from heaven after His coronation as King of the universe. "He has on His robe and on His thigh a name written: KING OF KINGS AND LORD OF LORDS."

Queen Victoria heard Dean Farrar preach a mighty sermon on the return of Jesus. Greatly moved, she said, "Dean, I would like to live until the Lord's return."

"May I venture to ask why?" he responded quietly.

"Oh, because I would like to lay my crown at His feet."

As Jesus, King of kings, rides forth from heaven to earth, John says, "I heard what sounded like the shout of a vast throng, like the boom of many pounding waves, and like the roar of terrific and mighty peals of thunder, exclaiming, Hallelujah (praise the Lord)! For now the Lord our God the Omnipotent (the All-Ruler) reigns! Let us rejoice and shout for joy [exulting and triumphant]!" (Rev. 19:6, 7, Amplified). A jubilant adoration will sweep over the entire universe when Jesus returns to earth as king.

Do you plan to lay the crown of your life at His feet?

DRG

CHRISTIANITY IS A RELATIONSHIP

And this is the real and eternal life: That they know you, the one and only true God, and Jesus Christ, whom you sent.
JOHN 17:3, MESSAGE.

For the past two weeks we have looked at the 14 pillars on which Jesus built a bridge with His own body. Now, how do we cross that bridge? To experience "real" life now and "eternal life" later, we must "know"—establish a relationship with—"the one and only true God, and Jesus Christ, whom [God] sent." To "know" Jesus is "to become acquainted with Him" in a deep and intimate relationship.

What happens in our present life when we establish such a relationship? "The experimental knowledge of God and of Jesus Christ whom He has sent, transforms man into the image of God. . . . It brings him into communion with the mind of the Infinite, and opens to him the rich treasures of the universe" *(Christ's Object Lessons,* p. 114).

How do we experience eternal life now? "Heaven is a ceaseless approaching to God through Christ. . . . And the more we know of God, the more intense will be our happiness" *(The Desire of Ages,* p. 331).

In his day people considered Phillips Brooks the prince of American preachers and a radiant Christian who possessed the powerful presence of Jesus in his life. A young pastor once wrote and asked him for his secret. He received this answer:

"I am sure you will not think that I dream that I have any secret to tell. I have only the testimony to bear which any friend may fully bear to his friend when he is cordially asked.

"The last years have had a peace and fullness which there did not used to be. I say it in deep reverence and humility. I do not think it is the mere quietness of advancing age. I am sure it is not indifference to anything which I used to care for. I am sure that it is a deeper knowledge and truer love of Christ.

"I cannot tell you how personal this grows to me. He is here. He knows me and I know Him. It is no figure of speech. It is the realist thing in the world. And every day makes it realer. And one wonders with delight what it will grow to as the years go on."

It is an experience that all who seek the personal presence of a living relationship with Christ may have. He is the answer to our every longing, the source of our every need.

DRG

JESUS LOVES US ALL

The woman of Samaria said to Him, "How is it that You, being a Jew, ask a drink from me, a Samaritan woman?" For Jews have no dealings with Samaritans.

John 4:9, NKJV.

Since I grew up in California when there was no visible prejudice against Blacks, my first visit to the South shocked me. I encountered separate restrooms for Whites and Coloreds and two drinking fountains, one labeled White, the other Colored. When I mentioned this to a graciously polite Southern man, his face hardened and his body stiffened.

History has rightfully credited Martin Luther King, Jr., with changing the attitudes of many Americans away from a racist mentality. King stated the goal of nonviolent Black marchers: "To awaken a sense of shame within the oppressor and challenge his false sense of superiority." He added: "The end is reconciliation; the end is redemption; the end is the creation of a beloved community." King's crusade for racial healing through nonviolent confrontations reached its climax on a bridge at Selma, Alabama. There mounted troopers charged a crowd of unarmed Black marchers, cracking heads and beating them to the ground. All the while White onlookers cheered them on. Scenes of the incident on TV shocked even racist Americans.

King's ideal echoed the example of Jesus. At the well outside of Samaria, "the woman of Samaria said to [Jesus], 'How is it that You, being a Jew, ask a drink from me, a Samaritan woman?' For Jews have no dealings with Samaritans" (John 4:9, NKJV). Jesus responded to the woman with kindness. He won her over, and as a result, "many of the Samaritans of that city believed in Him because of the word of the woman" (verse 39, NKJV).

The good news is that Jesus' approach to racial discrimination was a positive example of nonconfrontation. The lesson the disciples of Jesus learned that day must have become especially meaningful to them when, at the close of His ministry, Jesus commanded them to go "and make disciples of *all* nations" (Matt. 28:19, NIV). Have you learned that lesson?

DRG

MAKE THE GOOD NEWS ABOUT JESUS PERSONAL

> ***But He was wounded for our transgressions, He was bruised for our iniquities; the chastisement for our peace was upon Him, and by His stripes we are healed.***
>
> *Isa. 53:5, NKJV.*

A fatal disease struck an ungodly sea captain while he was in midocean. He summoned the ship's doctor. "Captain, you cannot live more than 24 hours," the physician explained. Terrified, the captain wasn't prepared to die. So he sent quickly for the first mate.

"Williams," the captain said, "the doctor declares I can't last more than 24 hours. I must have help! I'm going to die. I want you to get a Bible and read to me and pray with me."

"Captain," the first mate answered, "you've never given me an order in all these years but what I've carried it out to the letter, but I don't have a Bible and I don't know how to pray. But I've seen Willie Platt, the cook's boy, reading a Bible."

"Bring him in quickly."

So Williams went down to the kitchen and said, "Willie, get your Bible and go up to the captain's cabin."

When he arrived, the captain said, "I want you to read something about God having mercy on a sinner like me."

Willie turned to Isaiah 53 and began to read. When he came to the fifth verse, he repeated, "He was wounded for our transgressions, He was bruised for our iniquities; the chastisement for our peace was upon Him, and by His stripes we are healed."

The captain said, "That sounds like what I need. Read it again."

Encouraged, Willie asked, "Would you like me to read it the way my mother used to read it?"

"By all means," the captain answered. So in place of that word "our" Willie put the captain's name.

Slowly and reverently Willie read, "He was wounded for John Clout's transgressions, He was bruised for John Clout's iniquities; the chastisement for John Clout's peace was upon Him, and by His stripes John Clout is healed."

The captain fell back on his pillow and repeated the text again and again, putting his name in it. Finally he received the One who saves to the uttermost.

I want to put my name in that text, don't you?

DRG

JANUARY 23

CHRIST THROUGH ALL THE BIBLE

> ***And beginning at Moses and all the prophets, he expounded unto them in all the scriptures the things concerning himself.***
> *Luke 24:27.*

There is a Man whose entire life story was written more than 500 years before His birth. His story appeared in a book that was in existence before His lifetime. I have the Book. As I was reading it today, I found predicted the name of the Man's birthplace, His family name, and the work He would do. The Book foretells how the Man would minister to the sick. His own nation would despise Him, and one of His best friends would betray Him. The Book predicts the exact price paid to His betrayer and even when He would die. This remarkable volume also predicts that the authorities would bring the Man into court, that He would not hire a defense lawyer, and that He would be condemned to death as a criminal. Yet dying as a criminal and poor in our world's goods, He would make His grave with the rich.

Of course, the Man's name is Jesus, and the Bible reveals His history beforehand. The biblical authors wrote all the prophecies about Jesus from 500 to 1,000 years before His birth. We have cited only a few of the 333 prophecies recorded in the Old Testament. The Old Testament prophets accurately described every detail of Jesus' life, ministry, death, resurrection, and ascension into heaven. And, believe it or not, hundreds of years before He was born Jesus wrote His life story Himself! For it was the "Spirit of Christ" who was in the prophets that caused them to write (1 Peter 1:10, 11). The prophecies and promises in the Old Testament disclose the good news about Jesus, by Jesus. It should give us wonderful confidence in Jesus.

Jesus is the key player in the story of redemption as told in both the Old and New Testaments. History is His story. All history runs to and from Jesus' birth. Let's make Jesus, the focal point of history, also the focal point of our life today.

We have now laid a solid foundation by establishing the great truths about Jesus. From here on, except for holidays, we will trace the good news about Jesus through the Bible.

DRG

THE MASTER DESIGNER

God made two great lights—the greater light to govern the day and the lesser light to govern the night. He also made the stars.

GEN. 1:16, NIV.

In cooperation with the Father and the Holy Spirit, Jesus spoke the sun, moon, and stars into existence. "All things were created by [Jesus], and for him: And he is before all things, and by him all things consist" (Col. 1:16, 17). Jesus is the Master Designer not only of our world but of the entire universe.

Jesus had us in mind when He planned our world. We see His thoughts of us reflected in the minute detail of His creation. Take the moon, for instance. It is a satellite of the earth, the beautiful queen of the evening sky. Attached to the earth by the ties of gravity, the moon revolves around us. The average distance to the moon is about 240,000 miles, so reflected light from the moon comes to us in approximately one and one-third seconds.

The Holy Spirit, writing in Holy Scripture, declared that God brought the moon into existence as "the lesser light to govern the night." The Bible declares that the earth with its atmosphere, its strong gravity pull, its temperature, and its water, is perfectly designed for human existence. The Master Designer "formed [the earth] to be inhabited" (Isa. 45:18). The cold moon, with its lesser gravity, its lack of atmosphere and water, cannot support life, but, as the Bible declares, provides illumination for our world. Astronauts have been on the moon and left their footprints there, but people could not stay there permanently without great expense and effort.

Astronomers have carefully studied the moon, yet their scientific research has discovered nothing that contradicts the Word of God.

Just as Jesus designed our world for life and our enjoyment, He is the Master Designer of each of our lives. He fashioned us with designer genes and gives us every heartbeat. Beyond even that, He has a master plan for your life. So keep in constant contact with Him. God promises a fulfilling life when we do.

HMSR

JANUARY 25

GOD CREATED PEOPLE IN HIS IMAGE

So God created man in his own image, in the image of God he created him; male and female he created them.

GEN. 1:27, NIV.

I don't pretend to know in what form and shape God created beings on the other inhabited worlds throughout the universe. What is clear from Scripture is that God made Adam and Eve as unique beings for a vital purpose. His plan required creating mothers who could have children—in particular one Child, God's "one and only Son" (John 3:16, NIV). Without a mother created in God's image, God's Son could not have been born into our world.

Following the creation of Adam and Eve and their tragic plunge into sin, God promised to send His Son to our world. He would be born of a mother made in God's image (Gen. 3:15). The Creator fashioned both Adam and Eve in His image, and they both revealed His characteristics. Today let's look at the one trait of a mother that exhibits the most vital characteristic of God to us as human beings—He loved us enough to enter our world as a man, a human being, to die in our place.

A touching story of one mother's love for her child showcases the vital characteristic of a God of love demonstrated in a mother. The Nazis took the Rosenberg family—father, mother, grandparents, and sons David and Jacob—to a Nazi death camp. As long as they worked they would live, but when they could no longer work they would be gassed and thrown into an oven. The first to go were the grandparents. The Rosenbergs knew that the next to perish would be their disabled youngest son, David.

When father Rosenberg returned from work one day, he looked in vain in the crowded quarters for his wife and sons. Finally he spotted Jacob, his older son, bent over and crying. When he inquired about his mother and brother, Jacob sobbed out: "When they came to take David, he cried, and Mother said, 'Don't be afraid, David; I'll go with you.' So she went with him into the gas chamber."

Since the mother could not die in her son's place, she perished with him. But Jesus did die in our place, and through Him the Father also died with us. Both the Father and the Son were at the cross. They suffered a living death for us—you and me! That's the good news about the divine mystery revealed at Calvary.

DRG

THE NAMES OF JESUS

> ***And the Lord God formed the man*** **[adam]** ***from the dust of the ground*** **[adamah].**
> *Gen. 2:7, NIV.*

When I was 9 Mrs. Hayes, the pastor's wife, was my Sabbath school teacher. She took a special interest in me, chose me for special tasks, and invited me to their home. Several times when we were alone together she repeated with great earnestness: "Dare to be a Daniel. Dare to stand alone. Dare to have a purpose true. Dare to make it known."

During Israel's exile in Babylon, the Babylonian leadership chose Daniel, my namesake, for three years of special training in the king's palace. He "resolved not to defile himself with the royal food and wine" (Dan. 1:8, NIV). After he became one of the three highest officials in Babylon, an order went out that for 30 days no one was to bow down to any god or person except the king. While everyone else followed the king's order, Daniel continued to pray openly on the roof of his home three times a day. Even though the king could find no way of saving Daniel from the lions' den, the prophet's God protected him from the beasts. Our pastor's wife was challenging me to live up to my namesake, to have a purpose in life and to make it known even if, like Daniel, it meant standing alone.

Throughout the Old Testament a name reflects a person's nature or an outstanding character trait. When God created the first man, He formed him from the ground and called him Adam, a word related to the Hebrew *adamah,* meaning "ground." "Adam named his wife Eve [living], because she would become the mother of all the living" (Gen. 3:20, NIV).

The many names of the Father and of Jesus His Son are also character descriptions. An outstanding example is Isaiah 9:6 in which Isaiah predicts the birth of Jesus, who "will be called Wonderful Counselor, Mighty God, Everlasting Father, Prince of Peace" (NIV). The name Jesus itself means "the Lord saves," His most vital character trait to lost people needing salvation. So extensive are His character traits that Scripture refers to Jesus by more than 200 names. Watch for them and list them as you read your Bible through. Then ask yourself as a Christian, Do I live up to my name? Is Jesus supreme in my life?

DRG

JANUARY 27

THE PROMISED SEED

I will put enmity between you and the woman, and between your seed and her Seed; He shall bruise your head, and you shall bruise His heel.

Gen. 3:15, NKJV.

The entire Bible depicts this promise being fulfilled. It was both a curse on Satan and a promise of deliverance for those who accept Jesus, the Promised Seed. Eve had just made the fatal mistake of listening to the serpent and falling prey to Satan. Foretelling the effects of sin on the descendants of Adam and Eve, God informs Satan of the enmity that will exist between those following him and those faithful to God. The struggle climaxes when one of the woman's descendants, her "Seed," bruises Satan's head—a clear reference to Jesus' victory over Satan at the cross. The NKJV recognizes that Jesus is the Seed by using a capital S.

Genesis 3:15 points to Jesus' threefold role in our salvation. 1. It predicts Christ's incarnation. Notice that the Seed is from a woman, not a man. The biblical world believed that only men had seed. The image is a clear allusion to Jesus' virgin birth. 2. The passage in Genesis reveals Jesus' suffering and His death on the cross. Satan will "bruise" Christ's "heel." 3. Finally, the promise announces Jesus' victory over Satan. Christ "shall bruise [Satan's] head." Satan's scheme to put Jesus to death backfired. The cross dealt a deathblow to Satan's head—his destruction became a certainty. What Jesus did on the cross was a victory for everyone who accepts Him as their Saviour from Satan and sin.

The impact of this first gospel promise came home to me in a unique way. When our youngest daughter was 3, she caught her finger in a folding chair, splintering the bone. As we rushed her to a doctor, her loud cries of pain really tore at our hearts. After the doctor cared for her finger and put her to bed, her sister, who was two years older, sobbed, "Oh, Daddy, I wish it could have been my finger!" When we were crushed by sin and condemned to die eternally, Jesus said, "Oh, Father, I wish it could have been Me." And the Father gave Jesus His wish at the cross. This is the essence of the gospel. Is that good news creating gratefulness in your heart?

DRG

OUR DELIVERER FROM SIN

> ***Enoch walked with God: and he was not; for God took him.***
>
> *Gen. 5:24.*

From the lips of Adam Enoch heard the dark story of humanity's fall and the cheering promise that God would send a deliverer. Enoch lived 65 years and fathered a son. After that he walked with God for 300 years. Before his first son's birth Enoch loved, feared, and obeyed God. But afterward Enoch experienced an even closer relationship with God. His walk with God was not in a trance, but in all the duties of his daily life. His life was one of trust in God, for "without faith it is impossible to please him: for he that cometh to God must believe that he is, and that he is a rewarder of them that diligently seek him" (Heb. 11:6).

Enoch lived during a time of spiritual rebellion and skepticism, but instead of becoming a hermit and shutting himself off entirely from the world, he remained steadfast and served the Lord. As a result of such a life, "by faith Enoch was translated that he should not see death; . . . for before his translation he had this testimony, that he pleased God" (verse 5). His experience is what we need today as we prepare for translation at the Lord's coming.

If you are having a tough time right now and need encouragement, remember Enoch went through similar frustrations. The world had become corrupt, as sin had spread like a deadly leprosy. But through it all Enoch remained faithful to God. If you have become discouraged and feel that perhaps Jesus doesn't hear your prayers, or if you are tempted to even doubt the imminence of Christ's coming to end all trouble in this world, then I want to assure you that your feelings do not change the truth of the promises in God's Word.

What made possible Enoch's translation? His faith in the promise made to Adam and Eve that the Messiah would come as the Man Christ Jesus, deliver people from sin, and assure them of translation and eternal life. God fulfilled that promise to Enoch, and He will fulfill it to you. Jesus is reliable. Put your faith in Him. He will see you through now and give you the confidence you need. Why not thank Him this very moment?

HMSR

THE PROMISE

> *I will make you a great nation. . . . And in you all the families of the earth shall be blessed.*
> *Gen. 12:2, 3, NKJV.*

How do you view your mission as a Christian? "Do you sometimes wish your life could count more for God . . . that you could have more of an impact for good in the lives of those around you? . . . How many lives do you touch each day? Make a mental list. The number might surprise you. Your spouse, your parents, the kids, the boss, the teacher. Don't forget the neighbors, the people in your office, the mailman, the cashier. Select one name and one way God could use you to touch that life with a smile, a kind word, a thoughtful act. Then allow God to use you today . . . for good" (*Daily Walk* [Colorado Springs, Colo.: Walk Thru the Bible Ministries, Inc.], reading for Jan. 17, 1995).

Are you aware that events in the Garden of Eden long ago determined your life? God promised that Adam and Eve's "Seed" would conquer sin and Satan and save the world (Gen. 3:15, NKJV). Two thousand years later God reaffirmed His promise and told Abraham that He would fulfill it through his "seed" (Gen. 15:5). God expanded on the promise by telling Abraham: "I will make you a great nation. . . . And in you all the families of the earth shall be blessed" (Gen. 12:2, 3, NKJV). Then He renewed the promise to Abraham's son Isaac and his grandson Jacob (Gen. 28:13-15).

Think of the anticipation that must have existed during the 2,000 years from Adam to Jacob. People must have wondered, Why doesn't God fulfill His promise? When Jacob went down into Egypt at Joseph's request, people must have questioned the accuracy of God's promise that Abraham's descendants would become a "great nation," since at that time all the combined families of Israel numbered only 70 people (Gen. 46:27). But the "great nation" began to take shape in Egypt. Four hundred years later Israel had grown to a large size (Ex. 12:37).

About 1,500 years later the promise to Abraham came into focus. Jesus, a direct descendent of Abraham, was victorious over Satan through His death and resurrection. Since some of the literal offspring of Abraham rejected Jesus, Christians are "Abraham's seed, and heirs according to the promise" (Gal. 3:29, NKJV). God's mission for you and me, as Christians, is that "in you all the families of the earth shall be blessed."

DRG

JESUS THE PROBLEM SOLVER

> ***Then the Lord said to Abraham, . . . "Is anything too hard for the Lord?"***
>
> *Gen. 18:13, 14, NIV.*

While Abraham sat at the entrance of his tent, pitched near the oak trees of Mamre, "the Lord appeared to Abraham" with two angels (Gen. 18:1, 2, 22; 19:1, NIV). In the spirit of ancient Near Eastern hospitality Abraham invited the three "men" to share a meal. During the conversation the Lord said to Abraham, "I will surely return to you about this time next year, and Sarah your wife will have a son" (Gen. 18:10, NIV). Sarah overheard it and "laughed to herself" (verse 13, NIV). After all, she was 90.

Sarah was not the only skeptic. Sometime before, God had appeared to Abraham and covenanted with him to make a great nation of his offspring through a son born to Sarah (Gen. 17). To Abraham the thought seemed incredulous, and "he laughed and said to himself, 'Will a son be born to a man a hundred years old? Will Sarah bear a child at the age of ninety?' " (verse 17, NIV). So the Lord addressed them both when He said to Abraham, "Why did Sarah laugh and say, 'Will I really have a child, now that I am old?' Is anything too hard for the Lord? I will return to you at the appointed time next year and Sarah will have a son" (Gen. 18:13, 14, NIV).

If the Lord can enable a 100-year-old husband to impregnate his 90-year-old wife, is anything too difficult for God? Was creating the universe too hard for Him? "Ah, Sovereign Lord, you have made the heavens and the earth by your great power and outstretched arm. Nothing is too hard for you" (Jer. 32:17, NIV). Is saving the rich, totally absorbed in their wealth, beyond God's power? When the rich ruler turned down Jesus' offer of salvation, the disciples wondered if any wealthy person could be saved. Jesus responded, "With man this is impossible, but with God all things are possible" (Matt. 19:26, NIV).

Is solving your problems and answering your prayers too hard for the Lord? Whatever your difficulties, desires, or needs, nothing is beyond Jesus! He can transform the shattered lives of straying children and restore disintegrating marriages. God can build on past failures and transform dismal self-images. Always at our side, He is only a prayer away.

DRG

JANUARY 31

THE SILENT LAMB

Abraham took the wood for the burnt offering and placed it on his son Isaac, and he himself carried the fire and the knife. As the two of them went on together, Isaac spoke up and said to his father Abraham, "Father?" "Yes, my son?" Abraham replied. "The fire and wood are here," Isaac said, "but where is the lamb for the burnt offering?"

Gen. 22:6, 7, NIV.

In this, the Bible's first dramatic portrayal of the gospel, Scripture puts the good news about Jesus into human terms. The story touches us deeply, because we see God's love acted out in the lives of real people like ourselves. The story begins when God appeared and told Abraham to take his "only son, Isaac" and "sacrifice him" on Mount Moriah "as a burnt offering" (Gen. 22:2, NIV).

What thoughts would go through your mind if God told you to offer your only child as a sacrifice on Mount McKinley? Since God promised that the Messiah would be born through Isaac, "Abraham reasoned that God could raise the dead" (Heb. 11:19, NIV).

Great relief must have flooded Abraham's mind and heart as, when he stood over the young man with knife in hand, "the angel of the Lord called out to him from heaven, 'Abraham!' . . . Do not lay a hand on the boy. . . . Now I know that you fear God, because you have not withheld from me . . . your only son'" (Gen. 22:11, 12, NIV). The drama then focuses on a stray ram, fulfilling Abraham's conviction that "God himself will provide the lamb for the burnt offering" (verse 8, NIV). In time God provided Himself as the Lamb!

In New Zealand, as we watched a man shearing a sheep, it stood motionless. We couldn't keep back the tears as we thought of our heavenly Father, who gave His "one and only Son," and of Jesus, who was "led like a lamb to the slaughter, and as a sheep before her shearers is silent, so he did not open his mouth" (Isa. 53, 7, NIV). The Father offered His one and only Son, and Jesus gave His life quietly, without protest, for your sins and mine!

DRG

TAKE IT BY THE TAIL

Then the Lord said to Moses, "Reach out your hand and take it by the tail" (and he reached out his hand and caught it, and it became a rod in his hand).

Ex. 4:4, NKJV.

Born a slave, condemned to death before he was born, Moses was saved by a loving mother who dared to disobey the death decree of the cruel king of Egypt. She placed her infant in a tiny boat hidden among the papyrus on the bank of the Nile. A princess discovered and adopted him as her son. She gave him the superb education of a royal prince. He was evidently destined for the throne. But at 40 he ran for his life to the Sinai desert, and he herded sheep for 40 years while Israel endured bondage as Egyptian slaves. Then at 80, when he was way beyond retirement age, God called him to begin 40 years of service that changed all history.

At the burning bush God instructed him to return to Egypt and demand freedom for Israel. Moses didn't refuse, but he was afraid. He suggested to God, "Unless I am able to give the Egyptians and Israel proof by extraordinary works as well as words, they will not believe that You sent me." So the Lord told Moses to cast the rod in his hand to the ground. He did, and it became a serpent. Then the Lord said, "Take it by the tail." When Moses picked it up, "it became a rod" again. The serpent, a threat to his very life, turned into an instrument of deliverance as he faced the mighty Pharaoh.

What gave Moses such courage? "By faith Moses" turned his back on the throne and chose to deliver his people Israel, "esteeming the reproach of Christ greater riches than the treasures in Egypt; for he looked to the reward" (Heb. 11:24-26, NKJV). Moses knew the difficulties he would face, but his faith in the coming Messiah caused him to reach out and take the serpent by the tail. Whatever the opposition, however fierce and threatening the test, by God's grace may we also grasp it by the tail.

HMSR

FEBRUARY 2

PEACE IN YOUR LIFE

The Lord bless you and keep you; the Lord make his face shine upon you and be gracious to you; the Lord turn his face toward you and give you peace.

Num. 6:24-26, NIV.

The three segments of the Aaronic blessing begin with the name Lord. It appears in capital letters in many versions, indicating that it is from the Hebrew word Yahweh. Scholars believe the root of the word Yahweh is "I am," and Jesus is also "I am" (John 8:58). By repeating the blessing the priest is appealing for the Lord to pour out a threefold blessing on all Israel (Num. 6:23). The blessing climaxes by requesting "peace" for each Israelite. Recently I read a letter in *Reflections* (published by the Singapore Voice of Prophecy). It captures the importance of peace to the Christian: "I work in a government school in Kiulu, Sabah, as a teacher. When I finished my university degree in Malaysia, I requested a teaching post in Sabah. Here I fell in love with a beautiful Sabahan girl and married her. I was a Hindu, but my bride was a Seventh-day Adventist. Through her influence and also through studying the Voice of Prophecy lessons I came to know the true God and the Bible. I was eventually baptized into the SDA Church and my life has been so very different. I have peace and joy within my soul since Christ came into my heart."

This newborn Christian speaks of peace of heart accompanied by a joy within. In courtship and marriage the experience of falling in love is exciting and intense at first. Then, when it matures, love becomes mellow and satisfying with a sense of belonging. The peace of heart and joy within that comes from the Lord is also a positive state of well-being. It results from understanding the objective reality that Jesus died for our sins, and the accompanying subjective experience of inviting Jesus to come and live in our hearts (John 16:22, 33). On the objective side Jesus' willing death for our salvation assures us that Jesus saves us from our sins. On the subjective side the peace and joy Jesus gives us when we receive salvation lead to an outpouring of heavenly peace and joy. Are you experiencing such peace and joy in your relationship with Jesus? It's available to you and me—to everyone—today and every day!

DRG

HOPE ONLY IN JESUS

The Lord said to Moses, "Make a snake and put it up on a pole; anyone who is bitten can look at it and live."

Num. 21:8, NIV

I have adapted the following anonymous montage titled "Hope Only in Christ."

Assyria was not saved by its cities.

Egypt was not saved by its wisdom and its prowess.

Israel was not saved by a covenant of works.

Babylon was not saved by its power and authority.

Medo-Persia was not saved by its armies.

Greece was not saved by its art and philosophy.

Rome was not saved by its laws.

France was not saved by liberty, equality, and fraternity.

Japan was not saved by its emperor.

China was not saved by its ancient dynasty.

Russia was not saved by revolution and Communism.

The United States will not be saved by the mighty dollar.

Jesus is the only hope of saving the world. When Israel complained against God and Moses for bringing them into the desert the Lord sent venomous snakes, and people began to die. When they repented, "the Lord said to Moses, 'Make a snake and put it up on a pole; anyone who is bitten can look at it and live.' " Why a snake? Because a snake is a symbol of sin and Jesus became "sin for us" (2 Cor. 5:21, NIV).

And according to Jesus, "just as Moses lifted up the snake in the desert, so the Son of Man must be lifted up, that everyone who believes in him may have eternal life" (John 3:14, 15, NIV). When a person focuses on Jesus, things begin to change. The whole human outlook alters. Our hope is in looking to Him. So for happiness in this life and for eternal life in the next we need only look and live. We can face the crises of our personal lives and of this age with courage if we will only turn to Jesus. In Him you'll find salvation, forgiveness, acceptance, power, and guidance.

HMSR

FEBRUARY 4

THE APPLE OF JESUS' EYE

For the Lord's portion is his people, Jacob his allotted inheritance. In a desert land he found him, in a barren and howling waste. He shielded him and cared for him; he guarded him as the apple of his eye, like an eagle that stirs up its nest and hovers over its young, that spreads its wings to catch them and carries them on its pinions. The Lord alone led him.

DEUT. 32:9-12, NIV.

When I was a small boy my mother went with me to get my immunization shots. It greatly comforted me to have her squeezing my hand when the doctor stuck my arm with the needle. Then when I was 12 my father had his first stroke, and I became the truck driver for the family business. Since I had a restricted license, for several years my father had to sit next to me in the cab of the truck. We became very close. His death devastated me, and I didn't want to be with anyone except my mother, my brothers, and my sisters. None of us talked much. Just being in each other's presence was enough. As we face some difficult time in life we crave having someone close to us. Whether it be a job interview, a tax audit, the need to straighten out a misunderstanding, or some other trauma, we need support.

When Israel miraculously crossed through the Red Sea, then faced hunger, thirst, and armies with giants, God repeatedly assured them, "I am with you." Through it all "they drank from the spiritual rock that accompanied them, and that rock was Christ" (1 Cor. 10:4, NIV). According to today's text, Jesus Christ "shielded" and "cared for" Israel as devotedly as an eagle teaching her eaglets to fly, catching them with her wings when they faltered. Christ "guarded" Israel "as the apple of his eye." The apple, or pupil, of the eye is very sensitive, so a poke in the eye is extremely painful. The pupil of the eye is not only delicate, but essential to our vision, and for that reason we must carefully protect it. Jesus "shielded" Israel from being poked in the eye to protect them from pain and to keep their vision of the Promised Land clear and steady before them.

Jesus promises us, "I am with you always" (Matt. 28:20, NIV). We are "the apple of his eye." Whatever we face, He is with us to protect, shield, guard, and care for us. His wings hover underneath us in every time of need. He leads us to the Promised Land.

DRG

JESUS OUR INTERCESSOR AND FRIEND

Even now my witness is in heaven; my advocate is on high. My intercessor is my friend as my eyes pour out tears to God; on behalf of a man he pleads with God as a man pleads for his friend.
Job 16:19-21, NIV.

I remember when James Earl Ray, the convicted assassin of Martin Luther King, Jr., came before the parole board for the first time. The TV news that evening showed a clip of the hearing with Ray asserting his innocence. It is hard to tell if a person is guilty or innocent, because everyone denies guilt. If it is obvious that the person has committed a crime, the defense attorney often uses a "the devil made me do it" defense. Adam excused his eating of the forbidden fruit by blaming both Eve and God for causing him to do it. Eve tried to shift responsibility to the serpent, the devil. Blaming someone else for our actions is a common defense: "The people I grew up with made me do it." "The abuse by my father made me do it." "My husband battered me, resulting in my being temporarily insane, so he really made me do it."

You may have heard the story about the official visiting a prison. As he went from cell to cell he heard all the prisoners proclaiming their innocence. Finally he came to a prisoner who told the official about his guilt, his tormented conscience, and his sorrow over the crime he was guilty of committing. The official called the warden and directed, "Release this man quickly before he contaminates all these innocent prisoners."

Job's case is unusual in that his protests of innocence were really true. He didn't need an excuse. When he was in despair over being falsely accused, Jesus was his hope. The patriarch exclaimed: "Even now my witness is in heaven; my advocate is on high. My intercessor is my friend as my eyes pour out tears to God; on behalf of a man he pleads with God as a man pleads for his friend." Jesus lived a perfect life in our place, then in our place He died for our sins. How thankful we should be that Jesus our Saviour is our witness, our advocate, our intercessor, and our friend! "He pleads with God" for us "as a man pleads for his friend."

DRG

FEBRUARY 6

HUMANITY'S FOOTPRINTS ON THE MOON

When I consider . . . the moon.

Ps. 8:3.

I was in Hope, British Columbia, with our crusade team. It was almost time for us to go on the platform for the evening meeting. We had been listening to the radio and watching the news on TV. Finally we heard a voice chanting: "You are 'go' for landing. Over. . . . Roger, I understand. Go for landing. . . . 3,000 feet. . . ." Then, after some rapid speech by two different voices, we heard: "One hundred feet, 3½ down, 9 forward . . . 75 feet . . . guys looking good . . . down a half . . . lights on . . . picking up some dust . . . faint shadow, 4 forward, drifting to the right a little . . . down a half, 30 seconds . . . contact lights . . . OK, engine stop . . . engine override off.

"We copy you down, Eagle."

"Houston, Tranquility Base here. The Eagle has landed!"

Those few seconds I can never forget. It couldn't be true, yet it was. Neil Armstrong and Edwin Aldrin, Jr., had landed on the moon. At last a human being had reached the moon—in fact, two of them. And a few hours later they were making tracks in the moon dust—footprints on the moon! "I'm going to step off the LM. . . . That's one small step for a man, one giant leap for mankind," Armstrong exclaimed after his first step on the moon.

For a moment the realization of what they had accomplished made one proud to be a human being. Then the words of Scripture kept pushing into my consciousness—"When I consider . . . the moon." The moon reveals God's glory. It belongs to God. Notice: "When I consider thy heavens, the work of thy fingers, the moon and the stars, which thou hast ordained; What is man, that thou art mindful of him?" (Ps. 8:3, 4). Human beings landed on the moon, but God created the moon. Why should God notice Armstrong and Aldrin landing on the moon?

The Father, Son, and Holy Spirit created our world—and humanity (Gen. 1:1-3, 27). What are human beings in the eyes of an infinite, omnipotent Creator? They are so important to God that He gave His Son, and Jesus willingly came to our world to die to save you and me from sin (John 3:16). "When I consider . . . the moon" that our Creator shaped, I bow in reverent thanksgiving because of what Jesus has done for me.

HMSR

CHRIST'S FOOTPRINTS ON EARTH

For I know that my redeemer liveth, and that he shall stand at the latter day upon the earth.
Job 19:25.

In his elation at the wonderful feat of the three lunar astronauts, President John Kennedy described the days of the *Apollo 11* triumph as the greatest week since Creation. His enthusiasm evidently made him forget a far greater event than the moon walk. The supreme event after the six days of Creation week was not the ascent of a couple men to the moon but the descent of the Lord Jesus Himself from the highest heaven to Bethlehem of Judea. Job referred to this when he declared with confidence: "For I know that my redeemer liveth, and that he shall stand at the latter day upon the earth." Our Redeemer's "stand" on the earth as a man, and His other deeds, including His atoning death on Calvary's cross and His resurrection from the dead on the third day, are the mountain peaks of history. They far overshadow the feat of any human astronaut.

Christ's footprints on this earth are more wonderful than human footprints on the moon. Included in Job's "latter day" are both the first and second coming. As Jan Scott, a columnist of the Toronto *Telegram,* put it immediately following the moon landing: "The biggest space story is still to come." On the day before humanity placed its footprints on the moon this Christian newswoman wrote: "All being well, I shall be watching the touchdown of the first man on the moon, but this promised event does not excite me nearly as much as the anticipation of one day seeing the clouds open to reveal the Lord. . . . Today the newspapers and other communications media are clearing the channels in readiness to tell the world the story by word and picture of the most spectacular event to date. But thousands of viewers who are familiar with Scriptures are priming themselves for Jesus visiting the earth a second time, as an angel declared: 'He shall so come in like manner as ye have seen him go.' "

Miss Scott is right! The biggest space story is still to come. The day will arrive when the redeemed will take the greatest space journey of all time as Jesus transports the redeemed to His heavenly home. We've got to be on that space ship!

HMSR

MORE THAN SATISFIED

> *As for me, I will see Your face in righteousness; I shall be satisfied when I awake in Your likeness.*
> Ps. 17:15, NKJV.

Before my great-grandmother died, these were the words she requested my father to use in preaching her memorial service—"I shall be satisfied when I awake in Your likeness." Then all the scars and warps of sin will be gone. Those who awake in Jesus' presence will feel joy at sharing His likeness.

While we will find many things to complain about in this old world, we can always be satisfied with Jesus—here and hereafter. To the Christian, God promises a wonderful life beginning now. It will still have trouble and heartache, but with Jesus by our side we will have a deep joy within regardless of circumstances. God also assures us of a wonderful future life for the Christian. It will be a life without trouble or sorrow, without tears or heartache. Looking toward that day, the psalmist David said, "I shall be satisfied when I awake in Your likeness."

To wake up someday in Jesus' likeness is no idle dream—it is a solid biblical fact, a divine certainty. Why? Because, just as the psalmist said, "I will see Your face in righteousness." Not my own righteousness, but His righteousness. Because it is His righteousness, we will rise from the dead satisfied that we reflect His righteous likeness. And we will rejoice just as the psalmist did.

Paul clearly reveals the certainty of waking up with a character like that of Jesus. He challenges the Christian to live a changed life now: "For you died [to being a sinner], and your life is hidden with Christ in God," and "when Christ who is our life appears, then you also will appear with Him in glory" (Col. 3:3, 4, NKJV). The resurrection of Jesus makes forever sure the resurrection of all believers in His likeness at His second coming: For "now Christ is risen from the dead, and has become the firstfruits of those who have fallen asleep. . . . For as in Adam all die, even so in Christ all shall be made alive. . . . Christ the firstfruits, afterward those who are Christ's at His coming" (1 Cor. 15:20-23, NKJV).

Like my great-grandmother, I'm satisfied with His likeness for eternity—much more than satisfied. I'm jubilant! Are you?

HMSR

HAPPY IS THE PERSON WHOSE SINS ARE FORGIVEN

Blessed [happy] is he whose transgression is forgiven, whose sin is covered. Blessed [happy] is the man to whom the Lord does not impute iniquity, and in whose spirit there is no guile.
Ps. 32:1, 2, NKJV.

It's after dark. The great city is quiet, with only a few people on the streets. Down a narrow side street someone walks on his way to the night shift. Out of a darkened corner looms the shadow of a man. A scream and a scuffle echo off nearby buildings.

Soon, though, the police catch the mugger, and he whines out excuses for his life of sin. He says he grew up in a broken home, or he has a resentment complex because of what his parents did to him, or he is neurotic. After all, it wasn't his fault.

What a condition we have come to today! Sin has become only another kind of sickness. Why should anyone blame us if we succumb to the germ of evil? In fact, we don't call it sin anymore—it's just maladjustment. So we slip into a morally indolent deck chair and take a rosy view of our comfortable life. Why do we refuse to face up to the real problem? Why can't we say, "Yes, it is my fault, all my fault. I am to blame. I have sinned"?

The terrible turmoil in many hearts today would completely disappear if individuals were only willing to say, "Yes, I am at fault. I need forgiveness. I am willing to follow God's will." The psalmist assures us: "Blessed [happy] is he whose transgression is forgiven, whose sin is covered." Happy is the person who admits to sin and asks Jesus to forgive and cover those sins.

"Blessed [happy] is the man to whom the Lord does not impute iniquity, and in whose spirit there is no guile [deceit]." The person whose heart is without "guile" and therefore admits to sin rather than hiding behind heredity or environment, or claiming "the devil made me do it," is "blessed"—happy! Why? Because when we let Jesus cover our sins with His saving blood, He clears our record of sin. We don't have to feel guilty any longer.

Here is a tremendous opportunity for you and me today! We need only ask to be forgiven, and our happiness is assured.

HMSR

FEBRUARY 10

TASTE AND SEE FOR YOURSELF

> *O taste and see that the Lord is good: blessed [happy] is the man that trusteth in him.*
>
> *Ps. 34:8.*

A hard-hearted, bitter, and dying man in London had long resisted any efforts to lead him to God. Finally he took to his bed for the last time. When one of his friends went to him with a Bible, the man snapped, "So it's you, with that Book again. Take your old Bible away from here. I want nothing to do with it."

Sadly the friend returned to his home and told his wife about what had happened. Having overheard the conversation, their little girl went to her room, took her own new Bible, tucked it under her arm, and started off for the unbeliever's home. After knocking on the door, she heard the old man's voice inviting her in. As she entered the sickroom, he asked, "And what do you want, little girl?"

The child replied, "Well, Daddy said you didn't want his old Bible, so maybe you will take my new one." Then, bursting into tears, she laid her precious Bible on the table by the bed and hastened from the house.

Not long afterward the old man died. When the undertaker removed his body, he found the little girl's Bible under the pillow, together with a piece of paper stained with tears. It contained this verse:

"I've tried in vain a thousand ways
My fears to quell, my hopes to raise;
But what I need, the Bible says,
Is ever, only Jesus.
My soul is night, my heart is steel,
I cannot see, I cannot feel;
For light, for life, I must appeal
In simple faith to Jesus.
He died, He lives, He reigns, He pleads;
There's love in all His words and deeds;
There's all a guilty sinner needs
Forevermore in Jesus.
Though some should sneer, and some should blame,
I'll go with all my guilt and shame:
I'll go to Him because His name,
Above all names, is Jesus."

—James Proctor

—HMSR

"I AM THY SALVATION"

> ***I am thy salvation.***
>
> *Ps. 35:3.*

Satan declared, "I will exalt my throne above the stars [angels] of God. . . . I will be like the most High" (Isa. 14:13, 14). His designs are all self-centered—the big I, the braggadocio I.

In contrast the I AM's of Jesus center on you and me. "I am thy shield" to protect you from the darts of Satan (Gen. 15:1). "I am the God of Bethel" who comes to assure you of My intimate presence with you (Gen. 31:13). "I am thy salvation" from your self-centered nature and your sins that condemned you to death (Ps. 35:3). "I am the rose of Sharon," spreading My fragrance of delicate loveliness to enrich your life (S. of Sol. 2:1).

Moving on to the New Testament, Jesus again presents images of His care and concern for us. "I am the bread of life" who can sustain you not only physically, but eternally and spiritually (John 6:48). "I am the light of the world," giving brightness, hope, and salvation to all who bathe in My healing beams (John 8:12). "I am the door," the only way to My kingdom of wealth and splendor, where you will be content and happy for eternity (John 10:9).

"I am the good shepherd," your protector who is leading you to your heavenly home (verse 11). "I am the resurrection and the life," who will raise you at My second coming from the dead with a vibrant healthy body (John 11:25). "I am the way, the truth, and the life," who looks out for your best interests and assures you of eternal life (John 14:6). "I am the true vine," but you are a branch so closely knit to Me that I dwell in you and sustain you spiritually (John 15:1). "I am . . . the bright and morning star," marking the way to heaven, and your groom who is standing at the gate inviting you to "come" (Rev. 22:16, 17).

Our Saviour understands us because He is the Son of Man, a human being like us, who assures us repeatedly of His presence. "I am with you alway" (Matt. 28:20).

DRG

YOUR LIFE BELONGS TO ME

You shall receive power when the Holy Spirit has come upon you; and you shall be witnesses to Me in Jerusalem, and in all Judea and Samaria, and to the end of the earth.
Acts 1:8, NKJV.

During the Civil War a soldier in the Union army, William Scott, fell asleep while on duty at Chain Bridge. A court-martial tried and sentenced him to death. His mother approached President Lincoln and pleaded for her boy's life. Lincoln went to the guardhouse and found the young soldier. In a tone of sympathy he asked, "William, did you fall asleep? You know what might have happened if the enemy had marched over the bridge and killed hundreds of our boys? Did you get a fair trial? Do you deserve to die?"

With tears running down his cheeks, Scott said, "Yes, Mr. President, I'm guilty and deserve to die."

Then Lincoln, his heart moved with still deeper sympathy, said, "William, I am going to let you go. But remember, your life belongs to me."

Just before Jesus left our world, He reminded those for whom He had just given His life that their sin-cleansed lives belonged to Him. He instructed them, "You shall be witnesses to Me . . . to the end of the earth."

After Lincoln pardoned Scott, the young man went back to his company. Later, at the Battle of Gettysburg, he fell to the ground mortally wounded by enemy fire. He drew a deep breath and said to the comrade who bent over him: "John, when this war is over, they are going to take you soldiers and march you through Washington in a victory march. If you get a chance, I want you to fall out of the ranks, look up Abraham Lincoln, and tell him that William Scott gave his life back to him at Gettysburg."

Our pardon from Jesus cost Him something far greater than it did President Lincoln to pardon Scott—it demanded a life of suffering and a cruel death on Calvary. Jesus is not asking us to die for Him, but to live for Him as witnesses to what He has done in our lives. He wants us to reveal to others not only what our life was without Him, but most of all what it has been since He gave us a new and better life.

HMSR

SUPERMAN OR SUPER GOD?

O Lord, . . . the mighty oceans thunder your praise. You are mightier than all the breakers pounding on the seashores of the world!
Ps. 93:2-4, TLB.

Etched into my mind is the photograph of a very close friend, standing on the seashore, savoring an awe-inspiring sunset and contemplating the wonders of creation. Her experience must have been similar to that of David when he wrote: "O Lord, . . . the mighty oceans thunder your praise."

Later things changed in her life when her teenage son began to drift away from God. Now she stood in the same spot looking out on the waves breaking at her feet. As any parent would, I'm sure she wondered, *Lord, what about Your promise: "I will contend with him that contendeth with thee, and I will save thy children" [Isa. 49:25]? After all, "You are mightier than all the breakers pounding on the seashores of the world!"*

How is it that children coming from a model Christian home rebel and break their parents' hearts? Surely it's not because Satan is stronger than Jesus, for Jesus is "mightier than all the breakers pounding on the seashores of the world." Our Saviour is greater than the billions of atoms in the billions of waves that have pounded on the thousands of miles of seashore since Creation. Jesus is more than man, more than Superman—He is Super God.

Don't stop by just dwelling on His immeasurable greatness. Focus on His love. Jesus is infinitely more interested in the salvation of our children than we are. Think of His inexhaustible ability to attend to detail. He has counted each hair on each of their heads and knows each of them by name. Christ weeps over our children just as He wept over those living in Jerusalem as He walked down the road from the mountain where He could see Golgotha, the place where He would die to save people from sin, including our children. Intimately acquainted with each of them, He constantly seeks to lead them to accept the gift of salvation. Thank Him for watching over them and guiding their footsteps home!

DRG

FEBRUARY 14

LOVE IS A TRIANGLE

"I have loved you, O my people, with an everlasting love; with lovingkindness I have drawn you to me."

JER. 31:3, TLB.

God woos us with the tender message of today's scripture. His love is so strong, so deep, so passionate, that speaking of His greatest love, His church, the Bible says, "He gave his very life to take care of it and be its Savior!" (Eph. 5:23, TLB). "And you husbands, show the same kind of love to your wives as Christ showed to the church when he died for her" (verse 25). Courtships and marriages need that devotion today—of being willing to die for your spouse. And Valentine's Day is a good time to think about it and express it to the one you love!

The Song of Solomon is a poem about a pair of committed lovers and their expressions of their love to each other. "It is a song about love, courtship, and marriage. . . . These poetic verses describe a couple's desire for one another, the struggles they overcome, the tender feelings that love awakens in them, the joy they find in being together" (introduction to the Song of Songs in the *Life Application Study Bible).*

Listen to a young man speaking to his beloved: "O most beautiful woman in all the world . . . How lovely your cheeks are, with your hair falling down upon them! . . . Your lips are like a thread of scarlet. . . . The perfume of your love is more fragrant than all the richest spices" (S. of Sol. 1:8-4:10, TLB).

Now listen to a young woman's response: "Seal me in your heart with permanent betrothal, for love is strong as death. . . . Many waters cannot quench the flame of love, neither can floods drown it. If a man tried to buy it with everything he owned, he couldn't do it" (S. of Sol. 8:6, 7, TLB).

Such love comes about only by experiencing Christ's love for us—which enriches our love for each other. Courtship and marriage are like a triangle—with Jesus, the husband, and the wife represented by its angles. Like the angles in a triangle, the closer a husband and wife each come to Jesus, the closer they will approach each other. God intended courtship and marriage to have Jesus as the third party. With Christ's presence, every home is "a little heaven to go to heaven in" *(Review and Herald,* Apr. 21, 1891). In this sort of home, love grows more and more by being expressed more.

DRG

RICHES AT YOUR FINGERTIPS

Oh, that men would give thanks to the Lord for His goodness, and for His wonderful works to the children of men! For He satisfies the longing soul, and fills the hungry soul with goodness.
Ps. 107:8, 9, NKJV.

Pagodas glimmered in the tropical sunlight. Priests dressed in flaming orange robes held out their begging bowls. Children's chanting voices drifted over the sunbaked courtyard from the temple school. Glass squares hanging from the temple's turned-up eaves tinkled gently. Morose, soul-hungry worshipers with deep lines in their golden-brown perspiring faces stood before food-laden altars at the temple of the Golden Buddha, Bangkok's most valuable Buddha. Five tons of solid gold make the image worth millions of dollars.

Only recently was its value discovered. Hundreds of years ago surrounding kingdoms sent warriors to Thailand to plunder the wealth and carry back the beautiful Thai women to become their wives. To protect their temple treasures the Thais hid them beneath mounds of earth. Then they built brick pagodas over the mounds. They coated the Golden Buddha with plaster, making it appear valueless. Years later, when they moved the image to a new location, they accidentally dropped it, and the plaster cracked away. To their amazement, underneath was solid gold. For years the temple had untold riches at its disposal, but no one had discovered and tapped them.

We all have untapped riches at our fingertips—riches far more valuable than the Golden Buddha, resources that can supply our every need, wealth found only in Jesus. "He satisfies the longing soul, and fills the hungry soul with goodness."

Across the city from the Golden Buddha is the Bangkok Adventist Hospital. During the Week of Prayer I conducted for the nursing students, a young woman from a Buddhist home came to the counseling room. Her face was radiant. From a heart overflowing with joy she said, "I love Jesus. I've found Him as my Saviour, and I have such a peace in my heart." She had broken through the plaster and discovered gold—the unsearchable riches of Jesus. Through establishing a satisfying friendship with Jesus—and enriching it with many daily contacts—that same wealth of spiritual riches is available to you and to me.

DRG

FEBRUARY 16

GOD OF THE MOUNTAINS

> *I lift up my eyes to the hills. From whence does my help come?*
>
> *Ps. 121:1, RSV.*

Fuji-san, the Japanese delight in calling her. The sacred mount seems almost alive and is believed to be the home of the goddess of beauty. From the veranda of the Japanese inn where we were staying we saw Fuji's majestic cone-shaped front reflected in the still waters of Lake Kawaguchi. For years I had wanted to climb Fuji. Now my dream was to become a reality. After eating lunch at a low Japanese-style table, I took a bus to station five, then ascended the steep slope. Climbing over the loose volcanic rock was almost one step forward and two steps back.

That evening, weary from the climb, I sat on the veranda of the inn. The pink tinge of the setting sun set Fuji's cap on fire. As I pondered the faith of millions in this sacred mount, Psalm 121 came to mind. The psalmist may have had mountains sacred to idolaters in mind when he said, "I lift up my eyes to the hills." Then he asked, "From whence does my help come?" It was as if he had said, "Is my help in the gods of a sacred mountain?" No, is the implication of his answer. "My help comes from the Lord, who made heaven and earth" (Ps. 121:2, RSV). Salvation and aid do not come from a mountain—beautiful as it may be—but from the Lord who made the mountains.

My God is mountainlike in that He is awe-inspiring and eternal. But He is much more; He is the living Creator who is able to help us in every time of need. Not for a single moment does He forget us. "He will not let your foot be moved, he who keeps you will not slumber" (verse 3, RSV). God is ever near to protect us in the day of prosperity and in the night of adversity. "The Lord is your keeper; the Lord is your shade on your right hand" (verse 5, RSV). Our Redeemer Lord will protect and sustain us for eternity. "The Lord . . . will keep your life. . . . The Lord will keep your going out and your coming in from this time forth and for evermore" (verses 7, 8, RSV).

If troubles crowd upon you and it seems there is no way through them, or if you are wondering *Where is God? Why is He not keeping me from evil?* then look to Calvary, to Jesus dying there. What was God doing? He and His Son were transforming Satan's evil attack against Him into victory for the universe—for you and me. If Jesus and His Father can do all this, is any trouble you are currently experiencing too hard for God to handle?

DRG

JESUS WATCHES OVER US

The Lord keeps watch over you as you come and go, both now and forever.

Ps. 121:8, NLT.

Bill Harbour, a close friend since college, relates an experience that D. W. Hunter told him happened when the latter was a missionary in India. "Elder Hunter boarded a plane on his way to an important church meeting. It was urgent to be there on time because he had a whole series of other meetings scheduled to follow on his itinerary. Just before the flight was about to begin he was tapped on the shoulder by a hostess and was told that he would have to get off. A maharajah of great importance needed to be on that flight, and he had a higher priority than Hunter. There was no choice in the matter, so very reluctantly he gathered his bags and returned to the airport waiting room.

" 'O Lord,' he cried out as he paced the floor. 'How could You do this to me? I am Your servant, and I am giving my life to Your cause, and if I don't get to that council on time the results for Your work could be disastrous.'

"After a time of fuming and waiting he was approached by an Indian gentleman who appeared to be very wealthy and was heading for the same destination. The man said, 'Why don't you ride with me? I have my own plane. There is plenty of room and it won't cost you a penny.' So in a little while they were off, but this time Hunter was seated on this big plane in the midst of luxury and opulence, and the trip was free of charge.

"When they were about to land Elder Hunter noticed off to the side of the runway a big roaring fire and billows of black smoke. When they landed he learned that it was the plane he had been scheduled to be on. The plane had crashed, and all on board had been lost" (*The Last Amen,* pp. 8, 9).

Have you ever experienced a similar disappointment? Often we see only confusion, disappointment, and frustration. At such times we find ourselves tempted to wonder *Does God really care about me? If so, why did He allow this to happen to me?* Weeks, months, even years may pass without our understanding why circumstances led us in a certain direction. We may, in fact, never discover the reason for some great disappointment. But through it all, this comforting message of assurance is ours: "The Lord keeps watch over you as you come and go, both now and forever."

DRG

FEBRUARY 18

JESUS OUR SUBSTITUTE

> *All of us have strayed away like sheep. We have left God's paths to follow our own. Yet the Lord laid on him the guilt and sins of us all.*
>
> *Isa. 53:6, NLT.*

Abraham Lincoln was legendary for his honesty, but that is not the thing that impresses me most. Rather, it was his compassion. An elderly man whose son had been convicted of gross crimes came to plead with Lincoln for leniency. Since the boy was the man's only son, Lincoln was sympathetic. However, he had just received a telegram from a military officer named Butler: "Mr. President, I beg you not to interfere with the court-martials of this army. You will destroy all discipline in the army." Lincoln handed the old man the telegram, then watched the disappointment in his face as he read it. Lincoln suddenly blurted out: "Butler or no Butler, here goes!" He wrote out an order and handed it to the father: "Job Smith is not to be shot until further orders from me. Abraham Lincoln."

"Why," the father said, "I thought it was going to be a pardon. You may order him to be shot next week."

"My old friend," said Lincoln, "evidently you do not understand my character. If your son is never shot until an order comes from me, he will live to be as old as Methuselah."

On at least one occasion a soldier who had no family came to Lincoln and requested that he be able to die in the place of another soldier with several children. Lincoln allowed him to substitute himself for the other man. In Stroudsburg, Pennsylvania, on the headstone of a Civil War soldier appear the words: "Abraham Lincoln's substitute." With thousands falling in Lincoln's place on the battlefield, he chose to honor one soldier and make him his substitute, as a symbol of all the soldiers dying so that others might live.

We can rejoice that even though "we have left God's paths to follow our own . . . the Lord laid on [Jesus] the guilt and sins of us all." Jesus died as our substitute. "It was our weaknesses he carried; it was our sorrows that weighted him down. . . . He was wounded and crushed for our sins. He was beaten that we might have peace. He was whipped, and we were healed!" (Isa. 53:4, 5, NLT). Thank You, Jesus, for being my substitute!

DRG

JESUS' CONSTANT PRESENCE

> *Those who trust in the Lord are like Mount Zion, which cannot be moved, but abides for ever. As the mountains are round about Jerusalem, so the Lord is round about his people, from this time forth and for evermore.*
>
> Ps. 125:1, 2, RSV.

As we stood on Mount Zion in Jerusalem, our guide took out his pocket Bible and read aloud: "Those who trust in the Lord are like Mount Zion, which cannot be moved, but abides for ever." It was a wonderful assurance! Those who trust the Lord can face life with the stability and constancy of Mount Zion, the very hill that we were on.

Our guide then pointed out the higher ridges surrounding Mount Zion. To the south rose the Mount of Evil Counsel and to the east the Mount of Offense. To the northeast loomed the Mount of Olives, from which Christ had looked out over Jerusalem—the city that was rejecting Him—and wept. To the north lay Mount Moriah, where for more than 1,000 years God's people offered sacrifices that pointed to Jesus' death for us on the cross. And to the northwest was Calvary, where Jesus gave His life for the sins of the world—for your sins and my sins. After I viewed the hills that surrounded us, my heart filled with inspiration as our guide read: "As the mountains are round about Jerusalem, so the Lord is round about his people, from this time forth and for evermore."

Today mountains of assurance surround the Christian. Just as surely "as the mountains are round about Jerusalem," Jesus "is round about his people." We have full assurance in Him. We can place our full confidence in Christ. As surely as the mountains silently encircle Jerusalem, the Lord Jesus is still present, silently watching over us every moment of our lives. He sees every tear that falls and is interested in every tiny happening in our lives. The weeping Christ of the Mount of Olives is ever present with us. He promises to be with us "from this time forth and for evermore." Seek Him with all your heart, and He will become as real to you as the mountains around Jerusalem.

DRG

FEBRUARY 20

HAPPINESS PLUS!

Happy is he that hath the God of Jacob for his help, whose hope is in Jehovah his God.
Ps. 146:5, ASV.

Fanny Crosby became blind when she was very young. Blindness is one of life's greatest physical handicaps; yet Crosby has been an encouragement and a joy to many through her wonderful hymns and her witness for Christ. She has pointed the way to Jesus to many confused and lost people. "I am the happiest soul living," she once exulted. "If I had not been deprived of my sight, I would never have received so good an education, nor cultivated so fine a memory, nor have been able to do good to so many people."

What is true happiness, anyway? Is it having a healthy bank account or a new car or a new home or good health or lots of friends or social prestige or a full stomach? If happiness means the absence of pain, disappointment, and trouble, we cannot possibly be happy from the moment we enter life until our sunset years.

I believe Henry Ward Beecher gave a good definition of happiness: "The strength and the happiness of a man consists in finding out the way in which God is going, and going in that way too." Beecher's definition of happiness is similar to the psalmist's: "Happy is he that hath the God of Jacob for his help, whose hope is in Jehovah his God."

Jesus is uniquely qualified to meet our needs. He has been tested and tried. As A. B. Bruce said, "I am far within the mark when I say that all the armies that ever marched, and all the navies that were ever built, and all the parliaments that ever sat, and all the kings that ever reigned, put together, have not affected the life of man upon this earth so powerfully as has this One Solitary Life."

Many of us face deep disappointments in life. When the strong winds of strife blow through our lives, life may seem hopeless, with no possibility of happiness. If you feel that way just now, be of good courage—I have some good news for you. The words of comfort Jesus gave to His disciples on the Sea of Galilee when they trembled with fear are His message to you as you face this day: "Take courage! It is I. Don't be afraid" (Mark 6:50, NIV).

HMSR

WRAPPED IN CHRIST'S BANNER OF LOVE

He brought me to the banqueting house, and his banner over me was love.
S. of Sol. 2:4.

More than a century ago an Englishman was living in Cuba. He had been in America for a while and had become a naturalized American citizen. After he had been in Cuba for some time, civil war broke out there in 1867. The local authorities arrested him as a spy, tried him, and found him guilty. An order went out for his execution. The trial had been conducted in the Spanish language, and the man did not know what was going on. Finally, when he understood that he had been found guilty and would be shot, he sent for both the American and English consuls. He told them the whole story, stressing his innocence, and claimed protection as a citizen of another country.

The American and English consuls examined his case and found that he was indeed telling the truth. They went to the Cuban general and said, "This man whom you have condemned to death is an innocent man. He is not guilty." But the general said, "He has been tried by our law and found guilty. Therefore, he must die." Modern rapid communication did not exist yet, so these men could not consult with their respective governments.

The morning came for the execution. Soldiers dug a grave and rolled in a coffin on a cart for the man. They placed the condemned man upon it and put a black cap on his head and pulled it down over his face. As the soldiers awaited the order to fire, the American and English consuls rode up. The English consul sprang out of the carriage and took the Union Jack, the British flag, and wrapped it around the man. The American consul did the same with the Star Spangled Banner. Then he turned and challenged the Cuban officers. "Fire upon these flags, if you dare!" They could not take the risk. The flags represented two great governments, saving the man's life.

We are all guilty and have all been condemned to death. Each of us stands before the firing squad; but Jesus has already died our death. His blood covers our lives. He died because of His great love for us—a love that we cannot understand, a love that surpasses any human feelings or understanding. "His banner over" us is "love." Thank You, Jesus!

HMSR

FEBRUARY 22

ASK IN JESUS' NAME—THEN REJOICE!

> *Most assuredly, I say to you, whatever you ask the Father in My name He will give you. . . . Ask, and you will receive, that your joy may be full.*
>
> JOHN 16:23, 24, NKJV.

During the winter of 1777-1778 General Washington's army camped at Valley Forge. His men were barefoot and in rags, with hardly enough food to survive. Washington faced not only the complaints of his men throughout that long winter of semistarvation, but the antagonism and sometimes the outright disloyalty of his generals. Desertions increased, and the public wanted an easy victory. Congress had fled in panic from Philadelphia and had gone into hiding in central Pennsylvania.

One person, and one person alone, held the government, the army, and the people to their task: George Washington, a man who believed in prayer. The eloquent statesman William Gladstone, of Britain, said, "George Washington is the noblest figure that ever stood in the forefront of a nation's life."

Where did the Father of His Country obtain his steadfastness of purpose and courage? He himself declared that it was the God of the universe who sustained and strengthened him in many a trying hour. After winning an overwhelming victory, General Washington turned his commission as commander in chief of the armed forces back to Congress, which assembled to receive it. In the closing words of his address he said: "I consider it an indispensable duty to close this last solemn act of my official life by commending the interests of our dearest country to the protection of Almighty God; and those who have the superintendence of them, to His holy keeping."

No wonder Washington met with success, even under the most trying circumstances, since Jesus promised, "Whatever you ask the Father in My name He will give you."

For Washington, true prayer was communion with God, speaking with Him as one would with a friend. When we love someone, we want to talk and associate with that person, not just to get something from them, but to enrich our own life. We like to associate with others for the simple reason that we love each other. Love is based on giving, not receiving. Jesus encourages you to ask in prayer, "that your joy may be full."

HMSR

A NAIL-PIERCED HAND IS KNOCKING

I slept but my heart was awake. Listen! My lover is knocking: "Open to me, my sister, my darling, my dove, my flawless one. My head is drenched with dew, my hair with the dampness of the night."

S. of Sol. 5:2, NIV.

Many see the prospective bride here as the church and Jesus the groom. Because of His love for the church, He stands outside the bride's home "knocking" because He wants to enter. A parallel passage in Revelation 3:20 pictures Jesus knocking at the door of the Laodicean church. He promises to come into the hearts of all who will open the door.

The knocking hand is a nail-pierced one. The magnetism of Jesus' drawing power is Calvary. There sin pierced His hands so that He could destroy the devil and deliver us from the bondage of fear and death (Heb. 2:14, 15). The nailprints account for Jesus' amazing triumph over Satan, sin, suffering, and even death itself. It is the source of His strength (Hab. 3:4).

After knocking, standing, waiting, hoping, listening—finally Jesus calls to His bride (S. of Sol. 5:2). But His sleeping saints in the Laodicean church do not respond. Then He makes one final attempt to unlatch the door. In response His bride soliloquizes, "My lover thrust his hand through the latch-opening; my heart began to pound for him" (verse 4, NIV). But the bride is slow to let Him enter. Finally she rouses herself and opens the door to Jesus, only to find that her lover has gone (verse 6). Then follows the cry of utter despair at being too late: "I looked for him but did not find him. I called him but he did not answer" (verse 6, NIV).

With nail-pierced hands Jesus now stands knocking at the door of every Laodicean heart. Soon the judgment hour will close and it will be forever too late for salvation—too late to open the door and let Jesus in. The whole universe looks on in breathless anxiety, wondering, asking us: Have you opened the door of your Laodicean heart to let Jesus in? Are you in the service of your King? Is your union with Him strong and steadfast?

It's folly for us to reject Jesus' offer to enter our hearts and live in us, for He is mighty to save.

DRG

FEBRUARY 24

WALKING AND TALKING WITH JESUS

How gracious he will be when you cry for help! As soon as he hears, he will answer you.

Isa. 30:19, NIV.

The late Dr. Alexis Carrel wrote much on the subject of prayer and healing. An unpublished manuscript on prayer found after his death contained this statement: "A doctor who sees a patient give himself to prayer can indeed rejoice. The calm engendered by prayer is a powerful aid to healing. It is by prayer that man reaches God, and that God enters into him. Prayer appears indispensable to our highest development." Yes, prayer certainly does bring healing and power into our lives. Scripture promises: "How gracious [the Lord] will be when you cry for help! As soon as he hears, he will answer you."

Jesus invites the weary and burdened: "Come to me, . . . and I will give you rest" (Matt. 11:28, NIV). That promise surely includes all of us. Who is not at one time or another weary and burdened? Jesus wants us to pause in His presence. Too often we rush through our prayers when we need to spend time walking and talking with Him.

Listen to this testimony by Horace Bushnell, a master preacher who believed in prayer: "I fell into the habit of talking with God on every occasion. I talk myself asleep at night, and open the morning talking with Him."

The first enemy of prayer is time—the lack of time, that is. Have you ever tried to find time for prayer and then had so many things overwhelm you that you just gave up? You know, like getting the children ready for school and your spouse off to work, then rushing off to a special appointment. Hurry! That is the greatest enemy of prayer today.

Other enemies of prayer include worry, pessimism, doubt, and fear. They can ruin our prayer life, but the most effective antidote we have for them is to pray—just talking to our God and Saviour, Jesus Christ, and cultivating His presence. The prayer habit doesn't grow by itself. Persons of prayer power do not become such in a moment.

If today you find yourself weary and burdened, come to Jesus. He will give you rest. It may seem incredibly fantastic, but it is also wonderfully real.

HMSR

WHEN JESUS SPEAKS, LISTEN!

Your ears will hear a voice behind you, saying, "This is the way; walk in it."
Isa. 30:21, NIV.

Matilda Miller, my wife's mother,* lived on a homestead next door to her brother. She was a schoolteacher and took her brother's children to school.

One morning she dashed across the field to her brother's place to get the children and head for school. She had gotten a late start for the day, and her mind was so absorbed with her class plans that she paid little attention to the path as she hurried along.

Suddenly what seemed like an almost audible voice commanded, "Stop!" Startled at the suddenness of such an order, she paused dead in her tracks. As she did she looked down at the path not three feet ahead. There coiled up, ready to strike, was a big diamondback rattlesnake.

Whose voice was it that stopped her in the middle of the South Dakota prairie? Without any doubt in her mind she knew that God had spoken to her that day, protecting her from possible death from the fangs of that poisonous snake. Matilda was a beneficiary of the promise "Your ears will hear a voice behind you, saying, 'This is the way; walk in it.' "

Sometimes Jesus intervenes in human affairs as He did for Matilda Miller. Other times He does not. When He steps into the realm of time and space He can abruptly change the course of human events. Perhaps He may even speak in an audible voice. More often He gets His message through to us by powerful impressions on the mind. Always He guides and protects us in the way He sees is best.

However He leads, we know we can trust Him to do what is best for us at any time and in any circumstance. "And we know that God causes everything to work together for the good of those who love God and are called according to his purpose for them" (Rom. 8:28, NLT). We can put our full trust in Jesus.

---

*Adapted from a story told by Bob Edwards.

DRG

FEBRUARY 26

PERFECT PEACE—1

> ***Thou wilt keep him in perfect peace, whose mind is stayed on thee: because he trusteth in thee.***
>
> *Isa. 26:3.*

During the German blitz against London during World War II, someone asked an elderly woman how she kept so calm from day to day. Her answer: "Every night I say my prayers, and when I begin to worry about what Hitler is going to do, I remember how the parson said that Jesus is watching. So then I go to sleep. After all, there is no use for two of us to lie awake."

When we place our trust in Jesus, it enables Him to solve our personal problems. He promises to give us trust, confidence, and the ability to face our problems. Before He ascended into heaven He told His disciples that we can have peace in our hearts: "Peace I leave with you, my peace I give unto you. . . . Let not your heart be troubled, neither let it be afraid" (John 14:27).

You can have this peace. One of the greatest blessings of being a Christian is the sense of trust and assurance that fills the life. Those who have such a blessed experience can say with the prophet: "God is my salvation; I will trust, and not be afraid" (Isa. 12:2).

Perhaps you are asking, How can this be my experience? The Bible tells us: "Thou wilt keep him in perfect peace, whose mind is stayed on thee: because he trusteth in thee." The New International Version translates this passage: "You will keep in perfect peace him whose mind is steadfast."

Our mind—our thinking—must focus on Jesus. We are to be "steadfast" in trusting Him. Remember, Jesus is your best friend. An empathetic listener, He wants to share your problems and your joys.

HMSR

PERFECT PEACE—2

> ***He will keep in perfect peace all those who trust in him, whose thoughts turn often to the Lord!***
> *Isa. 26:3, TLB.*

During Christ's ministry on earth He often visited the home of Mary and Martha. It seems that Mary spent much time talking with Jesus about her needs, and so she was at peace, whereas Martha became too busy with her duties. Jesus said to Martha: "You are worried and troubled about many things. But one thing is needed, and Mary has chosen that good part" (Luke 10:41, 42, NKJV). You see, Martha needed to spend more time with Jesus.

Yesterday we discovered that keeping our mind on Jesus is the answer to finding perfect peace in our lives. Today and tomorrow we will look at a fourfold prescription for focusing our mind on the Lord throughout each day.

Point one: At the beginning of each day give yourself to Jesus completely. "Consecrate yourself to God in the morning; make this your very first work. Let your prayer be, 'Take me, O Lord, as wholly Thine. I lay all my plans at Thy feet. Use me today in Thy service. Abide with me, and let all my work be wrought in Thee.' This is a daily matter. Each morning consecrate yourself to God for that day. Surrender all your plans to Him, to be carried out or given up as His providence shall indicate. Thus day by day you may be giving your life into the hands of God, and thus your life will be molded more and more after the life of Christ" (*Steps to Christ,* p. 70).

Point two: Keep in contact with Christ throughout the day. As you let Him dwell in your mind, it will preserve peace in your heart.

A friend of mine once told me how he always remained aware of Christ: "It might sound strange, Harold, but as I practice the presence of Christ, I realize each day how the power of Christ keeps me. When I open the door of my car to go somewhere, I always invite Christ to enter with me. So all through the day I am aware of His presence." Does that sound strange to you? It doesn't to me.

HMSR

PERFECT PEACE—3

> *You will keep in perfect peace him whose mind is steadfast, because he trusts in you.*
>
> ISA. 26:3, NIV.

Today we will continue to explore a fourfold prescription for letting Jesus maintain perfect peace in our lives.

Point three: When you pray, open your heart to Jesus, talk to Him just as you would to your best friend. After all, He is your best friend. He wants to share every aspect of your life with you, more than any human being could ever do.

Now, the fourth point: God's Word must be your daily guide. It is not enough to read it only casually. You must study the Bible as God's personal voice speaking to you.

A little girl took part in a special Sabbath school program. As she recited the books of the Bible she had difficulty pronouncing "Revelation." She said, "First, Second, and Third John, Jude, Revolution." You may smile at this, but listen! That is exactly what takes place in our life when we study the revelation of Jesus Christ through His Word. It changes our life completely. Fear and perplexity leave, "and the peace of God, which surpasses all understanding" comes in (Phil. 4:7, NKJV).

A ship started to head for port, but the channel was extremely treacherous. The captain anxiously peered from side to side. It was evident from his mannerisms that he did not want any interruptions, for it was a heavy responsibility. A few minutes later, however, the captain was laughing and chatting with the passengers on deck and appeared not to have a care in the world. All anxiety had vanished, although the ship was still passing through the dangerous channel. What was it that had brought this sudden change? The ship had stopped and a small boat had pulled alongside. Several men had climbed the rope ladder and come aboard. One of them was the pilot, who went immediately to the bridge and took over. The ship was now his responsibility. The pilot knew every rock and danger point in the channel. He had negotiated the treacherous passageway many times before. When Christ, our Pilot, has control of our lives, we can cast away all fear, for we will experience perfect peace.

HMSR

THE SMALL THINGS AND THE BIG THINGS

Lift your eyes and look to the heavens: Who created all these? He who brings out the starry host one by one, and calls them each by name.
Isa. 40:26, NIV.

When I was a boy I loved to plant a vegetable garden. I especially liked to watch beans grow. Plant a bean, and in a short time you see a curved stem poking through the ground. Then it sheds the two halves of the bean as two leaves become a large plant that blooms and produces beans. A small thing becomes a productive big thing.

A microscopic sperm unites with a tiny egg and soon a fetus forms that grows into a smiling, cooing baby that matures into a seven-foot-tall basketball player or a teacher or a physician or an evangelist. Two tiny things unite and become a big thing. When we consider the miracle of growth, we can't help wondering: "Who designed a basketball player? Who designed the brain of an Einstein? Who turns microscopic things into giants physically and intellectually?" God answers when He says to His Son and the Holy Spirit: "Let us make man in our image" (Gen. 1:26, NIV).

The seed of a giant California sequoia tree is one of the smallest, but it transforms into a giant tree over thousands of years. Now, contrast the tiny seed of a giant sequoia, and even the sequoia itself, to the vastness of the heavens. Looking into the sky at night, we can see about 3,000 stars. Many of them are giant suns with planets revolving around them. That soft white cloud across the sky behind the stars is the Milky Way, a giant galaxy of which we are a part. It consists of hundreds of thousands of solar systems. And beyond are untold billions of galaxies. The gigantic size of the universe is beyond our comprehension. And yet Isaiah tells us: "He who brings out the starry host one by one . . . calls them each by name."

Are we lost in a vast universe, dust under God's feet? Not at all. The same Saviour who calls each star by name knows our name. He is intimately acquainted with each of us. "Indeed, the very hairs of your head are all numbered. Don't be afraid" (Luke 12:7, NIV). Don't worry your head over being lost as dust among the stars. The same Saviour who knows all about the big things also knows about you, about every intimate detail of your life. And "his great interest is in you" (1 Peter 5:7, Moffatt).

DRG

MARCH 2

LOOK AND BE SAVED

> ***Look unto me, and be ye saved, all the ends of the earth.***
>
> *Isa. 45:22.*

Charles Haddon Spurgeon, of London, perhaps the greatest preacher of the nineteenth century, might have remained in darkness and despair if he had not been caught in a snowstorm on his way to church. He could go no farther toward his own church. So he turned into a narrow court and happened upon a Methodist chapel. It had only about 15 people in attendance. Because of the weather, even the pastor was not there. A humble, uneducated layman began to preach.

As his text he used "Look unto me, and be ye saved, all the ends of the earth." Although he did not pronounce all of his words correctly, the layman spoke with deep conviction. He opened his sermon by saying, "My dear friends, this is a very simple text indeed. It says, 'Look.' Now, lookin' don't take a great deal of pains. It ain't liftin your foot or your finger; it is just, 'Look.' Well, a man needn't go to college to learn to look. You may be the biggest fool, and yet you can look. A man needn't be worth a thousand a year to be able to look. Anyone can look; even a child can look."

Then the man followed up his text by declaring, "Jesus says, 'Look unto Me; I am sweating great drops of blood. Look unto Me, I am hangin' on the Cross. Look unto Me; I am dead and buried. Look unto Me; I rise again. Look unto Me; I ascend into heaven. Look unto Me; I am sittin' at the Father's right hand. O poor sinner, look unto Me! Look unto Me!"

After about 10 minutes he had no more to say. But he saw Spurgeon sitting in the back, and, gazing right at him, he shouted in primitive Methodist style, "Young man, you look very miserable. . . . Look to Jesus Christ! Look! Look! Look!"

Later, when recounting his experience, Spurgeon said: "Oh, I did 'look'! I looked until I could almost have looked my eyes away. The clouds disappeared when I looked from my self to my Saviour." Spurgeon, the sinner, became Spurgeon, the golden-tongued preacher of Jesus.

"There is life in a look at the crucified One.
There is life in a look there for me.
Then look sinner, look unto Him and be saved.
Unto Him who was nailed to the tree."

DRG

JUST ONE GLIMPSE OF JESUS

Look to Me, and be saved, all you ends of the earth! For I am God, and there is no other.
Isa. 45:22, NKJV.

Charles Haddon Spurgeon was only a lad of 16 when he caught a glimpse of Jesus at the primitive Methodist chapel in Colchester, England. When he saw "God . . . in Christ, reconciling the world unto himself" (2 Cor. 5:19) on Calvary, atoning for the sins of the world, something remarkable took place in his heart. He found salvation from both the guilt and the control of sin, and at once started to preach the gospel good news.

Within two years he had his own congregation. Three years later he moved into a larger church, then into a nearby music hall. In 1861 a huge church was built in London, called the Metropolitan Tabernacle, where for 30 years great crowds gathered to hear this "prince of preachers." The secret of his success, I believe, was that he never for one moment forgot the glimpse of Jesus that he received as a young man of 16. In his preaching he never lost sight of the words that had brought Him to Christ: "Look to Me, and be saved, all you ends of the earth! For I am God, and there is no other." Spurgeon realized that Jesus is the answer to all life's problems. And in every single sermon he directed his congregation's attention to Christ, the center and circumference of truth, the focal point of the gospel.

As we look around us in our decaying world we see the great bulwark of morality crumbling. Some call the new ways the "new morality." Actually, it is the old immorality in new dress. The basic unit of society, the home, is disintegrating. We have reached the end of an era and stand at the dawn of the new and apocalyptic day of the Lord. No one can gauge exactly the outcome of present conditions, but I'm of the firm conviction that a new epoch is about to begin.

A great vacuum exists in the hearts of millions that only a glimpse of Jesus can fill. It will provide true contentment and new meaning to life. Just such a glimpse of Jesus will also prepare each of us for the soon coming of Jesus to solve the problems that plague both our life and our sick world.

HMSR

FOOTPRINTS

> *Fear not, for I am with you, be not dismayed, for I am your God; I will strengthen you, I will help you, I will uphold you with my victorious right hand.*
>
> *Isa. 41:10, RSV.*

Some time ago we attended a "celebration of life" for a lifetime friend who died suddenly. The printed program included the meditation "Footprints," by an unknown author.

"One night a man had a dream. He dreamed he was walking along the beach with the Lord. Across the sky flashed scenes from his life. For each scene, he noticed two sets of footprints in the sand: one belonging to him, and the other to the Lord.

"When the last scene of his life flashed before him, he looked back at the footprints in the sand. He noticed that many times along the path of his life, there was only one set of footprints. He also noticed that it happened at the very lowest and saddest times in his life.

"This really bothered him, and he questioned the Lord about it. 'Lord, You said that once I decided to follow You, You'd walk with me all the way. But I have noticed that during the most troublesome times in my life, there is only one set of footprints. I don't understand why when I needed You most You would leave me.'

"The Lord replied, 'My son, My precious child, I love you and would never leave you. During your times of trial and suffering, when you see only one set of footprints, it was then that I carried you.'"

If you are going through a particularly difficult time, remember, Jesus promises, "I will uphold you with My victorious right hand." He will pick you up, take you in His arms, and carry you through any river of difficulty. If you are facing a traumatic confrontation with your boss, repeat our Lord's promise: "Fear not, for I am with you." Should you encounter what seems like an overwhelming temptation, don't forget that Jesus assures you, "I will strengthen you." Or if you are frustrated with training your children, and they are driving you to despair, claim His promise, "I will help you." Regardless of what you face or what you fear, the Lord says, "Fear not, for I am with you." Jesus cares about you!

DRG

JESUS NEVER FORGETS US

But Zion said, "The Lord has forsaken me, the Lord has forgotten me." "Can a mother forget the baby at her breast and have no compassion on the child she has borne? Though she may forget, I will not forget you!"

Isa. 49:14, 15, NIV.

Tim, the pastor of the church we attended, one time made the shocking statement that for years he had hated his mother. He went on to tell the congregation why. When he was 12 years old his mother came home drunk. His father hit her on the mouth with the back of his hand and knocked her down.

Staggering to her feet, her mouth bleeding, she cursed her husband, then shouted at Tim: "Get out of this house. Leave now. You are just like him!"

How could Tim's mother order him to leave her home and add insult to injury by accusing him of being just like the father who had hit her and drawn her blood? In her drunken stupor she had "no compassion on the child" born to her. So when his parents divorced, Tim went to live with his father.

During the years that followed, Tim found a Saviour who promised him, "Though she may forget, I will not forget you!" When those we love most in life fail us, we have a Saviour who still loves us. Or when things get rough and we are tempted to feel forsaken and forgotten, remember Jesus' promise: "Though [your mother] may forget, I will not forget you!" Jesus thinks of you at all times and in all places. He is always near to guide you in financial reverses, near to comfort you when you suffer trauma because of the people in your life, near to soothe you when pain tortures your body.

Why not breathe a little prayer right now and say, "Thank You, Jesus!"

This story has a happy footnote. Tim's love for Jesus melted his hatred for his mother. His mother joined Alcoholics Anonymous and overcame alcohol. When he was 17 and his father remarried, Tim returned to live with his mother. The day his mother came to take him to her home, they fell into each other's arms and hugged.

DRG

MARCH 6

ENGRAVED ON JESUS' HANDS

"Can a mother forget the baby at her breast and have no compassion on the child she has borne? Though she may forget, I will not forget you! See, I have engraved you on the palms of my hands."
Isa. 49:15, 16, NIV.

My wife's brothers accidentally fired up a kerosene stove with gasoline. It exploded. Lillian was standing nearby. As burning gasoline covered her body, flames engulfed her. Hearing the explosion and the screams, her mother rushed outside. When she saw Lillian burning like a flaming torch, she snuffed out the fire with her bare hands. Lillian had third-degree burns over much of her body and hovered between life and death. But through her mother's prayers, after months in the hospital, she survived. Her doctor called her his miracle child. To the day of her death, Lillian's mother carried scars on her hands from putting out the fire. Through the years when Lillian looked at those scarred hands, it reminded her of her mother's love. Her love for Lillian had engraved itself on the palms of her hands.

Unlike Lillian's mother, some mothers forget and lack compassion for their children. But Jesus never forgets. He promises, "I will not forget you! See, I have engraved you on the palms of my hands." Jesus can't forget us, for we are etched in His hands. His hands that were pierced for us constantly speak to Him of us, and those nail-pierced hands should ever testify to us of the loving sacrifice He made as our substitute.

If Jesus had not died, we would be lost in our sins, without hope and without God in this sinful world. Our death would be the end of the story. Instead, through Jesus' nail-pierced hands, we have the glorious hope of eternal life and everlasting happiness to look forward to. No wonder Habakkuk said of our Saviour: "He had rays coming forth from his hand; and there was the hiding of his power" (Hab. 3:4, ASV). His nail-pierced hands give Him the power to save us.

Today you may have a hard day ahead of you. You may feel defeated and forgotten. But remember, no matter what you face in life, or how dark the outlook, you have a Saviour who has "engraved you" in the palms of His hands. He will be with you in everything you face.

DRG

THE MORNING WATCH

He wakeneth morning by morning, he wakeneth mine ear to hear as the learned.

ISA. 50:4.

Accompanied by the mission president, I drove through Malaya, a tropical paradise of banana, coconut, and rubber plantations. The president suggested that we stop at a large rubber estate and see a friend of his. After the usual Asian courtesy of serving a cool drink, our host offered to show us how his workers tapped rubber.

Drawing a knife across the tapping panel on the trunk of a rubber tree, the estate manager sliced off a thick piece of bark. The white latex immediately began to ooze from the tree, ran down a ridge in the bark to a small metal channel, then dripped into a porcelain cup. The manager explained that tapping must be done early in the morning because heat, wind, and sunlight tend to dry up the latex and cut down the yield.

"The rubber tree is very much like the Christian, Mr. Tan," I said to the estate manager. "A Christian must seek God early in the morning before the cares of the day crowd in."

According to S. D. Gordon, "in the morning watch appointment, faithfully kept, lies the great secret of riding masterfully upon the tide that surges around so fiercely, instead of being sucked under by it." Isaiah found refuge in God each morning. "He wakeneth morning by morning, he wakeneth mine ear to hear as the learned." The psalmist prayed, "Cause me to hear thy loving-kindness in the morning; for in thee do I trust" (Ps. 143:8). "In the morning, rising up a great while before day," Jesus "went out, and departed into a solitary place, and there prayed" (Mark 1:35). When we meet Jesus in the morning, we tap His secret of experiencing a better day.

At the rubber plantation that day the estate manager also explained that one must do the tapping regularly or the yield will decrease. But when faithfully tapped again, a neglected tree, over several weeks, will gradually return to full yield. Just so, if a Christian's devotional life is intermittent, he loses his hold on Christ. And what a Christian loses through a few days' neglect may take many weeks to regain. But "if with all your hearts ye truly seek me, ye shall ever surely find me" is Mendelssohn's rendering of Jeremiah 29:13. How true it is!

DRG

MARCH 8

HIDDEN GOLD AT YOUR FEET

He has no form or comeliness; and when we see Him, there is no beauty that we should desire Him. He is despised and rejected by men, a man of sorrows and acquainted with grief. And we hid, as it were, our faces from Him.

Isa. 53:2, 3, NKJV.

Too often we judge individuals by their appearance. In his book *By Faith I Live* the late William A. Fagal tells a story about Mozart. He was engaged to a young woman who became unhappy with her choice and broke off their engagement. Later, when the world began to recognize Mozart's musical genius, she commented: "I knew nothing of the greatness of his genius. I saw only a little man."

The Bible says of Jesus, "When we see Him, there is no beauty that we should desire Him." So people turn away and hide their "faces from Him." They do not see what He is really like until the Holy Spirit reveals it to them and draws them to Jesus.

For centuries a large stone lay in the clear waters of a shallow brook in North Carolina. Indians often crossed the brook at this point. Later settlers, as they went back and forth on the trail, saw only an ugly dark lump of stone. They left it undisturbed until a farmer, who needed a stone to hold his door open, took the rough stone from the brook and carried it home.

The stone was in his house for a long time until a geologist passing through the country happened to stop by. He examined the stone and recognized it as more than a mere rock. It turned out to be the largest lump of gold ever found east of the Rocky Mountains. Everyone wondered how so many people could have seen it and failed to realize its value. Many look at Jesus with unseeing eyes. How can they receive a correct picture of Jesus and recognize His golden character of love? "God willed to make known what are the riches of the glory of this mystery . . . which is Christ in you, the hope of glory" (Col. 1:27, NKJV). Jesus wants to reproduce His character in us so it can then be copied in others. Because Christ dwells in us, we are the face, the eyes, the lips, the hands, and the feet through which people view Jesus. Do we measure up?

HMSR

OUR AMAZING SUBSTITUTE

He was pierced for our transgressions, he was crushed for our iniquities; the punishment that brought us peace was upon him, and by his wounds we are healed. . . . The Lord has laid on him the iniquity of us all.
Isa. 53:5, 6, NIV.

During the American Civil War the military arrested several Southern civilians and charged them with ambushing Union soldiers. They were all found guilty and ordered to be shot. After the sentence the general allowed them to draw lots and in this way selected a few for execution. They would be shot the following morning.

Among the number waiting in despair was a middle-aged man with a family. The fate awaiting him deeply distressed him. During the evening a young neighbor, who had himself been among those arrested but had escaped the death decree, announced, "I have no family to mourn my loss; I trust God and am prepared to die. I am willing, for the sake of your family, to die for you. The general says he will consent to the change and accept my death in place of yours."

The surprised and overcome man accepted the offer, and the substitute remained under guard until morning. In the morning soldiers led the young man to the parade ground with his fellow prisoners. A company of men with loaded guns faced them. As the bullets found their mark, he fell—dying voluntarily for another.

Christ died for us, as our substitute, tasting death for every person. He was the Sinless One, yet God "laid on him the iniquity of us all." "He was crushed for our iniquities," yours and mine. Volunteering to take the "punishment" for our sins, He was "pierced for our transgressions." By His fatal "wounds we are healed" and receive eternal life. Christ did not hesitate to pay the supreme price to redeem us. If necessary, He was willing to suffer eternal death so that through His death we might find our way to God. Christ accepted death in our place, receiving the just penalty for our sin and guilt. That's why He died—for you and me.

HMSR

CRUSHED BUT SATISFIED

We all, like sheep, have gone astray, each of us has turned to his own way; and the Lord has laid on him the iniquity of us all.

ISA. 53:6, NIV.

Several strokes disabled my father, then my brother went off to war. Caring for my father and carrying the full weight of running the family business exhausted my mother. She also suffered excruciating back pain. I remember her saying, when she had become totally debilitated emotionally and physically, "I don't know if I can take it any longer."

My mother's suffering was minute compared to that of Jesus. His neighbors turned against Him. The church leaders misinterpreted His mission. One of His 12 disciples betrayed Him, and He was dragged before religious and Roman authorities. His 11 remaining disciples left Him. In His hearing, Peter, one of three disciples in His inner circle, denied ever knowing Him. The Roman soldiers beat Jesus and made Him carry his cross until He fell exhausted beneath the load. When evil men jammed the cross into the ground, Jesus experienced excruciating pain as the nails tore at the nerves in His hands. Isaiah describes His emotional and physical pain: He was "despised," "rejected," "oppressed," "afflicted," "pierced," and "crushed" (Isa. 53:3-7, NIV).

In addition to Jesus' physical and emotional suffering, God "laid on him the iniquity of us all." Think of experiencing the emotional weight of the sins of the more than 6 billion people on earth today, then add the weight of the sins of all who have ever lived. Remember the guilt you suffer when you look back on some single sin you've committed, and multiply that by the sins of your lifetime. Then multiply your guilt by the guilt of billions of other people. Remember, Jesus endured all this—plus His own emotional and physical suffering. Add to it the disappointment resulting from billions of people rejecting salvation. (Every soul winner's heart aches over even one person who spurns salvation.)

Does Jesus consider it worthwhile to suffer so much to save us? "He will see the result of the suffering of his soul and be satisfied" (Isa. 53:11, margin, NIV). It is worth it all to Jesus, because sinners respond and He can "justify [save] many" (verse 11, NIV). Would it be worth it to you?

DRG

MY SENSE OF SIN AND MY NEED OF A SAVIOUR

We are the ones who have strayed away like sheep! We, who left God's paths to follow our own. Yet God laid on him the guilt and sins of every one of us!
Isa. 53:6, TLB.

A man wrote to me stating that he wanted to know what we are supposed to be saved from. In other words, he did not believe in the existence of such a thing as sin. Society calls sin "indiscretion." Some scholars label it "ignorance." Evolutionists may term it "a trace of the brute in humanity." Rationalists declare that we must "cull the defect." Liberals refer to sin as "an amiable weakness" or "a touch of selfishness." But God calls sin separation from Him (Isa. 59:1, 2), a transgression of His laws (1 John 3:4).

In 1933 Albert Einstein was visiting Beno Gutenberg, a noted seismologist at the California Institute of Technology in Pasadena. As the two strolled around the campus, they saw excited people rushing from the buildings. As Gutenberg recalled it sometime afterward, he said, "We had become so involved in seismology that we hadn't noticed the famous Los Angeles earthquake of 1933 taking place around us—the biggest I had ever experienced."

Many are so concerned about the hypocrisy of someone they know that they fail to realize their own great need for forgiveness and a new life. But every individual on the face of our planet is a condemned person. "We are the ones who have strayed away like sheep!"

Since "all have sinned" (Rom. 3:23), all need forgiveness, and God has "laid on [Jesus] the guilt and sins of every one of us!" Forgiveness comes only through the gospel, the good news of salvation through Jesus Christ. Modern opinions to the contrary, people are unable in their own strength to lift themselves from the mire and filth of sin. But heaven offers us pardon and salvation by the power and intervention of Jesus. If we have "left God's paths to follow our own" and our sin is adultery, murder, stealing, lying, Sabbathbreaking, or "the lesser sins" of exaggerating, overeating, overworking, Jesus can give us eternal acquittal. He can and will remove the sin—and the guilt.

HMSR

MARCH 12

JESUS' BORROWED GRAVE

> ***He made his grave with the wicked, and with the rich in his death.***
>
> *Isa. 53:9.*

Let us enter the grave of Jesus. It was a costly tomb, yet it was a borrowed one. With great labor the work crews carved it out of solid rock for a rich man and his family. But Jesus slept here, buried in another's sepulcher. A poor man, Jesus had nowhere "to lay his head" (Matt. 8:20). Having no house of His own, He rested in the homes of others. He borrowed a boat in which to preach and had to request a donkey on which to ride into Jerusalem for His triumphal entry. Yet He was buried in a rich man's tomb. The disciple Joseph of Arimathea had excavated it for his family vault. But Jesus made it the tomb of the King of the universe.

Joseph did not lose it by lending it to Jesus. He had it back, as one of God's servants said, with interest. He lent it only three days. Why was it a borrowed tomb? No doubt it was to show that as His sins were borrowed sins—they were our sins—so His burial was in a borrowed grave. Jesus had no sins of His own, having never committed a wrong. Although sinless, He took all my sin and all yours. He bore our grief and carried our sorrows in His own body on the cross. Therefore, since they were another's sins, He rested in another's grave. And since they were imputed sins, that grave was only imputedly His. It was not His, but Joseph's.

All men and women and boys and girls are sinners, and He submitted to death as every sinner must. Bowing His head upon the cross for our sake, He was "despised and rejected of men; a man of sorrows, and acquainted with grief" (Isa. 53:3), yet was still buried in a rich man's tomb. Our Saviour lay in His tomb a murdered man, and—how can we endure to say it?—we are His murderers. Each of us may acknowledge, "I slew Him—my hand stuck the dagger to His heart. My deeds put Christ to death. I took part in the crucifixion of my beloved Friend, who loved me with an unfailing love." The death of Another saves each one of us. We should greatly appreciate and love the One who rescued us!

HMSR

THE RESULT OF HIS SUFFERING

> ***He will see the result of the suffering of his soul and be satisfied.***
>
> *Isa. 53:11, NIV, margin.*

The physicians told Arlene that she would not survive much longer with dialysis, that she needed a kidney transplant. Blossom, her sister, agreed to give her a kidney. A surgeon removed one of Blossom's kidneys and transplanted it in Arlene, and she lived for 12 years. When someone asked Blossom, "If you had known that Arlene would survive only 12 years, would you have done it?"

She replied nostalgically, "We had 12 blessed years."

Jesus, our Elder Brother, knew we could not survive without a heart transplant, so He made the commitment to us: "I will give you a new heart and put a new spirit in you; I will remove from you your heart of stone and give you a heart of flesh" (Eze. 36:26, NIV).

The price Jesus paid to fulfill His promise was much greater than giving up a body organ that He could live without. The price was His very life. He gave His life so He could remove our old sinful heart and transplant a new heart in us. And now we have eternal life and a new spirit, His Spirit within us!

If you were to ask Jesus, "Was it worth it? Would You have done it if You knew so many potential recipients would reject You?" you would find His answer in today's scripture: "He will see the result of the suffering of his soul and be satisfied."

Is the story about Arlene and Blossom true? Yes, I know it's true, because Mary Zytkosky told it to us in church one Sabbath, and she is an honest, reliable person. I asked her about Arlene and Blossom and found that I had even met Arlene's husband, but had never heard her story.

More important: Is the story of Jesus giving us a new heart and placing His Spirit in our hearts' true? We know it's true, because Jesus' death for us is a historical fact. But even more important than that, has the story of Jesus changed your heart and mine? Has Jesus replaced your sinful, stony heart with a heart of flesh and given you a new spirit within? Then drop your head just now in silent prayer and thank Him for the good news of His almost unbelievable sacrifice.

DRG

DIAL HEAVEN

Evening and morning and at noon I will pray, and cry aloud, and He shall hear my voice.
Ps. 55:17, NKJV.

We have phones in our homes, in our offices, and in our pockets. Hundreds of millions of times a day Americans use their telephones. Travelers contacting their offices, businesspeople placing an order, engineers obtaining information for the next project, college students calling home, a husband checking with his wife, an invitation being given, a congratulation said, or a loved one phoning just to say hello—people communicating with people.

On a trip to South America to conduct evangelistic rallies celebrating the fiftieth anniversary of the Voice of Prophecy in Brazil, I telephoned my wife, and it seemed as if she was in the same room. Through the magic of satellite transmission, I can now direct-dial calls and reach my wife in just seconds from most cities around the world and even from an airplane in flight high over the Atlantic or Pacific Ocean. Not only are we able to talk with our neighbor down the street or our family across the ocean—today people are reaching into space, communicating with other human beings as they orbit the earth or land on the moon. But even more fantastic and wonderful is the fact that by dialing heaven, we can communicate with Jesus our Creator.

Yes, the Bible tells us that even without a phone in our pocket we can still talk with our Saviour and our heavenly Father at any moment and They can hear us. "Evening and morning and at noon I will pray, and cry aloud, and He shall hear my voice." And best of all, Heaven not only hears us when we pray, but according to Jesus, He and His Father are also eager to answer our prayers: "If you then, being evil, know how to give good gifts to your children, how much more will your Father who is in heaven give good things to those who ask Him!" (Matt. 7:11, NKJV).

It is infinitely comforting to know that when we dial heaven, the three great Powers of heaven are ready, willing, and eager to listen . . . and then answer our prayers! Your day will go much better, and your life will have reason and purpose, if you dial heaven right now.

HMSR

JESUS' QUEST TO FREE US

> *The Spirit of the Sovereign Lord is on me, because the Lord has anointed me to preach good news to the poor. He has sent me to bind up the brokenhearted, to proclaim freedom for the captives and release from darkness for the prisoners.*
>
> *Isa. 61:1, NIV.*

Henry Drummond was leaving a home in the hills of Scotland after taking a few days of rest from his strenuous evangelistic meetings. His hosts asked him to go alone to the railway station with their driver. They said, "Drink has brought our driver to the depths. He is a scholar and a gentleman, but he is helpless in the clutches of drink. Maybe you can help him."

Drummond climbed onto the seat with the driver and in his winsome way won his confidence. Soon the driver was confessing his weakness, sin, and defeat. "What if I were the finest horseman that ever drove a team; what if I could control the wildest span of horses, no matter how strong or restive; what if these horses were such a span, and they rushed around this mountain road, and you were unable to restrain them," Drummond commented, "and I said, 'Man, give me the reins, and I will control them.' What would you do?"

The driver saw the point and said, "Oh, Mr. Drummond, is that what Jesus proposes to do for a man defeated and down? Does He just want me to give Him the reins to my life?"

"That is it," Drummond replied. "Let Christ have the reins. He will fortify you with a strength that is superhuman." From that hour, that previously defeated man walked in the conscious strength of Jesus. He later filled one of Scotland's positions of trust.

Today's text forecasts the good news about Jesus' work "to bind up the brokenhearted, to proclaim freedom for the captives and release from darkness for the prisoners." Jesus came to deliver those locked up in the darkness of sin. He releases those imprisoned by the bondage of guilt, habits, doubts, and remorse and introduces them to the "glorious liberty of the children of God" (Rom. 8:21). Christ paid the penalty that our sins deserve. Unlocking the door, He frees us, takes control of our lives, and gives us hope and light. Is this your experience today?

HMSR

MARCH 16

LOOK TO JESUS AND BE SAVED

> *Who is this coming from Edom, from Bozrah, with his garments stained crimson? Who is this, robed in splendor, striding forward in the greatness of his strength? "It is I, speaking in righteousness, mighty to save."*
>
> Isa. 63:1, NIV.

Many years ago in a little village near Warsaw, Poland, a mother and father went to a nearby city one evening, leaving their two small boys home alone. A winter storm came up suddenly, and the parents were unable to return home that night.

The next morning they found their boys frozen to death. They had apparently gone out in the yard to play in the snow, and because of the ice they could not open the door to get back into the house. The older boy had taken off his coat and placed it on the younger. He had done all that was possible to save his younger brother from freezing to death.

Such heroism draws out our love and appreciation for what that older brother did. But his efforts did not save his brother. Even if he had succeeded, it would have resulted in only a few more years of life on earth.

Jesus, our Elder Brother, died that He might clothe us with His perfect garments of righteousness. The transfer of His spotless garments to cover us assures us not only of life, but of immortality! We owe a debt of gratitude to Jesus.

When Jesus comes riding forth from heaven with bloodstained garments, the cry sounds: "Who is this coming from Edom, from Bozrah, with his garments stained crimson? Who is this, robed in splendor, striding forward in the greatness of his strength?" Jesus Himself answers, "It is I, speaking in righteousness, mighty to save."

Spurgeon once exclaimed, "Oh, this is worth proclaiming! Oh, for a silver trumpet with which to blow a blast that might awaken all who slumber! There is salvation; salvation by a glorious person; salvation unto holiness; salvation by redemption; a salvation so perfect that those who receive it shall never be forsaken. O dear hearer, do you not wish to have this salvation? Do you not desire to obtain it at once?"

You do? Then look to Jesus and be saved now and forever.

DRG

JESUS LIVES IN US

They overcame him by the blood of the Lamb and by the word of their testimony; they did not love their lives so much as to shrink from death. Therefore rejoice, you heavens and you who dwell in them!

Rev. 12:11, 12, NIV.

Saint Patrick was born in a Christian community in England, the son of a Roman official. Savage tribes inhabited Ireland to the northeast, and at times they came to England for plunder. When Patrick was 16, an Irish tribe captured him. After six years of slavery he escaped to Europe in a trader's boat. In what is now France he lived for several years in a monastery. He then returned to England and after 17 years of study went as a missionary to the very people who had taken him captive and made him a slave.

Patrick risked life itself to carry the message of salvation to his former captors, winning many of them to Jesus "by the word of [his] testimony." Such was the nobility of his life that Ireland still reveres his name. He represents a whole army of men and women empowered by Jesus to overcome the devil during the darkest hours of the Christian Era.

The transforming power of the blood of the Lamb in a person's life motivates Christians to win the world for Jesus, not by words but by the testimony of their lives, their living witness to the power of Jesus in them. "Therefore rejoice, you heavens and you who dwell in them!" The devil "knows that his time is short" (Rev. 12:12, NIV). Jesus triumphed over Satan at the cross, and He is now triumphing over Satan through His worldwide church. He is now making effective in people what He accomplished for them at the cross. The dynamic witness of Jesus dwelling in us has made the church an extension of the incarnation of Christ. Because Jesus lives in us, we become living witnesses for Him.

DRG

MARCH 18

AN OUTRAGEOUS ACT OF LOVE

> *"The days are coming," declares the Lord, "when I will raise up to David a righteous Branch, a King who will reign wisely and do what is just and right in the land. In his days Judah will be saved and Israel will live in safety. This is the name by which he will be called: The Lord Our Righteousness."*
>
> *Jer. 23:5, 6, NIV.*

At our alumni meeting, an alumna told us her husband was often late getting home. He never bothered to call and was not apologetic when he arrived. Nag as she did, he would not change. Finally, after a showdown, her husband agreed to call any time he would be more than 30 minutes late.

One evening she attended a class. After class she lingered in the parking lot talking to a friend. She became so involved and excited that time slipped away, and before she realized it more than 30 minutes had passed. She didn't take time to locate a telephone and make her arrival home even later, but got into her car and raced home. On her way she memorized her apology. When she arrived, her husband was waiting at the door. As he took her in his arms, she began her memorized apology, but he ignored it. "You must have had a very hard and long day," he whispered.

"To me that was an outrageous act of love," she mused.

Commendable as it was, her husband's act sinks into insignificance in the light of what Jesus' outrageous love has done for us. Today's text is an Old Testament prophecy that predicts the coming of the Messiah as Jesus. Taking over David's throne and becoming King of the saved, He "will reign wisely and do what is just and right," and the redeemed "will live in safety." Jesus becomes "the Lord Our Righteousness."

Reflect on what it cost Jesus to become "Our Righteousness." He gave up His honored place in heaven. Coming to our world, He lived a righteous life in our place, then died for our sins. He did it so He could forgive our sins, cleanse us from them, blot out their record in the books of heaven, and in their place transfer to our account His righteous life. Truly we can rejoice, for He is "Our Righteousness," leaving us without guilt. What an outrageous act of love! How we should love Jesus in return, for love begets love.

DRG

CHRIST'S MIRACLES IN A MODERN WORLD

A new heart also will I give you, and a new spirit will I put within you: and I will take away the stony heart out of your flesh, and I will give you a heart of flesh.

EZE. 36:26.

Ernest Gordon, dean of the chapel at Princeton University, in his book *Through the Valley of the Kwai,* tells how during World War II the prisoners of the Japanese in Malaya slipped to a level lower than animals as they struggled to survive. They stole food from their fellow prisoners who were also starving. In desperation a group decided it would be good to reinvestigate Christianity. Because Gordon was a university graduate, they asked him to lead, even though by his own admission he was a skeptic, and those who asked him were also unbelievers.

They began reading and discussing the New Testament, chapter by chapter. Gordon with the others came to trust Christ as they became acquainted with Him through the uncluttered simplicity of the New Testament. How that group of scrounging, clawing, hopeless human beings transformed into a community of love is a touching and powerful story, demonstrating clearly the reality of God and of Jesus Christ.

Many others today, in less dramatic terms, have found the same reality. This miracle reveals the fulfillment of the promise by an ever-living and ever-loving Saviour: "A new heart also will I give you, and a new spirit will I put within you." God's greatest witness to our world is a Christlike life.

Many do not even believe in the possibility of miracles. But look at lives changed with new attitudes and new purpose! Just as Jesus promised, "I will take away the stony heart out of your flesh, and I will give you a heart of flesh." Complete cleansing is ours for the asking. "If we confess our sins, he is faithful and just to forgive us our sins, and to cleanse us from all unrighteousness" (1 John 1:9). Once you are willing to recognize Jesus Christ as sovereign Lord, through the good news of Calvary's cleansing power your life and my life can be a miracle!

HMSR

THE GREAT PHYSICIAN

> *I will heal their backsliding, I will love them freely.*
>
> HOSEA 14:4.

Skulls still hang over your head when you sleep in a longhouse on the island of Borneo. The eerie beat of the head hunters' drums still pierces the blackness of the jungle night. Bakusut, who lived deep in the jungle, was taking a Voice of Prophecy Bible correspondence course. When he was halfway through the lessons, he became sick. The neighbors warned him that the spirits were troubling him because he was taking Christian lessons. So, as the neighbors looked on, he scattered his lessons on the ground and burned them in a ceremonial dance.

But instead of gaining peace of mind, he began to worry. By now he couldn't sleep, eat, or work. Then one night in a dream he saw Jesus, the Great Physician, hanging from a cross set on a hill. And he seemed to hear a voice calling, "Bakusut, humble yourself at the feet of Jesus, the Great Physician. He alone can help you. He alone can heal you. And He alone can give you peace, joy, everlasting life."

The next morning Bakusut wrote to us at our Voice of Prophecy office in Singapore and asked again for the lessons he had destroyed. As he studied them, Jesus filled his heart. When he turned his back on devil worship, Jesus, the Great Physician, fulfilled His promise: "I will heal their backsliding, I will love them freely." And Bakusut became a lay preacher among his people, the Muruts, deep in the jungles of Borneo.

We are in constant need of the miracle medicine Jesus uses to heal our tendency to "backsliding," our "waywardness" (NIV). A skillful physician and surgeon, the Great Physician never makes a needless incision. Every cut of the scalpel is from His skillful hand. "He who is imbued with the Spirit of Christ abides in Christ. Whatever comes to him comes from the Saviour, who surrounds him with His presence. Nothing can touch him except by the Lord's permission. All our sufferings and sorrows, all our temptations and trials, all our sadness and griefs, all our persecutions and privations, in short, all things work together for our good. All experiences and circumstances are God's workmen whereby good is brought to us" *(The Ministry of Healing,* p. 489).

DRG

WHAT LOVE CAN DO

He had rays coming forth from his hand; and there was the hiding of His power.

HAB. 3:4, ASV.

No word picture can adequately describe it or photograph capture its beauty. Here is beauty beyond belief. More majestic in reality than in anticipation, it has been called "A poem in stone." Standing beside a reflecting pool looking on the Taj Mahal, I recalled the story of Shah Jahan's dream, captured here in gleaming white marble. And I exclaimed, "That's what love can do!"

Three hundred years ago Shah Jahan ruled a vast Muslim empire from his capital at Agra. As a young man of 21 he fell in love with the beautiful Princess Arjumand. After their marriage, the princess was a constant friend and companion to her husband. She was with him in the palace, on the battlefield, and even with him in exile for eight years.

When the shah became emperor, he called his empress Mumtaz Mahal—the Chosen of the Palace. When death suddenly claimed her, the shah grieved bitterly. How could he best perpetuate her memory? Summoning Ustad Isa, the venerable Persian architect, he unfolded his plan and commanded, "Make it as beautiful as she was beautiful. Make it as delicate as she was delicate. Make it the image and soul of her beauty." Twenty-two years elapsed. Finally the Taj Mahal—the Crown of Mahal—with its translucent white domes and graceful minarets rose from a massive marble platform. Inside, surrounded by a delicate screen of carved alabaster, fine as lace, are the marble-encased caskets of Shah Jahan and Mumtaz Mahal.

Human love erected the Taj Mahal. But the greatest love story of the ages is what divine love can do. God's love erected not a marble monument but a cross. The cross no longer stands, but the love remains—in the heart of God. Jesus' hands are an eternal monument to His love for us. "He had rays coming forth from his hand; and there was the hiding of His power." Throughout eternity He will carry the marks of the Crucifixion as an emblem of His love for us. God's love can change a life, and in such a transformed life "divine love has indeed come to its perfection" (1 John 2:5, NEB). Our altered lives become monuments to His love, not of marble, but of flesh and blood.

DRG

SUCCESS ASSURED WHEN YOU WITNESS

"Not by might nor by power, but by My Spirit," says the Lord Almighty.
Zech. 4:6, NIV.

One time when Dwight L. Moody, the Billy Graham of the nineteenth-century, preached in Chicago, two women came to him and said, "We are praying for you."

"Praying for me!" he said in surprise. "Why? Am I not preaching the gospel? Why don't you pray for those who hear?"

They told him that he was preaching the gospel, but without power! When he heard that, he asked them to continue to pray for him. It helped to revolutionize not only his preaching, but his life. He became "God's man in God's place doing God's work in God's way."

The Holy Spirit is the energy the church needs. It is the power you and I must have. Since Jesus promised to send the Holy Spirit as His representative, we can experience the strength of the Holy Spirit today! The Spirit will lead everyone who is willing to have this experience. "There is nothing that Satan fears so much as that the people of God shall clear the way by removing every hindrance, so that the Lord can pour out His Spirit upon a languishing church and an impenitent congregation. . . . When the way is prepared for the Spirit of God, the blessing will come" *(Selected Messages,* book 1, p. 124).

The good news about Jesus will not reach the ends of the earth by the might and power of people and organizations—only when the Spirit fills God's people. Being prepared for the final outpouring of the Holy Spirit means putting away all sin and selfish ambition. God must be able to perform a mighty transformation in our hearts. The hour is late. We must not delay. God needs you and me as witnesses to the good news. He is waiting to lavish the Holy Spirit upon each of us in greater measure. Are you, am I, ready and waiting to receive it?

We are to pray for a great outpouring of the Holy Spirit in these last days. Holy Scripture directs us: "Ask the Lord for rain in the time of the latter rain. The Lord will make flashing clouds; He will give them showers of rain" (Zech. 10:1, NKJV). Will you covenant with me today to pray daily for the might and power of the Spirit to be poured out in your life?

HMSR

JESUS SAVES

> ***And she will have a Son, and you shall name him Jesus (meaning "Savior"), for he will save his people from their sins.***
>
> *MATT. 1:21, TLB.*

One evening I sat in an easy chair in a large lonely house waiting for the telephone to ring. I was there taking emergency calls for a physician. Those days we had no answering services or machines or cellular telephones. To pass away the time, I searched the dial for interesting programs on the doctor's powerful radio. On that Sunday evening, scanning the dial, I heard the Voice of Prophecy quartet singing, "Lift up the trumpet, and loud let it ring: Jesus is coming again!"

Although born into an Adventist home, I had slipped away from the church during my early teens. Now 18 and far from the church, I felt Someone compel me to listen to the broadcast. Hearing H.M.S. Richards speak on Daniel 2 that evening, I mused, *If the Bible can outline the entire course of history in advance, and if Jesus is coming soon, then I must get ready to meet Him.* Then and there in that dark and lonely house, I decided to give my life to Jesus and become a minister. The next Sabbath I was in church for the first time in several years. The pastor must have been puzzled when I asked for baptism. The following fall I enrolled as a ministerial student at La Sierra College. So I know from personal experience that Jesus saves!

The angel instructed Joseph that the child to be born to Mary should be called Jesus, "for he will save his people from their sins." The word "save" derives from a Greek word meaning "to deliver." Jesus, our Saviour, is our deliverer from sin. I'm thankful Jesus reached down to me, a wayward youth, and saved me—delivered me from a frustrating humdrum life and from eternal destruction.

Jesus' deliverance from sin is real. I have seen Him change alcoholics and drug addicts into zealous Christians. He transformed a headhunter in Borneo into a respected village chief and a blind beggar in Thailand into a lay preacher. Repeatedly I have seen Him reach people on the brink of suicide and give them a new beginning. Jesus changes hearts hardened against all human emotion, and softens and fills them with love. He not only delivered me from sin and gave me the assurance of eternal life; He has made my life rich and full. And you?

DRG

THE NAME JESUS

She will give birth to a son, and you are to give him the name Jesus, because he will save his people from their sins.
MATT. 1:21, NIV.

When we were growing up, a radio program for children began each time with a raucous voice screaming: "Henry! Henry Aldrich!" Henry was a rather scatterbrained character. In those days parents no doubt thought twice before naming a child Henry, since we judge what a person is like by their name.

As a child I had an aversion to the name Henry, but then my uncle Henry, whom I had never before met, came for a visit. He was everybody's favorite uncle—kind, likable, generous, soft-spoken, with a heart of gold. After that when the name Henry came to mind, I no longer thought of Henry Aldrich, but Uncle Henry. I forgot Henry Aldrich the scatterbrain, because Uncle Henry transformed Henry to a favorite name.

When Joseph found out that Mary, the girl he was engaged to, was pregnant, he decided to dissolve their relationship quietly. But then "an angel of the Lord appeared to him in a dream" and told Joseph that the child conceived in Mary was from the Holy Spirit, adding, "you are to give him the name Jesus, because he will save his people from their sins" (Matt. 1:20, 21, NIV).

Jesus means Saviour, from the Greek, "Yahweh saves." Jesus received the name that most closely matched His dominant character trait. His bottom-line purpose for coming to our world was to save people from sin. For those who need saving—and all of us do, "for all have sinned" (Rom. 3:23)—Jesus "is the sweetest name" we know. Those who desire the best things in life—happiness, peace of mind, fulfilment, and much more—realize that such things are available only in Jesus. Those who desire eternal life recognize that "salvation is found in no one else, for there is no other name under heaven given to men by which we must be saved" (Acts 4:12, NIV). Why not bow your head this moment in prayer and say, "Dear Father in heaven, thank You for sending Jesus, Your one and only Son, to save me. And thank You, Jesus, for saving me!"

DRG

BAPTIZED WITH FIRE

With water I baptize those who repent of their sins; but someone else is coming, far greater than I am, so great that I am not worthy to carry his shoes! He shall baptize you with the Holy Spirit and with fire.

Matt. 3:11, TLB.

Just what does it mean to be baptized with fire? The prophet Isaiah declared that the Lord would cleanse His people from their iniquities "by the spirit of burning" (Isa. 4:4). Jesus Himself said, "I am come to send fire on the earth" (Luke 12:49). On the day of Pentecost "there appeared unto [Jesus' disciples] cloven tongues like as of fire, and it sat upon each of them. And they were all filled with the Holy Ghost" (Acts 2:3, 4).

Notice today's text does not say that Jesus "shall baptize you with the Holy Spirit or with fire," but "with the Holy Spirit and with fire." When the Holy Spirit takes possession of a person, the effect is in a sense similar to that of fire in the natural world. The searching, penetrating, consuming, energizing Holy Spirit purifies the individual.

As I was studying this subject, I was greatly interested in reading all the references in the Bible that speak of this fire. The Bible makes it clear that when a person receives the baptism with fire, the Spirit will reveal who that person really is. It will expose all pride, selfishness, love of position, touchiness, and meanness. Such fire consumes the dross and scum in a person's life. God says, "I will turn my hand upon thee, and purely purge away thy dross" (Isa. 1:25). "In all who submit to His power the Spirit of God will consume sin" (*The Desire of Ages,* p. 107).

When we are baptized by the Holy Spirit and with fire, it consumes the rubbish of sin in our lives—the selfishness that dominates our being so much of the time. "In all who submit to His power the Spirit of God will consume sin. But if men cling to sin, they become identified with it. Then the glory of God, which destroys sin, must destroy them" (*ibid.,* p. 107). Thank You, Jesus for sending the Holy Spirit—and the fire! Please make quick work of my sins!

HMSR

MARCH 26

THE DOVE WHO LEADS US HOME

And Jesus, when he was baptized, went up straightway out of the water: and, lo, the heavens were opened unto him, and he saw the Spirit of God descending like a dove, and lighting upon him: and lo a voice from heaven, saying, This is my beloved Son, in whom I am well pleased.

Matt. 3:16, 17.

The essence of human tragedy is in loneliness," wrote Thomas Wolfe, an American novelist. How true this is! Loneliness seems to exist within every human being. Have you ever wondered why? Because we have been alienated from our Creator, and through Jesus, God is trying to draw us back to Him. Sin is the basic reason for humanity's separation from God. Our sinful rebellion against our heavenly Father's will and our desire to place ourselves in the central place in life that belongs only to God have put an abyss between us and Him. Jesus sent the Holy Spirit to our world to convict us of sin and lead us back to God (John 16:8-14).

Scripture compares the Holy Spirit to the dove that descended on Jesus at His baptism. The imagery denotes the beauty of the Holy Spirit's character. Like the dove, He is gentle, loving, meek, innocent, forgiving. Since Pentecost the Holy Spirit has dwelled in the believer just as He abode on Jesus at His baptism. On this wonderful occasion the Father announced: "This is my beloved Son, in whom I am well pleased." The words from heaven embrace humanity! "God spoke to Jesus as our representative. With all our sins and weaknesses, we are not cast aside as worthless" (*The Desire of Ages,* p. 113.) "He hath made us accepted in the beloved" (Eph. 1:6).

I once read the story of a guide in the deserts of Arabia who was said never to lose his way. He carried with him a homing pigeon with a fine cord attached to its leg. When in doubt about the path to take or the direction to go, the man tossed the pigeon into the air, and the pigeon quickly strained at the cord as it tried to fly in the direction of home. So the pigeon always led its master home, and people called him the "dove man."

The Holy Spirit is heaven's dove who is able to draw us away from the loneliness of sin to salvation—and lead us home.

HMSR

HAPPINESS PLUS!

Blessed [happy] are the . . .

Matt. 5:3-12.

Today's scripture consists of what we call the Beatitudes. Each begins with the word "blessed," an old-fashioned word that some translate "happy." Those who gathered on the mountainside to hear Jesus were amazed because His teachings were so different. The masses thought that happiness consists in possessing things, and they coveted fame and honor. But Jesus spoke with certainty that, in spite of circumstances, we can be happy if we give ourselves unreservedly to serving Him and the people around us.

Jesus' prescriptions for true happiness were revolutionary teachings for His day. The Romans despised pity, and the Stoics lacked compassion. The commonly accepted explanation for suffering saw it as the deserved punishment for sin. But according to Jesus, the poor in spirit will inherit heaven, those who mourn will receive comfort, the meek will inherit the earth, those who hunger and thirst for righteousness will have their needs met, the merciful will obtain mercy, the pure in heart will see God, the peacemakers will be called children of God, and the persecuted will enter heaven.

After explaining what constitutes true happiness and how we may obtain it, Jesus pointed out to His disciples their duty as witnesses. He also spoke of persecution, and counseled, "Rejoice and be exceeding glad" (Matt. 5:12). Not only glad, but "exceeding glad." Happiness plus! If your life has been in the minus column up to now, ask Jesus to bring it into perfect harmony with His will. We can't be happy if we insist on living according to our wishes, but we can be happy if we give ourselves unreservedly to God.

Albert Schweitzer was an accomplished musician and a rising theologian with a promising career before him, but God had a special work for him to do. Schweitzer determined to give his life for something outside and beyond himself. After his thirtieth birthday he struggled through the medical course and spent the rest of his life giving of himself to the multitudes in Africa. He could not experience happiness by doing anything else. We too can change boredom and an empty life for a life of true happiness. If we give ourselves, happiness plus can be ours today!

HMSR

MARCH 28

JESUS ANSWERS OUR PRAYERS

But thou, when thou prayest, enter into thy closet, and when thou hast shut thy door, pray to thy Father which is in secret; and thy Father which seeth in secret shall reward thee openly.
MATT. 6:6.

When Jesus suggests a closet, He is not referring to walk-ins or fit-ins. He is referring to solitude. It can be your car or the back porch—or walking down the street alone beneath the stars. But it must be a place where it is just you and God, where it is quiet and there will be no interruption" (Neil Wyrick, Jr., *These Times,* July 1967, p. 12). Where you can "shut thy door," that is, block out the distractions.

As we contact God, remember that prayer, to be effective, must be a "no-holds-barred" contact with our Saviour. Prayer causes us to stand back and look at our lives in a new way. People who pray are different from those who don't. You resemble the company you keep, and if that company is Jesus, it has to make a difference.

Paul instructs us to pray "always" (Eph. 6:18). How can I "always" be praying? What would people think of me if they saw me kneeling down and praying all the time? Entering the closet and closing the door means that we should ever be in a prayerful frame of mind. As I'm driving along in the car, I often commune with God. Every morning when I wake up, the very first thing I do is talk with my Saviour and thank Him for the good night's rest He has given me. I tell Him I am His for that day, and to use me if He can. The day goes much better for me when I'm in contact with heaven.

If you follow Jesus' instruction to closet your mind in prayer, He promises that your "Father . . . shall reward thee openly." One of our Voice of Prophecy listeners wrote his testimony to the power of God as a result of prayer: "You will want to praise God with me, because He has answered our prayers for my daughter after six years. She sent me a letter asking me to forgive the hurts she has caused, saying she has found God. It was almost like hearing from the dead. I thank and praise God for His answer to our prayers." Isn't it good news that God our Father and Jesus our Saviour answer our prayers!

HMSR

WHEN YOU PRAY, KEEP KNOCKING!

Ask, and it shall be given you; seek, and ye shall find; knock, and it shall be opened unto you.
Matt. 7:7.

In his book *Prevailing Prayer* Dwight L. Moody tells of a student who asked his teacher, "Why is it that so many prayers go unanswered? I do not understand. The Bible says, 'Ask, and it shall be given you; seek, and ye shall find; knock, and it shall be opened unto you.' But it seems to me a great many knock and are not admitted."

"Did you never sit beside your cheerful parlor fire," the teacher replied, "on some dark evening, and hear a loud knocking at the door? Going to answer the summons, have you not sometimes looked out into the darkness, seeing nothing, but hearing the pattering feet of some mischievous boy who knocked but did not wish to enter, and therefore ran away? Thus is it often with us. We ask for blessings, but do not really expect them; we knock, but do not mean to enter; we fear that Jesus will not hear us, will not fulfill His promises, will not admit us; and so we go away."

"Ah, I see," the student said, his eyes shining with the new understanding. "Jesus cannot be expected to answer runaway knocks. He has never promised it. I mean to keep knocking, knocking, until He cannot help opening the door!"

If an answer to prayer does not come, seek to find out the reason. Ask yourself, Is there something in my life that should not be there?

Many years ago I read this advice by Neil Wyrick in *These Times:* "When prayer is what it should be, it is a time of examination of self by self and a cross-examination by God. We do not have time to be vague in our personal prayers. . . . Do not make vague mouthings about love until you have specifically prayed that He might improve your false pride and prejudice. Name people. Name places. Name events. Dig up yesterday if you were unrepentant. Wipe the slate clean, but put everything on the slate. If it is thanksgiving you feel, spell it out" (July 1967, pp. 12, 13). Jesus cares about you. So keep knocking!

HMSR

MARCH 30

"WHAT KIND OF MAN IS THIS?"

Without warning, a furious storm came up on the lake, so that the waves swept over the boat. But Jesus was sleeping. The disciples went and woke him, saying, "Lord, save us! We're going to drown!" . . . Then he got up and rebuked the winds and waves, and it was completely calm. The men were amazed and asked, "What kind of man is this? Even the winds and the waves obey him!"

MATT. 8:24-27, NIV.

What kind of man is this?" He is a man similar to us, but also very different from us. Like us, He got weary and needed sleep. But unlike us, He spoke and quieted "a furious storm." Like us, He was born as a baby by His mother; but unlike us, He had no human father, but is God's "one and only Son" (John 3:16, NIV). Like us, He became hungry; but unlike us, He could feed "four thousand" with "seven loaves" of bread (Mark 8:1-11). Like us, He was "tempted in every way," but unlike us, He "was without sin" (Heb. 4:15). Though people who should have known better mistreated Him, unlike us "he did not open his mouth" (Isa. 53:7). Like us, He must die, but unlike us, He died "not for himself" (Dan. 9:26), but for the sins of the entire world (2 Cor. 5:21). Like us, He had to be buried; but unlike us, He came out of the grave the third day (Luke 24:1-6) and announced: "I am the resurrection and the life. He who believes in me will live" (John 11:25, NIV).

"What kind of man is this?" The kind of Man who lived, died, and rose again to give us and all who believe in Him eternal life. The kind of Man who could save James and John, "the Sons of Thunder" (Mark 3:17). The kind of Man who could forgive even those who put Him to death (Luke 23:34) and forgive and save the hardened criminal on the cross next to Him (verses 40-43). And the kind of Man who is still saving everyone who puts their faith in Him—without regard to how sinful they are (John 3:16).

"What kind of man is this?" That is, How is He unlike us? The antithesis between Jesus and us leads me to ask myself the question: What kind of person am I? Will you venture to ask yourself that question today and then, whatever the answer, thank Jesus for coming to our world to save you and re-create you to be like Him?

DRG

COME SEE! GO TELL!

Come, see the place where the Lord lay. And go quickly and tell His disciples that He is risen from the dead.
Matt. 28:6, 7, NKJV.

With Mary and the other women we arrive early in the morning the first day of the week at the tomb in the garden. There the angel speaks, "Come, see the place where the Lord lay." Let us be quiet now as we approach the grave of the greatest of all men—the resting place of the Son of man, the restorer of our race, the one who conquered death and hell. People travel hundreds of miles to see the tomb of some great poet or soldier, but where can the Christian go to find a tomb of one as famous as Jesus?

It is the tomb of your Best Friend. Many go to graves of loved ones to weep, thinking over past days. They place flowers on their graves, or sit on the grass of a father's grave, a mother's grave, or that of a wife or husband. We now stand before the grave of One who "sticketh closer than a brother" (Prov. 18:24), who loved you enough to die for you.

Join the devoted women to see the place at the angel's request. The tomb is clean and sweet. No body has ever decayed in it. Jesus was the first one to be buried here, and His body saw no corruption (Acts 2:31). Stop a moment at this quiet, restful place of meditation. We have been so busy. You may be a traveler, a business person, a scientist, a househusband. Whoever or whatever you are, you need to calm yourself and think about heavenly things, so obey the voice of the angel and "see the place where the Lord lay." Examine the empty tomb. Meditate on its meaning. Jesus "is risen from the dead." It offers hope of life after death for us and the entire human race.

Notice especially that the angel said not only, "Come see," but also "Go and tell." So go today and tell your work associates, the clerk at the convenience store, and your companion on the bus the good news of the empty tomb.

HMSR

APRIL 1

JESUS WILL TAKE CARE OF YOU

Come unto me, all ye that labour and are heavy laden, and I will give you rest.

MATT. 11:28.

When Jim was only 8 years old, his father told him, "You are now old enough to buy your own clothes."

As Jim wiggled his toes, it reminded him that his shoes had a hole in each sole.

"Pa, won't you buy me one more pair?"

"No, Jim," his father answered. "You'll have to begin now to earn all those things for yourself. You'll find a way."

Jim's father believed he should teach his children self-reliance. He was a part-time pastor and a not very successful Missouri farmer who stressed to his family the importance of honesty, tolerance, and living by the golden rule.

When Jim was in his teens his father was unfairly asked to resign his pastorate, and it affected Jim deeply. He didn't attend church again until his late middle years, when he accepted Christ and was baptized as a result of an experience at the Battle Creek Sanitarium. By then Jim Penney had been a multimillionaire as the founder of the Golden Rule stores, later J. C. Penney stores. He entered the sanitarium during the Depression years, a broken man, for he had lost much of his fortune and was near a nervous breakdown.

Feeling helpless, desolate, and forsaken, he heard people singing, "Be not dismayed, whate'er betide, God will take care of you." With faltering steps he stumbled up the stairs to the mezzanine floor where the sanitarium employees had gathered for worship, and slipped into a back seat. After the song, the leader read these words of Jesus: "Come unto me, all ye that labour and are heavy laden, and I will give you rest." Then and there Penney surrendered his heart to Jesus and was miraculously healed. Later he said of the miracle that had taken place in his heart: "I came out of that room a different man, renewed. I had gone in bowed with a paralysis of spirit, utterly adrift. I came forth with a soaring sense of release, from a bondage of gathering death to a pulse of helpful living. I had glimpsed God" (*Fifty Years With the Golden Rule* [New York: Harper and Brothers Pub., 1950], p. 159). If you are feeling lonely, discouraged, or blue, you too can find the peace and comfort Jesus offers to those who come to Him. You need only open your heart to Him just now.

DRG

LISTEN TO JESUS

> ***Behold, a bright cloud overshadowed them [Peter, James, John, and Jesus]; and suddenly a voice came out of the cloud, saying, "This is My beloved Son, in whom I am well pleased. Hear Him!"***
>
> *Matt. 17:5, NKJV.*

Knott's Berry Farm in California has a little wayside chapel in which one may catch a glimmer of the grandeur of the living Christ. A restless, talkative crowd enters the chapel. As the place fills, the lights gradually dim to complete blackness. A double door opens before the audience, revealing a faint light. A dim figure in white stands with outstretched arms. Music provides a background as a quiet voice narrates an ancient description of Jesus. Gradually the figure begins to glow with phosphorescent brilliance. Then suddenly its intensity increases until Jesus stands there in all His glory. A soft gentle voice repeats with deep feeling, "[Jesus] was transfigured before them. His face shone like the sun, and His clothes became as white as the light" (Matt. 17:2, NKJV). The light fades, and the doors close. The audience is silent—awestruck!

If a mere human representation of the Transfiguration can so move an audience, what must have been the effect upon Peter, James, and John as they saw the scene in living reality on the mount? It must have given them great reassurance when they heard the Father announce: "This is My beloved Son, in whom I am well pleased. Hear Him!"

Here is the Father's testimony to the person of His Son, and an endorsement of His authority to teach. "Hear Him!" The Father calls for the sick languishing in pain to hear—Jesus is the great physician. God summons the distraught, frustrated, and troubled to hear—the Master is our peace. The heavenly Father urges the spiritually famished to hear—Christ is the bread of life. The heavenly voice asks those searching for knowledge to hear—Christ is the light of the world. And the Father requests the bereaved and sorrowing to hear—Jesus is the life-giver.

Whatever your need, your problem, your heartache, the cause of your indecision, or the reason for your heavy heart, the Father wants you to "hear Him!" Hear Jesus! Listen to Him! He can and will resolve whatever is troubling you.

DRG

APRIL 3

FABULOUS NEWS

For the Son of Man has come to save that which was lost.

Matt. 18:11, NKJV.

Think what it would mean to be lost when Jesus comes.

The plight of the lost impressed itself upon my mind when I once asked a church member, "How did you become a Christian?"

"I'll tell you," said Mr. Lomax. "I went to the Mojave Desert to do some shooting. After considerable difficulty finding somewhere to stay, I felt I had really struck it right when I found a place whose owner offered to go with me to do some shooting that very afternoon.

"We drifted apart from each other. After a long while I called but had no response. Then I shot in the air. Finally I headed in what I assumed was the direction of home, but found after some time that I had circled back to the same spot. Again I went in the direction I thought I was staying, but once more I wound up where I had started.

"Night began to fall," Mr. Lomax continued. "If you have been in the Mojave Desert only in the heat of the day, you may not realize that during the winter months the temperature can get down well below freezing at night. So my fear increased with the falling sun. A cold wind began to blow across the warm desert sands. I feared I would freeze to death. The coyotes began to howl, and I became frantic!"

At this point in the story Mr. Lomax cleared his throat, mist filled his eyes, and his voice broke as he said, "You know, it's a terrible thing to be lost! I decided right then and there to give my heart to Jesus."

How thankful we can be that "the Son of Man has come to save that which was lost." It is a terrible thing to be lost, but it is a glorious thing to find salvation.

Finding salvation is fabulous news, because it means we are no longer slaves to Satan. We are free in Christ. And the guilt of sin ceases to torment us, for Christ forgives us and becomes our assurance. Jesus not only seeks for us until He finds us and forgives us, but He declares us righteous and assures us of a happy life here and eternal life in a land of beginning again. What is your response to a Saviour who searched for you until He found you and has given you a satisfying life as well as the promise of eternal existence?

DRG

JESUS IN OUR FAMILY

Where two or three are gathered together in my name, there am I in the midst of them.
Matt. 18:20.

"The family that prays together stays together" has been more than a meaningless cliché in the Richards' family, for prayer has always been an integral part of my life ever since I can remember. I remember how when I was 5 years old Father would call the family together for worship. I would sit on his lap while he read a Bible story. Then we would sing a hymn and kneel together while he prayed. Often each of us would pray.

The example of my parents has helped to establish our family altar on a firm foundation. Prayer in our family has meant much. We wouldn't be without family worship. While our three children were still young we all looked forward to it, especially on Friday evenings when the Sabbath came. On winter evenings we gathered around the fireplace and sang some of the grand old hymns. Then each member of the family would relate what God had meant to them during the past week. Sometimes each of us would quote a favorite Bible text. Finally we would all kneel together in the family circle, join hands, and pray.

If family life is not what it should be and dissension and distrust has crept in, gathering the family together and praying together establishes a healing bond. Family worship binds family members together, secures domestic harmony, and wields a permanent influence for good. I shall never forget what it meant to me, as a young man, to hear my father pray for me. Just to know that he was concerned about my well-being has influenced my life immensely.

When a Christian family gathers to pray, Jesus promises, "There am I in the midst of them." The song is true: "With Jesus in the family, happy, happy home." Worshiping together draws a family to Jesus. That's why Jesus appeals to us, "Come unto me" (Matt. 11:28) and pause in My presence.

We just rush about too much today. The plane is leaving, school is starting, the whistle is blowing, the horn is honking—it's time to go! Many just don't take time to call the family together and kneel down and talk to God; but when we do, something happens in our families. Jesus draws us together when we pray together.

HMSR

APRIL 5

"IS ETERNAL LIFE FOR ME?"

It is easier for a camel to go through the eye of a needle, than for a rich man to enter into the kingdom of God.

Matt. 19:24.

Jesus made this statement to His disciples after the rich young ruler turned down salvation. Some commentators see in the image the small needle gate a person had to go through after the gates to the walled city of Jerusalem closed at night. A small camel, if relieved of the load on its back and kneeling down on all fours, could sometimes with great difficulty slowly shuffle through a needle gate on its knees. Others consider it just another way of saying something was impossible without God's help.

When the disciples heard what Jesus said, "they were exceedingly amazed, saying, Who then can be saved?" (Matt. 19:25). And Jesus assured them, "With men this is impossible; but with God all things are possible" (verse 26).

Under what condition will the promise of eternal life be fulfilled to each of us? Jesus answered that question by promising: "Whosoever believeth in [God's only Son] should not perish, but have everlasting life" (John 3:16). Is eternal life for you and for me? Yes, if we believe—if we are willing to follow the One whom we love and do what He wants us to do. It does not mean that by doing something we may earn salvation, but we do Christ's will because when we become involved with Christ, His will is in us.

The word "believe" means so much, and at times it's so hard to comprehend. Eternal life comes by believing and being willing to trust and follow Christ. The simplicity of it all is what baffles so many people. It requires no elaborate preparation, no purification rites, no painful penance, no ceremony.

When William, Prince of Orange, handed a chosen man a written pledge of a high position in his government if the man would support him, the man declined it, saying, "Your Majesty's word is sufficient. I would not serve a king if I could not trust his word."

Jesus pledged His word. We may rely on it—His word is good and will be fulfilled. He asks us for total dependence upon Him. If you believe in Christ completely, then eternal life is for you!

HMSR

CAN WE REACH GOD THROUGH PRAYER?

And all things, whatever you ask in prayer, believing, you will receive.
Matt. 21:22, NKJV.

For centuries skeptics have scoffed at the idea of a prayer-hearing and a prayer-answering God. Meanwhile, as Christians, we have clung tenaciously to the Bible teaching that we can hold constant communication with a God in heaven through prayer. Today, through the invention of satellite technology, we can hear and see around the world. If human beings can do that, surely God can hear and answer our prayers.

Jesus testified during His sojourn on earth: "And all things, whatever you ask in prayer, believing, you will receive." John states that "this is the confidence that we have in [the Son of God], that, if we ask any thing according to his will, . . . we know that we have the petitions that we desired of him" (1 John 5:14, 15). Modern Christians bear a similar testimony. Ellen G. White writes: "Keep your wants, your joys, your sorrows, your cares, and your fears before God. You cannot burden Him; you cannot weary Him. He . . . is not indifferent to the wants of His children. . . . Take to Him everything that perplexes the mind. Nothing is too great for Him to bear, for He holds up worlds, He rules over the affairs of the universe" (*Steps to Christ,* p. 100).

When I attended college I became ill with undulant fever. After I had experienced the disease's acute phase my joints ached so badly that the pain would awaken me night after night. Doctors administered all the known treatments. They informed me that they had no cure and that it would take several months, possibly years, for the disease to "wear out."

I didn't want to drop out of school, so in desperation I went to Meade McGuire, a man of God, and told him my plight. He read a few scriptures, talked about faith and the power of prayer, and added that whatever God's will would be, we should be ready to accept it. Then he offered a quiet prayer—and I was healed! Since then I have witnessed answers to hundreds of prayers. Nothing can shake my belief that we can communicate with God through prayer.

DRG

JESUS IS HERE FOR YOU!

If you believe, you will receive whatever you ask for in prayer.
MATT. 21:22, NLT.

John Welch, son-in-law to John Knox, was one of the most ardent men of prayer our world has ever known. He counted a day wasted if he did not spend seven or eight hours alone with God in prayer and study of Scripture. Speaking of Welch after his death, someone said, "He was a type of Christ."

All of us need continual contact with our Saviour. We are not to be like the boy who said he prayed only at night, for in the daytime he could take care of himself. Communication with Jesus both day and night is our lifeline to the Divine. Our Saviour is constantly endeavoring to draw us to Himself. He promises, "If you believe, you will receive whatever you ask for in prayer."

Here are a few things someone has said that prayer is not:

First, prayer is not a blank check bearing God's signature that guarantees us anything we might like to have.

Second, prayer is not a rabbit's foot to preserve us from all misfortune.

Third, prayer is not an emergency door that opens instantaneously, offering us an exit in case of disaster.

Fourth, prayer is not a letter to Santa Claus.

Prayer is fellowship with God. It opens the door to the throne room of the universe, where we converse with God as with a friend. Can you imagine finite people being able to talk with the Creator of the universe as a personal Friend? Well, it's possible—yes, it is!—through prayer.

True prayer is communing with the Father through Jesus on the highest level, a warm intimate sharing of our deepest feelings and desires. It promotes our spiritual growth as almost nothing else can. Through prayer we discover God's will for our lives and receive directions from the Saviour throughout each day. Praying as David did uncovers our hidden sins (Ps. 139:23, 24). And through prayer we confess our sins and receive forgiveness (1 John 1:9), and the Lord delivers us from evil, danger, and emotional upheavals (Ps. 107:6). In every dilemma, in every challenge we face, we can pray, and our loving Saviour will listen and answer. Jesus is here for you today!

HMSR

UNDER JESUS' WINGS

O Jerusalem, Jerusalem, the city that kills the prophets and stones God's messengers! How often I have wanted to gather your children together as a hen protects her chicks beneath her wings, but you wouldn't let me.

MATT. 23:37, NLT.

Dan and his sister acquired a pet duck at Easter time. Everywhere that one of them went, Donald Duck was sure to follow. When Donald was lonely, much to the distress of the neighbors, he'd quack loudly until someone came to keep him company.

Then one day the strangest thing happened: Donald began to lay eggs—one every day. But the Donald tag stuck anyway. And when Donald made it clear that she wanted to nest on the eggs, the family put a male duck in the pen. Donald became very protective of the eggs, and when they hatched and a half dozen ducklings graced the nest, Donald became agitated when anyone came near, even Dan and his sister. Intent on protecting her ducklings, Donald would run and peck at any intruder.

Jesus depicted Himself as a mother hen, intent on protecting His chicks. He said to Jerusalem, "How often I have wanted to gather your children together as a hen protects her chicks beneath her wings, but you wouldn't let me." You can almost feel the anguished sorrow in His voice. Christ wants to protect us from life's cares and disappointments. Although He wants to hover over us and protect us under the shadow of his wings—"You wouldn't let me."

Kathy had a pet hen. One day when Kathy was away from home, her house, garage, and the chicken pen behind the garage burned to ashes. When she returned home to find all her belongings gone, what else was there to do but weep? As she walked with swollen eyes through what had been the chicken coop, she listlessly kicked a small mound of charred feathers. And what do you suppose happened? Several baby chicks came scampering out. That mother hen had died protecting "her chicks beneath her wings." Her death pictures the sacrifice Jesus made at the cross. He died there so He could protect us from the certainty of eternal death and give us eternal life.

Jesus shelters us under His protective wings from life's day-to-day hard knocks as well as from eternal death. What a Saviour!

DRG

TO ALL NATIONS

And this gospel of the kingdom shall be preached in all the world for a witness unto all nations; and then shall the end come.

MATT. 24:14.

When Jesus promised His disciples that the gospel would go to all nations, it must have seemed impossible to them. Maybe to Spain in the west, but could the gospel really go to unknown countries in the East? Twenty years ago, even with modern transportation and communication, it seemed an almost hopeless task to reach the billions of earth. But, through the power of the Holy Spirit, nothing is impossible. The Spirit is now moving on hearts, opening the entire world to the gospel.

Before the Berlin Wall fell (which surprised everybody) the spread of the gospel moved at a snail's pace at best in Eastern Europe. Now, through the Spirit's power touching hearts, tens of thousands are responding to the three angels' messages. For instance, in four short years church membership quadrupled in Russia. In 1969, when I last visited Cambodia, we had only one tiny church, and the members were nearly all Chinese, not ethnic Cambodians. Cambodians were almost impossible to reach, since becoming a Christian meant turning your back on your family traditions, culture, and country. It meant dishonoring your dead relatives by not offering food, flowers, and money to help them transmigrate to another, better life.

During the seventies Pol Pot's armies practiced genocide, killing more than a million rich or educated Cambodians. Many fled to refugee camps in Thailand, where the gospel reached thousands. Now they are back, and Adventist congregations are thriving throughout the country.

Fifty years ago one of my college professors felt Daniel 11:41 exempted Muslims from receiving the gospel as promised by Jesus. Now we see a widening door opening to Muslims in many countries and hundreds accepting Jesus. Jesus gave His prophecy in Matthew 24:14 not so we can make sensational detailed predictions about the future, but to assure us that God will accomplish His plans in amazing ways. Rest assured, the gospel will spread to all the world, and soon Jesus will come again. In Eastern Europe, Africa, India, China, Russia, and around the world we see the gospel racing on, reaching hearts that once seemed sealed. The good news about Jesus is triumphing!

DRG

THE CERTAINTY OF JESUS' SECOND COMING

Immediately after the tribulation of those days the sun will be darkened, and the moon will not give its light, and the stars will fall from heaven, and the powers of the heavens will be shaken.
MATT. 24:29, RSV.

In 1836 a Doctor Lardner of London said emphatically, "I maintain that no steamboat can cross the ocean, and I will write a book to prove it." He did produce the book, then lived to see it brought across the Atlantic Ocean to America on a steamship! Some have composed books that denounced the idea of Christ's return. But the coming of Jesus is certain, and some of those who make fun of the idea will live to see His return.

Jesus predicted four great events that would precede His coming: (1) the great tribulation, (2) the darkening of the sun, (3) the dimming of the moon, and (4) the falling of the stars.

Following that event "the powers of the heavens will be shaken," and then we "will see the Son of man coming on the clouds of heaven with power and great glory" (Matt. 24:30, RSV). Each of the four events has actually happened just as He said it would. One day soon the Lord Jesus Christ will appear in the heavens just as He told us He would. The great tribulation took place during the Dark Ages. The great Lisbon earthquake shook mightily at 9:30 a.m. on November 1, 1755, and half the world felt its convulsions. On May 19, 1780, occurred the great Dark Day. Herschel, the great astronomer, spoke of it as "one of those wonderful phenomena of nature which will always be read with interest, but which philosophy is at a loss to explain." The next night the moon became a blood-red color. When the stars fell on November 13, 1833, many thought the end of the world had come.

Since we have four spectacular prophecies occurring in definite sequence just as Christ predicted, this has to be more than coincidence. Surely the coming of Jesus is near.

Are you waiting expectantly for Jesus' return? G. Campbell Morgan, a well-known British preacher, said: "I never begin my work in the morning without thinking that perhaps He may interrupt my work and begin His own. I am not looking for death. I am looking for Him! Are you?"

HMSR

IT'S GETTING LATER EVERY MINUTE

So you also must be ready, because the Son of Man will come at an hour when you do not expect him.

Matt. 24:44, NIV.

Tongue in cheek, my father delighted in reminding us, "It's getting later every minute." When Jesus tells us we "must be ready, because the Son of Man will come at an hour when you do not expect him," He is expressing His concern that we be prepared for His return at any minute.

Signs of the Times ran an article titled "How Do You Set Your Watch for the End of Time?" (April 1994). In a letter to the editor (July 1994) a reader responded: "Attaching much importance to the end of the world robs individuals of the realization that they only have their own lifetime in which to achieve their goals for this life and any hereafter. The real end is when a person gives up the breath of life. That could be any day" (Joy Churchward, Lincoln, California).

The end of time for us may come at our death, or at Jesus' second coming. It really is getting later every minute. Every minute we are one step nearer to hearing the voice of Jesus call us out of our chaotic sin-drenched world. And that's good news! Whether the summons is to lift our eyes to the sky and see Him arriving in the clouds of glory, or to close our eyes in sleep until Jesus returns, the result will be the same: "the Son of Man will come at an hour when you do not expect him."

Think of what Jesus will deliver us from when He appears for us: Feelings of inadequacy. Driving pain. That "dead-tired" feeling. Depression because we live in a chaotic world. Worry about an unknown future. Fear of rampant crime. The threat of losing a job. And the list could go on and on. It includes everything frustrating, unpleasant, disagreeable, or repulsive.

On the other hand, imagine what Jesus will deliver us to. Try to grasp the place Jesus is preparing for us. It will be beyond our fondest hopes or wildest dreams—and best of all, Jesus will be there with us.

Let's rejoice today in the good news that it's getting later every minute, that Jesus is coming for us soon! It could be today!

DRG

"IS THIS A TRUE STORY?"

He saved others; Himself He cannot save. If He is the King of Israel, let Him now come down from the cross, and we will believe Him.
Matt. 27:42, NKJV.

As Dr. Charles Goodell was preaching in his New York congregation, a man stood and in a strident voice asked, "Say, mister, I'm a bad man. I just got out of the penitentiary. I did all they said I'd done and a good deal they never found out. I've been listening to what you have to say about this Jesus person, how He can take a fellow and make him clean and decent, and I want to know: Is this a true story, or are you making it up as you go along?" The man wasn't crazy or drunk, but desperately serious.

"Well, my man," the pastor replied, "this is a true story; I am not making it up." Goodell led the man to Jesus, who transformed his life.

The story of the cross really does seem too good to be true. Blasphemers passed by, wagging their heads, and the chief priests also mocked Jesus, saying, "He saved others; Himself He cannot save." Because Jesus did not come down from the cross, they refused to accept what He had taught. Mockers continued to taunt, "If He is the King of Israel, let Him now come down from the cross, and we will believe Him."

Jesus claimed to be, and was, the expected Messiah. The authorities put Him to death with common criminals. They identified Him with the wicked in an attempt to counteract the mighty influence of His spotless life. The Romans crucified Him between two thieves. All His enemies numbered a person who was holy with the unholy, a righteous being with the unrighteous.

In derision those at the foot of the cross cried out, "He saved others; Himself He cannot save." Never were truer words spoken. Jesus could not save us from eternal loss and also escape suffering and death. He must die for the lost if He was to save them. His death was their life as He took their place and died for their sins—and yours and mine. Thus He could not save Himself and save us, too. Because of His love for lost men and women and boys and girls, He died, and we can be forever thankful He chose to suffer just for us.

HMSR

COUNTDOWN TO ETERNITY

> ***When he had received the drink, Jesus said, "It is finished." With that, he bowed his head and gave up his spirit.***
>
> *John 19:30, NIV.*

STAND BY . . . T–10, 9, 8, 7, 6, 5, 4, 3, 2, 1, 0, LIFTOFF!" A countdown from Cape Canaveral has became so routine that we seldom see one even in a sound bite on the evening news. Another countdown took place about 2,000 years ago. Involving the whole universe, it was headed not by some modern shuttle captain but the Captain of our salvation, Jesus Christ. The location was not at Cape Canaveral but at the apex of all history—the cross at Calvary . . . 3 . . . 2 . . . 1 . . . victory! "It is finished." The news of Christ's divine act of sacrifice for the human race reverberated throughout the universe.

Christ's death on Calvary brought God and humanity, who had been separated by sin, back together. The people in Galilee knew what John the Baptist was saying when he spoke of Jesus in this way: "Behold the Lamb of God, which taketh away the sin of the world" (John 1:29). In Christ's death for our sins He stood in the guilty sinner's place. He died my death that I might live His life! The cross meant much to the apostle Paul. When others asked him what his message was, he replied, "We preach Christ crucified" (1 Cor. 1:23).

Today many have forgotten the greatest event of all history—the countdown to the cross! Many are looking for human-made panaceas or searching for ultimate wisdom and happiness in New Age philosophies. Humanity today is wrestling with the same philosophical problems that concerned Plato and Aristotle. But there is absolutely no way out of the sin problem except the cross. It is our only hope. At the cross we find God's justice perfectly manifested, the mercy of God wonderfully extended to the sinner.

Jesus died that you and I might live. "With His own merits, Christ has bridged the gulf which sin had made, so that the ministering angels can hold communion with man. Christ connects fallen man in his weakness and helplessness with the Source of infinite power" (*Steps to Christ,* p. 20). Today, when Christians around the world are taking another look at the cross, may Christ's countdown to eternity grip our lives!

HMSR

THE TWO RESTS OF JESUS

There remains, then, a Sabbath-rest for the people of God.
HEB. 4:9, NIV.

Some time ago we enjoyed Sabbath dinner and fellowship at the home of our friends Doyle and Paulene Barnett. When Palmer Wick lifted his plate to be served the entrée, he said, "Oh, I've discovered a secret under my plate." Doyle had typed out a question for each of us, followed by a quotation from Ellen White giving the answer. After dessert he asked each of us to read the slip under our plate and comment on it. It was a wonderful way to guide the conversation into Sabbath topics! That Sabbath became very special, because we entered into the spirit of Sabbath rest.

After creating the world in six days, our Creator rested on the Sabbath and established it as a day of rest for us to enjoy His creation. Thousands of years later, after guaranteeing a new life for us at the cross, our Redeemer rested again on the Sabbath day in Joseph's new tomb and established salvation rest as a daily celebration of our salvation. The book of Hebrews delineates the two rests of Jesus—Sabbath rest and salvation rest—and ties them together in Hebrews 4.

The term *Sabbath-rest* appears only once in the New Testament, in Hebrews 4:9 (NIV). How meaningful it must have been to those who received the book of Hebrews to read that "there remains, then, a Sabbath-rest [Greek, *sabbatismos*] for the people of God." Hebrews tells them that Sabbath-rest is grounded in God's rest after He created our world. "On the seventh day God rested [Greek, *katapauomai*] from all his work" (verse 4, NIV). God's rest was one of fantastic daylong companionship with Adam and Eve. Just think, they were only one day old, their world was fresh and new, and their Creator was there to bring it all to life!

Those who have heard the gospel, knelt at the foot of the cross, and believed enter into a rest that is closely related to Sabbath-rest: salvation-rest, *katapausis* in Greek (verses 2, 3). We truly experience salvation-rest only when we cease attempting to earn salvation and rest in the finished work of Christ on the cross, placing full confidence in Him every moment of every day. Why not avoid spiritual exhaustion by trusting Jesus and entering His rest?

DRG

"YOU'LL MAKE IT"

On my account you will be brought before governors and kings as witnesses to them and to the Gentiles.
MATT. 10:18, NIV.

The Kings Heralds Quartet and I were in an African airport waiting for our plane. We had an appointment with the king of Benin. A crowd of people stood in line with us, waiting, when an airport official came to the front and said, "Attention, please. The flight today has been canceled." After the crowd scattered, I went forward to talk with the man. "We have an appointment to appear before the king of Benin. As you know, if a king asks you to be there, you'd better be there. Is there any other plane?"

"No," he answered, "no plane until tomorrow."

"Is there a private plane, a train, any way that we can get up there?" While I was talking with him a man over in the corner shook his head, smiled, and said, "You'll make it." I said, "I certainly hope so."

Several times the quartet members urged me to go talk to the official again. Each time the man in the corner said, "You'll make it." Finally the quartet urged me to go just one more time.

"I'm sorry to bother you again," I told the man. "My friends wanted me to ask just one more time."

"I'm sorry, there is no plane until morning. Please don't ask me again."

Just then the phone rang. "Airport here. British Airways? What time? You have five seats available? Thank you." The official turned to me. "You're in luck," he said. "British Airways will be here in about one hour. They have five seats available for you."

When we walked up the steps to board the plane, that fellow in the corner had his hands folded. With a satisfied smile on his face, he said, "I told you you'd make it." We didn't know who he was, but we had an idea. After all, it was Jesus Himself who promised His messengers, "On my account you will be brought before governors and kings as witnesses to them and to the Gentiles." In every dilemma, in every challenge we face, our loving Saviour is near. He is here for you today!

HMSR

THE CERTAINTY OF JESUS' RESURRECTION

They told the soldiers, "You must say, 'Jesus' disciples came during the night while we were sleeping, and they stole his body.' "

Matt. 28:13, NLT.

Joseph, a rich man from Arimathea," placed Jesus' body "in his own new tomb, which had been carved out of the rock" (Matt. 27:57, 60, NLT). Jesus slept where never a human being had rested before. No one could claim that some old prophet had been interred in the place, and that Christ rose because He had touched the prophet's bones. (Remember Elisha's burial place? As someone hurriedly buried a man there, the body touched the prophet's bones and he came back to life [2 Kings 13:20, 21].) Christ touched no prophet's bones, for none had ever slept there. The Monarch of the earth rested in a new chamber during those three days.

Notice, too, this tomb was cut into the rock. Why? The Rock of Ages was buried in a rock. It was impossible for anyone to steal His body with the great stone at the door sealed and the guards watching. Does it not symbolize the fact that my sins rolled from my shoulders into His tomb—buried forever to have no resurrection?

As we reverently consider these things, stoop down and look into the tomb. Notice the graveclothes all wrapped and laid to one side, the napkin folded up by itself. His enemies said His body had been stolen. Surely grave robbers would not have stopped to wrap up the graveclothes in such an orderly fashion. In too much haste to get away, they would never have thought of such a thing. Why was this done? No doubt to demonstrate to us that Christ did not leave in a hurried manner. He came not "with haste, nor . . . by flight" (Isa. 52:12, NKJV).

When Mary Magdalene reached the tomb, she wept so deeply that she didn't notice the presence of Jesus, but thought He was a gardener. As we think about these images heralding the certainty of Jesus' resurrection, it seems to me that we too should approach the tomb with our emotions deeply stirred and with our faith greatly strengthened. We should today come to that empty tomb in full surrender.

HMSR

APRIL 17

THE TENDER HEART OF JESUS

And the King will answer them, "I solemnly say to you, every time you did a good deed to one of these most insignificant brothers of mine, you did a good deed to me."
Matt. 25:40, Williams.

One day as I drove along the freeway hoping to hear the traffic report on news radio, the newscaster reported on an incredible incident. A burglar had entered a Sears store the previous evening. He piled several pieces of electronic equipment outside by his car. When he went back in for more loot, he noticed the beds and lay down and relaxed. When the police came, he told them, "It was so warm and comfortable here, I just couldn't leave."

His comment was an indictment on society! How many lawbreakers find themselves driven to crime by the need just to be warm and have a place to sleep? No wonder Jesus placed so much emphasis on helping outcasts. He told the crowd who pressed around Him, "Every time you did a good deed to one of these most insignificant brothers of mine, you did a good deed to me." "When I was hungry, you gave me something to eat, when I was thirsty you gave me something to drink, when I was a stranger you welcomed me to your homes, when I needed clothes you put them on me, when I was sick you looked after me, when I was in prison you came to see me" (Matt. 25:35, 36, Williams).

When I once complained to a millionaire about Congress wanting to lower taxes on the rich and cut programs affecting the underprivileged, she retorted: "We earned our money." We all earn whatever money we have, but were we all born equal—with equal talents, an equal IQ, equal opportunities, equal physical energy, equal environments, equally loving and concerned parents? If we were born equal, that attitude might be acceptable. But we are not all born equal.

The good news about Jesus is that He cared for people—all kinds of people. Downtrodden, sullen people. Cold, hungry people. Even people driven to crime for lack of a warm, comfortable bed. And He desperately wants to reach beyond their temporal needs into the hearts of those He loves and give them unparalleled joy and eternal life. What is your deepest desire for the people you rub shoulders with each day?

DRG

A LIFE-CHANGING RELATIONSHIP

Surely I am with you always, to the very end of the age.

MATT. 28:20, NIV.

Christianity is not merely a set of doctrines. It is a passionate, life-changing relationship. Paul Young, of Reston, Virginia, responding to an article on the Holy Spirit in *Christianity Today,* wrote to the editors: "Today, as never before, there is a yearning in the hearts of people to know Christ personally, experientially. Christianity is more than a belief system or a behavioral system. It is a dynamic relationship with a person, God (the Father, Son, and Holy Spirit). To miss out on this relationship is to miss out on the whole thing" (Nov. 14, 1994, p. 10). Well said!

In Jesus' final commission to His disciples He instructed them to go into all the world and teach people the gospel, make disciples of them, and baptize them (Matt. 28:18-20). But Jesus did not stop there. Immediately after giving the Great Commission, He emphasized the need for the disciples and their converts to establish a relationship with Him: "Surely I am with you always, to the very end of the age."

Through the Holy Spirit, Jesus is present with us every moment of every day. He promised: "I will pray the Father, and he shall give you another Comforter, that he may abide with you for ever; even the Spirit of truth; . . . he dwelleth with you, and shall be in you. I will not leave you comfortless: I will come to you" (John 14:16-18).

Thus through the Holy Spirit Jesus is personally with us now, today! It should give us great comfort to know that He is always near through the divine Comforter, not just in time of difficulty or trials. The Christians of the book of Acts maintained a living, dynamic relationship with Jesus through the Holy Spirit. Through our inner relationship with Christ we will grow closer to Him day by day, and the living Christianity of the book of Acts will also thrive in our hearts. What a transformation it makes in our lives to have Jesus present through the Spirit of holiness.

DRG

GO PREACH THE GOOD NEWS

> ***Here begins the Good News about Jesus the Messiah, the Son of God.***
> *MARK 1:1, NLT.*

William Carey, a shoe cobbler who became a preacher, was so thirsty for knowledge that he kept a book open beside him while repairing shoes. In the process he became an expert in theology, Hebrew, and Greek. Finally a church appointed him a lay pastor, then a regular pastor.

While attending a conference of ministers, he stood and expressed his burden for a world dying without Christ. After urging the ministers to heed the instruction of Jesus to go into all the world and preach the gospel, he expressed his willingness to go himself.

The old chairman said, "Sit down, young man; you are a miserable enthusiast. When God wants to convert the heathen, He can do it without your help."

Carey kept agitating. Finally someone sent him to India, and he became the father of modern missions. Despite financial difficulties, his wife's insanity, and non-Christian prejudice, Carey remained firm. After years of working he finally won a convert, then others, and yet still others. He translated the Bible and founded a university. His life and ministry illustrate the power of the good news in a receptive heart.

As Mark starts to write his Gospel, he states, "Here begins the Good News about Jesus the Messiah, the Son of God." He concludes his Gospel with Jesus' final instruction to His disciples: "Go into all the world and preach the Good News to everyone, everywhere" (Mark 16:15, NLT).

Like Carey, those who saturate their lives with the good news about Jesus sense an urgency to "Go . . . and preach the Good News to everyone, everywhere." Immersing ourselves in the good news acts as a stimulus to tell others about Jesus. The news is so good that we can't keep it to ourselves, but we must share Jesus.

DRG

JESUS TOUCHED ME

> ***Filled with compassion, Jesus reached out his hand and touched the man.***
>
> *Mark 1:41, NIV.*

When Dr. Paul Brand, a leprosy specialist, was examining a leper in India, he placed his hand on the man's shoulder as he explained the treatment for the disease. The leper started crying. Brand asked his translator, "Have I done something wrong?" After questioning the leper in Tamil, the translator said, "No, doctor. He says he is crying because you put your hand around his shoulder. Until he came here to you no one had touched him for many years."

In Jesus' day society banished a leper from town. Outside the town wall he needed to stay at least six feet away from everyone and announce, "Unclean, unclean." "A man with leprosy came to [Jesus] and begged him on his knees, 'If you are willing, you can make me clean' " (Mark 1:40, NIV). It must have shocked His disciples and the entire crowd when, "filled with compassion, Jesus reached out his hand and touched the man." Think of how that leper must have felt when, like Dr. Brand, Jesus touched him. The Saviour said, " 'I am willing. . . . Be clean!' Immediately the leprosy left him and he was cured" (verses 41, 42, NIV). Joy must have overflowed from the leper's heart. He could now go home and be hugged by those he loved.

Jesus healed not only those with physical leprosy, but also untouchables suffering from the leprosy of sin. Religions such as Buddhism offer no spiritual cure, but Jesus heals those suffering from sin. Keo Sareith had been a soldier in two armies in Cambodia. He could no longer be a Buddhist, because according to Buddhist law, if a man killed anyone he could not be saved. Then Keo read John 3:16 in his brother-in-law's Bible, and with hope exuding from his entire being, he exclaimed, "When I heard the story of Jesus, I thanked Him very much because He has the power to save a man like me."

The good news for you and for me is that even though we are afflicted with the leprosy of sin, Jesus reaches out, puts His hand on our shoulder, and whispers words of forgiveness and cleansing. He can save a man or a woman like you and like me! Do you feel His touch today?

DRG

APRIL 21

JESUS' POWER TO FORGIVE

"That you may know that the Son of Man has power on earth to forgive sins"—He said to the paralytic, "I say to you, arise, take up your bed, and go your way to your house."

Mark 2:10, 11, NKJV.

Unable to walk, the paralytic had to have his friends carry him everywhere. His four friends placed him on a stretcher. We don't know how far or how long they walked—perhaps several days. Looking for Jesus, they finally found Him. But He was in a house so filled with people that they couldn't even get in the door. But where there is a will, there is a way. When we are determined to see Jesus and have faith in what He can do, we will find ourselves able to enter His presence.

So they climbed up to the flat roof. The men carrying the stretcher removed part of the roof and made a hole big enough to let the man down with ropes into Jesus' very presence. "When Jesus saw their faith, He said to the paralytic, 'Son, your sins are forgiven you' " (Mark 2:5, NKJV). The biblical world considered sickness punishment for sin. Jesus knew what the paralytic thought and eased his mind by forgiving him. When we turn to Jesus, He forgives our sins, and as a child of God, we then can endure the suffering. Jesus can heal us immediately as He did the paralytic, or at a later time, or maybe not at all—whatever He sees will be for our eternal good.

Theologians in the crowd accused Jesus of blasphemy. Because they did not acknowledge Him as the Son of God, they said, "Who can forgive sins but God alone?" (verse 7, NKJV). Jesus, knowing how they reasoned, said, "Which is easier, to say to the paralytic, 'Your sins are forgiven you,' or to say, 'Arise, take up your bed and walk'? . . . He said to the paralytic, 'I say to you, arise, take up your bed, and go your way to your house' " (verses 9-11, NKJV). The people in that crowded house were "amazed and glorified God" (verse 12, NKJV). Whether our sins are little or big, respectable or despicable, secret or blatant, Jesus can and will forgive them!

HMSR

A GIFT OF LOVE FROM JESUS

The Sabbath was made for man, and not man for the Sabbath. Therefore the Son of Man is also Lord of the Sabbath.

MARK 2:27, 28, NKJV.

Through Jesus "all things were created" (Col. 1:16, NKJV). According to the first two chapters of Genesis, Jesus created the world in six days and rested on, blessed, and sanctified the seventh day as the Sabbath. He made the Sabbath for us, thus "sanctified," set apart, it as holy, for our benefit (Gen. 2:1-3).

Note the triangular literary structure of Genesis 1:3 to 2:3:

	The Sabbath 2:1-3 Day 7	
1:9-13 Land and Plants	Days 3 and 6	Animals and Humans 1:24-31
1:6-9 Sea and Sky	Days 2 and 5	Fish and Birds 1:20-23
1:3-5 Light	Days 1 and 4	Sun and Moon 1:14-19

The land and plants, which God created on day 3, are complemented on day 6 by the animals and human beings, who enjoy and feed on them. Sea and sky, created on day 2, have the fish and birds, made on day 5, which swim and fly in them. Light, created on day 1, is manifested on day 4 by the sun and moon, which bathe the earth with light. Now, notice carefully: the entire Creation week builds toward the Sabbath. The Sabbath is at the top of the triangular structure of Genesis 1 and 2. The pinnacle of Creation week, it is the crown of Christ's creative work. Now you understand better why Jesus said, "The Sabbath was made for man, and not man for the Sabbath. So the Son of Man is also Lord of the Sabbath."

Our Saviour gave us a great gift of love when He established the Sabbath for us! He knew our needs. What better could there be to look forward to at the end of a frazzled week? The Sabbath provides for us a day to cease from routine weekly activities and be "rested" and "refreshed." It offers the joys of worship and fellowship with other Christians. And it allows us time to do thoughtful acts of kindness, to strengthen family ties, to enjoy creation and think about our Creator, and to deepen our relationship with Jesus. Let's explore to the full the joys and benefits of the Sabbath. How much nearer to heaven can we get than this!

DRG

SECURE IN JESUS

> *Be of good cheer: it is I; be not afraid.*
> MARK 6:50.

We desperately search for security, but it is hard to find when so much threatens the human race. Years ago, when a reporter asked Einstein, "Do you know what weapons will be used in World War III?" Einstein answered, "No, but I know what will be used in World War IV—rocks." That same threat remains today.

Years ago President Lyndon Johnson stated: "In the first nuclear exchange 100 million Americans and more than 100 million Russians would be dead. And when it was over, our great cities would be ashes, our fields barren, our industry destroyed, our dreams vanished." Now Americans and Russians are less hostile toward each other, but the nuclear threat hangs over our heads with even greater uncertainty because of the proliferation of nuclear weapons to countries that are more willing to use them than Russia ever was.

Not only do nuclear weapons endanger us, but an expanding population and food production race each other. Problems in food distribution have led to famines and deaths in too many countries around the world.

Consider also the breakdown of moral standards as wealthy investors bilk retirees out of their life savings and greedy politicians fleece society while we pile up billions in national debt. Divorce, homosexual marriages, and unmarried couples living together undermine the family as society's basic building block. The breakdown of morality has destroyed nations before us. Never before have the very foundations of our existence been threatened as now.

But there is a place we can find security. The same place the disciples discovered when the storm and an eerie figure in the misty darkness frightened them on Galilee. We can obtain security in the presence of Jesus, who announced to His disciples: "Be of good cheer: it is I; be not afraid." According to the psalmist, "God is our refuge and strength, an ever-present help in trouble. Therefore we will not fear, though the earth give way and the mountains fall into the heart of the sea" (Ps. 46:1, 2, NIV). Jesus is our security, so "be of good cheer!" He will be near you today, so whatever you face that seems intimidating or threatening, "be not afraid!"

HMSR

ARE YOU READY FOR JESUS TO COME?

At that time men will see the Son of Man coming in clouds with great power and glory. And he will send his angels and gather his elect from the four winds, from the ends of the earth to the ends of the heavens.
Mark 13:26, 27, NIV.

At 4:31 on a Monday morning in 1994 a violent shaking awakened us. We listened to our battery radio to find out where the 6.6 earthquake had centered. Its epicenter was in Northridge, about 30 miles from our home. Because of the extensive damage it created, many tagged it the worst natural disaster in United States history.

On the Sabbath morning following the earthquake our congregation invited its members to tell how the quake had affected them. Several told about their terror and fear. Then Tony spoke. He and his wife had lost a son several months before. Tony told us that when he was awakened by the earthquake, he began to praise God, thinking to himself, *At last, Lord, You have come to put an end to this old world! Thank You!* When Lillian told a friend about Tony's testimony, she exclaimed, "Oh, that gives me goose bumps!"

In a world trembling with death and destruction a soon-to-come "earthquake" will bring good news. For "at that time men will see the Son of Man coming in clouds with great power and glory." Think what it will mean when that worldwide earthquake strikes, and the word goes out that Christ has come. It will end corrupt politicians, crooked bankers, hardened criminals, random gunshots, genocide, and countless other horrors. The fears of the jobless, the homeless, the lonely, the sick, and the sorrowing will all melt into hope—Christ is come! "And he will send his angels and gather his elect from the four winds, from the ends of the earth to the ends of the heavens."

Christ will return as unexpectedly as the Northridge earthquake. And after He arrives, "there will be no more death or mourning or crying or pain" (Rev. 21:4, NIV). So keep your courage high, Tony, and all who are reading this, and "be ready, because the Son of Man will come at an hour when you do not expect him" to deliver you from our depressing, frustrating world (Matt. 24:44, NIV).

DRG

IN PARTNERSHIP WITH CHRIST

Go into all the world and preach the good news to all creation. Whoever believes and is baptized will be saved, but whoever does not believe will be condemned.
Mark 16:15, 16, NIV.

Having finally reached the island of Mussau, I had at last realized one of my lifelong ambitions. It was the island where missionaries named Oti and Salau had landed so many years before. They had responded to the message: "Your mission, if you choose to accept it, will be a dangerous one. The risks are high. Your assignment—to take the message of Prince Immanuel to the inhabitants of Mussau. You and Salau will not be alone. You won't see Me, but I will be with you."

The two missionaries had changed the people of the island. No more war canoes set out for other islands to ravage and rape. Instead more than 2,000 happy church members all lined up along the long trail that led up to the top of the hill where the church and mission school are now located. They all were singing, "We're happy today; we're happy today!" And then as a special greeting, they all began to sing, "We welcome you! We welcome you to Mussau!"

How wonderful to hear those 14 choirs waiting for us. Our hosts told us that when Oti and Salau came to Mussau, the governor of the territory gave them no assurance that he could protect them, because the islanders were so fierce. When Oti and Salau first met the inhabitants, the two missionaries began to sing to them. Music was not a part of the culture on Mussau, so it attracted people, and they begged the men to teach them how to sing. It wasn't long before Sabbath schools began and a request went back to mission headquarters for more help. We will never forget our day on Mussau.

In response to God's challenge to Oti and Salau to "go into all the world and preach the good news," an entire island now rejoices with new life. One person beautifully portrayed it in his prayer: "O God, before we did not know You. We had never heard Your name until the missionary came. Now we have heard of Jesus and intend to hold on to You forever!"

Oti and Salau faced an impossible task, but their mission was possible, because they were in partnership with Jesus, who had promised, "I am with you always" (Matt. 28:20, NKJV).

HMSR

JESUS HEALS A PARALYTIC

When Jesus saw their faith, he said, "Friend, your sins are forgiven."
Luke 5:20, NIV.

Jesus was teaching in a packed house in Capernaum. Curiosity seekers, hostile Pharisees, and some who were eager to know more about Jesus crowded around outside. A paralytic had heard wonderful things about Jesus and persuaded four friends to carry him on his mat to Jesus. But when they reached the house, the crowd pressed tight against the door and they could not get in. So, as we saw earlier this month, they climbed up on the roof, made an opening, and lowered the paralytic's "mat through the tiles into the middle of the crowd, right in front of Jesus" (Luke 5:19, NIV).

If you had been that paralytic lying at the feet of Jesus, what would you have desired most? Physical or spiritual healing? Jesus knew his heart. Recognizing the paralytic's priorities, Jesus said to him, "Friend, your sins are forgiven" (verse 20, NIV).

"The burden of despair rolls from the sick man's soul; the peace of forgiveness rests upon his spirit, and shines out upon his countenance. . . . In simple faith he accepted the words of Jesus as the boon of new life. He urged no further request, but lay in blissful silence, too happy for words. The light of heaven irradiated his countenance, and the people looked with awe upon the scene" *(The Desire of Ages,* p. 268).

The Pharisees in the crowd missed the point, so Jesus drove it home by asking if it is easier to heal a person physically or spiritually. Then turning His attention again to the disease victim, He said to the paralyzed man, " 'I tell you, get up, take your mat and go home.' Immediately he stood up in front of them, took what he had been lying on and went home praising God. Everyone was amazed and gave praise to God" (verses 24-26, NIV).

"Oh, wondrous love of Christ, stooping to heal the guilty and the afflicted! Divinity sorrowing over and soothing the ills of suffering humanity! Oh, marvelous power thus displayed to the children of men! Who can doubt the message of salvation? Who can slight the mercies of a compassionate Redeemer?" *(ibid.,* p. 269).

DRG

APRIL 27

JESUS IS GENEROUS WITH US

Give, and it will be given to you. A good measure, pressed down, shaken together and running over, will be poured into your lap. For with the measure you use, it will be measured to you.

LUKE 6:38, NIV.

Jesus here tells us that if we dispense something, we should use a large scoop and give liberal portions, for if we do, we will receive amply in return. When the person who dishes out the wheat presses it down in the measuring container, shakes the container, and fills it to overflowing, the result is a generous measure of wheat "poured into your lap."

The principle applies when we give tithes and offerings. Scripture tells us, " 'Test me in this,' says the Lord Almighty, 'and see if I will not throw open the floodgates of heaven and pour out so much blessing that you will not have room enough for it' " (Mal. 3:10, 11, NIV). Jesus is generous with us when we are generous with Him.

When giving, we must make two decisions: How much to give, and to what. For the tithe it's easy, for God directs that we are to give one tenth of our increase (Lev. 27:30-32; Deut. 14:22); and that we "bring the whole tithe into the storehouse" (Mal. 3:10, NIV)—the church. When presenting offerings we have more flexibility. We are to devote the offerings to helping people and spreading the gospel, so we know where to give them, but how much should they be? Even though Jesus taught that we can't outgive the Giver, we must make some kind of a practical decision.

When Lillian and I first married, we decided that in addition to the tithe we would give at least 10 percent in offerings. We also determined to divide our offerings equally between God's work overseas and His work locally. For more than 50 years we have experienced the wonder of seeing Jesus fulfill His promise to us: "Give, and it will be given to you. A good measure, pressed down, shaken together and running over, will be poured into your lap." He has blessed us materially, but even more important, He has blessed us spiritually. God has become more important to us every year that has gone by. Every moment of every day He has satisfied every need and longing of our hearts. And we are grateful!

DRG

JESUS' POWER OVER DEMONS

Then they went out to see what had happened, and came to Jesus, and found the man from whom the demons had departed, sitting at the feet of Jesus, clothed and in his right mind.

Luke 8:35, NKJV.

Demons possessed two men in Gadara, east of the Sea of Galilee. Both demoniacs had fled society and civilized life and lived in ancient tombs in this desolate part of the country. They made things so unsafe that people were not able to use the road that went that way. Although the authorities had chained them up several times, the demons that controlled them drove them to break the chains, tear off their clothing, and escape into the wilderness. There the men wailed through the desolate countryside, cut themselves with stones, and frightened everybody. No human agency could subdue them, for they were under the more powerful control of demons.

As Jesus and His disciples stepped off their little boat onto the shore of the lake, the men charged toward them. When the disciples fled back toward the boat, Jesus did not. One of the demoniacs approached Him and demanded in a loud voice, "What have I to do with You, Jesus, Son of the Most High God? I beg You, do not torment me!" (Luke 8:28, NKJV). Jesus cast the demons out of both demoniacs; and a crowd came "out to see what had happened." They found one of the men "sitting at the feet of Jesus, clothed and in his right mind" (verse 35, NKJV).

Demons still possess people. Paul warns: "In latter times some will depart from the faith, giving heed to deceiving spirits and doctrines of demons" (1 Tim. 4:1, NKJV). Many people in today's prisons have under demonic influence raped and murdered and mutilated the bodies of innocent people. Respected business executives, possessed by demons, have greedily bilked people out of millions, sometimes their entire life savings. Politicians under evil influence have sold out to political action committees to hold on to their office and their affluent lifestyle. Some of us, possessed by the respectable demons of the drive to be well off, or possessed of uncontrolled appetite or workaholic impulses, need to come to Jesus, sit at His feet, and allow Him to clothe us with His righteousness and restore us to a balanced "right mind."

HMSR

FACING DEATH UNAFRAID

Jesus . . . took Peter, John and James with him and went up onto a mountain to pray. As he was praying, the appearance of his face changed, and his clothes became as bright as a flash of lightning. Two men, Moses and Elijah, appeared in glorious splendor, talking with Jesus. They spoke about his departure, which he was about to bring to fulfillment at Jerusalem. . . . A voice came from the cloud, saying, "This is my Son, whom I have chosen; listen to him."
LUKE *9:28-35, NIV.*

On the Mount of Transfiguration Jesus knew that He faced death, and as a man "of like passions" (Acts 14:15), He hungered for human solace. He had taken three of His disciples along for comfort, but they were extremely sleepy. So Jesus' Father met the need by sending Moses and Elijah to talk with Christ about His death and to comfort Him. Moses faced a similar situation when he climbed the lonely mountain of Nebo alone, knowing he would die there. The Hebrew leader would have a natural death, but Jesus faced His fate at the hands of His nation's leaders. So Jesus' Father added a message of encouragement from heaven: "This is my Son, whom I have chosen; listen to him."

More than 50 years later, on the lonely isle of Patmos, Jesus appeared to John as "the Son of Man" (Rev. 1:13, NKJV), still retaining human nature, and thus identifying Himself with John. A thrill must have surged through the disciple. He was not comforted by two men who had come back to earth, but by a God-man who proclaimed, "Do not be afraid. . . . I am He who lives, and was dead; and behold, I am alive forevermore. Amen. And I have the keys of Hades and of Death" (verses 17, 18, NKJV).

All of us may face death before Jesus returns. The words of Jesus, "Do not be afraid. . . . I am He who lives. . . . I have the keys of . . . Death," are for each of us. Because He is alive, we too shall live. The resurrection of Jesus is not simply the story of a temporary escape from death and the grave. Jesus did not live to die again. His world-shaking proclamation, "Behold, I am alive forevermore," is a Conqueror's ringing words of permanent victory over death. Because Christ as a living God-man burst asunder the grave, we can face death unafraid!

DRG

LET THE FIRE FALL

Then [Jesus] said to them . . . "Which of you fathers, if your son asks for a fish, will give him a snake instead? Or if he asks for an egg, will give him a scorpion? If you then, though you are evil, know how to give good gifts to your children, how much more will your Father in heaven give the Holy Spirit to those who ask him!"
Luke 11:5-13, NIV.

On my dad's way north to hold an evangelistic meeting, he suggested that we spend a day in Yosemite Valley. At 9:00 that evening I remember our family standing in Camp Curry waiting for a very special event to take place. Hundreds of feet above on Glacier Point the rangers had built a fire with a special kind of bark and let it reduce itself to red-hot coals. At 9:00 sharp the rangers called down from Glacier Point: "Camp Curry, are you ready?" Back echoed the answer, "Camp Curry is ready. Let the fire fall!" At that the rangers pushed the coals over the precipice, and those of us below saw a great fire-fall of coals and embers.

What the church needs today is for the cry to go out: "Let the fire fall!" Jesus once asked: "If a son requests his father for food, will he give him a snake or a scorpion?" The only plausible answer is "Of course not." Jesus continued: "How much more will your Father in heaven give the Holy Spirit to those who ask him!"

When was the last time you asked for the Holy Spirit? We should not be reticent to do so. "The time is not far off now when men will want a much closer relation to Christ, a much closer union with His Holy Spirit, than ever they have had, or will have, unless they give up their will and their way, and submit to God's will and God's way. The great sin of those who profess to be Christians is that they do not open the heart to receive the Holy Spirit" *(Selected Messages,* book 2, p. 57).

Jesus is with us through the Holy Spirit. Every day we should pray, "Fill me with Your Spirit today, Lord, use me. Let the fire fall!" God wants to reveal Himself to the world through the power of the Holy Spirit in our lives. He seeks for us to enter a deeper relationship with Christ through a closer union with the Holy Spirit, because with the Holy Spirit of Jesus in our lives we would have a greater love for the Word, a greater love for each other, and a greater desire for Jesus to come.

HMSR

MAY 1

THE NEED TO BE SOMEBODY—1

He came to himself.
LUKE 15:17.

A young man in an Eastern country was dissatisfied with life. He wished to leave home and become somebody. Wanting position, fame, and a sense of personal significance, he requested his inheritance from his father and journeyed into a far country. Here was a young man with the means to enjoy the good things of life and with no one to restrict whatever he did. Through the influence of godless companions he spent all his money and soon found himself without friends. He had "wasted his substance with riotous living" (Luke 15:13).

The young man finally realized that he was among strangers who did not care about him. Before long his clothes were dirty and his hair unkempt. His body smelled of swine, for in his desperation he had accepted the menial and degrading work of a swineherd. The youth who had boasted of his freedom and his desire to be somebody now found that he was really a slave. The glitter and tinsel that enticed him had disappeared, and he began to feel the weight of the chains of sin that bound him.

We can just about see him—his dirty clothes, unkempt hair, twisted and matted beard. He has lost weight, and hunger pains constantly gnaw at his empty stomach. No longer does he resemble the son of a prosperous man. His carefree companions, who once flocked about him, have vanished. Life had lost its glow. "With money spent, with hunger unsatisfied, with pride humbled, with his moral nature dwarfed, with his will weak" (*Christ's Object Lessons,* p. 200), finally, "he came to himself." "He came to his senses" (NIV). He realized that he was squandering his powers of mind and heart and soul, that he was bankrupting himself for eternity, that he had made the wrong choice, and that he should return home and make things right.

If we want to be "somebody," we must first realize that without Jesus we are "nobody," for any attempt to live apart from Him leads only to meaninglessness. Before we can ever become somebody we must first realize our sinful condition and that Jesus waits for us to recognize our need of His presence in our lives every moment of every day. We then become somebody—His son or His daughter!

HMSR

THE NEED TO BE SOMEBODY—2

When he was yet a great way off, his father saw him, and had compassion, and ran, and fell on his neck, and kissed him.
Luke 15:20.

When the prodigal son realized he was squandering his powers of mind and heart and soul, and was bankrupting himself for eternity, "he came to his senses" (Luke 15:17, NIV). He acknowledged his condition and returned to his father to confess his errors, to ask forgiveness, and to request to become a hired servant. Instead, his father welcomed him back as a son. His father eagerly waited to receive him (Luke 15:18-24). "When he was yet a great way off, his father saw him, and had compassion, and ran, and fell on his neck, and kissed him."

His father accepted and forgave him and directed the servants to bring the best robe, put the ring of authority on his finger, and prepare a great feast. "For this my son was dead, and is alive again; he was lost, and is found" (verse 24).

"In his restless youth the prodigal looked upon his father as stern and severe. How different his conception of him now! . . . He whose eyes have been opened by the love of Christ will behold God as full of compassion. He does not appear as a tyrannical, relentless being, but as a father longing to embrace his repenting son" (*Christ's Object Lessons,* p. 204).

Many believe they are not important to God, but this is not true. Everyone has a deep need and longing to be loved, to be respected, and to feel significant. Jesus emphasized the importance of each of us as individuals in the parables of the lost sheep and the lost coin, and especially in the parable of the lost son. He waits for us, just as the loving father waited for his prodigal son to return. Christ welcomes back both the prodigal who is deep in sin, and also the prodigal Christian. Both are of great worth in His eyes.

Sometimes it is difficult for us, even as Christians, to realize that Jesus is interested in us. We may have disappointed Him by falling into "respectable sins." Or we may have slipped and wandered into wrong paths. But remember that the Saviour, who accepted the repentant prodigal, will certainly forgive and accept the repentant Christian. You are of great worth to Jesus.

HMSR

WHEN PRAYER WHEELS TURN

Men always ought to pray and not lose heart.
LUKE 18:1, NKJV.

Jesus tells us to "ask, and it will be given to you; seek, and you will find; knock, and it will be opened to you" (Luke 11:9, NKJV). But if God knows all things, why should we pray to Him? Does the Lord need a reminder of what He is already aware of?

The heart of every person desires to communicate with the Divine. From the Tibetans high in the Himalayas, with their prayer wheels constantly turning, to the Hindus bathing in the Ganges, to the American child in the bedroom upstairs, people realize the importance of communication with the God of the universe. Our strength as Christians comes not from something on earth, but from God. Human wisdom is not enough, and that's why Jesus urges us to ask, seek, and knock.

Like Jesus, the apostle Paul reminds us of our need for constant, persistent, overcoming prayer: "Pray at all times in the Spirit. . . . Keep alert with all perseverance" (Eph. 6:18, RSV). Realizing our natural frailties, he admonishes us to put all our energy into prayer. Why do Jesus and Paul emphasize that "perseverance" in prayer is vital?

First, because we are battling against the powers of evil. "We wrestle not against flesh and blood, but . . . against spiritual wickedness in high places" (verse 12).

The second reason for constant, persistent, overcoming prayer is that it is God's appointed way for us to obtain knowledge of His perfect will for us, and the strength to act upon it.

Third, if our spiritually dead loved ones are to rise to a new life, we must contact God and receive His power to witness to them.

Fourth, the leaders in the early church gave themselves "continually to prayer, and to the ministry of the word" (Acts 6:4). Here we find the secret of the tremendous success the early church had carrying the gospel to the then-known world.

Last, we are to persevere in prayer because Jesus appointed it as the means of protecting us from the cares of this life and preparing us for His soon coming (Luke 21:34-36). Everywhere around the world our families desperately need help, so why not start talking with God more persistently right now?

HMSR

DOES JESUS ALWAYS ANSWER OUR PRAYERS?

Watch therefore, and pray always that you may be counted worthy to escape all these things that will come to pass, and to stand before the Son of Man.

Luke 21:36, NKJV.

Jesus made the sweeping promise to His disciples that He would answer their persistent prayers for safety and salvation. He also assured them that if they prayed, "your Father who sees in secret will reward you openly" (Matt. 6:6, NKJV). Yet the question persists: "Does God really care for me? After all, it seems as if many of my prayers receive no answer." Often we become despondent because we feel God doesn't respond, and doubts creep in. When we talk to our Saviour, we must believe that as we reach up to Him, He reaches down and meets us more than halfway. "Rest in the Lord, and wait patiently for Him" (Ps. 37:7, NKJV).

During Jesus' prayer in Gethsemane He allowed His Father the freedom to act according to the best scenario for all the people of the world. Jesus prayed to be delivered from dying on the cross, but He was resigned to God saying no—that is, if God could not save Him from the cross and save us too (Matt. 26:39).

At times God will say no instead of yes as He responds to our requests. One little boy prayed for God to make Jacksonville the capital of Florida. When someone asked why he was praying so intently, he explained, "Well, that's the answer I put on my test paper this morning." At such times God's intervention would be impractical and unwise.

Sometimes our prayers receive their answer only after a long delay as God waits in the wings and directs events. Years ago in Ohio a little church had difficulty growing. Factions developed. The discouraged minister resigned. Finally it closed its doors. The church died—except for one man who patiently and persistently held a prayer vigil on the church steps each Wednesday night. People thought he was foolish, but he persevered in prayer until one man joined him, then one person after another. Finally the group called a pastor, and today this church lives and ministers to that community. When we pray, Jesus answers.

HMSR

MAY 5

YOU CAN DEPEND ON JESUS

Then Jesus said to him, "Receive your sight; your faith has saved you."
Luke 18:42, NKJV.

Bartimaeus, a blind man, sat by the side of the main highway between old Jericho and new Jericho. When he heard the noise of the excited crowd beginning to pass, he was sure it was Jesus approaching. The Master had healed many, and no doubt some were trying out their ability to walk, to jump, and to run, since the power of Jesus had straightened their legs. Some swung their previously withered arms. Others looked here and there and everywhere, trying out their new eyesight. Still others rejoiced at hearing the wonderful voice of Jesus for the first time. No wonder they were happy!

Somebody assured Bartimaeus that Jesus of Nazareth was passing. His ears could hear a lot, since he could not see. "And he cried out, saying, 'Jesus, Son of David, have mercy on me!' " (Luke 18:38, NKJV). The crowd tried to shush him up, because the phrase "Son of David" was a political slogan, referring to ancient Judean royal family, and could have directed the wrath of Rome down on them. "But he cried out all the more, 'Son of David, have mercy on me!' " (verse 39, NKJV). Did anyone ever try to shush you up? They have me at times. But when you come with a desire in your heart for God's blessing, don't ever let anyone silence you. Like that blind man, shout all the more, "Jesus, have mercy on me!"

Jesus brought the whole crowd to a halt and had the blind man brought to Him. When Bartimaeus reached Him, Jesus asked, " 'What do you want Me to do for you?' And he said, 'Lord, that I may receive my sight.' Then Jesus said to him, 'Receive your sight; your faith has saved you.' And immediately he received his sight, and followed Him, glorifying God" (verses 41-43, NKJV). Not only did Bartimaeus receive his eyesight, but God was glorified by him and all those who saw it.

Let us call to Jesus, the healer, the blesser, the Saviour, the Son of God, and He will hear our prayer. We do not see many physical healings today because most often Jesus says, "My grace is sufficient for you" (2 Cor. 12:9, NKJV). Nevertheless, spiritual healing for the troubles and difficulties that arise for all of us is always granted in answer to the persistent prayer of faith.

HMSR

THE POWER OF JESUS' RESURRECTION

Salvation has come to this home today.
LUKE 19:9, TLB.

Once I went to a concert by Michael Harris, a gospel singer with a deep bass voice. He told how God had saved him and his wife from drug addiction. On their way to Las Vegas, while under the influence of cocaine, he fell asleep at the wheel. His car overturned, throwing his wife through the windshield and breaking her neck. As a paraplegic, she turned to Jesus. His guilt led him deeper into drugs. She left him and returned to her roots in Fiji, all the while praying for him.

One day Michael looked in the mirror and saw nothing more than a beast. That led him to God. When he called to give his wife the news, she knew her prayers were being answered. She returned to the United States. Both of them surrendered to Jesus and were baptized. They could truly say, "Salvation has come to this home today." At their baptism Michael gave this testimony: "Instead of cocaine running through my veins, I have the blood of Jesus in my veins. Instead of dealing in dope, I have hope!" Like the prodigal son, Michael "was dead and has returned to life" (Luke 15:24, TLB). Jesus does the same for every willing heart!

Michael experienced "the power of [Jesus'] resurrection" (Phil. 3:10, NKJV). Or, as *The Living Bible* translates this expression, he began "to experience the mighty power that brought [Jesus] back to life again." The moment he received Jesus as his Saviour, Jesus' resurrection power began to work in his life. He "crossed over from death to life" (John 5:24, NIV).

Jesus' promise to each of us, "Because I live, you also will live" (John 14:19, NIV), is not just an assurance of life after death. Jesus is here describing His gift of a new life now through "the power of His resurrection." The power of the risen Saviour transforms each of us who become a Christian, sustains us each day of our lives, and assures us of both resurrection from death and eternal life. We die to a frustrating, destructive life of sin and are spiritually resurrected to live a new, more satisfying life. So no matter what we face in life, with the power of Jesus' resurrection working in and through us, how can we fail?

DRG

JESUS SAVES THE LOST

> *For the Son of man came to seek and to save the lost.*
> LUKE 19:10, RSV.

One evening when Genene, our oldest daughter, was 4 years old, she jumped up on my lap, and out came the usual "Please tell me a story, Daddy." I told a story I'd heard from George Vandeman about a little girl standing on a street corner in London with a torn dress and matted hair. Lost, she cried as if her heart would break.

At this point in the story Genene began to rub her eyes, and a tear trickled down her cheek. I continued by telling about two kind police officers who came to the girl's aid. They suggested many landmarks in an attempt to find out what part of the city she lived in—all dead ends. Then one of the officers asked her, "Do you know where that big white church with the high steeple with a cross on it is?"

"Oh, yes, yes," responded the lost girl, "take me to the cross. I can find my way home from there."

To drive the point home for Genene, I moralized: "That's the way Jesus feels about us when we are lost, and that's why Jesus came to die, so that we might be found."

After the story came Genene's usual "Please tell me another story, Daddy"; but this time she added, "Tell me a better story." Before I could ask what she meant by a better story, she continued, "Please tell me a story that won't make me cry."

I had dwelled too much on the lost girl's frustration and fear while lost and not enough on her happiness after she found the way home by being led to the cross. The cross of Jesus brings tears of sorrow, because our sins caused Jesus to suffer and die. But the cross also calls for tears of gratitude, because Jesus "came to seek and to save the lost." The cross reminds us not only that Jesus died for our sins, but also that He arose from the grave a conqueror over sin and death. We do not worship a dead Saviour buried in a dusty tomb. The tomb is empty. Jesus is alive and active in our lives. He came to take us home. We receive love, hope, and a bright future. The story of the cross should make us cry, but the story of the resurrection causes us to smile. The cross is good news only if Jesus came back from the grave. And He did—and He is alive!

DRG

THE WEEPING CHRIST

> ***And when he was come near, he beheld the city, and wept over it.***
> *LUKE 19:41.*

Here is a strange text of Scripture—Jesus weeping! He comforted the brokenhearted, brought joy to the downcast and heavy-laden, gave peace to the troubled and hope to the discouraged—and yet He Himself is weeping. Why? The occasion is one of great rejoicing for those crowding about Jesus. Joy and music are in the air. "The whole multitude of the disciples . . . rejoice and praise God with a loud voice for all the mighty works that they [have] seen; saying, Blessed be the King that cometh in the name of the Lord: peace in heaven, and glory in the highest" (Luke 19:37, 38). His disciples have placed Him on a colt and at His direction are leading Him down the Mount of Olives to Jerusalem, where they hope to crown Him king.

In the midst of the rejoicing throng Jesus looks out over the city of Jerusalem glistening in the sunlight, and to the amazement of all, weeps over it. Why? He is sobbing over Jerusalem's inhabitants who have rejected Him, and over a city soon to be destroyed by Roman armies as a judgment for her sins (verses 42-44).

It was not Jerusalem alone that brought His tears. "Jesus, looking down to the last generation, saw the world involved in a deception similar to that which caused the destruction of Jerusalem" (*The Great Controversy,* p. 22). He wept over a lawless, judgment-bound modern world. Christ shed tears over some of your neighbors, friends, and family members. Finally, our Saviour was weeping over every lost person in our modern world whom He longs to save and whom He could save if only they were willing.

Someday soon the tears of the weeping Christ will be eclipsed by a smiling Christ. Surely Jesus will smile broadly as He looks upon the redeemed as they with joyful hearts stand on the sea of glass singing praises to His name. Jesus' suffering will be over, and as He now lovingly gazes upon those whom He died to save, "He shall see of the travail of his soul"—the suffering and pain it cost Him to redeem us—"and shall be satisfied" that it has been worth it all (Isa. 53:11). Is this not ample cause for a smile? Do you prefer to be a source of tears for the weeping Jesus, or of joy for the smiling Christ?

DRG

MAY 9

"STAND STRAIGHT AND LOOK UP!"

The courage of many people will falter because of the fearful fate they see coming upon the earth. . . . Then the peoples of the earth shall see me, the Messiah, coming in a cloud with power and great glory. So when all these things begin to happen, stand straight and look up! For your salvation is near.

LUKE 21:26-28, TLB.

I remember one woman who found a special gleam of hope in the teaching of the soon coming of Jesus. She had said to me, "I am so afraid. Such terrible things are happening in the world. My father just died of a heart attack. I'm sure the fear of world conditions caused his attack."

In reply I read the striking description of our times that Jesus gives in Luke 21:25, 26: "Upon the earth distress of nations with perplexity; . . . men's hearts failing them for fear, and for looking after those things which are coming on the earth."

"Oh, is that in the Bible?" she asked in surprise.

"Yes," I said. "It sounds like the daily newspaper, doesn't it?"

She agreed and seemed to relax visibly as we read together the following verses: "And then shall they see the Son of man coming in a cloud with power and great glory. And when these things begin to come to pass, then look up, and lift up your heads; for your redemption draweth nigh" (verses 27, 28). Her face lit up with a glow of hope as the thought of the soon coming of Jesus brought release to her fear-burdened heart.

If you are depressed because you suffer a debilitating illness or you have lost a loved one, the hope of Jesus' return is for you. Or if your family is falling apart and you need Someone to lean on, Jesus' hope-filled message is for you: "Stand straight and look up! For your salvation is near." To a world that is sick, to a world full of people paralyzed with fear, Jesus, the Great Physician, challenges us, "Look up, My coming is near. Soon all trouble, sickness, and fear will be banished. It's almost time to go home with Me. Your pain is soon to be over. Death is soon to end. Bright days await ahead. There is hope for the future. 'Stand straight and look up!' "

DRG

WHO KILLED JESUS?—1

> ***Jesus said, "Father, forgive them, for they do not know what they are doing."***
> *LUKE 23:34, NIV.*

Just before He died, Jesus spoke these words to His heavenly Father. He prayed for those who had condemned Him and the men who had actually crucified Him. Notice that they did not know what they were doing. They did not understand what was taking place—why He was dying—though they were involved in it.

Paul also emphasizes this important point. He speaks about the mystery of what God is doing for the lost world through the gospel. "None of the rulers of this age understood it, for if they had, they would not have crucified the Lord of glory" (1 Cor. 2:8, NIV).

Have you ever thought much about the meaning of this text? People in general did not know what was happening. Even the "powers that be" who put Him to death—the ecclesiastical and political leaders and the soldiers who nailed Him to the cross as well as those who jeered at Him—did not realize to any great extent what was taking place.

That being true, who then really crucified Jesus? "[Jesus Christ, the Righteous One] is the atoning sacrifice for our sins, and not only for ours but also for the sins of the whole world" (1 John 2:1, 2, NIV). Who then is responsible for Jesus' death on the cross? The Judean leaders? Yes, they had a part in it. They were sinners. The Romans? Yes, Pilate and his soldiers had a role in it. They too were sinners. But don't stop there. Don't stop at Jerusalem. What about the people of Rome, of Moscow, Washington, San Francisco, Beijing, Montevideo, Cape Town? What about you? What about me? We all crucified Jesus, putting Him to death by our sins.

How thankful we can be for Jesus' prayer to His Father: "Father, forgive them." Let's ask Him to forgive all our sins so that His death will not be in vain. Can we do less when we consider the magnitude of His gift and the magnanimity of His prayer for forgiveness?

HMSR

WHO KILLED JESUS?—2

He was delivered over to death for our sins and was raised to life for our justification.

ROM. 4:25, NIV.

An Army chaplain described the terrible destruction from the World War II bombardment of Liège, Belgium. Four days and nights the rescue party worked desperately, trying to find those who might still be living under the rubble of the fallen buildings. Just when they thought they had discovered everyone, they heard a feeble cry. Surely no one could have survived so long in the cold, least of all a child—and yet it was a baby's cry. They dug deeper. Sure enough, the little fellow was there; and when they got him out they found him still conscious, though he hadn't had food or water for four days. How could he possibly have lived? Because he was sheltered beneath his mother's body. It was a miracle of a mother's love and sacrifice. She curved her strong body above her child. The building collapsed, and she took the full weight of the crushing stones. Although she was dead, her child was alive. As John Masefield, the poet laureate of England, wrote: "Oh, Mother, when I think of thee, 'tis but a step to Calvary."

It is a long step, of course. Jesus died for the salvation of all people. "He was delivered over to death for our sins and was raised to life for our justification." Our Saviour's life, death, and resurrection is the greatest story ever told. It will change the life of any person who will let it. After dying for our sins, Jesus rose from the dead to make our justification possible. God cannot justify our sinning, but He can by His grace justify us—account us righteous.

God sacrificed Himself to save us—even His enemies, even those who hate Him. "God commendeth his love toward us, in that, while we were yet sinners [enemies], Christ died for us" (Rom. 5:8). So if Jesus died for us, our sins really killed Him. He became "sin for us, who knew no sin; that we might be made the righteousness of God in him" (2 Cor. 5:21). How can we thank Him? By living our life for Him today—one day at a time.

HMSR

A MOTHER'S INFLUENCE

And I heard a voice in the heavens above me saying, "Write this down: . . . Yes, says the Spirit, they are blest indeed, for now they shall rest from all their toils and trials; for their good deeds follow them to heaven!"

Rev. 14:13, TLB.

When the followers of Jesus die, "their good deeds follow them to heaven." Their influence for good does not stop at the edge of the grave—it goes on and on and blesses the world. A Christian mother may come to the end of her journey here on earth and feel that her life's work is a failure, because her boys and girls have never turned to God and lived a Christian life. But her death may lead a daughter—who has held out against all her pleadings—to a decision. A son finds his mother's Bible and reads the verses underlined with pencil and discolored with tears, while the Spirit speaks to his heart. He can't resist, and surrenders to Jesus. The mother's works follow her. She "being dead yet speaketh" (Heb. 11:4). By her remembered example, at some time of crisis, her boy makes a decision for Christ, and one of her daughters turns to God for help.

Heaven never forgets a mother's prayers for a wandering boy. In a faraway land in the midst of a great battle, his mother's words come to him: "Someday, when you are in great trouble, if you call on your mother's God, you will find help. I will pray for you as long as I live." He sees that wrinkled face, and those worn hands folded in prayer. God has not forgotten her last petition: "Oh, Lord, I put him in Thy hands. Bring him to Jesus at last." And there in a foxhole, he turns to his mother's Saviour. Her works do follow her, and God answers her prayers.

It will be a wonderful reunion when in the presence of Christ, by the beautiful gate of the City of God, a mother receives the rewards of her labors with "all the children in." Yes, it's true: "They shall rest from all their toils and trials; for their good deeds follow them to heaven!" A mother's prayers follow her children in this world, and on through the gates of the New Jerusalem into the eternal world to come. And that is good news for every Christian mother—and father!

HMSR

WHO KILLED JESUS?—3

This Jesus, delivered up according to the definite plan and foreknowledge of God, you crucified and killed by the hands of lawless men.

ACTS 2:23, RSV.

Jesus went to His death according to God's plan, not humanity's. Christ, the one whom the Romans nailed to the cross, was actually handed over to be crucified "according to the definite plan and foreknowledge of God." God the Father gave His Son willingly, and God the Son died willingly. God took the responsibility and chose to die for your sins and mine. He gave Jesus "to be sin for us" (2 Cor. 5:21). When Jesus died on the cross, the heavenly Father was not receiving a gift from Jesus—He was making a gift to us. "God was in Christ, reconciling the world unto himself" (verse 19).

Dr. Loraine Boettner in the book *The Atonement* quotes from a Jewish scholar addressing an American-Jewish audience in answer to the question "Who killed Christ?" At the conclusion of his speech he said that in a larger sense the death of Jesus was not an accident. The greed of the mercenary priests and the weakness of Pontius Pilate were merely incidental to His death. He said, "The New Testament teaches that the death of Christ was a divine act, that His death was sacrificial." The intelligent follower of Jesus Christ will never shift the blame to the shoulders of the Jewish people, nor to the Roman government, but will assume equal responsibility with every other person in the world for the tragedy that took place there on Golgotha. Dr. Boettner goes on to quote a Christian litany: "Who was the guilty? Who brought this upon Thee? Alas, my treason, Jesus, hath undone Thee. 'Twas I, Lord Jesus, I it was denied Thee: I crucified Thee."

Not until the realization that we ourselves crucified Jesus hits home in our heart can we really ever understand God's love and saving mercy. His love, not Roman nails, held Him there. Should we not beat our breasts and plead for God's forgiveness? Should we not live for Him and show by our lives of humble obedience that we do love Him who first loved us?

HMSR

WITH JESUS IN PARADISE—1

And he said, "Jesus, remember me when you come into your kingdom."
LUKE 23:42, RSV.

Jesus was not crucified alone—the Romans executed two others with Him. His persecutors put Him between two condemned criminals to cast contempt upon His claim to the throne of Israel.

Just look at those three crosses on Calvary! A strange darkness gathers over the earth, and the shadows deepen around Golgotha. "One of the criminals who were hanged railed at him, saying, 'Are you not the Christ? Save yourself and us!' But the other rebuked him, saying, 'Do you not fear God, since you are under the same sentence of condemnation? And we indeed justly; for we are receiving the due reward of our deeds; but this man has done nothing wrong' " (Luke 23:39-41, RSV).

One of the dying thieves takes up the ridicule of the rulers and hurls it at the dying Saviour. Suddenly the other rebukes him: "Do you not fear God? In such an hour as this, when we have nothing more to fear from others, can you not recognize purity? We reap the just reward of a life of crime while this Man suffers unjustly."

Then the dying thief turns toward Jesus. Can you see him trying to pull himself closer to Jesus? He turns away from the world and his wasted life, away from the taunts of the listening crowd. In earnest tones he pleads, "Jesus, remember me when you come into your kingdom."

He knows that he is not prepared for eternity. At the supreme hour of Christ's rejection, when religious leaders have repudiated His claims and even His disciples have forsaken Him, the dying thief calls out to Jesus. At some time or other the thief has heard of the kingdom that Jesus preached. Possibly in Pilate's judgment hall he listened to Christ declare that He was a king. Now on a cross, crucified next to Jesus, he witnesses the taunts addressed to the Saviour and asks to be remembered.

The good news for the thief and for us today is that when things look dark, discouraging, and hopeless, Jesus promises, "Yes, I will remember you!" (see verse 43).

HMSR

WITH JESUS IN PARADISE—2

Jesus turned His head toward him and said, "I promise you today, when I return with the glory of my Father, I will take you home with me to paradise."
LUKE 23:43, CLEAR WORD.

One of two thieves dying on each side of Jesus' cross knew that sometime in the future Jesus would have a kingdom, and he requested that Christ remember him then. Jesus was dying by his side, but He would come into His kingdom. He would be King! And the dying thief asked to be a part of that kingdom.

Men might nail Jesus to a cross, but they could not keep Him from doing good. Those feet, always on errands of mercy along the dusty roads of Palestine, and those hands always bringing healing to pain-racked bodies and peace to broken hearts—they could nail them to the cross. They could push a crown of thorns down over His brow. But they could not keep Him from being a Saviour. "Jesus, remember me when you come into your kingdom," gasps the dying thief (Luke 23:42, RSV). And from the bruised lips of Christ there comes the promise "I will take you home with me to paradise."

"Today," the very day when it looked as if Jesus would not have a kingdom, He promised the thief: "You will be with me in Paradise" (verse 43, RSV). Jesus emphasized the time of His promise. "In this day of My humiliation, you have faith in My exaltation. In this day when all others have forsaken Me, you call Me Saviour. In this day of your extremity, when you throw your helpless soul upon a dying Saviour, I promise you. Today, I declare it as a royal decree from the cross, as from a throne: You will be with Me in Paradise!"

The thief was a prisoner, but he was a prisoner of hope—the blessed hope. A crown awaits the penitent thief. It will be his when Jesus sets up His kingdom. This is the triumph of faith.

With this wonderful example of Jesus' willingness to save the person who comes to Him, even in the most extreme trouble, you and I should never fear to turn to Him. Jesus is near to help us now. He gives us forgiveness and power to live for Him in our everyday life. It's absolutely true. You can depend on it.

HMSR

WAS CHRIST'S DEATH NECESSARY?—1

Was it not necessary that the Christ should suffer these things and enter into his glory?
Luke 24:26, RSV.

Three days after Jesus died, Cleopas, one of Christ's disciples, along with a companion, believed by some to have been his wife, journeyed from Jerusalem to Emmaus. About eight miles west of the city they discussed the things that had happened three days before—the Crucifixion, the burial, the fact that the disciples had found Jesus' tomb empty that very day.

As they walked along in sadness, suddenly a stranger joined them. Interested in their conversation, he asked, "Why are you so sad?" After explaining the reason for their concern about the prophet whom Rome had put to death, they told him how others had discovered His tomb to be empty. Some claimed the prophet was still alive, while others argued that thieves had stolen His body.

The stranger told the two that they were slow to believe and dull of understanding. "Was it not necessary that the Christ should suffer these things and enter into his glory?" He asked. "And beginning with Moses and all the prophets, he interpreted to them in all the scriptures the things concerning himself" (Luke 24:27, RSV). His theme was the most stupendous in all the Word of God—Jesus "in all the scriptures." No wonder the hearts of His listeners burned within them.

The words of special significance in Jesus' short Bible study with Cleopas and his companion consisted of His opening question: "Was it not necessary that the Christ should suffer these things?" Didn't the prophets look forward to Messiah's coming? Didn't they foretell a suffering Messiah? Didn't they point to a Christ who would come and die and then rise from the dead? Why should the two be sorrowful about His rejection and death? Wasn't this expected? Jesus probably included in His answer this prophecy: "He was wounded for our transgressions, he was bruised for our iniquities: the chastisement of our peace was upon him: and with his stripes we are healed" (Isa. 53:5). Yes, it was necessary for Jesus to suffer and die to save the world and you and me from sin and eternal death.

HMSR

WAS CHRIST'S DEATH NECESSARY?—2

And beginning with Moses and all the Prophets, he interpreted to them in all the scriptures the things concerning himself.

LUKE 24:27, RSV.

When the two on the way to Emmaus talked with Jesus, they did not recognize Him. As the evening shadows spread across the land and they reached their home, they invited Him to stay for the night. Suddenly, as they began the evening meal, they realized that He was Jesus, and He vanished out of their sight. They hurried back to Jerusalem to tell the other disciples they had seen Him.

As they had walked along the road listening to every word this stranger spoke, something inside them responded. Had they recognized Jesus from the beginning, they would not have heard anything He had to say. Instead, they would have been too full of happiness to comprehend His words. But they listened to the first Christian sermon, preached by Christ Himself on the day of His resurrection, not in the Temple or Jerusalem, but to two Jewish peasants out on a country road.

The Old Testament Scriptures, which Christ preached from, are full of Jesus. They contain prophecies that He has fulfilled and will fulfill through His life, death, resurrection, ministry above as our High Priest, and eventually His second coming. The Old Testament prophecies told why He would die. For instance, in Isaiah 53, written centuries before Christ appeared, we read: "And the Lord hath laid on him the iniquity of us all. . . . For the transgression of my people was he stricken. . . . [He died to] justify many; for he shall bear their iniquities" (Isa. 53:6-11).

Jesus explained to the two disciples on that country road why it was necessary for Him to suffer and die. Prophecy explained that if people were to be saved, God must give His Son so that all believers might have everlasting life. And the Son died "to give his life a ransom for many" (Matt. 20:28). How many? "For the sins of the whole world" (1 John 2:2). Jesus had to die as our Sin-bearer, our Lamb, the one great Sacrifice, that even though we are sinners we might be counted righteous and therefore find salvation. Let us enter His presence and thank Him just now!

HMSR

THE UNNATURAL ACT OF FORGIVING

Father, forgive these people, because they don't know what they are doing.

LUKE 23:34, NLT.

When an IRA bomb went off in Belfast in 1987, it trapped George Wilson and his daughter under the rubble. The last words he ever heard his daughter speak were: "Daddy, I love you very much." She died a few hours later. As he recovered, he said from his hospital bed: "I have lost my daughter, but I bear no grudge. Bitter talk is not going to bring Marie Wilson back to life. I shall pray tonight, and every night, that God will forgive them." Later, on a news broadcast over the BBC, when he told his experience, "the world wept."

In a sinful world, forgiving those who were responsible for killing Wilson's daughter and causing his own suffering was an unnatural act, rooted and grounded in divine love. When an unruly, hate-filled mob beat, mocked, and spit on Jesus, He cried out, "Father, forgive these people, because they don't know what they are doing." Jesus planted that same kind of love in the heart of George Wilson. We can exercise the unnatural act of forgiving only by receiving Christ's love first. When you find yourself holding back or unwilling to forgive, remember the cross! As you meditate upon it, try to realize that it is "a revelation to our dull senses of the pain that, from its very inception, sin has brought to the heart of God" (*Education,* p. 263).When you are wronged or misunderstood or suffer at the hands of misguided enemies or even friends, remember Christ's love! While our sufferings last for but one short lifetime, the Father and the Son have continually suffered every moment sin first darkened Their universe.

Our suffering always injures Jesus' heart of love. As a Father who loves us dearly He suffers along with us and seeks to turn all of our suffering into stepping-stones to a more abundant life. Become charged with Jesus' love and forgive!

DRG

JESUS' FINAL HOURS—1

> ***The Son of man must be delivered into the hands of sinful men, and be crucified, and the third day rise again.***
>
> LUKE 24:7.

Think of the tens of thousands of people during the past few decades who have jumped every time they heard a rap on the door at night. If it's midnight, it might be the police! The very thought of such incidents disturbs us. Many centuries ago, just outside the eastern wall of Jerusalem at the western base of the Mount of Olives, police arrested Jesus at midnight in the Garden of Gethsemane. It was a strange climax to His years of love-filled service for others!

Jesus and His disciples had gone to the garden after the inauguration of the first Communion in the upper room. It was late at night. He had been praying and had sought the companionship of the disciples nearest to His heart. Then came the confused noise of the approaching mob, led by officials and a military guard, along with the police, to arrest Him at midnight. With armed men surrounding Him as though He were a criminal, Jesus made no resistance. When Peter, His intimate friend, tried to defend Him with a sword, Jesus told him to put it away, then healed the wound that Peter had just caused.

The mob was no surprise to Jesus. Long before, He had declared that the time would come when He would be turned over to hostile authorities. Jesus was fulfilling a divine purpose in His life. Nothing took Him by surprise. As a man He was well acquainted with the Old Testament prophecies written centuries before. They clearly show that the Messiah, the Christ, long expected by the chosen people, would be rejected, "delivered into the hands of sinful men, and be crucified, and the third day rise again." While still in Galilee with His disciples, by that beautiful lake, Jesus had remarked: "The Son of man shall be betrayed into the hands of men: and they shall kill him" (Matt. 17:22, 23). Facing certain death, He let Himself be arrested without resisting—for you!

HMSR

JESUS' FINAL HOURS—2

Then Jesus said unto the chief priests, and captains of the temple, and the elders, which were come to him, Be ye come out, as against a thief, with swords and staves? When I was daily with you in the temple, ye stretched forth no hands against me: but this is your hour, and the power of darkness.

Luke 22:52.

Jesus' arrest took place at night because of a fear that the people would rush to His rescue, for He was quite popular at the time. Tens of thousands had heard of Him or had actually seen His miracles and listened to His wonderful sermons or knew someone that He had healed. In fact, many of them at one time wanted to take Him by force and make Him king. But Jesus, knowing this, had retired to an isolated spot. None of these events surprised Jesus, since He understood the prophecies. And as the Son of God, He of course was aware of what people were thinking and what they would do.

According to John 18, each member of the mob that came to arrest Jesus had some evidence that Jesus was more than merely a man, that He was divine, and that the power of heaven was upon Him. When they approached Him, armed as they were, He asked whom they were looking for. They said, "Jesus of Nazareth." When the Saviour said, "I am he," the Scripture declares they fell to the ground helpless (John 18:5, 6). Jesus could have escaped, but did not take advantage of the opportunity.

To the disciples He Himself had said that He could have called for 12 legions of angels (about 72,000), to protect Him (Matt. 26:53). The hosts of glory could have surrounded Him and delivered Him from our world of darkness and injustice. But He remained here. He came to suffer for us, to be treated as we deserve (we who are indeed sinners), that we might at last be treated as He, the holy, harmless, righteous Son of God, deserved to be treated.

Think of what He suffered that night—for you!

HMSR

JESUS' FINAL HOURS—3

Jesus kept silent. And the high priest answered and said to Him, "I adjure You by the living God that You tell us if You are the Christ, the Son of God." Jesus said to him, "It is as you said."

Matt. 26:63, 64, NKJV.

Jesus not only permitted wicked men to arrest Him but let Himself be tried at midnight before several tribunals, something apparently contrary to the practice of the time. Think of that long night and His preliminary hearing before Annas, the former high priest, then the one before the Sanhedrin, the supreme court of the land. Since it lacked authority to execute the death penalty, they dragged Jesus before Pilate, the Roman governor, to seek a death sentence.

The Sanhedrin should have been a pattern for true justice the world over. It demanded at least two witnesses for any prosecution and condemnation (Deut. 17:6). The court must examine each witness separately, and their evidence must agree. The judicial body considered a person innocent until evidence proved them guilty. Under no circumstances could it use an individual's own testimony against him or her. The case must begin with arguments in favor of the prisoner. Even if the Sanhedrin judged a defendant guilty of death, it could not pronounce the condemnation until the day following the trial, to give time for an appeal. Therefore, a trial could never take place on the day before the Sabbath. Such trials never convened at night.

But the Judean rulers did not observe these rules in Jesus' hearing. In their attempt to destroy Christ, His accusers had condemned Him before the trial began. The trial took place first before Annas and later before Caiaphas. It reached its climax when Caiaphas demanded, "I adjure You by the living God that You tell us if You are the Christ, the Son of God." Jesus' answer amounted to: "Yes, I am the Son of God." In addition to claiming divinity, Jesus added more than the high priest expected: He announced that Caiaphas would someday see Him coming back to earth as king.

As Christians, we need the courage of Jesus to stand up for who we are and what we believe. How courageous are you?

HMSR

JESUS' FINAL HOURS—4

When Pilate saw that he could not prevail at all, but rather that a tumult was rising, he took water and washed his hands before the multitude, saying, "I am innocent of the blood of this just Person. You see to it."
MATT. 27:24, NKJV.

When Jesus stood trial before the Sanhedrin, the court broke up when the mob condemned Jesus as guilty and deserving of death. At this point Caiaphas turned the Saviour over to the mob. We can only imagine Christ's sufferings at their hands. Before daybreak the religious authorities brought Him to Pilate, the Roman governor, who demanded to know the charges against Him. Since blasphemy was a purely religious matter and did not satisfy the Roman official, Christ's opponents raised the charge of treason. They charged Him with perverting the nation, claiming to be king, and forbidding others to pay tribute to Caesar—each a deliberate untruth.

Learning that Jesus was a Galilean, Pilate took advantage of the fact and turned Jesus over to Herod, the ruler of Galilee. Pilate and Herod had been enemies, but the death of Jesus led them to become friends (Luke 23:12). Herod sent Jesus back to Pilate. The Roman official could not get rid of the prisoner as easily as he had hoped. Again the crowd surged before him, demanding crucifixion. In the middle of it all, he received a message from his wife relating a dream and warning, "Have nothing to do with that just Man" (Matt. 27:19, NKJV).

Pilate was convinced of Jesus' innocence. Since it was the custom to pardon a prisoner to the people at the time of the Passover, he offered to release Jesus. But the mob chose Barabbas the murderer instead and demanded Jesus' crucifixion. The Roman official gave up his attempt to save Jesus and symbolically washed his hands of it all. He was not strong enough to resist the chant of the crowd: "If you let Jesus go, you are not Caesar's friend." That was dangerous talk, and Pilate knew it. He could not be just and save his position.

He had Jesus scourged, brought Him bleeding before the crowd, and "delivered Him to be crucified" (verse 26, NKJV). Jesus was handed over because of our sins, as our substitute. He died for us, erasing the account we never could pay. There was no other way for us to be saved. His atoning death brings us eternal life.

HMSR

JESUS' FINAL HOURS—5

About the ninth hour Jesus cried out with a loud voice, saying, . . . "My God, My God, why have You forsaken Me?"
Matt. 27:46, NKJV.

Think of what Jesus suffered during the final hours before His crucifixion—His hands bound tightly, no food, no sleep, the terrible tension of it all. The ignominy. The shame. The blows. The whipping with a Roman scourge until bones appeared through His flesh. The crown of thorns. The spikes through His hands. Above all, the sense of His separation from God, causing Him to cry out: "My God, My God, why have You forsaken Me?" Jesus suffered what the lost will endure when they realize they have eternally separated themselves from the life and forgiveness of God.

While our Saviour possessed miraculous power to heal the sick and to raise the dead, He worked no miracle to save Himself. He used only power available to us today. Power that comes from God through prayer and God's Word. In Jesus' final hours He willingly accepted the crushing weight of our sins and the sins of the world.

After His death He spent a full day and parts of two others in the tomb. Then came an earthquake and a brilliant light followed by two angels announcing: "He is not here, but is risen! Remember how He spoke to you when He was still in Galilee, saying, 'The Son of Man must be delivered into the hands of sinful men, and be crucified, and the third day rise again' " (Luke 24:6, 7, NKJV).

The women the angels spoke to ran back to the upper room and reminded the disciples that Jesus had said He "must" be delivered into the hands of sinners, must be crucified, and must rise again the third day. What happened in Jesus' final hours was according to a plan devised by God. Jesus was arrested in the darkness of the garden, tried at night before hurriedly gathered courts, whipped, and forsaken by all His disciples—one of them even cursed and swore and denied he knew Him. And then—the cross! Jesus did all this for you and me—everybody. The suffering and death of Jesus means salvation, love, and power, for He is alive today! He is your personal Saviour and best friend. He promises His strength for our weakness, His courage for our timidity, and His love for our receptive heart.

HMSR

JESUS' FINAL HOURS—6

He said, "It is finished!" And bowing His head, He gave up His spirit.
JOHN 19:30, NKJV.

It was the ninth hour when Jesus loudly cried, "It is finished!" He then bowed His head and died. The ninth hour was 3:00 in the afternoon, the very time the priests offered the lamb in the Temple, but Jesus' death on the cross was the real sacrifice. He is the Lamb of God to which all the ancient sacrifices pointed.

When soldiers came to break the legs of the three crucifixion victims to hasten their death, Jesus was already dead (John 19:33). The guards smashed the thieves' legs, but because Jesus was dead, they did not touch His legs (verse 36), thus fulfilling the prophecy: "Not one of [His bones] shall be broken" (Ps. 34:20, NIV).

Christ died a conqueror, His mighty shout, "It is finished," directed to His Father. Jesus had finished the work He came to do. With the universe reconciled, He had opened the way into heaven for all who would accept His grace. God had made provision to take away the sins of the world. The Saviour gave His life for those who did not know Him or even hated Him. Sinners can be saved if they turn to Christ, the Lamb of God, for salvation (John 1:29). Here is the everlasting gospel. God doesn't downplay sin or ignore it. Far from it. If anyone desires to know what God thinks of sin, look at the cross. God hates sin but loves the sinner. Calvary judged sin and destroyed its power in the universe forever. The cross is a ladder that reaches from earth to heaven. It reveals God's everlasting love and forgiveness. That triumphant cry of Jesus still rings throughout the universe: "It is finished!" The power of sin and death is finished. Christ accomplished a full and complete atoning sacrifice at the cross. The door to the city of God stands open to those who are disappointed with life, with themselves, with the world's philosophies, efforts, and sorrows. Through that open door God invites all to come to Calvary and really look to Jesus. Once we love Him, our life is never the same again. He gives us joy that nothing can ever take away. And that's good news!

HMSR

"POWER FROM HEAVEN"

And now I will send the Holy Spirit upon you, just as my Father promised. Don't begin telling others yet—stay here in the city until the Holy Spirit comes and fills you with power from heaven.
LUKE 24:49, TLB.

One day Alec Wyton, organist of the Church of St. John the Divine in New York City, was to play a dedicatory program in the majestic new Westminster Presbyterian Church in Greenville, South Carolina. He began to play and everyone waited for the first note, but no sound came from the great organ. Realizing what had happened, he turned toward the people and said, "Folks, one thing we cannot do without is power. We know the notes and the music, but without the electrical power we cannot play. Will someone please turn on the power?"

You may have everything our world has to offer, but without the power that comes from God, you cannot really live, you cannot have freedom and joy. You will be playing soundless notes unless you have the power of God in your life through His Holy Spirit.

I've often wondered what would happen if we celebrated as joyfully the advent of the Holy Spirit as we do the coming of Jesus at Bethlehem. To commemorate the arrival of Jesus, the second person of the Godhead, we give gifts, sing songs, and festoon windows with bright tinsel at Christmastime. But how many of us are as thankful for the advent of the Holy Spirit, the third person of the Godhead?

The coming of the Holy Spirit in your life affects not only you, but your whole family. Yes, even the neighbors next door. It is easy to think of Jesus and the Father as persons. We can visualize them in some way. But the Holy Spirit exists on a more mysterious level—invisible, intangible, secret. And yet the Holy Spirit identifies with Jesus in character, purpose, and activity. On Jesus' departure from earth, the Comforter arrived with power. He can be in every place at one time. When we think of Him as a person, we will understand how to yield to Him so He can enter our lives and use us. So claim the promise of Jesus: "And now I will send the Holy Spirit upon you." Ask and pray "until the Holy Spirit comes and fills you with power from heaven." The Holy Spirit is Jesus' personal ambassador to you.

HMSR

ONE SMALL STEP FOR GOD

In the beginning was the Word, and the Word was with God, and the Word was God. He was in the beginning with God. All things were made through Him, and without Him nothing was made that was made. . . . And the Word became flesh and dwelt among us, and we beheld His glory, the glory as of the only begotten of the Father, full of grace and truth.

John 1:1-3, 14, NKJV.

On July 20, 1969, we sat on a straw mat in front of a shop house in Golden Sands, Malaysia, and watched Neil Armstrong step down from the lunar landing vehicle *Eagle* and become the first person to walk on the surface of the moon. The Malaysian villagers sitting next to us began to speculate on how such a movie had been made. As other villagers joined in the conversation, a lively discussion ensued. They just could not believe they were actually looking at the real surface of the moon and that human beings were really walking on it.

As Armstrong bounced step by step over the surface of the moon, in Malaysia 240,000 miles away we heard him announce, "That's one small step for a man, one giant leap for mankind." For Neil Armstrong and Buzz Aldrin to explore the lunar surface was certainly "one giant leap for mankind." But that moment shrinks into insignificance when placed alongside what Jesus accomplished at Creation when "all things were made through Him." Jesus not only existed before the innumerable island universes made up of billions of suns and worlds, but He brought all of them into existence.

After Jesus made our tiny world in His vast universe, Adam, the first man to walk on Planet Earth, might well have exclaimed: "That's one small step for God, one giant leap for mankind!"

When Adam and Eve sinned, the One who created us "became flesh and dwelt among us, and we beheld His glory, the glory as of the only begotten of the Father, full of grace and truth." We can now rejoice in the good news that Jesus came to our world as a man to die in our place, and then shout to the highest heavens, "That's one gigantic step for God, and one giant leap for mankind!"

DRG

MAY 27

A MEMORIAL DAY TO REMEMBER

> *For in six days the Lord made the heavens and the earth, the sea, and all that is in them, but he rested on the seventh day. Therefore the Lord blessed the Sabbath day and made it holy.*
>
> Ex. 20:11, NIV.

Have you ever forgotten a birthday or an anniversary? I have, and it can be most embarrassing. Of course, some dates we seldom forget, such as July 4, 1776, the birthday of the United States; or November 11, the eleventh day of the eleventh month, when the warring forces signed the armistice of World War I. We can all remember our own birthday. I was born the week the stock market crashed in 1929, and all who were old enough to experience their impact will never forget the Depression years. But one birthday the Creator told us to remember many have forgotten—the birthday of our earth. After creating the world in six days, Christ set aside the seventh day as a memorial of Creation, the birthday of our world. He "blessed the Sabbath day and made it holy."

Today the United States observes Memorial Day in memory of those who died for their country in war. And since Jesus died on the cross, the Sabbath has become not only a memorial of our creation by Him, but a memorial as well of our being re-created by our crucified and risen Saviour.

Christ created the world, and He re-creates sinful men and women through the redemption provided on Calvary. The One who flung the worlds into space is the One who died on the cross for you and me. The Christ of Creation is the Christ of Calvary. Every seventh day is a special day that He "blessed" and "made . . . holy." The birthday of our world is a memorial day to Christ as both our Creator and our Saviour.

Satan has tried to destroy the concept of Jesus Christ as Creator and Saviour. Why? Because "the Sabbath was made for man" (Mark 2:27, NIV), and Satan does not want people to experience the blessings that our Creator and Redeemer gives to those who truly remember Him on the Sabbath. Since Christ "blessed the Sabbath day" with His special presence, celebrating the Sabbath is a life-building experience. Those who truly desire to cultivate a friendship with Jesus will remember His holy day. Honoring Jesus on His holy holiday brings unlimited blessings.

HMSR

THE RIGHT TO BECOME GOD'S CHILD

He came to His own, and His own did not receive Him. But as many as received Him, to them He gave the right to become children of God, even to those who believe in His name.

John 1:11 12, NKJV.

A friend of mine told me of an elderly woman who realized her sinfulness and confessed all to Jesus. She testified: "Well, I ain't what I ought to be, and I ain't what I'm going to be, but anyhow, praise God, I ain't what I used to be!" She did not claim the right to be a child of God because of her perfect life, but because she had believed in and received Jesus. He had given her "the right to become" one of God's "children," and she was still on her way up.

Some dread failure in their spiritual life, especially after reading in the Scriptures the high standard God expects of them. But if we "believe" and "receive," Jesus gives us "the right to become children of God." The word "right" used here is a synonym for the word "authority." We can revel in the assurance that Jesus has given us permission to call ourselves sons and daughters of God.

But we must allow Jesus into our lives. The key word is "receive." Notice carefully that we do not simply accept a doctrine or belief; we receive Him. It's a person we let into our lives, the person of Jesus Christ. When we believe in Jesus and receive Him as our personal Saviour, we then understand the real meaning of life.

A 3-year-old child lived in a foster home, penniless and unloved. A wealthy couple fell in love with her and she with them, and they adopted the child. She became the gleam in their eyes, the treasure of their hearts. Believing that they were her parents, she received them as such. They told her that she was adopted, then reminded her that other people have to take what they get when a child is born, but they chose her. Designated their heir, she inherited their fortune. It was her right. Jesus chose you as His child. If you believe in Him and have received Him as your Saviour, you have "the right to become" a child of God and to become an heir to a heavenly mansion in which you will live eternally! What higher certainty can you receive than that?

HMSR

CHRIST BECOMES A MAN

The Word became flesh and made his dwelling among us. We have seen his glory, the glory of the One and Only, who came from the Father, full of grace and truth.
John 1:14, NIV.

I once heard H.M.S. Richards tell this touching story:

A mother had just put her son to bed and was about to leave the room when he called after her, "Mommy, you're not going to leave me here alone, are you? It's so dark in here!"

"Yes, I know it's dark, darling, but God is here all the time."

"Yes, I know God is here, Mommy, but I want someone with a face."

Alone in a dark world, we long for Someone with a face. Jesus gave God a human face. Through Jesus God came down in human "flesh and made his dwelling among us." In the Old Testament tabernacle God visited Israel in the Most Holy Place so He could "dwell among them" (Ex. 25:8). Then in New Testament times God became a human being whom the people of His day lived with, and who, through the Gospels, we can see with our own eyes.

Jesus' actions, teachings, and attitudes are the actions, teachings, and attitudes of God—for He is God. "The Word was God" (John 1:1, NIV). Christ, "the Word," existed before He visited our world. He "came from the Father." The name Christ designates Him as the long-awaited Messiah and as fully God. Christ "became flesh." The name Jesus refers to Him as the babe born in Bethlehem of a human mother. Thus He is fully man. Christ Jesus is both fully God and fully man. God became a man and lived among us.

By becoming a human being, Jesus emphasized the tremendous worth, the infinite value, that God places on each of us. He respects our dignity and cares when we suffer. Jesus empathizes when we need a listening ear and sympathizes when we hurt emotionally. After experiencing all this as a human being, He then died to assure us that we will someday experience a life forever free from disappointments and troubles. Thank God for that!

And thank God for a Person we can relate to now. Jesus is a real, living human being, just like us, whom we can follow, love, and enjoy.

DRG

JESUS CURES THE LONELINESS OF SIN

No one has ever seen God, but God the One and Only, who is at the Father's side, has made him known.

JOHN 1:18, NIV.

The most difficult moments for us as missionaries in Singapore were waving goodbye to our oldest daughter when she boarded the plane to attend college in America. After all, an ocean would now separate us. During that time a story H.M.S. Richards told moved us.

A college boy, the son of missionaries, was lonely at Christmastime. The principal asked him, "What would you like most of all for Christmas?"

The boy looked at the framed photograph of his father sitting on the desk and said, "I would like my father to step out of that frame." God stepped out of the frame when Jesus came to live in our world.

When Adam and Eve sinned, the external results of sin—the things seen—were hard to endure. But most difficult of all was the emptiness of heart they began to experience. Hidden longings, unsatisfied desires, painful yearnings, all began to bore their way into those hearts that had broken their tie with God. They were experiencing the loneliness of sin! Since the entrance of sin every human being has suffered from soul hunger, from hidden longings of the heart. Misinterpreting those cravings, people have sought relief with money, drink, evil companions, immorality, and a life of ease. But such false remedies have never brought happiness. Why? Because the hidden hungers of the human heart are symptoms of loneliness for God, hunger pangs for His love in our life.

Jesus, who is one with the Father, "became flesh and made his dwelling among us" (John 1:14, NIV). "No one has ever seen God, but God the One and Only, who is at the Father's side, has made him known." God stepped out of the frame and into our world when Jesus came and lived among us. That's why, when we form a friendship with Jesus, it satisfies the cravings of our heart. We begin to experience a satisfying life of rest and peace, hope and joy—that only He can supply.

DRG

THE CARING CHRIST

When the wine was gone, Jesus' mother said to him, "They have no more wine." "Dear woman, why do you involve me?" Jesus replied, "My time has not yet come."
JOHN 2:3, 4, NIV.

How embarrassing that on a festive occasion the punch bowl had gone dry. Jesus' mother must have been a deeply caring person, for she felt for the family and she turned to Jesus. His reply to His mother may seem rude, but in every act of His life Jesus had to keep His mind on His goal for coming to earth. According to the prophecy of Daniel 9, Jesus' inevitable destiny was to die for us so He could give us eternal life. Nothing must interfere with that plan. Christ told His mother plainly that the time for Him to die had not yet come. At least 10 times in John's Gospel Jesus repeats this truth.

Mary had every confidence that Jesus could avoid a premature crisis, that this man she had raised also possessed her same caring nature, and she told the servants, "Do whatever he tells you" (John 2:5, NIV). Jesus really cares: "Nothing that in any way concerns our peace is too small for Him to notice. There is no chapter in our experience too dark for Him to read; there is no perplexity too difficult for Him to unravel" *(Steps to Christ,* p. 100). He pays attention to our needs, our problems, and our happiness.

When we were in pastoral ministry, God gave us some wonderful, caring people in our congregations. People who felt deeply about other people because of their association with Jesus and their desire to be like Him.

In Huntington Park, California, we called Olive Castleman our "associate pastor." When someone was sick, in trouble, or needing a listening ear and we went to visit them, it was often the case that she had already been there or would come while we were there.

In Singapore God gave us Della Sorensen, the wife of the Far Eastern Division president. She was a mother in Israel to every member of our congregation. One member said to us, "You are not going to like this, but she is our first lady." Not like it—we loved it! And we loved Mrs. Sorensen because, like Jesus, she cared.

Do you care? Do you assist your pastors with their flock?

DRG

MASTER OVER THE IMPOSSIBLE

This, the first of his miraculous signs [turning water into wine], Jesus performed in Cana of Galilee. He thus revealed his glory, and his disciples put their faith in him.

JOHN 2:11, NIV.

Jesus' miracles were "signs" that "revealed his glory." Character is the English word that I believe best reflects the predominant meaning of the word "glory." Christ's miracles revealed His character as the Master over the impossible, and because of this "his disciples put their faith in him." We should never write off any person or problem as impossible if we trust Jesus. For "with God all things are possible" (Matt. 19:26, NIV).

We have seen firsthand Jesus, this God of the impossible, work miracles. The miracle of healing saved my wife Lillian's life when doctors said she was burned too badly to survive. Through prayer God healed me of undulant fever. After we prayed for a 5-year-old deaf child in our home in San Pedro, California, the boy and his mother walked out onto our front porch and for the first time the boy heard the whispering of the wind. He looked up at his mother in wonder and uttered, "Psssssssssss."

Thousands of times in our years of ministry we have witnessed the greatest miracle of all—Jesus changing broken lives and performing spiritual healing. We lived in Singapore for 12 years during the Vietnam war and often invited GIs on R&R to our home. Sitting at our table, Robert told us of being delivered from alcohol, tobacco, and every kind of vice. He observed a Seventh-day Adventist soldier in his outfit who was different, began asking him questions, and received satisfying answers. Finally this hardened army man surrendered everything to Jesus. His changed life and the lives of hundreds of others we have rubbed shoulders with testify that Jesus is the God of the impossible. Nothing is too big for Him to handle. We can put our "faith in him."

You may need courage, money, health, peace in your home. Jesus' resources are inexhaustible. The One who transformed water into wine can change your circumstances, your outlook, your ability to cope with life. Our human resources may fail, but Christ's are inexhaustible.

DRG

JUNE 2

THE GOOD NEWS ABOUT JESUS HITS HOME

Now there was a man of the Pharisees named Nicodemus, a member of the Jewish ruling council. He came to Jesus at night and said, "Rabbi, we know you are a teacher who has come from God. For no one could perform the miraculous signs you are doing if God were not with him."

John 3:1, 2, NIV.

In reply Jesus declared, 'I tell you the truth, no one can see the kingdom of God unless he is born again.'

" 'How can a man be born when he is old?' Nicodemus asked. 'Surely he cannot enter a second time into his mother's womb to be born!'

"Jesus answered, 'I tell you the truth, no one can enter the kingdom of God unless he is born of water and the Spirit' " (John 3:3-5, NIV).

Lillian and I were in Kiev, Ukraine, the third largest city of the former Soviet Union. We visited a new church of about 600 members, established as a result of an evangelistic series. All but 20 were brand-new Seventh-day Adventists. The series was one of hundreds of crusades by evangelists sent into the former USSR in a General Conference-sponsored evangelism program. God has poured out His Spirit in latter rain proportions and thousands have responded to "the good news about Jesus" (Acts 8:35, NIV).

That evening in Kiev, Bob Spangler, the originator of the evangelistic program, told the story of Nicodemus coming to Jesus by night. Jesus informed Nicodemus: No one can "see" or "enter" the kingdom unless he is "born again." In contrast: "Everyone who believes in [Jesus] may have eternal life" (John 3:15, NIV).

After the service an old man came to us and said with teary eyes and a broken voice, "I'm so glad I lived long enough to hear about Jesus." God's Spirit had moved upon his heart, and the miracle of the new birth had taken place. For 70 years the atheistic Soviet Union kept the door to the entrance of the gospel sealed. It then opened wide, and the elderly man rejoiced in "the good news about Jesus" and the assurance of eternal life in Him.

Do you have the assurance of eternal life in Christ? Has God's Spirit given birth to a new life in Christ for you? Are you rejoicing in the good news about Jesus?

DRG

CHANGED BY THE POWER OF JESUS

Jesus answered, "Most assuredly, I say to you, unless one is born of water and the Spirit, he cannot enter the kingdom of God. . . . Do not marvel that I said to you, 'You must be born again.' "
John 3:5-7, NKJV.

Bonifacio Sanchez, a wealthy man, owned the largest drinking house in town. Unfortunately, he was a victim of the drink he sold. Alcohol did its deadly work. His wife, driven to despair by the abuse she suffered, fled, taking their two children with her. The sudden loss of his family threw him into depression and led to further excesses. He walked about with a dagger hidden in his pocket, ready to kill the first enemy he found.

The friend who told me this story reported: "While in this state Bonifacio was invited to attend our meetings, but he said, 'No, that's not for me.' Finally the kindness and love of the man who was inviting him prevailed, and he came to my meetings to listen to God's Word. A great change began in his heart. God's love and mercy toward sinners and Jesus' pardoning grace gave him hope, and Jesus freed him from his angry thoughts. It renewed him in spirit, body, and mind. His wife heard about his conversion and rejoined him. He is now a sweet Christian and has become a dynamic witness for Christ."

Bonifacio owes God his life, for he found salvation and forgiveness in Jesus. He can't change the wrongs he once committed, but God forgave his sins. He has discovered a new life and has been born again by a miraculous gift from God. That's the type of experience Jesus told a highly esteemed theologian about in that midnight interview in Jerusalem: "You must be born again," not physically, but of "the Spirit." The new birth is the key to unlock "the kingdom of God."

No matter how hopelessly lost in sin a person is, our Saviour can help anybody who comes to Him with a sincere desire to be forgiven. No one is outside the circle of Jesus' love. He has the power to change all sorts of people—not only unsaved sinners, but also pious, respected church members. Those with trigger tempers or secret sins held in the darkest recesses of their heart, those with bad habits, and even those who are only a tiny bit proud can be saved by the power of Jesus.

HMSR

LOOK AND LIVE!

As Moses lifted up the serpent in the wilderness, even so must the Son of man be lifted up: that whosoever believeth in him should not perish, but have eternal life.
John 3:14, 15.

Some time ago I had a thrilling experience with a young sailor who had written to me from various parts of the world. One day I received a letter saying that he had given his heart to Jesus Christ and was looking forward to baptism. He had taken a Voice of Prophecy Bible course, and it had led him to the Saviour. Repenting of and confessing his sins, he had looked to Jesus and lived. Eternal life was now in his grasp. Later the young man came to me and told me how he had looked to Jesus in complete faith. As we talked, I could see the joy and complete satisfaction written across his happy face.

A person who looks to Jesus is saved by faith. When Israel sinned and hundreds were dying from serpents who sank their deadly fangs into them, God instructed Moses to make a bronze replica of a snake and put it on a pole. He told Moses, "anyone who is bitten can look at it and live" (Num. 21:8, NIV). "As Moses lifted up the serpent in the wilderness, even so must the Son of man be lifted up: that whosoever believeth in him should not perish, but have eternal life." "The lifting up of the brazen serpent was to teach Israel an important lesson. They could not save themselves from the fatal effect of the poison in their wounds. God alone was able to heal them. Yet they were required to show their faith in the provision which He had made. They must look in order to live. It was their faith that was acceptable with God, and by looking upon the serpent their faith was shown" (*Patriarchs and Prophets,* p. 430).

In the beginning a look caused the human race to be lost. Eve gazed at the forbidden fruit, and it plunged the human race into sin. Jesus provided a way for another look to save people. Look to Jesus. Focus your spiritual eyes on Him and live eternally! Do you have acquaintances or loved ones whom you wish to see saved for eternity? Point them to Jesus. The way is so simple. It's just "look" and "live." So lift the Saviour up!

HMSR

SOLVING THE MYSTERY OF LIFE

For God so loved the world that He gave His only begotten Son, that whoever believes in Him should not perish but have everlasting life.
JOHN 3:16, NKJV.

The Mystery of Life is the largest sculptured group in Forest Lawn Memorial Park in Glendale, California. Standing before the statue, listening to the recorded commentary, and contemplating what is in the minds of each of the people carved in marble is a moving experience. A small boy beholds the mystery of life as he watches a baby chick emerge from a broken shell. His grandmother, who he thinks knows everything, looks on with wonder in her eyes. In the background are two lovers who believe they have found the mystery of life in their devotion for each other. A girl graduate lost in her dreams seems not to be giving thought to this vital question. Next to her a troubled scientist muses on all his failed attempts to solve the mystery of life. A happy family seem unconcerned, but as they look at doves mating, the question in their minds appears evident. A learned philosopher scratches his head. A monk and a nun seem to have found the answer in their religion. An atheist by his expression apparently has no interest in the mystery of life at all.

Next to the statue on a plaque is a message from Hubert Eaton, the founder of Forest Lawn: "Gentle visitor, during the years that *The Mystery of Life* group was being carved, the sculptor and I discussed many interpretations, but the one I liked best is found in the words of Victor Herbert's immortal song, 'Ah, Sweet Mystery of Life.'" The answer found in that well-known song is: "'tis love, and love alone."

Love is the answer to the mystery of life—love that oozed from God's heart and led Him to give "His only begotten Son, that whoever believes in Him should not perish but have everlasting life." Love that led the Son of God to go willingly to Calvary and die for our sins. That divine love moves the hearts of children and their grandmothers, young lovers, college graduates, entire families, philosophers, the religiously inclined, and even atheists, and causes them to repent and give their hearts and lives to Jesus. Have you solved the mystery of life and responded to Jesus' incomprehensible love?

DRG

JUNE 6

TRANSFORMING THUNDER INTO LOVE

For God did not send His Son into the world to condemn the world, but that the world through Him might be saved.
John 3:17, NKJV.

During my first year in the ministry, I considered myself to be preaching the truth, blowing the trumpet in Zion, telling people what they must be and do. One day as I was out Ingathering with a doctor's wife, a very dedicated woman, she said, "Sometimes I wonder if it is worth trying to live the Christian life. It's so hard, and the preachers tell us we are so terrible."

As I realized that my preaching was discouraging her I began to face the fact that while people long for victory, they are fighting hard, stern battles with self. That experience changed my preaching. Rather than condemning people, I began to present messages of encouragement and hope. I refocused my preaching on Jesus. "For God did not send His Son into the world to condemn the world, but that the world through Him might be saved."

John shares the message of this scripture with us. According to Jesus he was a son of thunder (Mark 3:17). By nature John was far from lovable and lovely. He was short-tempered, intolerant, vindictive. But Jesus saw past what John was to what he could become. Jesus formed an intimate friendship with the young disciple and changed thunder into love. And John became the beloved disciple.

What transformed him? How did a son of thunder become an apostle of love? If we discover John's secret, we too can have a life of victory. Two great visions changed John: 1. A vision of the cross. He saw in Jesus' eyes, looking down upon him from the cross, Christ's all-consuming love for him. That love broke John's heart. 2. A vision of the empty tomb also transformed him. The risen, living Christ, who is with us always, gave John victory and preaching power.

If you sometimes feel discouraged with yourself or if you think your life is one of failure rather than victory, John's life has a message for you. "In adoration and love [John] beheld the Saviour until likeness to Christ and fellowship with Him became his one desire, and in his character was reflected the character of his Master" (*The Acts of the Apostles,* p. 545). Look to Jesus. Only He can transform the thunder in you and me into love.

DRG

ETERNAL LIFE CAN BE YOURS NOW

All who believe in God's Son have eternal life.
JOHN 3:36, NLT.

On Jesus' final night with His disciples, after sharing the Last Supper, He unburdened His heart. Christ felt great sadness as He realized what would happen the next three days and how much the disciples would need Him to face a hostile world. So Jesus promised to send the Holy Spirit to be their Comforter, then shared some intimate thoughts that would give them insight, courage, and hope over the weekend and beyond (John 14-16).

Then Jesus prayed: "Father, the time has come. Glorify your Son. . . . He gives eternal life to each one you have given him" (John 17:1, 2, NLT). The disciples must have wondered when they would receive eternal life. "All who believe in God's Son have eternal life." The moment we accept Jesus, we have it spiritually as an entirely new life begins. It's a done deal, a completed transaction. Jesus guarantees eternal life now. "All who see [God's] Son and believe in him should have eternal life—that I should raise them at the last day" (John 6:40, NLT).

The disciples also must have asked themselves how they could be sure they would have eternal life. So Jesus prayed: "And this is the way to have eternal life—to know you, the only true God, and Jesus Christ, the one you sent to earth" (John 17:3, NLT). How do we get eternal life? Knowing God through becoming acquainted with Jesus. "Whoever believes in God's Son has eternal life. He is all you need. You don't need to wait for eternal life because it begins the moment you believe. You don't need to work for it because it is already yours. You don't need to worry about it because you have been given eternal life by God himself—and it is guaranteed" (note on 1 John 5:12, *Life Application Study Bible*).

Eternal life begins for us the moment we accept Jesus as our Saviour. It commenced for Jim, a former crack addict, the instant Jesus became his Saviour. Eternal life began for Mary, a former prostitute, when she turned away from a life of sin to enter a new life in Christ. And eternal life can start for us now, this very moment, no matter how hard and sinful we may be. We need only accept by faith what Jesus did for us on the cross and at His empty tomb, and the gift of eternal life is ours.

DRG

YOURS FOR THE ASKING

> *But whoever rejects the Son will not see life, for God's wrath remains on him.*
>
> JOHN *3:36, NIV.*

President Andrew Jackson pardoned George Wilson, who had been sentenced to be hanged for murder. But the prisoner rejected the pardon and insisted it could never be valid unless he accepted it. President Jackson consulted the Supreme Court, and Chief Justice John Marshall rendered the verdict: "It is hardly to be supposed that one under sentence of death would refuse to accept a pardon, but if it is refused, it is no pardon. George Wilson must be hanged." Wilson died because he didn't accept the pardon.

God offers us life eternal on the ground of faith in Jesus: "Whoever believes in the Son has eternal life" (John 3:36, NIV). If we do not believe, we "will not see life." The only way to live forever with the redeemed is to accept Jesus' pardon. By expressing faith in Jesus, everlasting life becomes ours. It's ours for the asking. Our hope of eternal life depends entirely on Jesus. We cannot live eternally apart from Him. He is the life-giver. Jesus came to abolish death and bring "life and immortality to light through the gospel" (2 Tim. 1:10). The gospel reveals eternal life and immortality as God's gift to those who believe in Jesus. They are not our natural possession (Rom. 6:23). Through faith in Jesus we receive eternal life now, and at His second coming we will acquire immortality (1 Cor. 15:51-53). It is power-packed comfort to know that immortal life beyond is just as certain for the blessed dead as was the resurrection of Christ: "He which raised up the Lord Jesus shall raise up us also by Jesus" (2 Cor. 4:14). The longer and rougher the journey of life, the more these words of comfort mean to us. They guide our eyes heavenward in anticipation of our Lord's return. God offers us immortality on the ground of belief in Jesus. Our hope is entirely in Jesus, for "whoever rejects the Son will not see life, for God's wrath remains on him."

Do you have the Son of God in your heart today? Have you fully accepted His pardon? If not, take it! It's yours for the asking. And if you forget everything else, remember Jesus!

HMSR

LET'S TALK ABOUT FAITH

The man believed the word that Jesus had spoken unto him, and he went his way.

John 4:50.

How often we hear people say, "My faith is too weak. I don't know whether God hears my prayers or not. How can I develop faith? What can I do so it will grow?"

How about you? Do we really trust Jesus to do the things He promises to do for us? Do you accept His promises to forgive our sins and to guide us daily? Are you like the man of faith in John's Gospel who "believed the word that Jesus had spoken unto him, and he went his way"?

Read the story of the nobleman in John 4. He pleaded with Jesus to come to his house and heal his boy who hovered at the point of death. Jesus said to him, "Go thy way; thy son liveth" (John 4:50). The man believed and returned home. When he arrived at his house the next day, he discovered that at the exact hour when Jesus had spoken to him, the grip of his son's deadly fever had broken. Christ had honored his faith.

How can we develop the same kind of faith? The Bible reveals several secrets for increasing our faith. First, ask Jesus, as the disciples did: "Increase our faith" (Luke 17:5). Second, faith is a gift (see 1 Cor. 12:7-9), and by praying for increased faith, then acting on that faith, we gain greater faith. Third, we strengthen our faith by learning to rely not on our own faith, but on the power of God (1 John 5:14, 15). Fourth, another secret is to feed on the Word of God as a means of increasing our faith (Rom. 10:17). Fifth, the apostles strengthened their faith by regarding faith as invincible (1 John 5:4) and by walking in the road of obedience. Sixth, we gain greater faith when, after committed prayer, we receive the things for which we have asked (1 John 5:14, 15).

The present life is really a school of faith. We request greater and greater things of God, then honor Him by trusting Him. Remember, exercising faith is vital, for faith in Jesus our crucified and risen Saviour is the key to eternal life (John 3:14, 15). We must talk faith, live faith, and act in faith. Never talk discouragement, but hope and victory. Let us ever keep looking up, ever going forward in faith.

HMSR

WHAT IS YOUR MOST IMPORTANT THOUGHT?

Truly, truly, I say to you, he who hears my word and believes him who sent me, has eternal life; he does not come into judgment, but has passed from death into life.
John 5:24, RSV.

Daniel Webster, one of the world's greatest orators, attended a dinner with 20 other men at Astor House. Since Webster was secretary of state, the conversation dwelled on political issues. A momentary silence fell on the group, then a guest asked, "Mr. Webster, will you tell us what is the most important thought that ever occupied your mind?"

After a moment of reflection Webster answered, "The most important thought that ever occupied my mind was that of my individual responsibility to God." He stated a profound truth. Think about it.

We all have a case pending in God's court, and that decision will have no appeal. It can never be changed. No higher court will overthrow it. The apostle Paul declared, "God shall judge the secrets of men [not only their acts, not only their words, but their secrets] by Jesus Christ according to my gospel" (Rom. 2:16).

You may be saying in your heart, "Then there's no hope for me. I know I've not always done as I should. There are many things I'd like to forget, but they come back to me sometimes at night when I can't sleep."

Here is good news: your court case would not be so terrifying to you if you knew the judge was not only just, but kind and loving, and if you could have the assurance that you need not fear His decision. Jesus promises us something even better than that: "He who hears my word and believes him who sent me, has eternal life; he does not come into judgment." Believers do "not come into judgment." God's plan is to save everyone who will accept "the free gift" of "eternal life in Christ Jesus" (Rom. 6:23, RSV). Jesus doesn't want us to die—He wants us to live. So He paid the price for our guilt by dying for our sins. We now have "eternal life." Since Jesus takes our place at the judgment bar, we do "not come into judgment." How does that sound to you? It sounds wonderful to me!

HMSR

WHEN JESUS FORGETS

> *"Then neither do I condemn you," Jesus declared. "Go now and leave your life of sin."*
> *JOHN 8:11, NIV.*

Recently we spent the weekend in College Place, Washington, the home of Walla Walla College. Driving down College Avenue, we saw this maxim on a sign in front of Andy's Market: "God pardons like a mother who kisses the offense into everlasting forgetfulness."

That describes exactly what Jesus did for the woman caught in adultery and dragged before Him. When her accusers suggested that she be stoned to death, Jesus began to write their own personal sins on the ground. "At this, those who heard began to go away one at a time, the older ones first, until only Jesus was left, with the woman still standing there. Jesus straightened up and asked her, 'Woman, where are they? Has no one condemned you?'

" 'No one, sir,' she said.

" 'Then neither do I condemn you,' Jesus declared. 'Go now and leave your life of sin' " (John 8:9-11, NIV).

"This was to her the beginning of a new life, a life of purity and peace, devoted to the service of God. In the uplifting of this fallen soul, Jesus performed a greater miracle than in healing the most grievous physical disease; He cured the spiritual malady which is unto death everlasting. This penitent woman became one of His most steadfast followers. With self-sacrificing love and devotion she repaid His forgiving mercy. In His act of pardoning this woman and encouraging her to live a better life, the character of Jesus shines forth in the beauty of perfect righteousness. . . . The world had for this erring woman only contempt and scorn; but Jesus speaks words of comfort and hope" (*The Desire of Ages,* p. 462).

What Jesus did for that trembling woman, He does for each of us. The Bible reveals the extent of Jesus' forgiving forgetfulness: Isaiah exalted, "You have cast all my sins behind Your back" (Isa. 38:17, NKJV). According to Micah, He casts "our sins into the depths of the sea" (Micah 7:19, NKJV). Jesus puts our sins out of sight, out of His mind—yes, and out of existence. "I've blotted out your sins; they are gone like morning mist at noon!" (Isa. 44:22, TLB). It's good news for Jesus to "kiss my offense into everlasting forgetfulness."

DRG

THE LIGHT OF LIFE

"I am the light of the world. He who follows Me shall not walk in darkness, but have the light of life."
JOHN 8:12, NKJV.

After World War II the Wholesome Bakery in Tampa, Florida, bought a huge searchlight from an Army surplus depot. The bakery intended to use it for publicity, but the firm had no idea that the beam would become one of the most familiar landmarks on Florida's west coast—and a navigation aid to pilots of both private and commercial planes.

People became so dependent on this beam of light that shone heavenward each night that the bakery did not dare to turn it off. For example, one evening two men were out in the swamp along the Alafia River looking for a Christmas tree. After dark they discovered they were lost. One of them climbed a tree to see some landmark. He could see nothing—except the beam of light shining into the sky from the bakery in Tampa. Using the beam as a guide, the men found their way back to safety.

When Christ came to earth in human flesh, people did not dream that He would become the light of the world. He seemed just another boy born into a poor family. But Christ in the flesh became a beam of light to point the way to His Father's heavenly home.

This tiny Baby has been the guiding light to millions. Not only does the Light of the world bring the wanderer home, but He is also the light of life that guides and sustains the Christian in every time of need.

Jesus is concerned about our lives. "To His faithful followers Christ has been a daily companion and familiar friend. They have lived in close contact, in constant communion with God. Upon them the glory of the Lord has risen. In them the light of the knowledge of the glory of God in the face of Jesus Christ has been reflected. . . . They are prepared for the communion of heaven; for they have heaven in their hearts" (*Christ's Object Lessons,* p. 421).

Have you ever seen anybody whose face is just radiant, a person you know is now different? Christ, the light of the world and the light of life, is an actuality in that person's life. There's something about that kind of person that we cannot ignore. Such living faith in Christ beams light and life to others.

HMSR

JESUS THE REVOLUTIONARY

Jesus replied, "You are slaves of sin, every one of you. And slaves don't have rights, but the Son has every right there is! So if the Son sets you free, you will indeed be free."

John 8:34-36, TLB.

Years ago a young Revolutionary began a liberation movement. Jesus came from an insignificant town, but His teaching was new and radical—it contradicted the accepted philosophy of the day. He even encouraged people to forgive those who had harmed them. "Love your enemies, . . . do good to them that hate you" (Matt. 5:44). That's contrary to human nature!

This unique Revolutionary did not attack the political or social system of His day. Instead of getting people out of the slums, He constantly worked at getting the slums out of the people. He liberated people from sin! And He is still doing it today. Listen to His instruction: "You are slaves of sin, every one of you. And slaves don't have rights, but the Son has every right there is! So if the Son sets you free, you will indeed be free."

Another member of the Christian liberation movement put it this way: "Stand fast therefore in the liberty wherewith Christ hath made us free, and be not entangled again with the yoke of bondage" (Gal. 5:1).

Have you been liberated from the bondage of sin? Are you experiencing forgiveness and freedom just now? One day Konrad Schuman, an East German sergeant guarding the Berlin Wall, suddenly broke away from the group of Communist guards. With a submachine gun in his hand, Schuman leaped over the barbed-wire entanglement to freedom in West Berlin. As he tore off his Communist uniform, he exclaimed, "Thank God! I am free."

When we become a member of the Christian liberation movement, it rips off our robe of self-righteousness and replaces it with the robe of Christ's righteousness—Christ living out His life in us. It gives us the freedom, the liberty that our heart has cried for. Arthur Moore once said that in all human hearts are a cross and a throne. If people occupy the throne, they'll place Jesus on the cross. But if they nail themselves on the cross, they'll put Jesus on the throne. A true revolutionary will execute self on the cross, and enthrone Jesus in their heart.

HMSR

SET FREE BY JESUS

If the Son sets you free, you will be free indeed.
John 8:36, NIV.

Lillian and I arrived in Moscow exactly one week after the coup by Communist hard-liners that led to Gorbachev's overthrow and the Soviet Union's collapse. We asked our guide if the people were happy with their newfound freedoms and if they would continue to rejoice in their freedom if the food shortages continued. "Freedom is worth more than bread any day," she replied. Just two years later—during my sixth trip to Moscow and Lillian's second in connection with the General Conference-sponsored evangelism advance—the need for bread, the surge of crime, and the chaos led many Russians to long for the good old days when the government did their thinking for them and provided food, security, and a place to live.

When God delivered Israel from slavery in Egypt, He destroyed Pharaoh's pursuing army in the Red Sea. For 40 years He fed and clothed Israel in the desert. But all this was not enough, and the murmuring Israelites complained and longed for Egypt. Freedom from slavery and a full stomach were not sufficient. They wanted flesh to eat as in Egypt. Nostalgia for their former life now drew them back to the land of their slavery.

Do we as Christians face a similar danger? When we are in bondage to sin we escape responsibility and experience sinful pleasures. Are we in danger of turning our backs on God's blessings, of failing to trust Jesus, of longing for the attractions of our past sinful life? Not if we have a genuine experience with Jesus that we keep warm and alive every day. In our former life we did not change and grow, or fully love and live. But a wholehearted surrender to Jesus satisfies all our hungers, for "if the Son sets you free, you will be free indeed."

Jesus does not give us freedom to do as we please, but freedom to follow Him. We are not asked to journey from slavery in sin to the Promised Land alone. Christ is always near to guide us along life's journey. Depending on Him offers us real freedom. We are free from the fear of death that previously tortured us, free from the self-destructive, sinful habits that once enslaved us, and free from a meaningless life, for Jesus gives us hope for today and an eternal tomorrow to look forward to. And that *is* good news!

DRG

"MY SHEEP HEAR MY VOICE"

My sheep hear my voice, and I know them, and they follow me: and I give unto them eternal life; and they shall never perish, neither shall any man pluck them out of my hand.

John 10:27, 28.

When the King's Heralds Quartet and I were holding meetings in Albuquerque, New Mexico, we heard of a woman who had taken nurse's training in Battle Creek, Michigan. I said to Jack Veazey, "Let's go see her." Arriving at her home, we saw a sign in a window advertising a trailer for sale. We knocked, and her husband came to the door. I said, "I'm Pastor Richards, and this is Jack Veazey. We've come to see your wife." When he hesitated, I added, "I understand you have a trailer for sale."

"Yes, I do; would you like to see it?"

We went out the back door and into the trailer and discussed trailers for about 20 minutes. Then we returned to the house, and the wife asked, "Did you buy my husband's trailer?"

"No," I said, "that's not really what I had in mind." She inquired if we were new in the community. So I sat down and told her that I had once lived in Albuquerque, but that we were here for just a short time.

When she asked, "What are you doing in town now?" I responded, "Well, if you folks like good music like I do, this man with me is in a quartet. The quartet is holding a concert tonight at the civic auditorium. It's terrific."

"They are?" she inquired, then turning to her husband, she asked, "Honey, do you think we could go?"

"Well, if you want to."

Then she asked me, "What do you do?"

"Oh, I announce the songs." Which I did.

They came to the meeting that night, and the next night, and the next night throughout the series, and were baptized. Jesus led us to two of His sheep. As they came to the meetings, Jesus spoke to their hearts, just as He promised: "My sheep hear my voice, and I know them, and they follow me: and I give unto them eternal life." You just can't beat that offer! Praise God for a life-giving Saviour who longs to give everyone eternal life.

HMSR

OUR EVERLASTING FATHER

For unto us a child is born, unto us a son is given: and the government shall be upon his shoulder: and his name shall be called Wonderful, Counsellor, The mighty God, The everlasting Father, The Prince of Peace.
Isa. 9:6.

One Sabbath Tony offered the prayer at our worship service. Before he prayed, he said, "I had the greatest father in the world. We called him Papa. Before he died he told me, 'Tony, you'll never know real love until you have children of your own.'" Then Tony prayed. His heartfelt prayer mightily stirred and left me in tears. To understand why, you must understand what Tony and his wife have been through during the past few years. They had three children, two sons and a daughter. One of their sons died several years ago. Two years later their other son, a physician, perished instantly when a moose jumped in front of his car in Yellowstone National Park. When Tony prayed, he addressed God as Papa. Heaven came very near. You could almost hear the flutter of angel wings and sense the arm of Jesus reaching around Tony's shoulder. How meaningful that Tony could address Jesus, the everlasting Father, as Papa!

After the prayer Lillian expressed how we both felt: "I've had my blessing. If we had to, we could go home now."

As our everlasting Father, Jesus has a love for us that endures—it is everlasting. He provides for us as a father should. I had the same kind of father as Tony. Lillian didn't. For her and all those who lacked a warm, loving father, the other names of the predicted Messiah provide comfort and refuge. Our wonderful counselor, King Jesus assures us He is watching over the entire universe and can guide and direct our lives. As our mighty God, Jesus reminds us that He came to our world to live among us and die defending us. Fulfilling the title Prince of Peace, He brings peace and a sense of well-being to each of us right now in this life. And someday soon, He will restore peace to our world and to the entire universe. The devil will be a defeated foe. The ruin that threatens our tranquillity and dogs our world will soon be over, for the Prince of Peace is coming soon to reign!

What could be greater news than having a papa like that?

DRG

THE SECRET OF THE TOMB

Jesus said . . . , I am the resurrection, and the life: he that believeth in me, though he were dead, yet shall he live. And whosoever liveth and believeth in me shall never die.

JOHN 11:25, 26.

Some time ago I stood in a tomb that had held a secret for more than 3,000 years. We walked down the corridor to the antechamber of King Tut's tomb. He had been buried in the Valley of the Kings along with other great pharaohs. The Egyptians believed in an afterlife in which their kings would need all the possessions that had made their lives enjoyable on earth. So they placed the pharaoh's belongings in rock-cut rooms adjoining the burial chamber. The objects were for his use in his afterlife: luxurious furniture, royal chariots, weapons, clothing, and an abundance of food and wine.

Even though the builders had concealed the entrances to the tombs and cut deep shafts and incorporated puzzle passages to discourage grave robbers, the tombs had all been plundered—except the one where I was standing, that of King Tut. Grave robbers had for some reason not found the entrance.

In 1922 Howard Carter discovered Tut's tomb. When he opened the funeral chambers he found hundreds of objects made of gold and precious stones. Three inner coffins, the third and last made of gold and jewels, enclosed the body of the 18-year-old king.

More important than Tut's tomb is the one Christ's disciples investigated. It had no golden chariots, no jeweled sarcophagi. In fact, the tomb was empty. Jesus revealed the secret of this empty tomb when He said, "I am the resurrection, and the life: he that believeth in me, though he were dead, yet shall he live." Friends had placed Jesus in the tomb on Friday and He liberated Himself on Sunday, a conqueror over sin and death. The secret of the empty tomb is that Jesus died on the cross, was buried, and burst out of the tomb so we can be set free from sin and enjoy life with Him for eternity, just as He promised: "Whosoever liveth and believeth in me shall never die." Nor do we need to store things in our graves that we'll require in heaven, for Jesus is now preparing a furnished mansion for us there.

HMSR

JUNE 18

THE TEARS OF JESUS

> *Jesus wept.*
>
> JOHN 11:35.

A brave mother told us about the loss of her 7-year-old son. She described how her son loved Jesus and always thought of others first. Our church had been praying for the boy who had a mysterious illness. After several brain scans the physicians diagnosed his problem as cancer of the brain stem. When his mother went in to break the news, she took him in her arms and told him that the doctors said he had only a short time to live. The unusual boy's first thought was to comfort his mother, and he said, "Well, Mom, at least I've had seven good years."

I mentioned to the boy's grandfather that we dare not ask the question Why? "We shouldn't ask that question," he commented, "because there is no answer." In reality, there is an answer, but in the complex play and counterplay of human events we cannot now sort it out. We will not know the reason until, on the other side, we sit at the feet of Jesus and He puts the puzzle together for us.

In the meantime we can find comfort in knowing that when Jesus stood beside the grave of His friend Lazarus, "Jesus wept." The shortest verse in the Bible, it is poignant with meaning. Why did Jesus weep? Was it because Lazarus was one of Jesus' best friends? because Martha expressed confidence in Jesus by saying, "If you had been here, my brother would not have died" (John 11:21, NIV)? Did Jesus weep because Martha said, "I know that even now God will give you whatever you ask" (verse 22, NIV)? Or was it because Jesus saw Mary and others weeping and "was deeply moved" (verse 33, NIV)? Perhaps Jesus wept for all these reasons.

Perhaps Jesus was also weeping for this 7-year-old boy and his mother, and for all of us who suffer at various times and for many reasons. Jesus' tears at the graveside of Lazarus are only a microcosm of the pain He has experienced as He has watched the suffering human race. So if you are going through a difficult time right now—whether little or big—remember the tears of Jesus. He endured the cross so He can empathize with you and sympathize with you. You can take comfort and face life knowing that Jesus is close by your side.

DRG

WHAT'S IN YOUR FUTURE?

I am telling you now before it happens, so that when it does happen you will believe that I am He.
John 13:19, NIV.

One evening in India a friend of mine held a Bible study with a very bright non-Christian student from Calcutta University. The Christian Scriptures were an unknown book to him. As my friend talked with him, he turned to Daniel 2 and read the prophecy of the great image.

"Now," my friend said to the student, "how is it? Do you know from your study of history whether this ancient prophecy written in Babylon nearly 2,500 years ago is a true and accurate outline of events that have come to pass?"

This non-Christian student answered, "I know this outline is correct. It gives the history of the world in the exact order of events."

Then he turned, and in the light of the study lamp my friend saw a look of surprise and awe on the young man's face. A new thought had come to him. With the force of a sudden conviction, he looked up and said, "Only the living God could have written that before it came to pass!" This non-Christian student saw the true import and impact of divine prophecy.

It had the exact effect that Jesus said prophecy would have: "I am telling you now before it happens, so that when it does happen you will believe that I am He." The great historic prophecy of Daniel 2 bears witness to the living God and to Jesus, our Saviour. To give us faith and save us, God has piled evidence upon evidence in Holy Scripture. No book compares with it. There is no other Saviour like the One it reveals. Jesus not only knows the world's future, He knows your future and mine. What does the future hold? Many good things. Maybe some things we wish would never occur. If we knew everything that was going to happen to us and when, I'm afraid we wouldn't sleep much. But one thing is sure, and it is this: as long as the Saviour who guides the course of nations directs our lives, we can rest secure in Him. So take hold of Him this day. Trust Him. And be at peace.

HMSR

TROUBLED HEART? JESUS IS COMING

Let not your heart be troubled. . . . I will come again.
JOHN 14:1-3, NKJV.

Many years ago Los Angeles had streets named Faith, Hope, and Charity. Because of the changing face of Los Angeles, with the multiplication of freeways and urban renewal and city beautification, two of the street names vanished, but one of them still remains—Hope Street. Really, hope is just about all we have left in our decaying, troubled world—hope for something better, a better future.

During a Voice of Prophecy radio evangelistic series in the San Joaquin Valley of central California, an outstanding couple met me at the door of the theater in which we held the meetings. They told me they had thought for many years that politics was going to bring utopia to our world, and that they had been politically active in their district and precinct. Now they realized that politics would not produce any hoped-for utopia. Only Christ Jesus could bring peace to our old earth. And they were certainly correct, for only Christ can give real meaning to life. "The Lord Jesus Christ" is "our hope" (1 Tim. 1:1, NKJV).

How wonderful it is that we can approach Christ and on bended knee ask, "Lord Jesus, really, are You coming back? Many thousands of men and women and boys and girls do not know which way to turn. Is there an answer to all the world's problems and to my personal problems?"

His answer is "Let not your heart be troubled." There is hope for you here and now. "Now may the God of hope fill you with all joy and peace in believing, that you may abound in hope by the power of the Holy Spirit" (Rom. 15:13, NKJV). And there is hope for your future and the future of our world in His hope-filled pledge: "I will come again." His promise is sure. He is the Lord of the Advent. If we make Him Lord of our hearts, we shall gladly welcome His return to earth again.

HMSR

"LOOK!" JESUS IS COMING

Let not your heart be troubled; you believe in God, believe also in Me. In My Father's house are many mansions; if it were not so, I would have told you. I go to prepare a place for you. And if I go and prepare a place for you, I will come again and receive you to Myself; that where I am, there you may be also.
JOHN 14:1-3, NKJV.

One day while driving I listened to Dennis Prager on KABC talk radio. A medical oncologist called in, almost in panic. When Prager asked why, he said it was because of his concern for his patients. He went on to say, "I don't know what to tell those dying of cancer. I feel helpless because I can't cure many of them."

As Christians we have a Saviour who comforts the dying and who will someday come again and put an end to sickness, sorrow, and death. He admonishes us, "Let not your heart be troubled."

Have you ever thought how disappointing it would be if Jesus did not return? If He didn't, the starving people of Africa and elsewhere in the world would continue to die. The genocides that put millions to death in Pol Pot's Cambodia, the former Yugoslavia, and countless other places would repeat themselves again and again.

How thankful we can be for Jesus' promise, "I will come again." His second advent is a divine certainty! And what a day that will be as He breaks up every cemetery in the world. He will raise the dead and unite us for eternity with our loved ones. Jesus promises both those who are resurrected and those who are alive, "I will come again and take you to be with Me where I am." Frustrated, lonely lives will awaken to friendship with Jesus throughout eternity.

Jesus promises to take us to the place He has prepared for us in His Father's mansions. John describes our new abode: "Look, the home of God is now among his people! He will live with them. . . . He will remove all of their sorrows, and there will be no more death or sorrow or crying or pain. For the old world and its evils are gone forever. . . . Look, I am making all things new" (Rev. 21:3-5, TLB). I can hardly wait! How about you?

DRG

REACH OUT FOR LIFE

Jesus said to him, "I am the way, the truth, and the life. No one comes to the Father except through Me."
JOHN 14:6, NKJV.

A kaleidoscope of changes swirls in every area of our society, whether it be social, economic, political, or scientific. It makes it difficult, if not impossible, for many of us to cope with the problems that face us. Everything is so transient . . . so temporary! We are all experiencing supernormal rates of change.

Today people orbit our earth at 18,000 miles per hour, and life seems to be accelerating just as fast. So many today find themselves confused. Which direction should they go? People consider themselves out of control, spinning and careening into a future of hopelessness. Have you ever felt that way? Many of us have.

But here is good news. You can enjoy a meaningful direction for your life. Perhaps you have been searching frantically for a way to cope with some personal difficulty, or a problem with your family. You have contacted many services for help, but they have all failed. Jesus' reassuring promise, "I am the way, the truth, and the life," has given me personally and every member of my family peace every day and a purpose and direction that has really led us to a new lifestyle! Christ not only knows the way—He is the way. He is the only way that makes sense. His invitation to you and me today is: "If any man will come after me, let him deny himself, and take up his cross daily, and follow me" (Luke 9:23). That's the right direction to go.

Christ knew the right direction to go in the garden the night of His betrayal by a human being. He knew the right direction to go in the court that day when a human being judged Him. My Jesus knew the right direction to go that afternoon when human beings finally crucified Him. And my Lord knew the right direction to go early that morning when He arose from the grave, victorious over death—by the power of God! Our Saviour knows the right direction for you and for me to go today, each day, each week, each month. Take His hand just now. And reach out for life . . . in the right direction!

HMSR

JESUS REVEALS THAT GOD CARES

Jesus said to him, "Have I been with you so long, and yet you have not known Me, Philip? He who has seen Me has seen the Father."
John 14:9, NKJV.

The richest man in ancient history, Croesus, one day asked Thales, the wisest philosopher of his day, "What is God?"

Thales, the wise man, asked for a day to study his answer. Then he asked for another, and another, and still another day. Finally he went to Croesus and admitted that the more he studied God, the more mysterious the question became.

Tertullian of the early church referred to this experience and said that no one can know God who does not first know Jesus Christ.

God has revealed Himself to us through Jesus. The Bible presents Christ, our Creator and our Saviour from sin, as the "express image" of God (Heb. 1:3, NKJV). He existed with the Father in Old Testament as well as New Testament times. Jesus Himself said, "He who has seen Me has seen the Father."

When looking at the Father through Jesus' life and ministry, we discover not only an all-powerful Creator but an infinitely loving Friend. He is someone we can lean on in every time of need, someone who gives us security, someone whose promises we can believe and rely on in confidence. Jesus and His Father devised the plan for our redemption. God loved us so much He gave us His Son, and Jesus loved us so much He gave His life to assure us of eternal life.

Jesus is not only the world's hope but also the hope for you and me. Have you felt exhausted? Have the mundane duties of life become drudgery for you? Is life just a rat race with no finish line? Then listen to what Jesus promised: "Come to Me, all you who labor and are heavy laden, and I will give you rest" (Matt. 11:28, NKJV). For those searching for peace, security, and contentment, but who have found their hopes thwarted—consider Jesus. He will forge new hope for the youth as well as the aged and provide purpose and meaning to life. And, as a gigantic bonus, eternal life.

Jesus, please do all this for me today!

HMSR

JUNE 24

JESUS OUR LOVING FATHER

Don't you believe that I am in the Father and the Father is in me? The words I say are not my own but are from my Father who lives in me. And he does his work through me.

John 14:10, TLB.

A blind boy stood on a busy street corner waiting for his father. A passerby, chancing to see the boy, offered to help him cross the street. "No, thank you," the boy said. "I'm waiting for my father."

"Do you think you can trust your father to come and get you?"

"Yes, my father takes care of me. He leads me all the time, and when he has my hand, I feel perfectly safe."

"Why do you feel safe?" the man questioned.

With a serene smile of perfect trust, the boy answered, "Oh, because my father knows the way. He can see the way, but I am blind."

We have Jesus as our Father. Sin has blinded us, but our Father can see. Taking us by the hand and leading us, Jesus promises, "Fear not, for I am with you; be not dismayed, for I am your God. I will strengthen you, yes, I will help you, I will uphold you with My righteous right hand" (Isa. 41:10, NKJV). What could be better news than to have a Father like that? John speaks of Jesus as "the Father," of us as "the sons of God," and of Jesus being "manifested to take away our sins," an evidence of the "manner of love" Jesus bestows upon His children (1 John 3:1-5). While this passage reveals sin as "the transgression of the law," note that it also discloses sin to be the violation of a sacred personal relationship—the Father-child relationship, a relationship based on mutual love. We do not sin against Sinai granite, or even against a great moral ideal, but against our Father's heart of love.

So let's lay our sins on Jesus. Ask Him to forgive us. Then luxuriate in His loving presence. He wants that kind of loving relationship with us. Jesus has toward us "an exceeding tenderness, as far surpassing what our father or mother has felt toward us in our helplessness as the divine is above the human" (*The Desire of Ages,* p. 327).

DRG

CAN WE REACH GOD THROUGH PRAYER?

I go to My Father. And whatever you ask in My name, that I will do, that the Father may be glorified in the Son.
John 14:12, 13, NKJV.

For centuries skeptics have scoffed at the idea of a prayer-hearing and a prayer-answering God. Meanwhile, as Christians we have held tenaciously to the Bible teaching that we can hold constant communication with a God in heaven through prayer. The invention of radio provided a scientific analogy for the Christian's position on this matter.

Ethel Romig Fuller wrote:

"If radio's slim fingers can pluck a melody
From night—and toss it over a continent or sea;
If the petaled white notes of a violin
Are blown across the mountains or the city's din;
If songs, like crimson roses, are culled from thin blue air—
Why should mortals wonder if God hears prayer?"

Today, through the invention of satellite technology, we can hear and see around the world. If human beings can do that, surely God can hear and answer our prayers.

Jesus testified while on earth: "And whatever you ask in My name, that I will do." John witnessed: "Now this is the confidence that we have in Him, that if we ask anything according to His will, He hears us. And if we know that He hears us, whatever we ask, we know that we have the petitions that we have asked of Him" (1 John 5:14, 15, NKJV). James added his firm conviction: "If any of you lacks wisdom, let him ask of God, who gives to all liberally, . . . and it will be given to him" (James 1:5, NKJV).

Ellen G. White wrote: "Keep your wants, your joys, your sorrows, your cares, and your fears before God. You cannot burden Him; you cannot weary Him. He who numbers the hairs of your head is not indifferent to the wants of His children. . . . Nothing is too great for Him to bear, for He holds up worlds, He rules over the affairs of the universe. . . . There is no chapter in our experience too dark for Him to read, there is no perplexity too difficult for Him to unravel" (*Steps to Christ,* p. 100). Nothing can shake my belief that we can communicate with God through prayer. After all, Jesus testified that we can.

DRG

JUNE 26

"LORD, YOU ARE STILL HERE!"

> *You can ask for anything in my name, and I will do it, because the work of the Son brings glory to the Father. Yes, ask anything in my name, and I will do it!*
>
> *John 14:13, 14, NLT.*

I have a lot to be thankful for. Some time ago I lay in a hospital with a very severe case of herpes zoster, better known as shingles. The doctors hoped that I wouldn't get meningitis as well. My mouth was full of ulcers. The pain was so intense that I could have anything I wanted to relieve the pain. But not a pain pill in the world would help. For months the pain afflicted me.

At times like that we find ourselves tempted to ask, "Where is God?" I'm reminded of an atheist who wrote across the wall in big letters, "GOD IS NOWHERE!" A little girl in her innocence began to read, "GOD IS . . . ," but the long word "NOWHERE" had her stumped. So she began to sound it out, and from her mouth came the wisdom of an innocent child: "GOD IS NOW HERE."

When I lay down at night and tried to go to sleep with my face and my torso racked with torturing pain, I wondered, *Lord, are You anywhere around?* Desperately longing for a good night's sleep, I prayed, "Lord Jesus, if You could just do a little something and let me have no pain when I sleep, I would appreciate it." The throbbing pain finally went away. I didn't have to wonder any longer, *Lord, are You anywhere around?* I couldn't hold the tears back. "Lord, You are still here!" And I dropped into a sound sleep.

Don't ever get the idea that Jesus doesn't answer your prayers. He does! For me He took the pain away. Praise God! The experience made me appreciate as never before the promise of Jesus: "You can ask for anything in my name, and I will do it, because the work of the Son brings glory to the Father. Yes, ask anything in my name, and I will do it!"

HMSR

OUR LOVE RELATIONSHIP WITH JESUS

If you love me, you will keep my commandments.
JOHN 14:15, RSV.

In the Magnolia Gardens of Charleston, South Carolina, I saw a striking evidence of a loving relationship with Jesus. These Edenlike gardens are the fulfilled dream of a Dr. Drayton, who spent his years of retirement from the ministry enhancing their beauty. In the memorial section a plaque inscribed in memory of the doctor states: "And he heard the voice of the Lord God walking in the garden in the cool of the day and he went out to meet Him and was unafraid"—the result of Dr. Drayton's love relationship with Jesus. His experience was a marked contrast to that of Adam and Eve, who "heard the sound of the Lord God walking in the garden in the cool of the day, and . . . hid themselves from the presence of the Lord God among the trees of the garden" (Gen. 3:8, RSV).

Adam and Eve violated a direct command from God, and their sin short-circuited their relationship with Him (Gen. 3; see Isa. 59:1, 2). That very day Jesus came to restore that relationship and to give the prophetic promise of restoration to all humanity (Gen. 3:15). Through removing the separating wedge of sin by dying to take away our sins, Jesus has successfully repaired the broken union between Himself and His children. The love of the Father and Son motivated the agony at Calvary that restored our relationship with the Divine. So our sin is more than transgressing the law—it spurns divine love. Sin violates a sacred personal relationship, one vital to our happiness.

Love begets love. Jesus' love for us stimulates love in us. As we look to our dying Saviour, we respond to Jesus' love, and God's love fills our hearts (Rom. 5:5). It restores our union with God when we establish a love relationship with Jesus. Because God engraves His law of love on our hearts (Heb. 10:16), we become lawkeepers. Jesus longs for such a love relationship with each of us. His plea is: "If you love me, you will keep my commandments." In fact, when God's "law is within my heart," I will "delight" to do His will (Ps. 40:8). Those who do not yet experience this mandate of freedom should accept Jesus' offer at once, for through union with Jesus our relationship with heaven is rich, full, and complete.

DRG

JESUS IS NOW WITH YOU

I will pray the Father, and he shall give you another Comforter, that he may abide with you for ever; even the Spirit of truth; . . . he dwelleth with you, and shall be in you.

John 14:16, 17.

In a little upper room in Jerusalem sat a small group of men who had followed their Lord through the years of His public ministry. Many things had happened that they could not understand. Their Master had fastened a towel about His waist and had knelt down before each of them and washed their feet. They had shared the broken bread and the poured-out wine—the symbols of His approaching death. Judas had already left the group. Now Christ was alone with the 11. Sadness filled their hearts. Christ had tried to point out to them the great object of His mission on this earth.

But they knew that shortly He would be separated from them, and fear fell on them. They had looked to Him for help in all their difficulties and sorrows and disappointments. But now the time had come for Him to leave. Pressing close to Him, they listened to every word that He said. He gave them hope by telling them that He would prepare a place for them in heaven and would return to take them there (John 14:1-3). But what would they do in the meantime? Philip asked a question, and Jesus answered it. Then He proceeded to unfold to them the wondrous provision of a Comforter who would be with them and in them.

Jesus would not leave the disciples orphans, with no divine parent to protect and help them. He promised the Comforter, His personal representative. The Holy Spirit had always been with people, but from Pentecost forward God purposed that the Holy Spirit "shall be in you" as a sacred reality. The Christian is to realize the personal indwelling of the Spirit. "By the Spirit the Saviour would be accessible to all. In this sense He would be nearer to them than if He had not ascended on high" (*The Desire of Ages,* p. 669). "With you, and . . . in you." What a fantastic opportunity for us to come near to Jesus today!

HMSR

YOUR PERSONAL COMFORTER

> *I will ask the Father and he will give you another Comforter, and he will never leave you.*
> JOHN 14:16, TLB.

L. E. Froom tells of a wonderful chime player named Gadsen who lived many years ago in Charleston, South Carolina. "When the city was shaken by an earthquake, terror and despair possessed all minds. Men were fleeing for their lives. The air was filled with the crash of falling buildings and the shrieks of the wounded. Gadsen rushed to his post, and sent pealing forth through the darkness the strains of 'Rock of Ages,' to hush and calm the hearts of men. It proved a mighty, steadying, assuring force" (*The Coming of the Comforter,* p. 203).

We live in a time when political corruption, violence, lewd conduct, and every kind of evil shake society's foundation. We need a mighty steadying, assuring presence. Jesus promised to ask His Father to send just such a presence—the Comforter. And the echo of Jesus' steadying presence through the Holy Spirit is pealing forth above the darkness to hush and calm our hearts.

The first and second persons of the Godhead—God the Father and God the Son—now hold Their residence on earth through the third, the Holy Spirit. The presence of the one involves the presence of the others. Do you see how important it is for us to have the Holy Spirit within us? "The work of the Holy Spirit is immeasurably great. It is from this source that power and efficiency come to the worker for God; and the Holy Spirit is the comforter, as the personal presence of Christ to the soul" (Ellen G. White, in *Review and Herald,* Nov. 29, 1892).

Do you have the Comforter with you? Have you received an outpouring of the Holy Spirit in your life? What would happen to you, to your family, to those in your neighborhood, if you had that special outpouring of the Holy Spirit, the Comforter of God?

Why not make this the prayer of your heart today:

"Holy Spirit, light divine,
Shine upon this heart of mine,
Chase the shades of night away,
Turn my darkness into day."
—Andrew Reed

HMSR

JUNE 30

PANACEA FOR A TROUBLED LIFE

I am leaving you with a gift—peace of mind and heart! And the peace I give isn't fragile like the peace the world gives. So don't be troubled or afraid.

John 14:27, TLB.

A volcano erupted on the little island of Tristan da Cunha in the South Atlantic. The inhabitants did not want to leave their island home, but the British authorities finally persuaded them to do so. A passing ship picked them up and took them to England, where the crowds overwhelmed them. They just couldn't cope with the bustle, the noise, and the traffic of city life, and the everlasting struggle to make ends meet. One of them said, "It's money, money, money; worry, worry, worry, all the time."

They began to think about their rocky little island, where nobody bothered about taxes or money, and which had never had liquor, written laws, or crime. They finally decided they would rather face volcanic eruptions than live in the distracting civilization of London. So the main body of 198 former inhabitants of Tristan da Cunha went back to their rocky island—back to isolation and no buses, electrical gadgets, television, or any of the rest of civilization's "assets." Back to the potatoes and fish, back to peace. With no island to move to, however, we must live on in modern civilization. But there is a way to find peace of mind and heart—His name is Jesus. He promises us "a gift—peace of mind and heart!" We tap into His gift of peace by cultivating His presence in our lives, talking with Him, and allowing Him to speak to us daily and moment-by-moment throughout the day.

The poet T. S. Eliot commented: "Where is the knowledge we have lost in information, endless invention, endless experiment? . . . Where is the life we have lost in living? Where is the wisdom we have lost in knowing? In order to keep our fidelity to Christ we need to take time each day to pray. Don't let the noise and false standards of this world distort your view of life. Prayer provides perspective. Prayer provides the power that you and I need." More and more people today are discovering that human wisdom is not sufficient to solve their problems, and when they come face to face with Jesus, they receive the gift of peace.

HMSR

JESUS AND THE MISSING BABYLONIAN

I have told you these things before they happen so that when they do, you will believe [in Me]."

JOHN 14:29, TLB.

Have you ever seen a Babylonian? I haven't. I have looked over the roster of countries participating in the United Nations and have not seen the Babylonians listed or even mentioned. Why do no Babylonians exist today? The Babylonian Empire was one of the great world empires of ancient history. Its capital had one of the seven wonders of the ancient world—the beautiful hanging gardens of Babylon.

Founded by Nimrod more than 2,000 years before Christ, the Babylonian Empire was known as the golden kingdom of a golden age. "She invented an alphabet; worked out problems of arithmetic; invented implements for measuring time; . . . discovered the art of polishing, boring, and engraving gems; knew how to reproduce faithfully the outlines of human and animal forms; attained high perfection in textile fabrics; studied successfully the motions of the heavenly bodies; conceived of grammar as a science; elaborated a system of law; saw the value of exact chronology. In almost every branch of science she made a beginning. Much of the art and learning of Greece came from Babylon. No, never had the world seen such a city. . . . Its lofty palaces and temple towers stabbed the sky above the towering walls and thrilled the approaching traveler while he was yet miles away" (E. A. Rowell, *Prophecy Speaks,* p. 51).

After a 70-mile journey by car from Baghdad, we arrived at the site of ancient Babylon. Its tremendous walls have collapsed. The magnificent city of the golden empire is in ruins. A desolate, forbidding wasteland was all I saw. Why? What happened? Why was it destroyed?

Because Bible prophecy centuries before predicted Babylon's destruction and eventual abandonment (Isa. 13:19-22). Cyrus of Persia invaded that seemingly impregnable city in 539 B.C., just as predicted (Isa. 45:1). As I stood there looking at those ruins, my confidence in Jesus strengthened, for He announces the destinies of cities and nations "before they happen." Why? According to His own words: "So that when they do, you will believe [in me]." The good news is that we can trust Jesus!

HMSR

JESUS IS NEAR TO ANSWER YOUR PRAYERS

> ***If you abide in Me, and My words abide in you, you will ask what you desire, and it shall be done for you.***
>
> *John 15:7, NKJV.*

Communion with the heavenly Father affected the life of the late Madam Chiang Kai-shek. "I used to pray that God would do this or that," she once wrote. "Now I pray that God will make His will known to me." Just as we are willing to hear the requests of our children, God is willing and waiting to hear and answer our prayers. Jesus promised: "Ask what you desire, and it shall be done for you." So it is up to us to ask.

Note the condition Jesus places on answering our prayers: "If you abide in Me, and My words abide in you." To receive answers to our prayers it's necessary to stay close to Jesus and be immersed in His Word. The Lord listens to honest prayer. If you mean it, say it; but if you don't, don't say it. Sometimes we just mouth the words of prayer while thinking about something completely different. Our prayers must be meaningful and the result of walking closely with Jesus.

An important point to remember is that prayer does not change God. "Like the stars in the vast circuit of their appointed path, God's purposes know no haste and no delay" (*The Desire of Ages,* p. 32). At times He may have alternate ways of working or may permit choice, as when He allowed King David to choose one of three punishments: seven years of famine, three months of defeat in battle, or three days of pestilence (2 Sam. 24:12-14).

God's purpose never alters, but prayer does transform things. Prayer can clear away difficulties, heal the sick, reunite families, change the entire course of a person's life, even redirect history; but it is because we are the ones transformed. Prayer brings a person into harmony with God. We become His partner. Forgetting about what we had been so intent upon getting, our mind now focuses upon what God wants for us. When we are in God's hands, we know He will work things out for our best good (Rom. 8:28). Some implore God to do their will and respond with anger or disappointment when God does not answer their prayer. But when we remain close enough to Jesus to ascertain God's will, our problems will be solved.

HMSR

"ARE THERE ANY REAL CHRISTIANS IN THE WORLD?"

> ***This is to my Father's glory, that you bear much fruit, showing yourselves to be my disciples.***
>
> *JOHN 15:8, NIV.*

Are there any real Christians in the world, Mr. Hull?" David Ben-Gurion, premier of Israel at that time, asked William Hull, director of a Christian mission in Jerusalem.

Before Hull could answer, the prime minister continued: "I have read the New Testament, and I am deeply moved by what I find there. Its teaching and standards are wonderful. But where are the people who live up to it? Can this book really produce what it sets forth? Are there any real Christians in the world?"

The Israeli premier had confused the idea of a Christian nation with Christian people. There are no Christian nations. A Christian is one who accepts Jesus as the Son of God, the Saviour of the world, and receives Him with true faith as a gift of God. And through the Holy Spirit a Christian allows the living Christ to penetrate his or her life. The true Christian will "bear much fruit"—that is, give evidence of being a disciple of Jesus.

Hull went away from his audience with the prime minister with the conviction that one of the greatest obstacles to the spread of Christ's gospel is Christians themselves. While other factors also hinder Christianity's progress, who can deny that some Christians—or shall we call them professed Christians?—are among the best arguments against Christianity?

One may be perfectly orthodox in doctrine and not be an actual Christian in life. It takes more than belief in doctrinal truths to change a human life; it takes faith in Jesus Christ, an absolute surrender and dedication of our life to Him (Heb. 11:6).

"Christ is seeking to reproduce Himself in the hearts of men; and He does this through those who believe in Him. The object of the Christian life is fruit bearing—the reproduction of Christ's character in the believer, that it may be reproduced in others" (*Christ's Object Lessons,* p. 67).

"There is nothing that the world needs so much as the manifestation through humanity of the Saviour's love" (*ibid.,* p. 419). "This is to my Father's glory, that you bear much fruit, showing yourselves to be my disciples."

HMSR

GENUINE FREEDOM

Now the Lord is the Spirit, and where the Spirit of the Lord is, there is freedom. And we, who . . . reflect the Lord's glory [character], are being transformed into his likeness with ever-increasing glory, which comes from the Lord, who is the Spirit.
2 Cor. 3:17, 18, NIV.

While watching on Boston Common the July 4 celebration of the declaration of freedom from British rule, I heard the Boston Esplanade Orchestra play "Stars and Stripes Forever." The announcer indicated that more than 100 years ago John Philip Sousa wrote this crown jewel of all marches. If I were asked to write such a march, I could not do so, for such a composition must result from an innate something within. Just as writing "Stars and Stripes Forever" came from within Sousa, living a Christlike life can occur only as Christ lives in me. We are "being transformed into [Jesus'] likeness with ever-increasing glory, which comes from the Lord, who is the Spirit."

According to Peter, Jesus, our sinless Saviour, is our example, and we are to follow in His steps (1 Peter 2:21, 22). But through my human effort any attempt to live a sinless life is impossible for me, for at birth I came into this world "controlled by [my] sinful nature" (Rom. 8:8, NIV). However, the following verse resonates with the encouraging good news that after being born again, the Spirit of Christ "lives in you" (verse 9, NIV).

Because Christ died to pay the penalty for our sins on the cross, being forgiven for our past sins is now an objective reality. But living a Christlike life in the present is possible only when the Spirit of Christ "lives in you." Christ's Holy Spirit working in us breaks sin's power. The result: "where the Spirit of the Lord is, there is freedom." Truly, freedom from the power of sin is cause for a real Independence Day celebration.

To attempt to live a Christian life through our human effort is a dead-end street. For "when the kindness and love of God our Savior appeared, he saved us, not because of righteous things we had done, but because of his mercy" (Titus 3:4, 5, NIV). To have Jesus as our example is not enough; we need Him as our Saviour.

DRG

LIVING IN JESUS' LOVE

When you obey me you are living in my love, just as I obey my Father and live in his love.
John 15:10, TLB.

When I was growing up, I often heard my father and mother bragging to people about what a good boy Danny was. Since we had a strong love relationship, hearing their comments increased my bond with them. So when tempted to steal a peach from a neighbor's tree, I didn't reason: "I can't do this, because the commandments say, 'Thou shalt not steal' " (Ex. 20:15). Instead, because my parents' love filled my heart, I wasn't tempted to steal that peach. I wouldn't want to hurt them. Besides, their love for others had caught on in my heart, causing me to love our neighbors too much to rob them. My resistance to doing wrong did not come from what I had heard in church, what I had been taught in school, or what others expected of me, but from the love my parents had implanted in my heart as a result of my relationship with them.

That's the kind of relationship we are to have with Jesus. It's what He was talking about when He said: "When you obey me you are living in my love, just as I obey my Father and live in his love." Because of Jesus' love relationship with His Father, He lived in His Father's love. Jesus wants us to have that kind of relationship with Him. "I want you to obey me," He says, "because 'you are living in my love.' " He wants to change our nature to one that loves and obeys.

Jesus reminds us, "If you love me, you will keep my commandments" (John 14:15, RSV). The nature of love is to act as the person who is loved. Jesus was speaking from experience. His obedient life resulted from a Son's love relationship with His Father. It is a tremendous relief to realize that our task for today does not revolve around striving to obey a list of rules, but on getting to know Jesus better, loving Him more, having His love "shed abroad in our hearts" (Rom. 5:5), then living out that love in our lives.

DRG

WE ARE FRIENDS OF JESUS

I command you to love each other in the same way that I love you. And here is how to measure it—the greatest love is shown when people lay down their lives for their friends. You are my friends if you obey me.
John 15:12-14, NLT.

When people asked a man by the name of Charles Kingsley for the secret of his successful life, he answered, "I had a Friend." He had taken to heart Jesus' proclamation, "You are my friends." A friend of Jesus! I can't think of any higher honor or any greater privilege.

When the Scottish boy Robert Moffatt left home his mother walked a ways with him. Then she stopped to say goodbye and added, "Robert, I want you to promise me something."

"What?" he asked.

"Promise me something!" she gently urged.

"You'll have to tell me before I promise."

"Robert," she said, "it is something you can easily do. Promise your mother."

He looked her in the face and said, "Very well, Mother; I'll do anything you wish."

She clasped her hands behind his head, pulled his face close to hers, and said, "Robert, you are going out into a wicked world. Begin every day with God. Close every day with God."

She kissed him. That kiss made Christ Robert Moffatt's friend. And with his friend ever by his side, Moffatt became the man who conquered Africa for Christ.

Moffatt's preaching did not change Africa; it was his living. And the source of its power rested in the promise he had made to his mother to begin and end every day with God. The beginning and the ending determined the in-between.

In answer to those who charge that "Christ doesn't make much difference in the life," the very life of a person who is truly a friend of Christ's testifies: "It makes all the difference in the world." So when Jesus is your friend, He will change your world through you!

DRG

NO GREATER LOVE

> ***Greater love hath no man than this, that a man lay down his life for his friends.***
>
> *JOHN 15:13.*

What prompted Jesus to die for you and for me? It was His love for us. "Greater love hath no man than this, that a man lay down his life for his friends." Yet Christ also offered His life for His enemies, for those who hated Him, even for those who murdered Him. He gave Himself for you and for me.

His love is unchangeable. "Having loved his own which were in the world, he loved them unto the end" (John 13:1). Even though He knew which disciple would betray Him, He still loved Judas. It was Christ's love for him that broke Peter's heart and brought him back in penitence. It is impossible to comprehend such matchless love.

Once Niagara Falls stopped flowing because of an ice jam across the river. The rainbow faded, and the vast rush of the falls stilled. But there has never been a moment in which God's love toward His children has ever failed, because His love for you is greater than your mother's love or your father's love. No parents in the world ever loved their child as God does you and me. To think of offering one of my sons even to save a friend—I cannot comprehend it or fathom it! Yet God so loved our sinful world that He did something even greater. He sacrificed His Son, His only Son. I cannot understand that kind of love. Can you?

One thing that has helped me has been my experience with my own family. I loved my children before they knew anything about my love, and that is the way it is with God's love for us. He loved us before we ever thought of loving Him. "Herein is love, not that we loved God, but that he loved us, and sent his Son to be the propitiation for our sins" (1 John 4:10).

God loves you! He loves you so much that He gave, and His Son gave also. He has much planned for you if only you will accept that love. In the beginning God could have stamped out all sin, but then people in our world would not have had a choice. Our eternal destiny still hinges upon our own choice. If anyone is lost, it will not be because God does not love them, but a result of resisting the love of both the Father and the Son.

HMSR

THE TWO B'S

> *You did not choose me, but I chose you and appointed you to go and bear fruit—fruit that will last.*
>
> JOHN 15:16, NIV.

When David Hume, a philosopher in the Age of Reason, finished speaking at a university gathering, one student filing out turned to another and said, "He demolished everything, didn't he? He never left a shred of the faith." But the other young man replied, "He never touched my mother's religion."

When I was a young man during college days, I read arguments against the inspiration of the Bible and other pillars of the Christian faith. Then I'd think of certain people I knew, especially my parents. The thought would come to me, *Both of them are evidences and proofs of the truth of Christianity. They are so much like Christ that He, through His Spirit, must be living in them. The Bible must be true.*

To me that's an unanswerable argument. A genuine Christian is my proof of Christianity. A real Bible believer, guided by the Holy Spirit in the path of obedience, demonstrates the inspiration of the Scriptures. Such proofs live and walk about in the world everywhere today.

The evidence that the grace of God is operating in believers' hearts must be seen in their daily lives. Paul stated it this way: "Everyone who confesses the name of the Lord must turn away from wickedness" (2 Tim. 2:19, NIV). James said: "Faith without deeds is useless" (James 2:20, NIV). So we see the two B's in the Christian life—believe and behave. We cannot divorce them. They belong together, and we should not confuse them with each other.

Always we must remember that a person's acceptance in the sight of Jesus does not depend upon good works. At the same time we must also keep in mind that Jesus "chose" and "appointed" us to bear "fruit that will last." Here is the good news: True faith in Jesus includes accepting His death for our sins, but faith does more—it leads to a re-creation of life by the power of the Holy Spirit. As a result, Christians present this new life before the world as they live, act, and talk like Jesus.

HMSR

THE VICAR OF CHRIST

Nevertheless I tell you the truth; It is expedient for you that I go away: for if I go not away, the Comforter will not come unto you; but if I depart, I will send him unto you.
John 16:7.

Fear filled the disciples' hearts when Jesus told them He would be returning to heaven. So He assured them that He would not leave them as orphans, with no divine parent to protect and help them. He promised to send them His representative, the Comforter, the Holy Spirit—the Vicar of Christ, Christ's representative on earth. And the Spirit came to comfort the followers of Jesus, the disciples, and you and me.

While the New Testament mentions the Holy Spirit 262 times, many references to Him also appear in the Old Testament. In fact, He has played a very important role in humanity's life from the beginning of time. The Holy Spirit had a part in the creation of all things. He was active in convicting the antediluvians of their sins. In Judges we find the Holy Spirit filling the lives of Samson, Joshua, Gideon, and others. The prophets felt His influence. All through the Old Testament we see the Holy Spirit as the moving power of God functioning in the lives of people, convicting them, encouraging them, and leading them to a new consciousness of God.

This promise of the Holy Spirit, who was to come as a Comforter to the disciples, represented a special outpouring and indwelling not only for the early church, but for His contemporary church—for you and me! And the Holy Spirit did indeed come—not that He had not always been here on this earth, but people had not been able to receive Him in His fullness before that time. Then they saw the Holy Spirit function at Pentecost as never before in a dramatic, awe-inspiring, breathtaking way.

Have you ever stopped to ponder and appreciate the absolute necessity of the indwelling Spirit in your life? Really, your life doesn't mean a thing unless the Holy Spirit is guiding you! Without the Holy Spirit we cannot really experience Jesus in our life. So our daily prayer should ever be "Come, Holy Spirit, come. Make my experience with Jesus real today."

HMSR

THE POWER OF THE HOLY SPIRIT IN YOUR LIFE

Howbeit when he, the Spirit of truth, is come, he will guide you into all truth. . . . He shall glorify me: for he shall receive of mine, and shall shew it unto you.
JOHN 16:13, 14.

A man in a Southwestern city occasionally attended the church that I pastored. He really came out of deference to his wife and family. Many times as he left the sanctuary he would make a comment that was not exactly complimentary: The auditorium was too stuffy, or the choir sang too loudly. He had made no commitment to Christ. I had his name on the list of men for whom I was praying.

One day I received a telephone call from him. "Pastor Richards, I must see you," he said. "Shall I meet you at the church office at 3:00 this afternoon?" I assured him that I would be there. The businessman came promptly at the time he had suggested, and as we visited, I could tell something bothered him. So I asked him what it was. He moved closer to my desk and put his head between his hands. As he leaned his elbows on my desk, tears came to his eyes, and he blurted out, "Pastor Richards, I want to give my heart to Christ! I've been so empty inside."

Yes, the Holy Spirit was working with him. Just as Scripture says: "When he, the Spirit of truth, is come, he will guide you into all truth." The Holy Spirit always uplifts Jesus, for He "is the way, the truth, and the life" (John 14:6). He convicts us of sin and leads us to accept Jesus as our Saviour (John 16:8-11). Then through the Holy Spirit Jesus "dwelleth with you, and shall be in you" (John 14:17).

If Jesus is not dwelling in you through the Holy Spirit, you are not really living. You are a mere physical shell. Without the Holy Spirit we may have a physical existence, but only with the Holy Spirit can we live the spiritual life. Nor can we have spiritual power without the indwelling of Christ's representative on earth. You and I are really a channel for the working of the Holy Spirit. His power must flow through us. So let us invite Him into our hearts today and every day.

HMSR

"GOD SENT YOU HERE!"

> ***Ask and you will receive, and your joy will be complete.***
> *JOHN 16:24, NIV.*

"Don't pray, if you don't want God to answer," my wife, Lillian, told the congregation at church one day.

The church we attend had been planning an evangelistic meeting for the next year, and to prepare the way, some members were studying the "Good News for Today" Bible course with interested people in our community. One weekend Lillian asked God to help her find a person to study the Bible lessons with. Three days later He led her to a home. During her visit Jan (not her real name) told her about her burden for her three children because only the youngest was still attending church with her.

A few minutes later, while a friend waited in the car, Jan's 17-year-old daughter came in for some money. Her mother went to get the money, and Lillian talked with the daughter. She found a spiritual hunger in the girl's heart, and the daughter agreed to take the Voice of Prophecy Discover course. The mother returned and heard what was going on. After her daughter ran out the front door, she said, "I believe God sent you here in answer to my prayer!" Then Jan told Lillian that for the past several days she had been praying both for her children and for a deeper understanding of the Bible. She agreed to study the "Good News" lessons with Lillian—an answer to both their prayers.

Just then Jan's husband, who too had stopped attending church, returned home. When the telephone rang, Jan went to answer, and Lillian had an opportunity to talk with the husband. When the wife returned, he announced, "I think we should begin reading the Bible together each day." After relating this and other experiences, Lillian explained to the congregation that God had led her to six people that week that she had started Bible studies with. That's when she told the church members, "Don't pray, if you don't want God to answer." He answered, prepared the way, and put the right words into her mouth.

Jesus meant business when He said, "Ask and you will receive, and your joy will be complete." Lillian's joy appeared all over her face. The good news that Jesus will answer our prayers is available to each of us this very day.

DRG

REJOICE! JESUS ANSWERS PRAYER

Until now you have asked nothing in My name. Ask, and you will receive, that your joy may be full.

John 16:24, NKJV.

One day Lillian received a letter from her close friend Pearl Martin. My wife had shared a dramatic and specific answer to prayer with Pearl, who wrote: "It brought tears to my eyes when you described your experience. What a miracle!

"Your experience reminded us of a similar experience we had a number of years ago, not too long after we returned from Singapore. Charles [Pearl's husband] and I were walking by the ocean, enjoying the surf. He was in the water about up to his knees, I was nearer to the shore, when a big wave came and caught us off guard. It knocked Charles down, but I was able to escape it by jumping toward the sand. Anyway, his glasses flew off in the swirling water.

"He came out of the water toward me and told me what had happened. We were sick about it, because in those days before he had the cataracts removed he really had very poor vision without his glasses. Since we had the trailer at the beach, we didn't know how he could drive home. I had not pulled the trailer before and was extremely nervous about even attempting it.

"We asked the Lord for help. When we looked out at the ocean and the waves coming and going, we were not sure even where Charles was when he lost the glasses. I walked out into the water during a time when there was a lull in the waves. Putting my hand down in the water, I picked up the glasses as though I could see them and knew they were there! Oh, how we felt the presence of a loving, caring heavenly Father, for, like you, we felt it was a miracle. It is so thrilling that the Lord cares about the smallest details in our lives and delights to answer our prayers!"

If, like the disciples, "until now you have asked nothing in [Jesus'] name," "ask, and you will receive, that your joy may be full."

DRG

JESUS IS REAL

> ***Believe on the Lord Jesus Christ, and you will be saved.***
>
> *Acts 16:31, NKJV.*

Several times people have asked me, "How do you know Jesus ever existed?" Suppose your neighbor were to raise that question today—what would you answer? Here are a few thoughts that might be of help.

How do we know that Napoleon Bonaparte once lived? By what his friends and enemies said about him, the effect he had on history, the battles he won. And so it is with Jesus. We can trace the historical records called the four Gospels back almost to His time. Note also that records of the church extend back nearly to His century. Also, the Jewish people have continued from Christ's time, and few of them have ever doubted the reality of the historical Jesus.

Josephus, a first-century Jewish historian, in his *Antiquities of the Jews*—a historical writing that the Romans admired so much that they granted him citizenship—makes the following statement: "So he [Annas, the high priest] assembled the Sanhedrin of judges, and brought before them the brother of Jesus who was called Christ, whose name was James, and some of his companions. And when he had laid an accusation against them as breakers of the law, he delivered them to be stoned."

Four pagans wrote about Jesus. In the first century Tacitus recorded: "Christus, the founder of the name [Christians], had undergone the death penalty in the reign of Tiberius, by sentence of the procurator Pontius Pilatus." In the second century the historian Suetonius spoke of the followers of "Chrestus" being exiled from Rome. Pliny the younger, in a letter to Emperor Trajan about the year A.D. 112, told the emperor how he dealt with Christians. English translations with the full text of these historical references are available in libraries.

This leaves us with an even more important question than "Did Jesus really exist?" Does He exist in my heart? Does He dwell in your heart? The question is vital because of Jesus' promise "Believe on the Lord Jesus Christ, and you will be saved."

HMSR

WHEN TROUBLE COMES

I have told you these things, so that in me you may have peace. In this world you will have trouble. But take heart! I have overcome the world.
JOHN 16:33, NIV.

Jesus gives Christians a satisfying life even when troubles surround them. Take, for example, Mary White Rowlandson, a pioneer mother in colonial New England. During the Indian war in the winter of 1676 attacking Indians surrounded her cabin. They carried her and her three children away from the burning village as prisoners, and her youngest child soon died of exposure. For 11 weeks the Indians held her captive, then finally released her with her two surviving children.

Often in her journal she recorded God's goodness, and once she wrote these words: "God was with me in a wonderful manner, carrying me along and bearing up my spirit, that it did not quite fail." And, speaking of a sorrowful experience, she said: "As soon as I had an opportunity I took my Bible to read, and that quieting scripture came to my hand, Psalm 46:10: 'Be still, and know that I am God.' "

The Living Bible translation of today's verse is refreshing: "I have told you all this so that you will have peace of heart and mind. Here on earth you will have many trials and sorrows; but cheer up, for I have overcome the world."

Many have found this same "peace of heart and mind" that Jesus promises to those who are having "trials and sorrows." Why does the Christian experience peace of heart and mind despite going through many trials and sorrows? Because of the Saviour, who says, "Cheer up, for I have overcome the world." Their association with Jesus has encouraged them and carried them through many experiences of despair and heartache.

Christ's power can enable us to do the seemingly impossible. Yes, He enables us to live a life of peace when troubles surround us. "His divine power hath given unto us all things that pertain unto life and godliness" (2 Peter 1:3). Jesus strengthens us to live above the troubles that disturb the life of a non-Christian. We are "strengthened with all might, according to his glorious power" (Col. 1:11).

HMSR

JESUS OUR ANCHOR

Jesus spoke these words, lifted His eyes to heaven, and said: "Father, the hour has come. Glorify Your Son, that Your Son also may glorify You, as You have given Him authority over all flesh, that He should give eternal life to as many as You have given Him."
John 17:1, 2, NKJV.

It's an inspiring experience to visit the home of John Knox, the great Scottish Reformer. One of the most courageous men who ever lived, he seemed to fear no man, yet when he was about to die in that little house just across the street from St. Gile's Cathedral in Edinburgh, he called his wife and said, "Read to me." When she asked, "What shall I read?" he replied, "Oh, read to me from the place where I first cast my anchor."

She knew where the text was—John 17. And it was certainly a wonderful place to cast an anchor—a place that will truly hold. When we build our faith upon such a divine promise, we need never fear anything. Though waves rage and the ship of our life seems in danger, we just must see that our anchor has been secured in a promise of God like this, and we are safe, perfectly safe. God has given Jesus "authority over all flesh, that He should give eternal life to as many as" God has "given Him." Christ is our anchor, our "authority" who assures us of eternal life.

As our anchor Christ has authority that no one else in our world has. A long time ago in Palestine Jesus died on Calvary's cross for our sins, and that is true. But the real question is Does He live now in our hearts? Does He dwell in our homes? Is He the anchor of our being?

Jesus will not force His way into our lives. But when we give our hearts to Him completely, our lives change and become really worth living. Everything is different. None of us actually knows how wonderful life can be until Christ becomes our anchor. As our anchor He has "authority" over us. He is over all we think and do and has a right to decide our plans, our friends, our love affairs—everything. If we truly believe that Jesus is our anchor and that we are His disciples, everything that belongs to us is in His hands. We can rest secure in Jesus. With Him as our anchor, we can know without doubt that it will hold. Our place in heaven is secure.

HMSR

ETERNAL LIFE DEPENDS ON IT

Father, the time has come. Glorify your Son, that your Son may glorify you. For you granted him authority over all people that he might give eternal life to all those you have given him. Now this is eternal life: that they may know you, the only true God, and Jesus Christ, whom you have sent.

John 17:1-3, NIV.

According to Jesus' prayer to His Father, eternal life depends on our knowing God and His Son, Jesus Christ. "The knowledge of God as revealed in Christ is the knowledge that all who are saved must have. It is the knowledge that works transformation of character. This knowledge, received, will re-create the soul in the image of God. It will impart to the whole being a spiritual power that is divine" (*Testimonies for the Church,* vol. 8, p. 289).

Even little children can appreciate the benefits of knowing Jesus and receiving the assurance of eternal life. When Genene, our oldest daughter, was about 4 years old, I put her to bed one night. She put her arms around my neck and held me tight. "Nene, who do you love?" I asked her.

You know what I expected her to say, what I hoped she would say. But no. Instead, with a smiling yet serious face she replied, "I love Jesus."

In sober reflection I would rather that she gave this answer, for "this is eternal life: that they may know . . . Jesus Christ." After all is said and done, my human love could mean a happy life for her only for the present. Only Jesus can give her what I cherish most for her—eternal life. It is vital that we know the good news about Jesus, for eternal life depends on it.

DRG

JESUS' DARKEST NIGHT

> *He . . . went . . . out: and it was night.*
>
> *JOHN 13:30.*

Forget for a moment that you are sitting in your home, or wherever you may be. Imagine that you are in Jerusalem on the day before Christ's crucifixion. Notice that everyone in the street is staring at a man coming down the other side with 12 men. He has caused a great deal of discussion the past few days in Jerusalem. "That is the prophet from Galilee," people tell each other as they intently watch Him. It is the great feast of the Passover. Tens of thousands of people fill the city. Let's follow Him on down the street. Entering a common-looking home, He goes to an upstairs room, and His 12 disciples gather around Him to share the Passover meal.

Very quiet, He seems "exceeding sorrowful" (Matt. 26:38). Looking at His disciples, He says, "One of you will betray Me." Each man wonders if he is the one. One by one they ask, "Is it I, Lord?" "Is it I?" It seems they distrust themselves. At last it is Judas's turn. Even though he has already planned in his heart to betray Him, he inquires, "Master, is it I?" Jesus gives him to understand that it is and declares, "That thou doest, do quickly" (John 13:27). The others don't understand, though. They think Christ is sending Judas out to give something for the poor or to secure more supplies for the Passover feast. Nothing in all recorded history is more sorrowful than that parting. As Judas turns away from Jesus, we hear the door close and his steps going down the stairs. "He . . . went . . . out: and it was night." Yes, it was night. It was a nighttime meeting, and it was night in the heart of Judas as it had never been night before. Three long years with Jesus; three long years as a disciple! Think of the bands that bound those 12 together! Now Judas is gone—gone to sell Jesus to His enemies for 30 pieces of silver.

Think of what must be going on in the heart of Jesus as the steps of Judas fade in the distance. It is also His darkest night. You cannot help falling in love with Jesus when you see how much He suffered for you and me. So speak up now and tell Him that you love Him as you begin this day.

HMSR

BETRAYED BY A KISS

Judas then, having received a band of men and officers from the chief priests and Pharisees, cometh thither with lanterns and torches and weapons.
JOHN 18:3.

Imagine again today that you are in Jerusalem the night before Jesus' death. You sit in the upper room with Jesus and His disciples. Judas has gone to betray Him, and now Jesus comforts His disciples. He tells them that He is going away, but they do not need to be concerned, for He will prepare a place for them in His Father's home and return to take them there.

Next we follow along with Jesus and the disciples as they leave the upper room and head out the eastern gate of Jerusalem and across the little valley of Kidron to the Garden of Gethsemane. Watch as Jesus takes Peter, James, and John a little beyond the rest, and asks them to wait and pray. Jesus goes off by Himself, kneels, and begins to pray Himself. As He prays He sweats great drops of blood. Suffering for your sins and mine, He finds Himself under the very shadow of the cross. The sins of the world begin to rest heavily upon His heart. He has never sinned, yet He is soon to take the sins of the world on Himself as our substitute.

While He prays we see a band of men entering the garden with torches and weapons. Listen as Jesus calls out, "Whom seek ye?" (John 18:4). They answer, "Jesus of Nazareth" (verse 5). Then we hear Jesus say, "I am He. . . . If you seek Me, let these go" (verse 8, NKJV).

The disciples run away, but not before Judas rushes up and betrays Jesus with a kiss. When Jesus says, "Judas, betrayest thou the Son of man with a kiss?" (Luke 22:48), we can't help thinking, *This must be breaking Jesus' heart.*

What is taking place in your heart at this moment? My heart is subdued. Had I been there, would I have run away with the disciples or pressed close and comforted Jesus? If you'd been there, what would you have done?

HMSR

WHAT WILL YOU DO WITH JESUS?

Will ye therefore that I release unto you the King of the Jews? Then cried they all again, saying, Not this man, but Barabbas. Now Barabbas was a robber.
John 18:39, 40.

Pilate had attempted to pass to Herod the responsibility of condemning Jesus to death, but failed. Now he tried another plan to escape responsibility. He had a prisoner called Barabbas, a bandit guilty of murder. According to the custom of that time, Pilate could liberate during Passover someone who happened to be in prison. He brought Barabbas out and said, "Whom shall I deliver to you, Barabbas or Jesus?"

It seemed to him that Jesus, bleeding from the terrible Roman scourge and wearing on His head a crown of thorns, surely would excite the pity of the crowd. Barabbas looked the evil person he was. *Certainly,* Pilate thought, *they will choose Jesus.* "No, no," they shouted, "give us Barabbas, Barabbas. We want him released."

Pilate did not know what to do with Christ. "What shall I do then with Jesus which is called Christ?" he asked (Matt. 27:22). The Roman official had to decide, but didn't know which way to go. And every one of us must determine what we will do with Jesus. Either we receive Him as the one who died for us, or we nail Him to the cross.

"Let Him be crucified," the crowd roared. "Let Him be crucified" rang out over the streets of the city that day. Pilate was too weak to withstand the demand of the mob, and, washing his hands in front of them, he declared, "I am innocent of the blood of this just person" (verse 24). Christ was not guilty, and yet the Roman official turned Him over to be executed. All the waters of the seven seas could not wash the blood from Pilate's hands. Neither can it cleanse the blood from our hands. Since Jesus died for the sins of the whole world, then the sins of the whole world killed Him. Your sins were there as well as mine. His blood is on our hands. We all must answer the question: What will I do then with Jesus who is called Christ?

HMSR

JESUS DIED IN MY PLACE

> *Then delivered he him therefore unto them to be crucified. . . . And he bearing his cross went forth into a place called the place of the skull, . . . where they crucified him.*
> JOHN *19:16-18.*

Some years ago an 18-year-old University of California freshman commented, "Someone else died in my place. Of course, I feel wonderful to be alive, but I feel so bad about the other girl. Somehow, I can't feel nothing happened to me. I like life very much . . . but for another to die in my place is a hard thing to put into words."

Those words might have come as a testimony in a religious service, but they were not. They referred to the tragic crash of a United Airlines DCA and a Trans-World Airlines Constellation. The UC freshman, Leslie Picker, had a reservation on the ill-fated United Flight 226 for the Chicago-to-New York portion of her trip. Then she obtained a seat on a nonstop flight from California to New York a day earlier. An 18-year-old freshman, Katherine Post, took her seat on the original flight and died in the crash. We can all enter into the feelings of the young woman who escaped, with her mingled gratitude and grief. Because Jesus died in our place.

Jesus perished for us not by accident, but by the deliberate plan and foreknowledge of God. Wicked men led Jesus out to be crucified, but Jesus went willingly. "God commendeth his love toward us, in that, while we were yet sinners, Christ died for us" (Rom. 5:8).

The death of Katherine Post was unintentional. But Jesus' death was a voluntary, substitutionary, atoning death. Jesus willingly came all the way from heaven to earth to give His life for us sinners, to die in our place. Actually the death of Katherine Post did not save Leslie Picker—it only postponed her death. But those who put their faith and trust in Him will never have to face what Jesus endured at Calvary. His death was a substitution for ours. To accomplish that for us, He was more than willing to experience His darkest night on earth. We dare not allow Jesus' suffering and death for us to be in vain.

HMSR

WHAT JESUS FINISHED AT THE CROSS

When Jesus had received the vinegar, he said, "It is finished"; and he bowed his head and gave up his spirit.
John 19:30, RSV.

Just before Jesus died, He shouted one word in Greek, *teleo,* which means that something is finished; completed; attested to, just as though someone were signing an important document. What did Jesus mean? What was finished? Without doubt most, or even all, of the people present at the Crucifixion didn't know what He meant.

We must remember that Christ's great work as revealed in the Bible has a fourfold aspect: First, we speak of His finished work of creation when He fashioned the world. The Bible says that He made the world. Jesus, the Son of God, was the active agent in Creation as we read in the first few verses of John, the first chapter of Hebrews, and the first chapter of Colossians.

Second, there was His finished work of reconciliation on the cross, when He made an atoning sacrifice for the world's sins. Really, He brought the world back to God. It had wandered away because of human sins. Anticipating His final victory over Satan at Calvary, on the evening before the Crucifixion Jesus prayed to His Father: "I glorified thee on earth, having accomplished the work which thou gavest me to do" (John 17:4, RSV).

Third, we read in the Scriptures of His task of intercession when, as the great Judge of all, He will decide the destiny of every person. The Father has committed all judgment to Him (John 5:22).

Fourth, there will be His finished work of re-creation, when He removes all trace of sin and its resulting death, sorrow, pain, and destruction. Jesus will completely erase it from the world, and we will have a new earth—that forever world of tomorrow.

At the cross, for all intents and purposes, Christ finished His work by settling for all time His victory over Satan. The cross determined the final verdict on what will happen when Christ sets up His kingdom. Has that controversy been settled in your heart? Have you accepted the finished work of Christ for your salvation?

HMSR

CHRIST ATTENDS TO OUR INDIVIDUAL NEEDS

> *Peter was hurt because Jesus asked him the third time, "Do you love me?" He said, "Lord, you know all things; you know that I love you." Jesus said, "Feed my sheep."*
>
> *John 21:17, NIV.*

Jesus took a personal interest in every individual. The day prior to His crucifixion Peter told Him, " 'I will lay down my life for you.' Then Jesus answered, . . . 'I tell you the truth, before the rooster crows, you will disown me three times!' " (John 13:37, 38, NIV). The next morning in the courtyard of the high priest's home, after the disciple denied Christ three times, the rooster crowed, and "the Lord turned and looked straight at Peter" (Luke 22:61, NIV). It must have been a pained but forgiving look, because Peter "went outside and wept bitterly" (verse 62, NIV).

On the resurrection morning when the women came to the tomb and found it empty, Jesus sent an angel to tell them He had risen, and to instruct them, "Go, tell his disciples and Peter" (Mark 16:7). How loving of Jesus to tell the angel to mention Peter by name. Christ had forgiven Peter, and He wanted the disciple to know it. Later when all the disciples met Jesus, our thoughtful Saviour singled Peter out and instructed him, "Feed my sheep." He was letting Peter know that his past was no obstacle to the important work Jesus had for him to do.

Jesus is interested in every person's individual needs today. Take, for instance, Mark Guy Pierce, an obscure person you have probably never heard of. Though Guy was not a Christian, on his way to work one day he got to thinking about Jesus' question to Peter, "Do you love me?" and about Peter's answer, "Lord, you know all things; you know that I love you." He wished he could answer as Peter did. Later he wrote: "I could not say, 'Lord, You know that I do not love You,' and I found some comfort in that. At last I grew bold enough to look up and say: 'Lord, You know that I want to love You.' Then I began to think of His great love for me. I thought of His life, of His words, of His cross; and almost before I knew what I was doing, I looked up and said, 'Lord, You know that I do love You.' " Then and there on his way to work Guy's new life began. This same Jesus takes just such a personal interest in each of us—in you!

DRG

BAPTIZED BY FIRE

The Day of Pentecost had now arrived. As the believers met together that day, . . . what looked like flames or tongues of fire appeared and settled on their heads. And everyone present was filled with the Holy Spirit and began speaking in languages they didn't know, for the Holy Spirit gave them this ability.

ACTS 2:1-4, TLB.

Just as Jesus promised, the apostles received the baptism of the Holy Spirit. Before the Spirit's outpouring, they had been haggling among themselves, striving for supremacy, looking for position, trying to exalt themselves. But after Pentecost they completely lost sight of self. Jesus alone had first place in their thoughts, their actions, their lives. Before Pentecost they were afraid, weak, trembling human beings. Afterward they were on fire for Christ. Nothing could hold them back.

The baptism of fire can make us a new person in Christ. Put iron ore into the fire, and it will come out pig iron. Put the pig iron through another fiery process, and you will have high-quality steel. God wants to make a new high-quality person of you and of me. But often instead of yielding our lives to be changed, we make excuses for the way we are living. Just as the apostles needed and received the baptism of the Holy Spirit, it is imperative for us today to accept the Holy Spirit by recognizing our need, by believing the baptism of the Spirit is for us, by earnestly desiring it, and by continuing steadfastly in prayer, being wholly surrendered to God's will.

A great religious leader once tried to explain to one of his followers how to obtain salvation. They were near a large container of water, and the religious leader pushed his friend's head down into the water until just a few bubbles of air came up out of the water. Finally he removed his hand, and his friend came up gasping for air and demanding why he had done such a thing to him. The leader replied that until he desired eternal life as much as he had craved air, he would never get it. We must long for the baptism of fire more than anything else in the world or we will not receive it. Only Jesus is qualified to baptize us with fire. We are saturated with the bitumen of sin, and the only way to escape destruction in the fires of the last days is to be burned now with the Pentecostal baptism of fire.

HMSR

LIFE-CHANGING FIRE

They saw what seemed to be tongues of fire that separated and came to rest on each of them. All of them were filled with the Holy Spirit and began to speak in other tongues as the Spirit enabled them.

Acts 2:3, 4, NIV.

When we held a meeting in Chattanooga, Tennessee, we invited the people to surrender completely to Jesus. Among the many who responded was a middle-aged couple. They told me they had attended the meetings out of curiosity and had determined to find as much fault as they could with the services and the teaching and preaching. But something had happened. The Spirit of God had spoken to their hearts. A conviction had come to them so strongly that they just had to respond. What a thrill it was to see them walking down the aisle, hand in hand, tears running down their cheeks! The fire spoken of in this text had cleansed their lives. The thoughtless words, the proud tongue of self-promotion, the malicious tongue of prejudice and passion and condemnation—the power of God had cleansed all of it. That is the way to be made clean—by the penetrating, consuming, purifying baptism of the Holy Spirit.

We need to have the trash in our lives burned away! Remember, only the fire of God can do this. When that holy fire burns, it will consume the rubbish of pride and self-love. It will destroy the stubble of our questioning doubts and the sham of our un-Christlike activities. The Spirit of God will consume our prickly tempers and all the refuse of malicious jokes until Jesus, the Great Refiner, can see His image reflected in us. How much we need this today!

How many times have you asked for the baptism of the Holy Spirit that Jesus promised? Or how many times have you requested Jesus to cleanse your heart from the easy sins that penetrate our lives? We need the Pentecost experience today! So let us pray this prayer penned by the late LeRoy Froom:

"O fire of God, burn on, burn on,
Till all my dross is burned away;
O fire of God, burn on, burn on,
Prepare me for the testing day."

HMSR

CLEANSED, REFRESHED, AND AT PEACE

And it shall come to pass in the last days, saith God, I will pour out my Spirit upon all flesh: and your sons and your daughters shall prophesy, . . . that whosoever shall call on the name of the Lord shall be saved.

Acts 2:17-21.

The early and latter rainy periods of Palestine's wet season represent the outpouring of the Holy Spirit on the day of Pentecost. We can certainly say today that the human heart is as dry and sterile as the desert sand. It needs the outpouring of the Holy Spirit. God's rain from heaven brings life and a plentiful harvest to the parched earth, so the Holy Spirit can bring cleansing and peace to your heart and mine.

A group of farmers gathered to pray for rain. One of the men began, "We pray for rain, Lord, for rain we pray. We don't pray for a drizzling, fizzling rain, but for a regular gully-washer and ground-soaker!" When we pray for the Lord to fulfill His promise to send an abundant rain of His power, He always drenches us with His love. As we claim the promised gift of the Holy Spirit, the God of the universe will water our soul with His Spirit. We will have an abundant life, a more meaningful existence, for today's text indicates that after the Spirit cleanses us, Jesus becomes real in our lives, assuring our salvation.

God promised Israel of old, "I will give you rain in due season" (Lev. 26:4). If we are willing to obey God, then He will be able to fulfill His promise of a refreshed life with Jesus through the Holy Spirit's power. God also vowed that He "will give peace in the land" (verse 6). What would it be like today if we were all encircled by the peace Jesus offers?

HMSR

THE UPSIDE-DOWNERS—1

But when they did not find them, they dragged Jason and some brethren to the rulers of the city, crying out, "These who turned the world upside down have come here too."

ACTS 17:6, NKJV.

The apostle Paul was perhaps the most effective upside-downer who ever lived. It was following Paul's Sabbath sermon in the synagogue at Thessalonica that unbelieving Jews set the city in an uproar and complained to the rulers of the city that the Christians had "turned the world upside down."

During his preaching tour in Asia Minor in response to the leading of the Holy Spirit, Paul turned toward Europe. The gospel spread over Europe and eventually over the whole earth. What did Paul have that enabled him to penetrate Asia and Europe and turn "the world upside down"? Complete dedication. We find Paul's commitment in the fervent declaration he wrote to the church at Corinth: "For I determined not to know any thing among you, save Jesus Christ, and him crucified" (1 Cor. 2:2). As with Peter and John, those who listened to Paul "took knowledge of [him], that [he] had been with Jesus" (Acts 4:13).

David Livingstone, another pioneer missionary, turned Africa upside down. Even though a brilliant young physician, he determined to give himself to helping others in service to Jesus. In 1840 he set sail for Africa. During the years that followed he battled Africa's slave traffic with a courage born of heaven. When in 1862 his wife died, he did not lose courage but pressed on. For years the outside world lost sight of him until Henry Stanley, a famous newspaperman and African explorer, found him. During the four months Stanley spent with him, he discovered Livingstone's Saviour and became a transformed man.

God's plan has a place for each of us to serve as upside-downers who see the great need in today's world and determine to do something about it. It may not be as a full-time missionary in some far-off land, but right where you are—at home, at school in the locker room, at work, on summer vacation, on the street corner, at church, or wherever we are. God needs us as upside-downers for Him in today's world. We have so much to do for Jesus, the Saviour who did so much for you and me.

HMSR

THE UPSIDE-DOWNERS—2

Now when they saw the boldness of Peter and John, and perceived that they were unlearned and ignorant men, they marvelled; and they took knowledge of them, that they had been with Jesus.

Acts 4:13.

In a time when the world is wrong side up, Christ is calling for people who are willing to turn the world upside down—to get it back in place again. What prepares a person to do this? Being like Jesus. That's what enabled the disciples of Jesus to transform the world. When those on the street "saw the boldness of Peter and John, . . . they took knowledge of them, that they had been with Jesus." Only those personally acquainted with Jesus can dramatically alter the world. When the Holy Spirit filled the apostles' hearts, no amount of opposition could prevent them from preaching Jesus.

People in their day did not want to be disturbed. It was the age of Roman peace, and the imperial authorities dealt with anyone who threatened the status quo. But the apostles went on preaching, defying kings and princes. They even spoke to rulers upon their thrones, and as they entered cities the people cried, "These that have turned the world upside down are come hither also" (Acts 17:6). Yes, they were turning the world upside down, because it was wrong side up. It takes courage to be an upside-downer, not education and wealth. Peter and John "were uneducated and untrained men" (Acts 4:13, NKJV). It doesn't require education, wealth, or reputation, but courage, dedication, and commitment—all three under the guidance of the Holy Spirit.

The world in which we live today has never been so restless. Social strife and economic upheaval haunt every nation. Both young and old people strive to find the answer to life in pleasure and amusement or in political upheaval and rebellion. The world really is wrong side up, and God really needs people to turn the world upside down again. When Peter and John went out to right the wrongs by Christianizing the world, people saw their "boldness." Christ was with them, and the crowds "took knowledge of them, that they had been with Jesus." We too can turn our world upside down by reflecting Jesus.

HMSR

THE UPSIDE-DOWNERS—3

When the Council saw the boldness of Peter and John, and could see that they were obviously uneducated non-professionals, they were amazed and realized what being with Jesus had done for them!

ACTS 4:13, TLB.

Down through the ages dedicated men and woman have attempted great things for God, and have turned the world upside down—individuals such as William Carey, "the father of modern missions." Although just a simple shoemaker, as he grew in Christian experience a great burden for the non-Christian world pressed upon his heart. He felt a profound call from God to go to a foreign land. Carey gave 41 years of service to India, and lived to see much fruit from his hard labor and dedication to the people of that great country. Besides being the first to translate the entire Bible into Bengali, he and his associates printed Scripture portions in 40 languages and dialects. He wrote many religious works, grammars in five languages, and dictionaries in three. God used his monumental work to help turn the world upside down.

F. A. Stahl is another great stalwart who was willing to let God use him to transform part of the world. He heard of the great need among the Indians of South America, and he and his young wife gave their lives in service to the people of the highlands surrounding Lake Titicaca. One day while Pastor Stahl preached about Jesus to the Indians, an old chief stood up in the midst of the crowd and began to weep. Suddenly he raised his hand and said in a loud voice: "O my people, heaven has come to us. This is nothing less than heaven that has come to us!" The great multitude of his tribe began to echo those words again and again, "Heaven has come to us!" That is why many called Pastor Stahl "the apostle to the Indians of South America."

Those who turn the world upside down are not only completely dedicated, but they are totally willing to follow Jesus. People are amazed when they realize "what being with Jesus" has "done for them." The world's need and Jesus' power in a person's life remain the same as when the force of Christianity first exploded in the Roman world, India, Burma, or South America. If we stay close to Jesus, people will be awed at our boldness and realize "what being with Jesus" has done for us!

HMSR

REJOICING IN SUFFERING

They [the religious leaders] called the apostles in and had them flogged. Then they ordered them not to speak in the name of Jesus, and let them go. . . . Day after day, in the temple courts and from house to house, they never stopped teaching and proclaiming the good news that Jesus is the Christ.

Acts 5:40-42, NIV.

On a wide bend of the Volga River in Tver, Russia, is a university city of a half million people. Its wide streets and ornate buildings contrast with the small house on the edge of the city that Adventists have converted into a church. When I visited the church I saw two elderly women in a very small room correcting Voice of Prophecy Bible lessons. After I complimented them on their volunteer activity, one of them responded, "We are so happy to have the opportunity to do this work. During the Communist time four of us secretly operated a Bible school. We got caught, were arrested, and three of us women spent one year in prison, and my husband spent three years. We are delighted that we can now do this work openly and without fear!"

Persecution and prison did not deter the faithful during this dark era. Like the apostles, the pastors and lay members of the Soviet Union "never stopped teaching and proclaiming the good news that Jesus is the Christ." After Stalin's oppression of the church began in the 1930s, all of our 150 pastors, except two, at one time or another endured imprisonment. Most died in prison. But prison did not stop those who survived from continuing to spread the gospel after their release. The church grew during the Communist years from 14,000 to 35,000. With glasnost and the end of Communist rule, the membership doubled in two short years. The persecution and martyrdom of the dark years became the seed for the rapid spread of the church.

What would you and I have done if we had lived through those years of persecution? As I ponder this question I think of Dwight L. Moody's response to an admirer who suggested that he would like to have a martyr's faith just like Moody's: "Brother," Moody said, "I don't have a martyr's faith, but if called upon to die as a martyr, I believe God would give me a martyr's faith."

DRG

HEART PEACE

> *I'm sure you have heard about the Good News for the people of Israel—that there is peace with God through Jesus Christ, who is Lord of all.*
> *ACTS 10:36, NLT.*

The "peace with God through Jesus Christ" spoken of is not some transient feeling. It is a deep, lasting change that vibrates through our entire being. Since the heart is at the center of a person's faculties, its condition affects the emotions and the will. A marked contrast exists between the attitudes and actions of a sinful person and one who has heard and accepted the good news and is experiencing heart peace.

That fact forcefully impressed itself upon Lillian one day when she stopped by to see her friend Betty Voon. Betty was living with the Lim family. Her Christian witness had transformed their Buddhist home. When Lillian arrived Betty was not at home, and she found Mr. Lim praying. Since his wife was not yet a Christian, the Buddhist altar was still in a prominent place in their living room. Because of his still imperfect understanding of prayer, Mr. Lim was standing before the altar repeating the Lord's Prayer.

Lillian and Mr. Lim talked about prayer and about the change in his life since he had accepted Jesus. The glow on his face made it evident that He was rejoicing in his newfound faith in the Saviour. So Lillian asked, "Mr. Lim, what difference has it made in your life now that you have become a Christian?" Without hesitation he pointed to his heart with his index finger and said, "I have such a peace in here!"

One unfailing mark of a Christian is the reality of heart peace. When Jesus went away He promised, "Peace I leave with you, My peace I give to you" (John 14:27, NKJV). Nothing He could have done for us would have been more needed or more appreciated than peace of heart. Contrast His gift and the fleeting pleasures of our world. They may satisfy for a few years, but then follows the bitter aftertaste and the gnawing depression. The heart peace Jesus gives us is lasting and satisfying, an antidote for anxiety and fear, a guarantee of stability and assurance. It is far more wonderful than we can explain. And it can be yours by experience!

DRG

HEATING OIL TO SMOOTH YOUR LIFE

God anointed Jesus of Nazareth with the Holy Spirit and with power, who went about doing good and healing all who were oppressed by the devil, for God was with Him.

ACTS 10:38, NKJV.

The Holy Spirit was the oil that anointed Jesus at His baptism. The Spirit descended upon Jesus, and He was a bright and shining light for God in our world. The biblical world used oil as fuel in lamps. Besides illuminating, it heals, comforts, and consecrates. Bible times also employed olive oil to anoint prophets, priests, and kings. The Holy Spirit anointed Jesus at His baptism as our prophet, priest, and king.

In the Old Testament God instructed Moses in the preparation of holy anointing oil (Ex. 30:22-33). The sacred oil typified the Holy Spirit and the holiness of His character as He equips believers for service. The divine Holy Spirit anointed the human Christ, preparing Him to serve us and give us salvation.

When we surrender to Jesus—and seek the Holy Spirit's power to cleanse our lives, teach us, lead us, and fill us for God's service—the oil of the Spirit will smooth the way. The great English Baptist preacher, Charles H. Spurgeon, said: "Organizations without the Holy Spirit are like mills without power."

If you are dissatisfied with your present life or if its cares crowd out the things of God, at your sincere request Jesus will pour out the holy anointing oil of the Spirit on your heart. And your day will go much better—in fact, this coming week can be the best week you have ever had.

HMSR

IS THERE AN ANGEL IN YOUR HOUSE?

And [Cornelius] shewed us how he had seen an angel in his house, which stood and said unto him, Send men to Joppa, and call for Simon, whose surname is Peter; who shall tell thee words, whereby thou and all thy house shall be saved.
Acts 11:13, 14.

From time to time during public gatherings someone will hurry to the platform, interrupt the speaker, and ask, "Is there a doctor in the house? If so, please come to the lobby. You are needed at once."

It's about time the people of God asked the question Is there an angel in the house? I certainly hope your house has an angel—and mine. I'm not referring to a good person, such as a loving mother or wife. Instead I'm referring to an angel of God.

Cornelius had an angel in his house—that is, an angel that appeared in bodily form as a man. A Roman officer in charge of a group of men in the Roman military headquarters at Caesarea, Cornelius learned of the true God and was worshiping Him according to his best understanding. Then the angel suddenly told him how to get more help. He was to send a message to Joppa, a town some miles south along the coastline. There would be a man staying at a seaside house owned by another man. Peter, the visitor, would come and help Cornelius.

The angel came to Cornelius as the Roman officer was praying. It's a wonderful thing to have an angel in your house. And as a follower of Jesus you have one in your house with you all the time. The book of Acts gives several instances of ministering angels. When the authorities in Jerusalem put Peter in prison, "an angel of the Lord stood by him" and brought about his release (Acts 12:7-10, NKJV). Afterward Peter went to the home where the church was praying for him, knocked at the door, and called for someone to let him in. Believing that he was still in prison, those in the house concluded that "it is his angel" (verse 15, NKJV). It is comforting to know that each follower of Jesus has a guardian angel. Is there an angel in your house today watching over you and guiding your life?

HMSR

THE MAN GOD ORDAINED AS OUR JUDGE

He has appointed a day on which He will judge the world in righteousness by the Man whom He has ordained.
Acts 17:31, NKJV.

Years ago I attended a session of the traffic court in Los Angeles, California. A man charged with speeding came before the judge. He pleaded guilty but asked for leniency because of his safe driving record, explaining that he had been on the same job for 25 years without a ticket or an accident. The judge questioned the man and discovered that he worked for a diaper service. In fact, the man delivered diapers to the judge's home. The judge suspended the fine!

A Hispanic boy, also charged with speeding, later appeared before the judge. The judge suspended his license. The boy's mother asked him at least to allow the boy the privilege of driving to school. The judge said sternly, "He can walk to school!"

When the bailiff called the next case, an attractive young woman went forward. I had overheard the bailiff and the girl talking in the hallway before the court session began. She was one of the chorus girls for the policeman's ball. At her hearing, the bailiff stepped up to the bench and whispered something to the judge. The judge asked her if she would drive more slowly if he let her go. "Yes," she said.

"Case dismissed," the judge concluded.

When all the inhabitants of this world stand before the judgment seat, would you like that man to be your judge? The Judge in that day will be eminently fair, for "the Man" the Father "has ordained" to judge us is Jesus. He understands all about us, having become a man, lived a perfect life in our place, then died for us on the cross.

In a dispute between two parties, a judge is a mediator who reconciles the two parties by bringing them together. Impartial, he seeks to be on an equally friendly relationship with both. As our judge, Jesus places one arm around us and with the other arm reaches up to the throne of His Father. He is uniquely qualified to bring the Father and us together, to restore our fellowship with God. His having lived and died among us enables Him to place His loving arm around us and draw us back to God. As our mediator Jesus is ever working to make His life and death a transforming power in our lives. Is Jesus your personal Saviour and mediator before God?

DRG

THE GOSPEL IS THE POWER OF GOD

For I am not ashamed of the gospel of Christ, for it is the power of God to salvation for everyone who believes.

Rom. 1:16, NKJV.

Here are three striking sentences handwritten at the bottom of a Voice of Prophecy Bible course test sheet: "I am on death row in Utah State Prison. Before I took this course I was lost, but now I have something to look forward to, and I have found a new love. I pray this will stay with me through the agony I must suffer until the end of this life I am in now."

On death row! Lost! Nothing to look forward to but the death chamber and ultimately eternal death. Then the gospel message reached his cell, Jesus entered his heart and life, and he could write: "Now I have something to look forward to, and I have found a new love."

What did this prisoner on death row discover? Good news! The gospel touched his hardened criminal heart. The gospel is not just good advice—it is "the power of God." The emphasis is on its source of power—God. It is "the power of God to salvation" exerted in people's minds and hearts, saving them. And the gospel's saving power is for "everyone who believes," even a prisoner on death row. God delights to save, to do the impossible. Christ takes apparently hopeless material and makes such people the subjects of His grace. The changes that happen in a hardened criminal on death row amaze even angels.

Notice that gospel power is available only to those who "believe" in Christ. For only Christ can save a person from sin's penalty, and only He can rescue a person from sin's dominion. A person has no power to resist Satan and sin. It takes something stronger—the power of God within. And everyone who believes on Jesus Christ will receive that power.

What does the gospel of Christ save a person from? It delivers us from sin and its guilt. Like an antiseptic the gospel protects us from a world infected by sin. It halts our downward path to destruction and eternal death. Eventually it will take us from this sinful world. The gospel is "the power of God" to save a person. Aren't you thankful for that!

DRG

FINDING LIFE THROUGH TRUSTING CHRIST

This Good News tells us that God makes us ready for heaven—makes us right in God's sight—when we put our faith and trust in Christ to save us. This is accomplished from start to finish by faith. As the Scripture says it, "The man who finds life will find it through trusting God."

ROM. 1:17, TLB.

Ridwan was once a Muslim in the Muslim state of Kelantan, Malaya. During the closing years of his attendance at a Malay school, he felt a deep longing for peace that he could not satisfy. After his graduation he taught for two years, then worked as a clerk in a shop owned by a friend. Someone came to the shop and gave him an enrollment card for the Voice of Prophecy Bible course. Through studying the Bible lessons he found the answer to his heart's longings. He accepted the truth of Jesus' soon coming and determined to accept Jesus as his Saviour.

One day his employer saw the framed certificate Ridwan had received after completing the Bible course. The man asked what it stood for. When Ridwan explained, the employer furiously drove him away without even giving him the opportunity to pack his things. The Muslim businessman had no time for a fellow Muslim who dared to study Christianity. What would his reaction have been if he had known of the young man's desire to accept Christianity?

Ridwan left Malaya to attend our college in Singapore. There I heard his story. He told me that he planned to tell his people about Jesus. Knowing that a Muslim's life is not safe when he becomes a Christian, I tested Ridwan by asking him, "What will you do when you graduate? Aren't you afraid to go back to Malaya?"

Without a moment's hesitation he answered, "Why should I be afraid? I have Jesus and His angels with me to watch over me." Truly the gospel good news had penetrated his life, and he had put his "faith and trust in Christ to save" him. Just "as the Scripture says it, 'The man who finds life will find it through trusting God.' "

DRG

AUGUST 5

JESUS—A GIFT OF GRACE

Righteousness from God comes through faith in Jesus Christ to all who believe. . . . All have sinned and fall short of the glory of God, and are justified freely by his grace through the redemption that came by Christ Jesus. God presented him as a sacrifice of atonement, through faith in his blood.

Rom. 3:22-25, NIV.

William Cowper, the famous poet, paced the floor in spiritual agony. Overwhelmed with a feeling of helplessness and hopelessness, in desperation he picked up a Bible that happened to be lying on a table nearby. The Bible fell open to the third chapter of Romans. After reading it, Cowper exclaimed:

"I received immediate power to believe. The rays of the Sun of Righteousness fell on me in all their fullness. I saw the complete sufficiency of the expiation which Christ had wrought for my pardon and entire justification. In an instant I believed and received the peace of the Gospel. If the arm of the Almighty God had not supported me I believe I should have been overwhelmed with gratitude and joy. My eyes filled with tears. . . . I could only look to heaven in silence, overflowing with love and wonder."

Like Cowper our greatest need is to establish a right relationship with God, for "all have sinned and fall short of the glory [character] of God." We are all hopelessly lost in sin, and no one is righteous. But at the cross God intervened! Christ's death on the cross was a "sacrifice of atonement"—a sacrifice of at-one-ment. It brings us back into one in our relationship with God. Even though we are unrighteous sinners, "righteousness from God comes through faith in Jesus Christ."

As human beings we cannot earn righteousness. It is a gift from a gracious God. We "are justified [declared righteous] freely by [God's] grace through the redemption that came by Christ Jesus." Through faith in Christ we accept His gift of righteousness and the result is freedom from sin and guilt. Christianity is the great leveler. Every person ever born has the same status—hopelessly lost in sin. Nor can we by trying to be good provide a righteousness that will satisfy God. But God takes us, sinful as we are, and declares us righteous. It's an incredible gift! What should our response be to a God who forgives our sins, declares us righteous, and assures us of a happy life here and eternal life in a land of beginning again?

DRG

THE GOOD NEWS OF THE CROSS

All have sinned and fall short of the glory of God, and are justified freely by his grace through the redemption that came by Christ Jesus. God presented him as a sacrifice of atonement, through faith in his blood.
Rom. 3:23-25, NIV.

In Singapore we often saw a snake charmer sitting with crossed legs and blowing his flute to tame a cobra. As people would watch him, the tension would mount, for an untreated cobra bite is almost certain death. The antidote to the cobra's poison must be administered at once to save a person's life. Sin is like the venom of a deadly cobra. Once infected by sin, humanity has only one remedy. The only antidote for sin is "faith in [Jesus'] blood" that He spilled at the cross.

You would think a cross—a diabolical instrument of torture—would be bad news. But the cross of Christ is good news for you and me! People lost in sin find themselves saved at the cross "through faith in [Christ's] blood." As a friend of mine expressed it, "only the silver of Christ's tears and the gold of His blood could pay for our sins." Christ's blood forgives us, and we no longer need to be tortured by sin's guilt.

Because sin is destructive, the blood of Jesus flowed to rid our lives and the world of it. Think of the magnitude of the burden of guilt Jesus felt weighing on His heart at the cross. Consider your own sins as well as those of your family and the billions in our world today. Besides that, Jesus carried the weight of all sin from Adam to the end of the world. Faith in Jesus' blood will forgive all such sin.

Since our sins caused the Saviour's death, are you willing to say, "I acknowledge my fingerprints on the nails that held Jesus to the cross"? Then make this your prayer commitment:

"When I survey the wondrous cross
On which the Prince of glory died,
My richest gain I count but loss,
And pour contempt on all my pride.
Were the whole realm of nature mine,
That were a present far too small;
Love so amazing, so divine,
Demands my soul, my life, my all."
—Isaac Watts

DRG

CAN YOU FACE YOUR LIFE RECORD?

He was delivered over to death for our sins and was raised to life for our justification.

Rom. 4:25, NIV.

During the Watts riots in Los Angeles a number of years ago, a Dr. Hill pastored a church in the area. Though he was sympathetic with the plight of the rioters, he denounced their violence and looting.

One evening the phone rang. During the call his wife noticed that Dr. Hill seemed troubled. Afterward she pressed him to tell her what was wrong. He tried to stonewall. But his wife persisted. Finally he told her the caller had told him that an undetectable car bomb at an unknown time and in an unknown place would kill him.

The next morning when he got up, Dr. Hill looked out the window. What he saw startled him. His car was missing from the carport. A few minutes later his wife drove in and entered the house. "Where have you been?" Dr. Hill asked. His wife replied in a matter-of-fact way that she had been checking out the vehicle.

Later, when telling this experience, Dr. Hill spoke with deep feeling when he said, "I have never again asked my wife if she loves me." Her willingness to die in his place demonstrated her undying love.

Even so, nothing can compare with the death and resurrection of Jesus as a demonstration of the infinite and unfathomable love of God. Jesus "was delivered over to death for our sins and was raised to life for our justification."

Justification means that first we are forgiven of our past life of sins. Second, Jesus cleanses our record of our past sins—it is as if we had never sinned. And as if that is not enough, Jesus takes one more action: Third, He puts the record of His perfect life of righteousness to our account in the place of the record of our sins. Not only does Christ's "death for our sins" forgive us and cleanse us from our sins, but Jesus "was raised to life for our justification." So when the final judgment takes place and the Judge examines our record, it is not a blank page. God sees our life characterized as the perfect life of Jesus. As a result, we are assured not only of a new life now, but of eternal life in the future.

DRG

WE HAVE PEACE WITH GOD THROUGH JESUS

Being justified by faith, we have peace with God through our Lord Jesus Christ.

Rom. 5:1.

A man riding a bus said to a Christian sitting next to him, "Why, you have nothing at all to rest your faith on. I can prove to you that your scriptures are wrong."

The humble Christian man replied, "Sir, I am not a learned man. I can't answer your questions, but I believe in Jesus. And I have experienced such a change of character, and I feel such a joy and peace in believing, that I wish you knew my Saviour too."

His seatmate responded, "You've got me there; I can't answer that." As Christians we have a peace that a Christian understands but cannot fully explain. We live a totally new life.

A disgruntled former church member once said, "Christianity doesn't make much difference in the life!"

Back came the reply from a true follower of Jesus: "It makes all the difference in the world." The change God performs in the life and emotional makeup of a person who is in Christ is a miracle of grace.

A religious skeptic once said to a Christian, "You read in the Bible about Jesus turning water into wine. But to me that is fiction. I've never seen anything like that taking place today."

The kindly Christian answered, "Well, I haven't seen Jesus turn water into wine, but I have seen Him turn whiskey into furniture. And to me that is an even greater miracle." Transforming the lives of people who are at war with themselves and giving them victory over sin and inner peace is also a miracle of grace.

On the Island of Borneo I saw shrunken heads hanging in the longhouses, a reminder of what the people were before they became Christians. They hunted heads and ate each other.

Things are different now. So different that neighboring villages began calling one Christian village Damai, which means peace. As Christians we have a peace that we understand and reflect but cannot fully explain. "Being justified by faith, we have peace with God through our Lord Jesus Christ." It gives us assurance of salvation, an entirely new life of happiness, and the hope of heaven. Why shouldn't our lives be saturated with a peace that passes all understanding, for our peace comes through a living Saviour living in our hearts?

DRG

GOD'S LOVE TO LOVE WITH

God has poured out his love into our hearts by the Holy Spirit, whom he has given us. You see, . . . when we were still powerless, Christ died for the ungodly. Very rarely will anyone die for a righteous man, though for a good man someone might possible dare to die. But God demonstrates his own love for us in this: While we were still sinners, Christ died for us.
ROM. 5:5-8, NIV.

Would you be willing to die for a hopelessly addicted drug addict with multiple charges of child abuse? You might be willing to risk your life by donating an organ to save your child who would die if you are not willing to take the risk, but would you perish for the abusing addict? Probably not. Yet God gave His Son to die "for the ungodly."

Consider and be amazed that "God has poured out his love into our hearts." "When we were still powerless" to live as Christ lived and to love as Christ loved, God gave us His love to love with. He offers us the kind of love Jesus had when "Christ died for the ungodly." The kind of love Jesus loved with when He cried out, "Father, forgive them, for they do not know what they are doing" (Luke 23:34, NIV).

Jac Colon, a Seventh-day Adventist evangelist, before his conversion was a United States Air Force fighter pilot in Vietnam. In 1991 he held a series of evangelistic meetings in Riga, Latvia. One of those baptized was a Soviet fighter pilot who had served on the opposite side in Vietnam. During Jac's evangelistic meetings the atheist gave his heart to Jesus. On the day of his baptism he said to Jac, "We were once mortal enemies who would have shot each other out of the sky, but now we are brothers in Christ." Then they hugged each other and silently wept with emotion.

Such a miracle could take place only because God had "poured out his love" into the hearts of the two men. "When men are bound together, not by force or self-interest, but by love, they show the working of an influence that is above every human influence. Where this oneness exists, it is evidence that the image of God is being restored in humanity, that a new principle of life has been implanted" (*The Desire of Ages,* p. 678). What a difference love—the love of Jesus—makes in a person's heart!

DRG

THROUGH THE NARROWS AT CALVARY

God showed his great love for us by sending Christ to die for us while we were still sinners.
ROM. 5:8, NLT.

Lillian and I stood at the Cave of the Winds staring through the mist at Niagara Falls with its impressive drop of 167 feet. Twelve million cubic feet of water per minute roar over the lip of the falls. We had seen beautiful Lake Ontario below Niagara and mighty Lake Erie, the source of these waters. Now we were at the narrows between the two great lakes looking on the most impressive scene of all—Niagara Falls.

Although two mighty lakes of suffering mark the centuries preceding and following the cross, the suffering of God because of our sin rushed through the narrows at Calvary. There in one concentrated glimpse history revealed on the human level God's suffering heart of love.

Since Eden every sin committed has pained the divine heart. Consider how the Lord must have felt when the man and woman He had created and loved committed the first sin. Imagine His pain knowing what sin would do to their lives and that of their offspring for thousands of years.

Finally, think about Jesus' suffering at the narrows of Calvary as the weight of the sins of the entire world came to rest on Him. "Having taken the responsibility of dying in the sinner's stead, His interests are identified with those of every member of the human family. And every evil deed, every transgression, every rebellion, whether of thought or action, pierces the heart of Christ" (Ellen G. White, in *Signs of the Times,* Feb. 3, 1898, p. 1).

"God showed his great love for us by sending Christ to die for us while we were still sinners." Jesus portrayed His love for us by choosing to die so that we could have eternal life and eternal happiness.

DRG

AUGUST 11

THE DEPTH OF GOD'S LOVE

But God commendeth his love toward us, in that, while we were yet sinners, Christ died for us.

ROM. 5:8.

A number of years ago an atheist declared to passersby, "If there is a God in heaven, I challenge Him to strike me dead in five minutes." Finally after five minutes had passed he said with a sneer, "You see, there is no God, or by this time He would have struck me dead."

A woman standing by heard him. As he began to leave, she stepped up to him and asked: "Do you have any children?"

The man replied, "Yes, one son."

"If your son gave you a knife to kill him, would you do it?"

"Of course not," he promptly answered.

"Well," she asked, "why not?"

"Simply because I love him too much."

Before she turned away, the little woman explained: "Mister, it's because God loves you so much, even though you are an atheist, that He refuses to accept your foolish challenge. He wants you saved, not lost!"

That's my kind of God. "While we were yet sinners, Christ died for us." It's something we mortals cannot comprehend. Why should God love us so much that He would send His own Son into the world, knowing that wicked human beings would reject Him, persecute Him, and finally nail Him to a cross? The cross no longer stands, but love remains.

One of the eyewitnesses at Calvary later wrote that "God so loved the world, that he gave his only begotten Son, that whosoever believeth in him should not perish, but have everlasting life" (John 3:16).

It has become the best-loved verse in the Bible, and it applies to you, whoever you are—atheist, struggling skeptic, lukewarm church member, frustrated mother, depressed wife, angry husband, or dedicated Christian. The love of God and of Jesus, His Son, can change your life—and your day. Today!

HMSR

RECONCILED BY JESUS' DEATH

> *When we were God's enemies, we were reconciled to him through the death of his Son.*
> *Rom. 5:10, NIV.*

God's great love in giving His Son to die for us astounds every devoted father. One father expressed his feelings this way: "Oh, I could give my life, but not my son." But that is exactly what our heavenly Father did, "for God loved the world so much that he gave his only Son so that anyone who believes in him shall not perish but have eternal life" (John 3:16, TLB). The Father's great love in giving us His Son to die for sinners has such magnetic power that it causes sinners to be "reconciled to him through the death of his Son."

A headline in our local newspaper stated one day: "Marsh Family Is Reunited by Tragedy." The article went on to say of the family members, "They vow never to be separated again." The story reveals the attempt of Mrs. Marsh to poison her husband, Tony, by putting caustic soda in his breakfast food. The court sentenced her to prison. During her confinement Tony had trouble finding someone to care for their five small children. One day while he was out looking for a baby-sitter, Cynthia, their 4-year-old daughter, was badly burned in an accident. She died a few hours later in the hospital, nearly breaking the father's heart.

Cynthia's mother was also heartbroken. As a result, when released from prison, she returned home to the remaining children and to her husband. The estranged couple fell into each other's arms and vowed to forgive and forget. The death of another had reconciled them.

Even so, "when we were God's enemies" and estranged from Him, "we were reconciled to him through the death of his Son"—not an accidental death, but the death of a willing Son agreed to by a willing Father.

DRG

SAVED BY JESUS' LIFE

For if, when we were God's enemies, we were reconciled to him through the death of his Son, how much more, having been reconciled, shall we be saved through his life!
ROM. 5:10, NIV.

When something breaks a relationship, reconciliation is necessary. Usually both parties are at fault. But in the falling out between God and humanity the blame rests on our side. When Adam and Eve sinned and severed the relationship, God's consuming love brought Him to the Garden of Eden to talk with them. Immediately His plan for winning the human race back to Him went into action. The cross was at the center of that plan to heal the rift sin caused. Human experience proves that the cross draws sinful people back to a relationship with God. That's why Jesus could promise: "I, when I am lifted up from the earth, will draw all men to myself" (John 12:32, NIV).

We are "reconciled to [God] through the death of his Son." And after being reunited to God at the cross, we are "saved through his life"! Someone has aptly said, "When a noble man dies, his life has an after-influence; but when Jesus died, His life had after-activity as well." After His death, Jesus immediately assumed His role as our mediator, making His death effective in human lives. "Therefore he is able to save completely those who come to God through him, because he always lives to intercede for them" (Heb. 7:25, NIV).

"The Elder Brother of our race is by the eternal throne. . . . He knows by experience what are the weaknesses of humanity, what are our wants, and where lies the strength of our temptations. . . . He is watching over you, trembling child of God. Are you tempted? He will deliver. Are you weak? He will strengthen. Are you ignorant? He will enlighten. Are you wounded? He will heal. . . . Whatever your anxieties and trials, spread out your case before the Lord. Your spirit will be braced for endurance. The way will be opened for you to disentangle yourself from embarrassment and difficulty. The weaker and more helpless you know yourself to be, the stronger you will become in His strength. The heavier your burdens, the more blessed the rest in casting them upon the Burden Bearer" (*The Desire of Ages,* p. 329).

DRG

WE CAN WALK IN NEWNESS OF LIFE

Do you not know that all of us who have been baptized into Christ Jesus were baptized into his death? We were buried therefore with him by baptism into death, so that as Christ was raised from the dead by the glory of the Father, we too might walk in newness of life.

Rom. 6:3, 4, RSV.

Daniel, a young man in a non-Christian land, after hearing the good news of the gospel, turned from his pagan ways and became a follower of Jesus. The new Christian went about his village inviting his friends to come to his home the next day to see a very special event. He told them he was to be buried in his front yard and wanted them all to be there. Of course, it didn't take long for word to reach the entire village.

The next day everyone wondered whether Daniel would actually die and be buried as he said he was. As the crowd began to gather, they saw him digging a large hole in his front yard. "What are you doing?" some asked.

"Why, I'm digging my grave," he replied.

By this time the villagers believed that he meant what he said. When the missionary arrived and helped fill the hole with water, the villagers gathered around to witness what to them was a strange sight. The missionary led Daniel down into the watery grave of baptism and immersed him, and the lad came out a new person in Christ. Daniel died and was buried, but a new Daniel now lived to give testimony to the transforming power of Jesus in his life.

Without this positive change, this transformation to live a new life for Jesus, baptism is meaningless. In our text for today Paul informs us that just as Jesus died, was buried, and was raised from the dead, so we are to die to sin, bury our past life of sin in the watery grave of baptism, and be resurrected to a new life in Christ. We are to "walk in newness of life."

I will never forget the day I was baptized and realized that I was dying to sin and self—just as if being laid in the grave and then rising to walk in newness of life. Jesus promises to raise us from the living death of a miserable sin-filled life so "we too might walk in newness of life." Is this your experience? Are you today walking in newness of life with Jesus?

HMSR

OUR NEW LIFE IN CHRIST

The death he died, he died to sin once for all; but the life he lives, he lives to God. In the same way, count yourselves dead to sin but alive to God in Christ Jesus.
Rom. 6:10, 11, NIV.

A boy stood gazing at a large painting of the Crucifixion. A man standing nearby pretended to know nothing about what it depicted.

"What is that painting about?" the man asked.

"Don't you know?" the surprised lad asked. "That's Jesus on the cross when He died for our sins."

"Oh, that's it," said the man as he walked away.

The boy went running after him and breathlessly shouted, "Sir, I wanted to tell you, He is alive!"

In the first five chapters of Romans Paul nails down the meaning of the cross. Then in chapters 6 through 8 he fastens our attention on the significance of a risen, living Christ in the experience of the believer. Like the little boy, Paul shouts, "Sir, I wanted to tell you, He is alive!"

Also in chapters 1 through 5 Paul teaches that justification results not from keeping the law, not from anything we do, but by faith alone. It is a gift of grace from God. Next in chapters 6 to 8 Paul makes it crystal clear that once we become Christians, we are to "count" ourselves "alive to God in Christ Jesus."

Paul first uses the expression "in Christ" in the book of Romans in our text for today. He describes a life "in Christ" as an entirely new existence with a new set of aims, ambitions, motives, and opportunities to serve. The change God produces in people who are "in Christ" is a life-changing miracle of grace.

How does such a vital connection come about? By being "united" with Christ (Rom. 6:5, NIV). How do we form a union with Christ? Grafting joins a bud to a tree. The bud and the tree grow together, and the bud becomes a fruit-bearing branch. When the Christian unites with Christ, they grow together. Through a life of union with Christ we become like Him. And we bear fruit to His glory, the fruit of "righteousness leading to holiness" (verse 19, NIV).

DRG

SAVED BY A GIFT OF LOVE

Now that you have been set free from sin and have become slaves to God, the benefit you reap leads to holiness, and the result is eternal life.
Rom. 6:22, NIV.

In the courtyard of Singapore's Hindu fire-walking temple amid heavy odors of burning incense and the pulsating rhythm of the drums, devout worshipers paraded about with huge gaudily painted wooden idols. Others, carrying heavy frames supported by needles inserted in their flesh, danced wildly in circles to the piercing tune of the flutes and the beat of hollow wooden drums. Groups of wild-eyed followers cheered the men who were to walk through the fire.

All day long piles of burning wood burned to red-hot coals. Men then raked them into a pit 10 feet wide, 25 feet long, and about one foot deep. At the end of this pit of red-hot coals was a smaller pit containing sacred cow's milk. All day long a continuous stream of devoted worshipers stopped to empty bottles of milk as an offering to the gods. Eager for understanding rather than ridicule, Mr. Ratnam, a tax collector for the government, told us, "Just as you Christians ask your God's forgiveness and have faith that He can do it, so we Hindus ask our gods and goddesses to forgive our mistakes, and we show our sincerity by running through the fire."

Swarming crowds of spectators jammed the temple. The fire-walkers swooned in a trance at the end of the pit. The crowds went wild as the first devotee dashed through the red-hot coals. One by one the glassy-eyed men and boys made their way across the pit—sprinting, leaping, dancing, or plodding through the sizzling coals. Not one fire-walker had burned feet.

They were sincere and devoted but deluded people. As my heart ached for them, I felt like climbing up on the temple roof and shouting, "You don't need to do this! There is a better way—Jesus, God's gift of love." Through faith in Jesus you and I are "set free from sin . . . , the benefit you reap leads to holiness, and the result is eternal life." Think of it: "For it is by his grace you are saved through trusting him; it is not your own doing. It is God's gift" (Eph. 2:8, NEB). Thank God for that "gift"! Jesus, God's gift, is the good news that we can receive salvation, not by walking on hot coals, but by faith in Him.

DRG

HOW TO LIVE FOREVER

For the wages of sin is death; but the free gift of God is eternal life in Christ Jesus our Lord.
Rom. 6:23, ASV.

Dr. Roy Anderson was a powerful Adventist preacher. As a lad of 17 he visited a city in Britain where a famous murder trial was in progress. He and another boy slipped into the courtroom just as the crown prosecutor had made his charges and the barrister for the defense began pleading for the life of his client, who was not much older than Roy and his friend.

Hour after hour they watched the young man's pallid face and twitching hands. They saw the look of despair on his face when the jury returned with the verdict—guilty. One reason the trial gripped Roy Anderson was that by coincidence the prisoner's name was the same as his. That made an impression on his young mind. Any murder trial has something frightening about it, for life and death hang on the jury's decision.

All of us have a case pending in God's court. "Every one of us shall give account of himself to God" (Rom. 14:12). As sinners we have all earned "the wages of sin," which "is death."

We all face condemnation in God's judgment, for we are all guilty. "All have sinned" (Rom. 3:23). Although God created us in His image, sin has partially defaced but not eliminated it. That's why we have an unquenchable urge, an eternal hunger for salvation in our souls. We are never at rest, never at peace, never satisfied until we find Jesus and accept His forgiveness for our past.

All of us "fall short of the glory of God" (Rom. 3:23, ASV). Nothing we do on our own can restore God's image, His glory, or His character within us to its condition before sin entered. We cannot cleanse our souls or lift ourselves up step by step on some ladder to heaven. Nor can we avoid the death sentence hanging over us until Someone takes our place and dies for us. Jesus is the only way of escape. Even though we deserve eternal death, God provided a solution—"the free gift of God is eternal life in Christ Jesus our Lord." Christ agreed to come into our death cell, take our place, and let us go free so He can pound the gavel and say, "Not guilty!"

HMSR

THE DIARY OF A STRUGGLING SOUL

What a wretched man I am! Who will rescue me from this body of death? Thanks be to God—through Jesus Christ our Lord!

ROM. 7:24, 25, NIV.

The word "law" appears 23 times in Romans 7. Looking in the mirror of God's law, the sinner sees himself or herself as a lawbreaker (Rom. 7:7-12). The legalist, on the other hand, is in agonizing conflict and laments, "I do my best to keep the law, but I continually fail." Paul seems to be speaking of his own experience. Judged by the letter of the law, he was a lawkeeper. But when he saw himself in the light of the spiritual nature of the law, he recognized the self-centeredness of his life. The realization disturbed the tranquillity of his legalism. He was exhausted by good works, by trying to keep the law (verses 15-24).

In that pitiful state Paul exclaimed, "What a wretched man I am! Who will rescue me . . .?" Paul himself answers in exultation, "Thanks be to God—through Jesus Christ our Lord!" Christ delivered Paul not only from the outward sins that others see, but from the internal sin—self.

This brings us to the Spirit-filled Christian's relationship to the law. We no longer try by human effort to obey the written code. Instead "we serve in the new way of the Spirit" (verse 6, NIV). Most of us have at one time or another observed, "No matter how hard I try to do right, I am continually doing wrong—why?" So for our encouragement Paul writes his own life story, the search of his soul, as he gropes his way through his frustrations as a legalist to a life of peace and assurance.

When the church at Rome heard Paul's letter being read to them, their ears must have perked up when they came to chapter 7. They must have recognized themselves in its diary of a struggling soul. I can imagine a woman sitting near the front listening. Tears roll down her cheeks as she thinks to herself, *I remember when I still felt I must strive to reach what seemed an unattainable ideal. Then victory in Christ broke in upon my soul. In Him I found full refuge, freedom from condemnation and guilt. I felt a new power, the power of the Spirit, take hold of my life. The Spirit cleansed the fountains of my desires, unified my life, and put me at one with myself.* It is a fantastic experience to discover the Spirit-filled life!

DRG

BANDIT MISSIONARY

> *There is now no condemnation for those who are in Christ Jesus, . . . who do not live according to the sinful nature but according to the Spirit.*
> ROM. 8:1-4, NIV.

It was a Wednesday night prayer meeting. The speaker's sentences were clear, his ideas lucid, his presentation logical. But above all, he spoke with deep conviction and sincerity. He had no notes. If he had any, he couldn't have used them. For he is blind. As he gave a stirring call to prayer, God's Spirit drew near.

That morning in a pastors' retreat we discussed the eighth chapter of Romans. "There is now no condemnation for those who are in Christ Jesus," verse 1 begins. We could have easily condemned the speaker. Before losing his sight, the man had been a terrorist. As an opium smoker, drinker, and gang leader he had led his men in plundering villages. "Give us your goods, or we will burn down your houses!" they constantly threatened.

Then the miracle happened. One day while visiting a Buddhist temple, he chanced to find a tract on Christianity that caught his interest. Some time later, after becoming blind from an eye infection, he came in contact with Seventh-day Adventist Christians among the Karen people on the border between Thailand and Burma. After a terrible one-month struggle he gained victory over opium and liquor.

But what about his past? What about restitution? As a blind man with little means of support, the best restitution he could think of was to preach Christ in the very villages he had once terrorized. When he returned to these villages, the people, seeing the remarkable change in his life, were kind to him. He would ask a villager as a favor to read to him from the Bible. Through this means he led many to a knowledge of Jesus. Two churches now stand as monuments to his dedicated work for Jesus.

For several years I had heard about "the blind man," as those who know him affectionately call him. Now after seeing for myself the dedication of this former bandit and listening to his Spirit-filled preaching, Paul's words came home to my heart with an even greater impact: "There is now no condemnation for those who are in Christ Jesus."

DRG

WHAT CHRIST CAN DO FOR THE CHRISTIAN

What the law was powerless to do in that it was weakened by the sinful nature, God did by sending his own Son in the likeness of sinful man to be a sin offering. And so he condemned sin in sinful man, in order that the righteous requirements of the law might be fully met in us, who do not live according to the sinful nature but according to the Spirit.

ROM. 8:3, 4, NIV.

Pastor H. L. Hastings once told an experience that illustrates the change that comes when a person forsakes the old life and lives an entirely new life in Christ: "A friend of mine visited the Fiji Islands in 1844, and what do you suppose a man was worth then? You could buy a man for a musket, or if you paid money, for several dollars. And after you bought him you could feed, starve, work, whip, or eat him. . . . But if you go to Fiji today, you could not buy a man for seven dollars, or even seven million dollars. There are no men for sale now.

"What made the difference in the price of humanity? The twelve hundred Christian chapels scattered over the island tell the story. The people have learned to read a book that says, 'You are not redeemed with corruptible things as silver and gold, but with the precious blood of Christ.' Since they learned that lesson, no man is for sale there."

Nothing thrills me more than hearing testimonies about transformed lives and individuals mightily used by Christ. Romans 8 vividly portrays what Christ can do for the Christian. God's forgiveness releases the sinner not only from future punishment, but from guilt and condemnation now! People's past lives need not point an accusing finger at them and torture them, because God sent His "own Son in the likeness of sinful man to be a sin offering." Christ does great wonders for a sinful person's past.

Now consider what Christ can do for the Christian in this present life. The sinful person is tyrannized by a sinful nature, while the Holy Spirit rules the righteous person. The sinner is a lawbreaker, while the Spirit-filled person is a lawkeeper. Why? Because "the righteous requirements of the law might be fully met in us, who do not live according to the sinful nature but according to the Spirit." The person in Christ is a lawkeeper because the Holy Spirit is a driving, motivating power within. Is this your experience?

DRG

LED BY THE SPIRIT OF GOD

Those who are led by the Spirit of God are sons of God. For . . . you received the Spirit of sonship. And by him we cry, 'Abba, Father.' The Spirit himself testifies with our spirit that we are God's children.

ROM. 8:14-16, NIV.

John Wesley, the founder of Methodism, at one time had no sense of assurance with God. On his voyage to America as a missionary he met the Moravians, who remained unafraid during a terrible storm. Spangenberg, one of their leaders, questioned Wesley about his spiritual state. "My brother," Spangenberg asked, "have you the witness within yourself? Does the Spirit of God bear witness with your spirit that you are a child of God?" Wesley was silent because he didn't know what to answer.

"Do you know Jesus Christ?" Spangenberg continued.

"I know He is the Saviour of the world," Wesley answered.

"True, but do you know He has saved you?" Spangenberg persisted.

"I hope He died to save me."

"But do you know, yourself, that He has saved you?"

Wesley answered, "I do," but eventually admitted, "I fear these were vain words."

Later at Aldersgate Wesley experienced the inner witness. After that he spoke with certainty. "I felt . . . an assurance was given me that Jesus had taken away my sins, even mine, and saved me from the law of sin and death."

Does God's "Spirit himself" testify with your spirit that you are one of "God's children"? Personal assurance is available in Christ through His Holy Spirit. Romans 8 uses the key word "Spirit" 20 times. The life of the sinner on its own is one of defeat. But the life of the person empowered by the Spirit is one of victory. Without the Spirit of Christ in us we would be nothing. But as "sons of God" with the powerful Spirit of Christ in us Christ can do everything in, for, and through us. We can cry out "Father, my Father" as sons and as "heirs of God and co-heirs with Christ" (Rom. 8:17, NIV). The Spirit makes us brothers and sisters of Jesus, sons and daughters of the King. When the Spirit enters our hearts with power, our hearts burn within us, stirring us to our very depths. And we cry out in response, "Father, my Father!"

DRG

IN THE LIKENESS OF JESUS

For those God foreknew he also predestined to be conformed to the likeness of his Son.
ROM. 8:29, NIV.

The fantastic privilege "to be conformed to the likeness of [God's] Son" gives us great destiny, opportunity, and responsibility as Christians.

Samuel Money, a departmental secretary for the Southeast Asia Union and a personal friend, illustrates how important it is to Jesus for us to reflect His "likeness." Money is a dark-skinned person of Indian descent. When his wife gave birth to their first child, she was in labor from Saturday night until Monday morning. In those days the hospitals in Malaysia would not allow the father to be in the delivery room.

"After the baby was born," Samuel reports, "I was naturally eager to see my newborn. I went to the nursery window and saw an array of Malaysian and Chinese babies, but spotted only one with dark skin like mine. I pointed to the baby and asked the nurse to hold it up so I could see it. When the nurse held up the baby, I saw its terribly deformed and grotesque face. I was so shocked I nearly collapsed.

"Then the nurse asked me to hold up my identity card. When she saw my name, she realized she had held up the wrong baby. When she brought the right baby, I could see its perfectly formed nose, forehead, and delicate features. What a relief!"

After telling his experience, Samuel commented, "Jesus looks into our faces to see His likeness there. It is a heartbreak for Him to see a deformed face!" When Jesus searches your face what does He see?

We are "predestined to be conformed to the likeness of His Son" and to be "among many brothers" of Jesus (Rom. 8:29, NIV). How can we ever reach such a high destiny? The context of today's verse should give us courage, for everything depends on God, not on us: "In all things God works for the good of those who love him" (verse 28, NIV). Those He predestined He calls, justifies, and glorifies (verse 30). We can depend upon and put our trust in our Father and our Brother. Why not lift up your heart in prayer just now and thank Them for that good news?

DRG

JESUS CARRIED YOUR CROSS

He who did not spare his own Son, but gave him up for us all—how will he not also, along with him, graciously give us all things?

Rom. 8:32, NIV.

After declaring Jesus innocent, Pilate sentenced Him to scourging and crucifixion. Crucifixion was a Roman punishment, while the Jewish mode of capital punishment involved stoning. After enduring more than 12 hours of shameful treatment, Jesus, the innocent One, "carrying his own cross . . . went out to the place of the Skull" (John 19:17, NIV). A cross could be in either a T or an I shape. If the cross were a T, studies in the field of archaeology have made it clear that the one to be crucified did not carry the entire cross, but only the cross beam. It would weigh possibly 100 pounds. Because of His abuse and lack of sleep, Jesus apparently fell beneath the load. The Roman soldiers drafted Simon of Cyrene to take Jesus' cross the rest of the way to Calvary.

Picture Jesus and two bandits staggering along with their cross beams. The two criminals had evidently been convicted earlier. Barabbas had been the third man condemned to death, but Pilate had released him at the crowd's demand. Jesus now stumbled under the cross that Barabbas should have carried.

A convicted murderer, Barabbas' name means "son of a father," and as such he represents all sons of all fathers of Adam's race—and that is all of us. Have we not all been bound over for sedition, convicted before God's holy law of sin, and are we not then subject to its penalty? The sentence of death hangs over us all as sinners. Without our doing a thing and while we were still under condemnation, something was done for us. Another took our place. One wonders what thoughts must have gone through Barabbas' mind as he saw Jesus walking off with his cross, moving toward Calvary and crucifixion!

And what sort of thoughts should we have as we realize that Jesus was not dying for Himself, because He was holy, harmless, and sinless? But for Barabbas and for us God handed Him over because of our sins. God "did not spare his own Son, but gave him up for us all."

HMSR

MORE THAN CONQUERORS

In all these things we are more than conquerors through him who loved us.

ROM. 8:37, NIV.

Paul tells us that the God who called and justified us, will also certainly glorify us (Rom. 8:30). It gives us fantastic assurance to realize that all heaven is working and waiting for our redemption—for the sons of God to come into their own (verses 26-30). Our wonderful Saviour seals with certainty the fulfillment of God's purpose.

Christ deals with our sinful past. Paul raises the question "Who will bring any charge against those whom God has chosen? It is God who justifies" (verse 33, NIV). Christ has justified us, and He is our judge. Who then can hold our past against us?

More than that, Christ also takes care of our present needs. Paul asks in verse 34: "Who is he that condemns? Christ Jesus, who died—more than that, who was raised to life—is at the right hand of God and is also interceding for us." The crucified and risen Saviour now represents us in heaven. His life record stands in place of our record. He makes Himself responsible for our actions. Who then can condemn us for our present life?

Finally, Christ provides for our future. "Who shall separate us from the love of Christ? Shall trouble or hardship or persecution or famine or nakedness or danger or sword?" (verse 35, NIV). The answer is a resounding "No, in all these things we are more than conquerors through him who loved us" (verse 37, NIV). Our salvation is assured!

No wonder Paul exults, "For I am convinced that neither death nor life, neither angels nor demons, neither the present nor the future, nor any powers, . . . nor anything else in all creation, will be able to separate us from the love of God that is in Christ Jesus our Lord" (verses 38, 39, NIV). The cross and the Resurrection guarantee that Jesus will come again. Our redemption is certain. The sons and daughters of God will come into their own.

We cannot comprehend the certainty of what Christ has done, is continually doing, and will do for the Christian. But we can comfort ourselves with the fact that the three great powers of heaven are working for us. No one can argue with a certainty founded on the entire Godhead. So let us explore all of heaven's activities and desires for us to the utmost!

DRG

GOOD NEWS THAT TRANSFORMS LIVES

Therefore, I urge you, brothers, in view of God's mercy, to offer your bodies as living sacrifices, holy and pleasing to God—this is your reasonable act of worship.
ROM. 12:1, NIV, MARGIN.

A young man complained about his pastor that "he preaches too much doctrine!" But he failed to take into account that what we believe affects how we live. His comment goes contrary to Paul's use of the word "therefore" in today's Bible text.

After arguing heavy doctrine for 11 chapters, Paul employs the power-packed word "therefore" to introduce the practical section of his letter to the Romans. For 11 chapters Paul reasons about complex doctrines such as atonement, reconciliation, justification, sanctification, and predestination. Now in chapter 12 he gets down to the everyday application of those doctrines. "Therefore," because of what you believe about such teachings, here is how you should live, how you should act toward and react to others. Then Paul dishes out a heavy dose to swallow. Christians are to "be patient in affliction," to "bless those who persecute you," to "live in harmony with one another," and much more (Rom. 12:2-16, NIV).

How is it possible for me to live like that? "By the grace given to me" and "in accordance with the measure of faith God has given you" (verse 3, NIV). Living such a life is not your doing, but God's. He gives us the faith and the power to do it! This is the good news about Jesus that Paul proclaims in chapters 1 to 11.

He begins by telling us that the gospel "is the power of God" to "everyone who believes" through God's gift of faith (Rom. 1:16, NIV). Faith is my response to God's activity to save me. What God does includes atonement (Jesus died to save me), reconciliation (He accepts me unconditionally), justification (He forgives my sins and declares me righteous), sanctification (He constantly seeks to make me as holy as He is), and predestination (He purposed that I be saved). Our part is to respond to His overwhelming grace through faith. No wonder Paul ends his long discourse on doctrine by shouting in triumph, "we are more than conquerors through him who loved us" (Rom. 8:37, NIV).

DRG

JESUS IS LORD OF ALL

For to this end Christ died and rose and lived again, that He might be Lord of both the dead and the living.

ROM. 14:9, NKJV.

Charles L. Slattery tells the story of a new pastor who visited a member's house. When the husband came home from his work, the wife said, "The new pastor called today."

"What did he say?" her husband asked.

"Oh," she answered, "he asked if Christ lived here. I didn't know what to say."

The man's face flushed. "Why didn't you tell him that we are respectable people?"

"Oh, I might have said that, but that was not what he asked me."

"Then why didn't you tell him that we say our prayers and read our Bibles?"

"But he didn't ask me that," the wife repeated.

The man grew more vexed. "Why didn't you say that we are always at church?"

The poor woman sobbed. "He didn't ask that, either. He asked only, 'Does Christ live here?' "

That husband and wife thought about this a long time. Unable to forget the question, they tried to imagine just what the pastor meant. Little by little their lives changed as they kept thinking about it. And little by little they grew to expect Christ, to think of Him as not being dead, but gloriously alive. And somehow, through great love and a willingness to be surprised by the mystery of His radiance and His presence, they really became acquainted with Jesus. Their lives altered, and through them He really did live there—and everyone seemed to feel it who entered that house.

Jesus is "Lord both of the dead and the living," that is, of all the people who have ever lived in the world and who are alive in it now. Dwight L. Moody was never a great orator. He had little schooling. Yet he was one of the greatest soul winners of the nineteenth century. When someone asked him the secret of his successful life, he said, "All I can think of is that the Lord has had all there is of me." That's the secret of success for any of us. Jesus must be Lord of all.

HMSR

AUGUST 27

GOD'S SECRET WISDOM

We speak of God's secret wisdom. . . . None of the rulers of this age understood it, for if they had, they would not have crucified the Lord of glory. However, as it is written: "No eye has seen, no ear has heard, no mind has conceived what God has prepared for those who love him" —but God has revealed it to us by his Spirit.

1 Cor. 2:7-10, NIV.

During World War II an exploding shell cost John Griffin his eyesight. After the war he earned a living writing books by dictating them on a wire recorder. Ten years later Griffin was walking toward the house on his parents' farm near Mansfield, Texas. Suddenly he began to see again. By the time the doctor arrived, Griffin was able to read. After becoming blind, Griffin had married and become the father of two children. Now, looking upon his wife and children for the first time, he said, "They are more beautiful than I ever imagined. I am astonished, stunned, and thankful."

Attempting to give unbelievers an adequate explanation of the meaning of the cross is like describing to a blind man the beauty of a fiery sunset or a spouse they have never seen. When for the first time God's Spirit gives us an insight into what our salvation cost our crucified Lord—spoken of in today's text as "God's secret wisdom" which "no eye has seen, no ear has heard, no mind has conceived"—we respond with surprised wonder: "God's plan for saving us is more beautiful than I ever imagined. I am astonished, stunned, and thankful." For no human eye, ear, or mind can fully comprehend, or even conceive of, the jam-packed meaning of the cross.

The meaning of the cross is a secret—a mystery—to the uninitiated. But when the Spirit reveals its significance to a receptive heart, we realize that God's plan to save us is beyond our fondest hopes or our wildest dreams. Only through the voice of the Spirit can we experience the full impact of our sins being forgiven through our Saviour's death and of our lives being changed and enriched by a living Saviour. Nothing can compare to the joy and the peace of heart that comes to those who, at the foot of the cross, experience Jesus' love for them and their love for Him. Are you astonished, stunned, and thankful for what Jesus did for you at the cross?

DRG

DREAMLAND OF TOMORROW

What no eye has ever seen, what no ear has ever heard, what never entered the mind of man, God has prepared all that for those who love him.

1 Cor. 2:9, Moffatt.

I once mentioned the hope of heaven to a young physician. He responded, "Oh, I don't want Jesus to come and take me to heaven, not yet. I have a lot of livin' to do. I want to make a success of my lifework. I want to travel and enjoy the beauties of earth. I want to get a Cadillac and own a nice home." My friend had become absorbed in the things of earth. He needed the timeless advice: "Is it gold you want? The streets up there are paved with gold!"

Yesterday we looked at the primary meaning of today's text: No human being can totally understand the full meaning of the cross. In a secondary sense the passage refers to the eternal reward of the saved. No one in the present life can fully grasp what heaven will be like. What God has prepared for those who love Him is beyond our fondest hopes or our wildest dreams, but "God has revealed it to us by the Spirit" (1 Cor. 2:10, Moffatt).

Think for a moment about God's description of the wonderful world He has prepared for us. In heaven we will be absorbed in creative thought and action. We will build beautiful homes of our own (Isa. 65:21, 22) and enjoy rivers, trees, gardens, and flowers in their Edenic beauty (Isa. 51:3). Each of us will eat homegrown fruits and vegetables from our very own garden (Isa. 65:21, 22). All of us will sing from a heart overflowing with love (Isa. 35:10). As real people who associate with family and friends (1 Cor. 13:12) we will experience a vibrant, healthy lifestyle (Isa. 33:24). Life will be so satisfying that human tears will never fall. The cold hand of death will never claim a victim, people will never speak bitter words, the elasticity of youth will remain forever, and human suffering will be unknown (Rev. 21:4). Best of all, Jesus will personally minister to the redeemed in this dreamland of tomorrow (verse 3).

Think of sitting down with Jesus face-to-face! To see and talk with our Saviour will be an experience of breathtaking wonder. I want to be there. What about you?

DRG

GIVING ALL

For he who was a slave when he was called by the Lord is the Lord's freedman. . . . You were bought at a price; do not become slaves of men.
1 Cor. 7:22, 23, NIV.

During a minister's visit in his home, the husband of a church member complained that "all the church wants is money." The pastor turned to his host and said, "No, my friend, that's not all the church wants. Nor is that all the Lord desires of you. He wants not only your money—He wants your wife, your children, your plans, your thoughts, your mind, and your heart." When we acknowledge that Jesus freed us from being "slaves" by purchasing us "at a price," we willingly give Him everything we have.

A Scripture statement that puzzles some appears in Isaiah 55:1: "Come, all you who are thirsty, come to the waters; and you who have no money, come, buy and eat! Come, buy wine and milk without money and without cost" (NIV). How can one buy something without money and without paying for it? An even greater conundrum concerns why Jesus purchased our freedom by paying the price with His life. But that's the kind of Saviour we have. He owed us nothing and gave us everything—His very lifeblood. We owe Him everything, and yet He offers us our heart's desires: a good life, freedom from slavery to sin, and eternal life—all without asking us for a single penny. Why? Because He wants us to become His sons and daughters and someday soon join Him in His heavenly home.

And here and now He longs for us to dedicate our time, our money, our talents, and live our lives according to His plans and purposes. Jesus wants us to be like the churches in Macedonia who "gave their own selves first to the Lord" (2 Cor. 8:5, NIV). When they presented God with their person, Christ became their passion, and they changed their world!

God owns the cattle on a thousand hills and all the silver and gold on earth, and each one of us belongs to Him. "You were bought with a price"—a high one, the very life of Jesus. Therefore, "you are not your own" (1 Cor. 6:19, NIV). Do you belong to Jesus completely? Remember, the One who bought us purchased us to set us free from sin. To each of us He has given life as a sacred trust. So spend it wisely!

HMSR

WHY DID JESUS DIE?

Christ died for our sins.
1 Cor. 15:3.

During a terrible drought on the island of Hong Kong, the Buddhists there held a seven-day prayer service for rain. They climaxed their session by freeing hundreds of sparrows, deer, monkeys, fish, and turtles that they had purchased at pet shops and markets. According to their way of looking at things, the drought resulted from Buddha's anger at human sin, and they could achieve an atonement by sparing the lives of the animals.

When I visited Hong Kong, I saw caged birds for sale in a market for this very purpose. The idea was that you pay for the bird, and the merchant opens the door and lets the bird out. It flies away to freedom, and thus you obtain atonement, forgiveness, or at least the smile of Buddha. But freeing a bird brings no real hope, no atonement, for the troubled human soul.

Only Jesus, the Son of God, grants atonement, and not on the basis of freeing birds or animals, but of His death. "Christ died for our sins." "We also joy in God through our Lord Jesus Christ, by whom we have now received the atonement" (Rom. 5:11).

Atonement appears in the King James Version of the English New Testament only in this one text. The Greek word actually means "reconciliation." The death of Jesus reconciles sinners to God. God made us perfect in the beginning. Then our first parents disobeyed God, breaking His divine law of love. Ever afterward we have been rebels against God, determined to have our own way and run our own affairs without regard to Him. The Bible calls this alienation from God sin.

Jesus came and took our place. Holy and perfect, He volunteered to give His perfect life in place of the life that we forfeited by our sins. On the cross He made the atoning sacrifice that provides us eternal life. Jesus, who is very God, by becoming a man could live a perfect human life here on earth, die in our place, become our substitute, make atonement for us, and reconcile us to God. We owe Him our life—for eternity!

HMSR

AUGUST 31

WHAT IF JESUS HAD NOT RISEN?

And if Christ is not risen, your faith is futile; you are still in your sins.
1 Cor. 15:17, NKJV.

A woman diagnosed with melanoma called the pastor to her bedside and told him she wanted to be buried with a fork in her hand. The pastor thought that strange, but felt it best not to react. After they were well into their conversation, she asked the pastor, "Wouldn't you like to know why I want to be buried with a fork in my hand?"

"Yes, I really would."

"When you've had a meal," she told her pastor, "and the host comes around and takes your empty plate and says, 'Keep your fork,' you know something substantial is coming. Not just Jell-O, but something like apple pie."

Because of Jesus' resurrection, this dying woman knew that something substantial is coming—our resurrection. That's good news, since "if Christ is not risen, your faith is futile; you are still in your sins." "But now Christ is risen from the dead, and has become the firstfruits of those who have fallen asleep" (1 Cor. 15:20, NKJV). And since Jesus was resurrected, "your faith is [not] futile; you are [not] still in your sins." All of that is worth keeping a fork in your hand.

How does the resurrection deliver us from our sins? "Therefore we were buried with Him through baptism into death, that just as Christ was raised from the dead by the glory of the Father, even so we also should walk in newness of life. . . . Knowing this that our old man was crucified with Him, that the body of sin might be done away with, that we should no longer be slaves of sin. For he who has died has been freed from sin" (Rom. 6:4-7, NKJV).

Through the twin miracles of Christ's death on the cross for us and then coming forth from the tomb, we through a third miracle are forgiven. Our past life of sin is cleansed, and we "walk in newness of life." Jesus arose from the dead as "the firstfruits of those who have fallen asleep." And because of Jesus' lavish display of love, we with our loved ones, those both living and dead who have known Jesus as their Saviour, can look forward to becoming immortal when Jesus returns. Something substantial is coming!

DRG

THE FULL GOSPEL OF JESUS

Moreover, brethren, I declare to you the gospel . . . by which . . . you are saved. . . . That Christ died for our sins according to the Scriptures, and that He was buried, and that He rose again the third day.

1 Cor. 15:1-4, NKJV.

Without the Resurrection the cross would be meaningless. Paul's gospel included both "that Christ died for our sins" and "that He rose again the third day." The cross and the Resurrection are Siamese twins. We must be "reconciled to [God] through the death of His Son" in order to "be saved through his life!" (Rom. 5:10, NIV). Through the cross millions have found their way back to God, but that would not be possible unless Jesus had risen. Both the cross and the Resurrection are at the heart of the gospel.

While visiting China, in Beijing we passed Temple Street. I asked the taxi driver, "Is there a temple on that street?"

"There used to be," he responded, "but it's now used as an auto repair shop."

In countries outside China—Taiwan, Hong Kong, and Singapore—we saw Chinese worshiping at shrines in homes, shops, and public parks. But we did not see one such shrine in China. The decline in traditional religions inside China contrasts with a thriving Christian church filled with Christians who pack the churches in much of the country. In addition, millions worship in home churches.

After returning to America, I mentioned to a friend the contrast between a thriving Christian church in China and the fading of the traditional religions.

"How do you account for a thriving Christian church when the other religions have dwindled?" he responded quizzically.

"Because," I said, "Buddha is dead. Confucius is dead. But Christ is alive!"

We do not serve a dead Saviour still on the cross, but a living one! He died, then broke out of His tomb to reconcile the people in our sin-cursed world to God. Our Saviour lives today in the hearts of millions of Christians around the world who "rejoice in God through our Lord Jesus" (Rom. 5:11, NIV).

DRG

SEPTEMBER 2

JESUS PROMISES US LIFE AFTER DEATH

> ***But now Christ is risen from the dead, and has become the firstfruits of those who have fallen asleep.***
>
> *1 Cor. 15:20, NKJV.*

Years ago in my hometown of Glendale, California, the lifeless body of a 73-year-old retired professor was frozen. He had just died of lung cancer. Members of the Cryonics Society took charge of a unique freezing process, using artificial respiration and external heart massage to protect the brain from oxygen loss or damage until it had frozen solid. As a safety measure, they drained all the blood from the body and replaced it with an antifreeze solution. After the body froze, they packed it in dry ice and flew it to another state. It is now stored there, frozen by liquid nitrogen at –321° F until science finds the cure for cancer. Then they plan to thaw the body, bring it back to life by artificial respiration and external heart massage, and cure the dread disease that caused the man's death in the first place.

It may sound to some like a fantastic idea. With it, of course, come many problems and complications. Is this the answer to the age-old problem of death? Will modern men and women return bodily from the dead, with the identical flesh they had before they died, simply by freezing, waiting, and reanimating? Will the Cryonics Society be successful in bringing the frozen body of the professor, and hundreds of others, to life when medical science finds a cure for cancer and other diseases? Is life after death in the hands of modern scientists, or is there a higher power who influences human existence?

Only through the assurance of a resurrected Christ do we have hope of being awakened out of the sleep of death. The risen Christ is only "the firstfruits of those who have fallen asleep" in death. Our risen Saviour has "the keys of Hades [the grave] and of Death" (Rev. 1:18, NKJV), and He promises to call from the grave "those who have done good, to the resurrection of life" (John 5:28, 29, NKJV).

Many of us with tear-stained eyes have stood by the grave of a loved one and asked the question Why? Take heart—the great resurrection morning is coming!

HMSR

JESUS THE LIFESMITH

Listen, I tell you a mystery: We will not all sleep, but we will all be changed—in a flash, in the twinkling of an eye, at the last trumpet. For the trumpet will sound, the dead will be raised imperishable, and we will be changed.

1 Cor. 15:52, NIV.

When the pioneer chemist Michael Faraday entered his laboratory one day, he found everything in great confusion. One of his workmen had accidentally tipped a beautiful silver prize cup into a jar of chemicals, where it dissolved and disappeared. Some accused the distressed workman of stealing it. But Faraday poured a liquid from a large bottle into the jar, and instantly the silver deposited itself as a fine powder on the bottom of the jar. He then poured off the liquid and sent the powdered silver to a silversmith, who returned a cup far more beautiful than the first.

When people die, their bodies dissolve to dust. It will take more than a chemist and a silversmith to put their bodies back together. And that is where the Bible promise comes in: "Listen, I tell you a mystery: . . . we will all be changed—in a flash, in the twinkling of an eye, at the last trumpet." Jesus, our lifesmith, will refashion our bodies, and we "will be raised imperishable." Our resurrected bodies will be eternal and far more beautiful than the first.

Jesus is our surety of life eternal. "Do not be afraid. I am the First and the Last. I am the Living One; I was dead, and behold I am alive for ever and ever! And I hold the keys of death and Hades" (Rev. 1:17, 18, NIV).

Because Jesus is risen and alive, our Saviour has the keys of the grave and of death, and He is waiting to save and bless. With those keys He will raise you and me—each of us—whoever we are and wherever we are, to a life that never ends. Not only does such a life change become effective when Jesus returns in glory, but it is also ours by faith now. Christ is both the resurrection and the life (John 11:25). You can begin a new and better life, yes, eternal life now—with Jesus as your Saviour, Companion, and Friend! (John 5:24).

HMSR

SEPTEMBER 4

HAVE YOU THANKED GOD FOR LOVING YOU?

> *Thanks be to God, who gives us the victory through our Lord Jesus Christ.*
>
> 1 Cor. 15:57, NKJV.

When Sadie Virginia Camp was 96 years old, she was living in the Virginia Hotel in Long Beach, California. Having seen a lot of history in the making, she had sewed baby clothes that went on Grenfell's expedition into Labrador. Now the Virginia Hotel gave her a beautiful party in honor of her ninety-sixth birthday. It was a gala occasion. The huge birthday cake, decorated with 96 candles, resembled a miniature forest fire.

Before anyone ate the cake, she asked, "Who baked the cake?" No one seemed to hear her. She repeated again, "Who baked the cake?" Someone told her it was Billy Blake, who had been the hotel baker for many years. After the party she went upstairs to her room and penned a thank-you note. She enclosed a $5 bill and had it taken to Billy Blake.

That evening she heard a knock at her door. When she opened it, there stood a man wearing his baker's hat. "I'm Billy Blake," he said. "I've been here baking for years and years and have made hundreds of birthday cakes, but this is the first time that anyone ever said thank you."

How long has it been since you have thanked God for giving His Son to die for you? Or how long has it been since you have thanked Jesus for dying for you? Real love makes a thankful, happy heart. Instead of always asking, we should express our thanks to our Father and His Son for the blessings that are ours each day. The expression "Thanks be to God, who gives us the victory through our Lord Jesus Christ" should be often on our lips. Love in the heart brings a sense of appreciation and thanksgiving.

In return for a love that resulted in Jesus dying for us, He deserves our unlimited, unceasing love. The love He showed us will prompt us to give Him our loyalty—loyalty of thought and speech, loyalty of heart and of our very being—gladly. Yes, the love that we cherish for our Lord should be far greater than our love for anyone else. Real love is unselfish. Christ's love is not dependent on our response, because it exists in His very nature—He is love. Why not bow your head just now and say, "Thank You, Jesus!"

HMSR

A LIVE BOTTLE OF PERFUME

Wherever I go, thank God, he makes my life a constant pageant of triumph in Christ, diffusing the perfume of his knowledge everywhere by me.
2 COR. 2:14, MOFFATT.

A little girl who had received a bottle of perfume took it outdoors to show to her playmates. She hid it behind her back and said, "You can't guess what I have!" Then in her excitement she held the bottle high above her head. Her little friends cried, "Fumery, that's what it is—fumery!"

Her playmates had read the label on the bottle. But one said: "Oh, that's just printin'. Why don't you take the cap off the bottle? Then we can tell if it is real or not."

When they removed the cap and they all had a good smell, one of them said triumphantly, "Say, that's the real stuff, all right!" There is a great need for Christians today to uncap the bottle and let the world breathe the fragrance of Jesus, the Rose of Sharon. When He lives in my heart, people know that I have been with Jesus, for I am "diffusing the perfume of his knowledge everywhere."

Note the imagery in this passage: "God . . . leads us in triumphal procession in Christ and through us spreads everywhere the fragrance of the knowledge of him" (2 Cor. 2:14, NIV). A note in the *NIV Study Bible* informs us: "The imagery is that of a Roman triumph in which the victorious general would lead his soldiers and the captives they had taken in festive procession, while the people watched and applauded and the air was filled with the sweet smell released by the burning of spices in the streets. So the Christian, called to spiritual warfare, is triumphantly led by God in Christ, and it is through him that God spreads everywhere the 'fragrance' of the knowledge of Christ."

A Christian is a living bottle of perfume. Our lives are to spread the sweet fragrance of Christ to those with whom we come in contact. People are not so much impressed with what we believe as with what we are and how we live. When we invite Jesus into our heart, He lives His life out in us, and those who are acquainted with us want what we have. As a result, when people look at your life and my life, they enthusiastically respond: "That's the real stuff, all right!"

HMSR

SEPTEMBER 6

THE JESUS FRAGRANCE

I live for God as the fragrance of Christ breathed alike on those who are being saved and on those who are perishing, to the one a deadly fragrance that makes for death, to the other a vital fragrance that makes for life. And who is qualified for this career?

2 Cor. 2:15-17, Moffatt.

Describing his 80-year-old father, Nathan Hatch wrote: "Dad has been no respecter of persons. He has naturally gravitated to 'little' people, the ungifted, the unattractive, those often regarded as unlovely, or troublesome, or unuseful. One deeply wounded person whom he counseled for years wrote, 'You have been Jesus in flesh and bone to me.' As an adolescent, I could never understand how the ministry of my shy and private father reverberated with such power in people's lives. When he taught, people listened, riveted. When he preached, people's views of God and themselves changed, often in dramatic ways. And when he counseled, broken people tasted healing. No amount of analysis can explain the contagious quality of love he radiates: he is a vessel simply brimming with the powerful love of Christ" (*Christianity Today,* Nov. 14, 1994, p. 34).

This man's father permeates with the Jesus fragrance Paul was describing when he says, "I live for God as the fragrance of Christ . . . a vital fragrance that makes for life. And who is qualified for this career?" The apostle qualified as one who spread "the fragrance of Christ." And in our day fathers like this and Christians who become "a vital fragrance that makes for life" diffuse Jesus' fragrance throughout the world.

Faith, hope, and love combine to form the Jesus fragrance—love being predominant (1 Cor. 13:13). When we apply this perfume, we permeate the world with His fragrance, because "God has poured out his love into our hearts by the Holy Spirit" (Rom. 5:5, NIV). Turn the negatives into positives in 1 Corinthians 13:4-8, and you will discover that a loving Christian is patient, kind, humble, courteous, thoughtful, even-tempered, generous, pure, buoyant, protective, trusting, hopeful, and consistent. Filled with "the fragrance of Christ," we circulate in flesh and blood a divine atmosphere around the world.

DRG

ALL THINGS FRESH AND NEW

All this is God's doing, for he has reconciled us to himself through Christ.
2 Cor. 5:18, Phillips.

Tan Sua Eng, of Phuket, Thailand, became addicted to opium while smoking during business deals with his lawyer. For years he tried to stop the habit, but remained firmly in the drug's clutches. Gradually he sold most of his land because opium was costing him the equivalent of the wages he paid to five laborers in his rice fields. "After 15 years of addiction to opium smoking," Sua Eng told me, "I came in contact with Christianity through some evangelistic meetings in our village. After attending three meetings, I decided to renounce Buddhism and become a Christian. I came to the conviction that to be a genuine Christian I must give up opium smoking."

Three months of agony followed, three months of unsatisfied cravings, but never once did Sua Eng return to the opium habit. Despite the terrible agony from the burning within his body, he vowed to overcome the addiction. He spent sleepless nights pacing the ridges in the rice fields. His friends warned, "You will die if you persist in your desire to give up opium." But nothing could deter him from his firm decision for Christ. Today he is "a new person altogether—the past is finished and gone, everything has become fresh and new."

I need not have asked the question, for his face was radiant, but I wanted to hear him say it, so I inquired, "Were you richer with all your cattle and lands, or are you richer now in Christ?" In his enthusiasm he ignored the first part of my question and literally beamed from ear to ear as he answered, "Oh, yes!"

At this point in the conversation his wife broke in, "He was so irritable and mean before he accepted Jesus that we were all afraid of him. But since he has found Jesus, he is happy all the time." Because of his changed life, Sua Eng's wife, five children, and several neighbors became Christians, and they established a church in his home. Truly, "all this is God's doing . . . through Christ." Sua Eng's amazing experience is available to you, to me, to all who choose to live "in Christ."

DRG

WHAT LOVE CAN DO

God was in Christ personally reconciling the world to himself—not counting their sins against them—and has commissioned us with the message of reconciliation. We are now Christ's ambassadors, as though God were appealing direct to you through us.
2 Cor. 5:19, 20, Phillips.

On an It Is Written telecast Josh McDowell told Mark Finley that he went away to university as an agnostic and returned home as a Christian. Josh now specializes in leading young people to find faith in Jesus Christ. His father was the town alcoholic, and Josh hardly ever saw him sober. McDowell's father would beat his mother so severely that she could hardly get up and walk. Two months before he graduated from the university, Josh heard his mother crying and asked, "What's wrong?"

"Your father has broken my heart," his mother answered, "and all I want to do is live until you graduate, and then I want to die." Two months later Josh graduated, and soon after his mother died. As a result, he hated his dad.

"After I made the decision to put my personal trust in Christ as Saviour and Lord and accept His forgiveness into my life," Josh said, "the love of God through Jesus Christ came into my life. He took that hatred and turned it upside down, and I found myself looking into my dad's eyes and saying, 'Dad, I love you.' The irony was that I didn't want to love him. Even as a new Christian, I didn't want to love my dad; for this reason: I wanted the joy of hating the man who had killed my mother. But all of a sudden I found myself, almost against my will, saying to my dad, 'I love you.' "

Christ had personally reconciled Josh, "not counting [his] sins against" him. Christ's act of love flooded Josh's heart, commissioning him to take "the message of reconciliation" to his father. It was as though God were appealing directly to his father through Josh.

As a result, his father came to him one day and said, "Son, how can you love a father such as I?" McDowell shared the good news about Jesus with his father and told him Jesus wanted to forgive him, come into his life, and live His life in and through him.

His father responded, "Son, if God can do in my life what He's done in yours, then I want to give Him the opportunity." What love did for Josh and his father, it can do for you and me!

DRG

I TALKED WITH A MIRACLE—1

When someone becomes a Christian he becomes a brand new person inside. He is not the same any more. A new life has begun!

2 Cor. 5:17, TLB.

Years ago on the Voice of Prophecy broadcast I interviewed Pastor Richard Hall, a missionary to Borneo, and Chief Ryong from the Iban tribe in Borneo. I asked Hall: "Do you think it is still important for us to invest in sending missionaries? You know, we have heard that primitive people are happy just as they are. Why disturb them?"

"Well," Pastor Hall answered, "I think the chief can answer that question. He knows much more about that than I do, because he was one of them. In fact, he was a headhunter, one of the so-called wild men of Borneo."

My heart thrilled as Chief Ryong told his story and Pastor Hall translated it for the radio audience: "Before a missionary ever came with the gospel to the Tatau River where I live, my heart, and the hearts of my people, were filled with devil worship. What the devil urged, through his witch doctors, was that we cut off human heads and use them in our worship. Then a missionary, Pastor Youngberg, came from America to Tatau. For three years we didn't accept him. We were afraid of what he had. In fact, when the missionary arrived, we wanted to cut his head off too. But Pastor Youngberg wasn't afraid, so we didn't cut his head. We waited to see what he would do.

"He began to take care of our children when they were sick, and he always helped them. They began to be friendly with him. Pastor Youngberg did so much good work for us that we began to love him. Then he began to teach us from the Bible and show us that it was God who was helping, and that this was what the Christian way of life was. After three years I accepted Christ, and five of us were baptized. When Jesus entered my heart, He drove Satan completely out. I have nothing to do with the devil anymore. Instead I have the spirit of Jesus in my heart. I don't cut off heads anymore. I go out to help my fellow human beings—a complete change in my life."

Chief Ryong's face radiated with the greatest of all miracles: When someone becomes a Christian, he becomes a brand-new person inside. He is not the same anymore. A new life has begun!

HMSR

SEPTEMBER 10

I TALKED WITH A MIRACLE—2

We look inside, and what we see is that anyone united with the Messiah gets a fresh start, is created new. The old life is gone; a new life burgeons! Look at it! All this comes from the God who settled the relationship between us and him.
2 Cor. 5:17, 18, Message.

Yesterday you read the eloquent testimony by Chief Ryong of how Jesus gave meaning to his life as well as power and strength to live a completely new lifestyle. Jesus in the chief's heart caused everything to change: "[His] old life is gone; a new life burgeons! Look at it!" The change in the chief's life caused his whole family to "look at it!" They became Christians, and more than 200 in his longhouse followed and gave their lives to Jesus.

When I interviewed him, the chief had a skull, a sword, and a hatchet with him. I asked Pastor Hall, who was translating for the chief, "Are these some of the things he used when he was worshiping the devil?"

"Yes," Hall answered, "this sword has cut off many heads. This skull is one of them. The hair is actual human hair. The headhunters believe evil spirits live in the skull and use them as objects of worship. But all that's changed. Chief Ryong uses these objects to show people the tremendous change in his life since Jesus came into his heart."

The chief is truly a powerful testimony to the truth of today's text. "We look inside, and what we see is that anyone united with the Messiah gets a fresh start, is created new. . . . All this comes from the God who settled the relationship between us and him." Ellen G. White comments on this text: "Through the power of Christ, men and women have broken the chains of sinful habit. They have renounced selfishness. The profane have become reverent, the drunken sober, the profligate pure. Souls that have borne the likeness of Satan have become transformed into the image of God. This change is in itself the miracle of miracles" (*The Acts of the Apostles,* p. 476).

At the close of his testimony the chief said of his village: "We are now happy in our service to God. I'm so thankful for the people who helped me by giving the gospel message so Jesus could come into my heart. The devil is forever out!"

HMSR

JESUS BECAME SIN FOR US

God made him who had no sin to be sin for us, so that in him we might become the righteousness of God.

2 Cor. 5:21, NIV.

As Everett Duncan, our Sabbath school teacher, was sharing some thoughts on this text, Tony, one of the members of our class, spoke up. He told us he was attempting to share Christ with one of his neighbors, an atheist, by telling him about Jesus who died for us. "What's the big deal about that?" his neighbor responded. "Millions of soldiers have died for their country."

The class entered a spirited discussion on the meaning of the cross to give Tony some ideas to use the next time he witnessed to his neighbor. Our teacher reminded us that "Jesus was the only person born into this world expressly to die." Jesus, God in human flesh, came to our world knowing that He would perish.

Someone pointed out that when Jesus became "sin for us" by dying on the cross, the weight of the sins of the entire world—"gillians" of sins—rested on Him. They not only bore down on His shoulders, but on His mind and heart. Every day of His life He faced the apprehension of His coming death for our sins.

When we sin, guilt pangs may plague us the rest of our lives. But that is nothing compared to the guilt Jesus suffered on Calvary. The most excruciating pain that Christ endured was the withdrawal of His Father's presence from Him at the very time the penalty and guilt of our sins were crushing the heart of Jesus. Finally Christ broke under their weight and died. As if that were not enough, Jesus continues to this day to grieve over the sins of those who neglect Him and eventually reject Him.

Why was Jesus willing to die, bearing our sins? "So that in him we might become the righteousness of God." Becoming the righteousness of God has two well-known aspects. 1. Jesus not only forgives and blots out our sins, but He credits our account in heaven with the record of His sinless life. 2. And as if that is not enough, He is with us every day, imparting His righteousness to us, enriching our lives with His presence as we grow up in Him. No other being in the universe could equal, let alone top all that!

DRG

THE TIME IS NOW!

Behold, now is the accepted time; behold, now is the day of salvation.

2 Cor. 6:2.

When he was in the West Indies, Pastor R. H. Pierson, former General Conference president, urged a physician friend to accept Christ as his personal Saviour.

"I feel fine," the doctor said. "I do not need to be overly concerned about religion just now. I'm good for at least 20 years yet. Come back 15 years from now and talk to me about salvation. There's plenty of time ahead for that. I want to enjoy life now."

The doctor failed to remember the uncertainty of life. He forgot blackwater fever, among other things that might snap the cord of human life. Within, not 20 years, but 20 days, the doctor was in his grave—unprepared to meet his God.

Millions today are so busy living, having what they call a good time or just going on in selfish and indifferent ways, that they forget the most important thing. Eventually, they say, they will turn over a new leaf. Someday, like the doctor, they will listen to God and accept Jesus as their Saviour. But someday never comes. They leave this life without God, without Christ, without hope (Eph. 2:12).

The setting of today's text reveals that Paul's admonition is not primarily to non-Christians, but to Christians. Paul, writing to the church at Corinth, declares: "As God's fellow workers we urge you not to receive God's grace in vain. . . . I tell you, now is the time of God's favor, now is the day of salvation" (2 Cor. 6:1, 2, NIV).

For the sinner to reject the call to accept salvation is a tragedy. An even greater tragedy is for a Christian "to receive God's grace in vain" by living for self, rather than for Jesus, the author of our salvation. Examine your heart today, and as you do, remember: "Now is the accepted time; behold, now is the day of salvation." Then take hold of Jesus' hand and live for Him today. The time is now! Today is your "day of salvation."

HMSR

I OWE GOD $3 MILLION

For you know the grace of our Lord Jesus Christ, that though he was rich, yet for your sakes he became poor, so that you through his poverty might become rich.
2 Cor. 8:9, NIV.

Three million dollars—that's a lot of money, isn't it? The author of a true story that appeared in a leading religious magazine says he stole $3 million during his career as a swindler and confidence man. He was so adept at crime that if he were dropped from a plane by parachute anywhere in North America, he said within 24 hours he could arrange some sort of swindle that would net him at least $1,000.

His family was not religious, and he grew up in poverty. But in one thing he was different from many boys living in such an environment: he loved school and stayed out of teenage gangs. He had the knack of getting along with people. In time he married, had two children, became vice president of a company, and earned a substantial salary.

But that didn't satisfy him. He wanted something more interesting. Crime seemed to offer the excitement he craved. Liking the intoxication of outwitting the law, he gave up his promising career, home, family, children, friends—everything—and embarked on a path of crime. In one of his major swindles he sold $600,000 worth of useless franchises. Traveling constantly, he lived like an emperor, with expensive automobiles, an airplane, and a yacht. But way down deep inside him was a tiny spark that we call conscience. Eventually the authorities caught and imprisoned him.

The burden of his guilt was so unbearable that he considered suicide. Just then a religious magazine showed up in his cell. He says something—or Someone—prompted him to read it. Writing to the editor, he asked how he could find God. The man who answered his letter told him about Jesus, the sinner's friend who died for all of us. The prisoner accepted Jesus and became a Christian.

He took his stand on the promise: "For you know the grace of our Lord Jesus Christ, that though he was rich, yet for your sakes he became poor, so that you through his poverty might become rich." Through the power of the Holy Spirit, his whole life took a 180-degree turn. His burden rolled away, and Clay Lawrence says he would not exchange the riches in Christ that are inside him now for $3 million.

HMSR

SEPTEMBER 14

LORD OF OUR THOUGHTS

Casting down arguments and every high thing that exalts itself against the knowledge of God, bringing every thought into captivity to the obedience of Christ.
2 Cor. 10:5, NKJV.

Our brains have 10 or 12 billion nerve cells, or neurons, that are constantly receiving messages from all parts of the body and transmitting them to the control center of the mind or brain. Our personal control centers record at least 100 million sensations a second, which means that in the past 12 hours 4,320,000,000,000 sensations have bombarded my brain. It would take a large computer chip to handle this number of connections. About 1 billion nerve cells participate in every move we make to keep our bodies vertical. Just think of the billions of nerve cells it must take to do creative thinking.

Someone has said, "You are not what you think you are; but what you think—you are." Thoughts harm us or help us. Therefore it is most important to know who is in control of our mind and thoughts: Christ or Satan. Face it, we will have unseemly thoughts, but we have power to change them through Christ in our lives.

To have wrong thoughts enter the mind is not sin, but if we entertain or encourage them, we place ourselves on dangerous ground. "For as [a man] thinketh in his heart, so is he" (Prov. 23:7). First comes the thought of evil, then the imagination makes the evil seem attractive, and finally it results in delight, consent, and action. To drive out evil thoughts, we must dwell on good thoughts, thus "casting down arguments and every high thing that exalts itself against the knowledge of God, bringing every thought into captivity to the obedience of Christ." In other words, cast out evil thoughts, then fill the vacuum with good thoughts through Bible reading, prayer, meditation, and song.

Sunlight has an antiseptic effect on bacteria, and exposure to the Holy Spirit and to Jesus Christ spiritually cleanses our hearts and minds, and They become the controllers of each of our lives. When Jesus becomes Lord of your thoughts, the great controversy in your life will end in victory for the right.

HMSR

ENCIRCLED BY CHRIST

> ***For as many of you as have been baptized into Christ have put on Christ.***
>
> *Gal. 3:27.*

One day as he walked down skid row in Chicago, Dwight L. Moody, the Billy Graham of the nineteenth century, paused now and then to speak a word of encouragement to those who would listen. An intoxicated man lying on the sidewalk looked up at Moody and asked, "Mr. Moody, don't you remember me?"

The great evangelist looked down at him quizzically for a moment, then replied, "No, I don't believe I do."

"Why, Mr. Moody," the drunk continued, "I am the man you converted down at the temple. Why, I am one of your converts, Mr. Moody."

Then the famed evangelist said, "Yes, I guess you are one of my converts, for if you were one of the Lord's converts, you wouldn't be where you are today."

If a person has been truly baptized "into Christ," that person has "put on Christ." *The Living Bible* says that we "are enveloped by him." The NIV declares that you "have clothed yourselves with Christ." To be baptized into Christ is to be robed with His righteous character and live as He lived. Such a transformation is not our doing, but entirely Christ's.

When Jesus asked John to baptize Him, John could not understand why Jesus, the sinless Saviour, should be baptized. Jesus was not a sinner. Why then did He request the rite? Because Christ's great purpose in coming to our world was to communicate the fullness of His righteous life to lost men and women so they can stand perfect in the presence of God in the judgment day. And the only way for a lost sinner to receive righteousness is through Jesus' sinless life, His glorious substitutionary death, and His majestic resurrection.

So when John objected to baptizing Him, Jesus said: "Thus it becometh us to fulfill all righteousness" (Matt. 3:15). By accepting baptism Jesus declared His willingness to commence His ministry of reconciliation through His life, death, burial, and resurrection. He did all this as our substitute, becoming "sin for us, who knew no sin; that we might be made the righteousness of God in him" (2 Cor. 5:21). Can you think of any better news than that?

HMSR

SEPTEMBER 16

"THE OLD ORCHARD TEST"

But the fruit of the Spirit is love, joy, peace, patience, kindness, goodness, faithfulness, gentleness and self-control. Against such there is no law.

GAL. 5:22, 23, NIV.

Paul here compares the Holy Spirit to a tree loaded with attractive fruit. If the Holy Spirit guides people, their lives will reveal proof of it. If I claim to be a Christian, a follower in the footsteps of Jesus Christ, and I am rude and unkind and selfish and unsympathetic, I am merely professing Christianity, not practicing it. Jesus is not living in my heart through the Holy Spirit. Some people call it "the old orchard test." "By their fruit you will recognize them" (Matt. 7:16, NIV).

Jesus reads the innermost heart of a person. As He looks into your heart and into mine just now, what does He see? After listing the fruit of the Spirit in Galatians 5:22, 23, Paul goes on to elaborate: "Those who belong to Christ Jesus have crucified the sinful nature with its passions and desires. Since we live by the Spirit, let us keep in step with the Spirit" (verses 24, 25, NIV). The passage reminds me of the old adage by Edgar Guest: "I'd rather see a sermon than hear one any day."

Christianity today meets the greatest challenge that it has ever faced. Human beings, moral rebels, demand freedom—freedom from all restraint, freedom to do as they please, freedom from all control. Men, women, and children declare, "No one is going to tell me what to read. I'll read what I want to read; I'll go where I want to go; I'll do what I want to do." People want their own way, but they are stumbling, fumbling, and grumbling in darkness, groping for a way out of the mire and the mess that they have gotten themselves into. Humanity wants to find its own answers.

As Christians we know there exists only one answer, only one way to real freedom, only one door to a happy life—yielding to the Spirit of God and living for Jesus, thus bearing a crop of attractive, tantalizing fruit. Grade A fruit. The fruit of an intimate day-by-day association with Jesus.

HMSR

THE TRANSFORMING POWER OF THE CROSS

But God forbid that I should glory except in the cross of our Lord Jesus Christ, by whom the world has been crucified to me, and I to the world.
Gal. 6:14, NKJV.

When Charles V ruled the Holy Roman Empire, he borrowed a large sum of money from an Antwerp merchant to meet a dire need of his government. When the promissory note came due, the emperor was bankrupt. He had no money. Knowing the king's need, the merchant invited His Majesty to a banquet. The great men of the kingdom gathered around the table awaiting a sumptuous feast. The wealthy merchant had a large platter brought in and placed in the center of the table. A servant lighted a fire on the platter. Taking the note from his pocket, the merchant held it over the flame until it was reduced to ashes. Charles V, seeing what his benefactor had done, jumped up, threw his arms around him, and wept for joy.

What the merchant did for Charles V is commendable, but it cost him only a small part of his wealth. What Jesus did for us far surpasses the merchant's generous act—He gave His life for us. We owe Jesus more than a hug and a few tears of joy—we owe Him our life.

Jesus suffered a cruel, torturous death for us on the cross. After they scourged Him twice, the soldiers placed the cross on His shoulders and forced Him to walk through the busiest part of town and suffer the taunts of the jeering crowd. Reaching Calvary, they laid Him upon His cross and nailed Him to it. Those skilled in execution knew exactly where to drive the nails to inflict the most pain to the sensory nerves. The slightest movement on the raised cross caused excruciating agony.

Jesus did not die from the pain or from exhaustion or from asphyxiation; He gave His life to save us (Matt. 20:28). Paul, that once dedicated persecutor of Christians who wrote today's text, testifies that through the cross "the world has been crucified to me, and I to the world." The powerful meaning of the cross suddenly transformed his life.

When we dwell on Jesus dying for us on the cross, we fall in love with Him, and our life is never again the same. He gives us a joy that nothing can ever take away.

HMSR

HOW TO BE BLESSED WITH GOD'S BEST

How we praise God, the Father of our Lord Jesus Christ, who has blessed us with every blessing in heaven because we belong to Christ.

EPH. 1:3, TLB.

Our pastor recommended that we read the Bible through. Each week he assigned the chapters to read and chose a passage from them for his sermon the following Sabbath. He suggested that we use the *Daily Walk* as a guide. Each day it gives a brief overview of the chapters to read and suggests practical applications to gain from the passages.

One assignment was Numbers 34 to 36. Israel is jubilant, for the nation is about to realize God's promise of the land of Canaan. *Daily Walk* suggests: "A good subtitle for today's reading might be 'How to Be Blessed With God's Best.'. . . As you look at the people whose lives seem to overflow with God's blessing, you may be tempted to think they have a special key to His storehouse which you don't possess. Turn to the New Testament and read the first 14 verses of Paul's letter to the Ephesians. There you'll find a reminder of just how rich you are as a Christian. Then on a deposit slip from your checkbook, itemize the parts of your spiritual inheritance that you own but are not presently enjoying" (reading for Monday, Feb. 20, 1995).

I turned to Ephesians 1 and itemized my spiritual inheritance described in one very long sentence in verses 3 to 14: 1. God chose me in Christ. 2. Through Christ He adopted me as His son. 3. In Christ He promised to make me holy and blameless. 4. He redeemed me from slavery to sin through Christ. 5. Jesus' blood forgave my sins. 6. By giving me Jesus, God lavished on me the riches of His grace. 7. Someday soon He'll bring all in heaven and earth together under the headship of Christ. 8. I am chosen to be the praise of God's glory—to be like Jesus in character. 9. Because I believe the gospel of Christ I am sealed by the Holy Spirit. 10. The Spirit of Christ is a deposit guaranteeing my inheritance in heaven. (And you will find much more in these verses.)

Truly God "has blessed us with every blessing in heaven because we belong to Christ"!

DRG

HOW MANY WAYS OF SALVATION?

In Him we have redemption through His blood, the forgiveness of sins, according to the riches of His grace.

Eph. 1:7, NKJV.

While standing in the courtyard in Singapore where the participants in a ceremony known as Thaipusum were preparing to march, the heavy odors of incense, the din of the chanting crowd, the screeching flutes, and the clanging gongs playing a chant to the gods all threatened to overwhelm me. One glassy-eyed devotee danced wildly in circles, fulfilling his vow to win the favor of the gods by carrying a kavadi.

The kavadi, a semicircular steel frame, is supported on the shoulders by steel bars held steady by long needlelike spears inserted into the bare flesh. Incantations, chanting, and the steady beat of music lull the devotee into a trance. He sits motionless on a high stool as others thread the needles through the kavadi's steel frame and thrust them into his chest and back. After someone jabs a silver needle through his protruding tongue, he is ready to join the stream of kavadi carriers in a five-mile walk to the Chettiar Temple. These worshipers puncture their skin and torture their bodies in order to win the favor of their gods.

As Christians we do not need to win God's favor, for His attitude is always one of grace—a free gift, not dependent upon human effort to please Him. To reveal His heart of grace, God sent His Son to our world. "In Him we have redemption through His blood, the forgiveness of sins, according to the riches of His grace." Here is the good news of the gospel. Christ's life, death, and resurrection laid bare God's heart for all to see. Through Christ we see that God is graciously disposed toward the sinner, that His attitude and nature are redemptive, and that His compassion is broad enough to include every sinner.

Christ reveals, as nothing else ever could, God's grace. That grace includes more than His attitude—it is an active, energizing, transforming power working to save us. We cannot earn forgiveness. Human achievement, striving to be good, can never gain God's favor. His grace is free, a gift. "There is therefore now no condemnation for those who are in Christ Jesus" (Rom. 8:1, NKJV). What a relief!

DRG

THE UNIVERSAL PANACEA

That . . . He might gather together in one all things in Christ, both which are in heaven and which are on earth—in Him.
EPH. 1:10, NKJV.

During the past century many have offered panaceas of various kinds for our sin-sick world, but they have all proved to be worthless. God's Word gives the real cure for all earth's problems—Jesus. God promises to "gather together in one all things in Christ, both which are in heaven and which are on earth." The ARV phrases it as: "to sum up all things in Christ." All things will be included in Christ and completed in Him—or, as we might say, consummated in Him. We speak of some certain individual as "summing up" a period of history, but no ordinary person has ever lived of whom it was seriously claimed that he or she summed up all things. But here are three reasons why Jesus gathers together, or sums up, all things.

First, He sums up truth. All false religions and philosophies carry some truth, but Jesus claims to be the Truth (John 14:6). Jesus was and is the source and personification of truth. In Him "are hid all the treasures of wisdom and knowledge" (Col. 2:3).

Second, Jesus encompasses all humanity. He is not simply the world's greatest teacher or a great psychologist. Christ is the Son of Man as well as the Son of God. Coming from above, He took upon Himself the likeness of humanity (Phil. 2:7). A person never really discovers himself or herself until he or she discovers Jesus in His fullness, for fullness and completeness occur only in Him.

Third, Jesus contains all power. "All power is given unto me in heaven and in earth" (Matt. 28:18). Nature reveals His power as He upholds all things (Heb. 1:3) and "by him all things consist" (Col. 1:17) and subsist. In the wonders of a Christian life we see His power. "In him we live, and move, and have our being" (Acts 17:28). We need Jesus, the universal panacea, for He who has the power to control the universe has the ability to give us fulfilled lives now and for eternity.

HMSR

WE CAN BELIEVE IN THE COLOSSAL

For it is by grace you have been saved, through faith—and this not from yourselves, it is the gift of God—not by works, so that no one can boast. For we are God's workmanship, created in Christ Jesus to do good works, which God prepared in advance for us to do.

EPH. 2:8-10, NIV.

Charles H. Spurgeon, the pastor of the Metropolitan Tabernacle in London during the mid-nineteenth century, told his students: "Some modern divines whittle away the gospel to the small end of nothing. They make our divine Lord to be a sort of blessed nobody. They bring down salvation to mere solvability, make certainty into probabilities, treat verities as mere opinions. . . . As for me, I believe in the Colossal—a need as deep as hell and grace as high as heaven. I believe in a pit that's bottomless, and a heaven that's topless. I believe in an infinite God, and infinite atonement, infinite love and mercy, an everlasting covenant, ordered in all things and sure, of which the substance and reality is an infinite Christ."

I too believe in the colossal, for I have seen sinners sunken in sin as deep as hell, forgiven and cleansed through grace as high as heaven. For instance, following the collapse of the Berlin Wall and the religious revival that swept over atheistic Russia, millions experienced the dramatic pull of God's grace and became Christians. Galena, who lives in Nizhni Novgorod, attended evangelistic meetings and surrendered her life to Jesus. With tears running down her cheeks, she said, "Before I came to these meetings, I was an atheist. I didn't believe in God. Now I have accepted Jesus. I am a brand-new person inside. The truths you have been teaching us from the Bible have opened my eyes."

What could be more colossal than the grace that saved Galena and millions like her? It is not of our own doing, but "the gift of God—not by works." Why not of works? Because our salvation is God's doing and His alone. After we are saved through faith in Jesus, we naturally do good works because "we are God's workmanship, created in Christ Jesus to do good works, which God prepared in advance for us to do." The new heart that Jesus created in Galena is an act of God, and that heart's very nature is to do good works. That is colossal! Are you experiencing the colossal in your life?

DRG

THE FELLOWSHIP OF THE MYSTERY

To [Paul] . . . this grace was given, that I should preach among the Gentiles the unsearchable riches of Christ, and to make all people see what is the fellowship of the mystery, which from the beginning of the ages has been hidden in God who created all things through Jesus Christ.
Eph. 3:8, 9, NKJV.

As two men argued, one asked the other, "Which evolved first in the process of evolution, the hen or the egg?"

"The egg," came the reply.

"Then," said the other, "there was one egg that did not come from a hen? Where did the egg come from?"

Seeing his predicament, the other apologized for his mistake and guessed it was the hen that came first.

"Very well, then there was a hen that did not originate from an egg. Where did the hen come from?"

The other person had to admit that he did not know.

For information on the only possible explanation of origins we must turn to divine revelation, where we read that God "created all things through Jesus Christ."

We need to remember constantly that all enlightened minds admit that both humanity and nature contain unsolved mysteries. Their solution evades the most profound intellects. Among them are the origin of the earth and living things. Modern science can't explain the beginning of anything. The mystery of creation is outside its realm. Scientists may advance opinions, theories, or hypotheses as if they were demonstrated fact, but these theories are frequently as vague as they are contradictory. Humanity did not yet exist at the time of the earth's origin. Therefore, we must depend upon divine revelation on this point.

But today's text speaks about an even more profound mystery—"the fellowship of the mystery," "the mystery of Christ," our Creator (Eph. 3:4, NKJV). It declares that Gentiles as well as Jews can be "partakers of [God's] promise in Christ through the gospel" (verses 5-8, NKJV). And the essence of the gospel is "the unsearchable riches of Christ" (verse 8, NKJV). These riches include the good news that "now in Christ Jesus you who once were far off have been made near by the blood of Christ. For He Himself is our peace" (Eph. 2:13, 14, NKJV). Thanks be for this saving gospel!

HMSR

THE ONE DOCTRINE THAT MATTERS MOST

> ***For us there is only one Lord, one faith, one baptism.***
>
> *EPH. 4:5, TLB.*

When Henry Ward Beecher began his ministry, he had a list of 100 great fundamentals (doctrines) a person should hold to be a true Christian. At 40 he said he had reduced the number to 65. At age 50 to 25. At age 65 to 10. On his deathbed he told his family, "I now have only one doctrine—the doctrine that I am a great sinner, and Jesus is a great Saviour."

Jesus also saturated the sermons of Pastor H.M.S. Richards. Whenever he preached, no matter what the subject, he focused on Jesus, our Saviour. He followed the admonition of Ellen White that "no discourse should ever be preached without presenting Christ and Him crucified as the foundation of the gospel" (*Gospel Workers,* p. 158). "Christ is the center of all true doctrine" (*Counsels to Parents and Teachers,* p. 453).

Just as "there is only one Lord," so there is only "one faith." Jesus is the foundation, the essence, and focal point of the gospel. In truth Jesus *is* the gospel! The good news about Jesus is the "one faith," the one doctrine every other doctrine in Scripture revolves around. The doctrine of Jesus is both the center and circumference, the hub and the rim of every other religious teaching. All other doctrines of Scripture are but spokes that lead us to Jesus. The one thing that really matters is "What do you think about the Christ? Whose Son is He?" (Matt. 22:42, NKJV).

The Pharisees tried to draw Jesus into a controversy over the doctrine of the law. He answered them in a nonthreatening way, then asked a question that diverted their attention to the one question that eclipses every other: "What do you think about the Christ?" Only a correct response to that question will open the way for a person to receive salvation.

What do you think about Jesus?

DRG

CHRIST'S LOVE IN FOUR DIMENSIONS

That Christ may dwell in your hearts through faith; that you, being rooted and grounded in love, may be able to comprehend with all the saints what is the width and length and depth and height—to know the love of Christ which passes knowledge; that you may be filled with all the fullness of God.

Eph. 3:17-19, NKJV.

In a human sense, we love individuals as long as we consider them worthy of our love. Then when we think they no longer are, we tend to cast them off. But it is not that way with God. A tremendous difference exists between human love and divine love. When Christ dwells in our hearts, He roots and grounds us in His love, and we are then "able to comprehend with all the saints what is the width and length and depth and height—to know the love of Christ which passes knowledge."

Sometimes we might feel that we have grasped something of God's love only as time goes along to discover that we really did not know one hundredth of what we should have understood. Columbus discovered America, but what did he know about its great lakes and rivers and forests, its mountains and deserts, and the wide expanse of its fertile valleys? He died without knowing much about what he discovered. Many times we have discovered something of the love of God, but its heights and depths and lengths and breadths are beyond our understanding. His love is infinitely beyond our experience.

At one time the civil authorities threw the bishop of Paris into prison and condemned him to be shot. Before they led him out to die, he observed that the window in his cell was in the shape of a cross. At the top of the cross he wrote "height," at the bottom "depth," and under each of the two arms "length." He was experiencing in-depth the meaning of the cross:

"When I survey the wondrous cross
On which the Prince of glory died,
My richest gain I count but loss,
And pour contempt on all my pride."
—Isaac Watts

When we want to know and understand the love of God, we should go to Calvary. The cross speaks most eloquently of God's love. There Christ died my death and yours that we might live His life.

HMSR

"YOU DON'T WANT TO HEAR IT!"

He who began a good work in you will carry it on to completion until the day of Christ. . . . So that you may be . . . filled with the fruit of righteousness that comes through Jesus Christ—to the glory and praise of God.
PHIL. 1:6-11, NIV.

When Pastor Lloyd Wyman was director of the Adventist Evangelistic Association, he told an experience to our church. During one of his evangelistic series a woman who had been a member of the church for 20 years asked him to visit her husband. She wanted him to join the church. Lloyd agreed to see her husband, but only on the condition that he would talk to him alone.

As Wyman invited the husband to become a church member, the man replied, "Oh no! Why would I want to do that? My wife comes home and criticizes the pastor and the members. Why should I join a church like that?"

After the visit the wife wanted to know the result. Lloyd answered, "You don't want to hear it!" When she insisted, he told her, then suggested that she begin to look only at the beautiful things happening at church and convey that to her husband. It worked! Before the evangelistic series ended the man gave his heart to Jesus and decided to be baptized. Instead of the woman detracting from Christ, she changed her relationship to Him and was "filled with the fruit of righteousness that comes through Jesus Christ."

Each of us should examine our own lives and ask: Would I want to hear what people have to say about the impressions my conversations have left on them? While we can't change the past easily, we can go to Jesus for help in the present and in the future. We can take refuge and comfort in the promise of Scripture that "he who began a good work in you will carry it on to completion until the day of Christ." It will increase our effectiveness for Jesus one-hundred-fold. "If we would humble ourselves before God, and be kind and courteous and tender-hearted and pitiful, there would be one hundred conversions to the truth where now there is only one" (*Testimonies for the Church,* vol. 9, p. 189).

DRG

"TO LIVE IS CHRIST"

For to me, to live is Christ and to die is gain.
PHIL. 1:21, NIV.

H M.S. Richards was a giant for God through his close relationship to Jesus. The Holy Spirit filled his life and preaching, because, like Paul, his stated purpose was: "for to me, to live is Christ." When he preached, the Holy Spirit moved mightily on his audiences.

It was a great privilege Lillian and I had to work at the Voice of Prophecy with this mighty man of God and his two sons. He once told us that each day when he climbed the hill above his home, he looked out over Glendale and prayed for the lost men, women, and children in his town. By his Christ-centered, Spirit-filled preaching and by his prayers and his exemplary life, he constantly testified that "for to me, to live is Christ."

Paul did not say, "For to me, to live is to preach the gospel." Nor did he declare, "For to me, to live is to do evangelism," or "For me, to live is to raise up churches." Instead the former persecutor and hater of Christians said, "For to me, to live is Christ." Christ now lived in Paul. His life was an example of the lifestyle he wanted for the Philippians. Such a life doesn't result from self-effort—it "comes through Jesus Christ," so "the glory and praise" belong to God (Phil. 1:11, NIV).

The *NIV Study Bible* comments on the passage: "Christ was the source and secret of Paul's continual joy (even in prison), for Paul's life found all its meaning in Christ." Then the commentary adds: "The gain brought by death is 'being with Christ,' so that here Paul is saying that his ultimate concern and most precious possession, both now and forever, is Christ and his relationship to Him."

The good news is that we can all live such a life if we are willing to establish a similar relationship with Jesus. What kind of relationship with Jesus do you desire to have today?

DRG

"TO DIE IS GAIN"

For to me, to live is Christ and to die is gain.
PHIL. 1:21, NIV.

No one knows for certain what was in Paul's mind when he said that "to die is gain." Why would dying be a gain to him? Perhaps after being torn apart inside by mediating the various factions in a divided church, he might feel that falling asleep in Jesus would be preferable to such conflict. On his release from captivity Paul felt duty bound to return to Philippi "so that through my being with you again your joy in Christ Jesus will overflow on account of me" (Phil. 1:26, NIV). The satisfaction would be great for Paul, but the trauma of leading a strife-torn church back to unity in Christ would also be painful.

The apostle's entire life was no picnic. The suspicions of some church leaders constantly concerned him. Judaizers dogged his footsteps. He suffered from what may have been a painful eye disease, possibly from the bright light that blinded him on the Damascus road. And he was in prison for no good reason. Could it be that the thought of relief from all this might have lurked in Paul's mind when he wrote that "to die is gain"? Probably not. Paul's sights were lifted much higher than physical, mental, and emotional torture. His overriding desire was "to depart and be with Christ" (verse 23, NIV). Paul's motivation was not what he would be delivered from, but what he would be delivered to—the very presence of Jesus.

If for us "to live is Christ," then "to die is gain." Why? Because after what will seem just a moment, the next thing we will hear will be the triumphant voice of Jesus awakening us. Death is like a sound sleep without any consciousness of the passage of time until the gentle voice of Jesus wakes us up. H.M.S. Richards compared death to going through a door into a brighter tomorrow where Jesus will welcome us. When Jesus comes, the first face we will see is His. Think of being welcomed by Jesus into a brand-new world and a brand-new life. We can't even begin to imagine what that good news will mean. For "what no eye has ever seen, what no ear has ever heard, what never entered the mind of man, God has prepared all that for those who love him" (1 Cor. 2:9, Moffatt).

DRG

SEPTEMBER 28

REFLECTING THE MIND OF JESUS

> ***Let this mind be in you, which was also in Christ Jesus.***
>
> *PHIL. 2:5.*

In the days before prenuptial agreements I recall reading about a young woman who lived in Chicago. One day she could not have bought a dollar's worth of anything, but the next day she could purchase a thousand dollars' worth of whatever she wanted. What made the difference? She had married a rich husband. The young woman had fallen in love with the man, and all he had became hers. She was involved in part of his life.

Belief in Christ includes involvement. It means accepting His Word with unquestioning obedience. If Jesus says, "This is the way, walk ye in it" (Isa. 30:21), then it is the path I must walk, with no argument, no halfhearted following from a long way off. Should He command, "Love your enemies" (Matt. 5:44), such an attitude must become a natural part of my life. Or if He announced, "I will come again" (John 14:3), then I must direct my whole life to living as if I believe absolutely that His arrival is imminent.

Paul instructs us: "Let this mind be in you, which was also in Christ Jesus." I must become so involved with Jesus that my mind meshes with His. As a result, I must think as He thinks, believe as He believes. His faith must be my faith, His standards my standards. Jesus believed wholeheartedly in the Scriptures as the Word of God. He made no exceptions and no conditions. Christ believed in the resurrection of the dead, in His own visible and literal return, in giving tithes and offerings.

Jesus practiced the law of kindness in forgiving sinful people. When they brought the woman taken in adultery before Jesus and condemned her to die by stoning, Jesus won her to Himself by the sheer force of His compassionate forgiveness.

Even when nailed to the cross, Jesus freely forgave His persecutors and cried out: "Father, forgive them; for they know not what they do" (Luke 23:34). And here is the good news: Jesus extends that same forgiveness to you and me and to all who accept the invitation to think as He thinks, to love as He loves, and to forgive as He forgives. Does your life reveal today that the mind of Jesus is "in you"?

HMSR

THE DEPTHS OF JESUS' LOVE

God exalted him to the highest place and gave him the name that is above every name, that at the name of Jesus every knee should bow, in heaven and on earth and under the earth, and every tongue confess that Jesus Christ is Lord, to the glory of God the Father.

Phil. 2:9-11, NIV.

As a young man, the great painter Quentin Matsys was a blacksmith with hardened, callused hands. He could swing the heavy hammer, and was rough and untutored. Then he fell in love with the beautiful daughter of an artist who laughed at the idea of a blacksmith marrying his highly accomplished, educated daughter.

"You may have my daughter," he said when Matsys asked for her hand, "if you will become a great painter!" The father chuckled to himself; he thought she was safe enough now. Could such a demand stop Matsys' love? He got an easel and some pigment, and he painted for years until he became a recognized artist. Today art galleries around the world exhibit his paintings. When asked how he became so skilled an artist, he answered: "Love made me a painter." And he got the girl, too.

Jesus and Matsys had one character trait in common: they were both motivated to accomplish their objective by love. But there is a great difference as well. Matsys started as an uneducated laborer and became a skilled artist, while Jesus began as God, equal with the Father, and became "nothing, . . . a servant, . . . in human likeness" (Phil. 2:6, 7). He was "a man, . . . obedient to death, . . . on a cross!" (Phil. 2:8, NIV). Herbert Douglass wrote about this text: "Its mind-stretching, heart-tugging focus on the incredible cascade of eternal love poured out in Jesus' becoming man, is unsurpassed in religious literature" *(Adult Sabbath School Lessons,* July 10, 1994).

Jesus too got what He was after—our salvation. Because of His willing humiliation, "God exalted him to the highest place . . . , that at the name of Jesus every knee should bow, . . . and every tongue confess that Jesus Christ is Lord."

HMSR

"THE SURPASSING GREATNESS OF KNOWING CHRIST"

I consider everything a loss compared to the surpassing greatness of knowing Christ Jesus my Lord, for whose sake I have lost all things. I consider them rubbish, that I may gain Christ and be found in him.
PHIL. 3:8, 9, NIV.

In 1847 Dr. James Simpson, a Scottish physician, pioneered the science of anesthesiology when he used chloroform to put patients to sleep during surgery. In his declining years one of his students at the University of Edinburgh asked him, "What do you consider the most valuable discovery of your lifetime?" The student probably expected him to reply, "Discovering the benefits of chloroform for surgery." Instead he answered, "My most valuable discovery was when I discovered that I am a sinner and Jesus Christ is my Saviour."

In a similar viewpoint Paul makes clear in our scriptural passage for today that the most valuable discovery of his lifetime was "the surpassing greatness of knowing Christ Jesus my Lord." When Paul speaks of "knowing Christ," he has in mind a lifelong relationship with Him. Christianity is a relationship. That is Paul's primary point in Philippians 3. His emphasis here is not on knowing facts, but on experiencing an intimate relationship with Jesus, being "found in him."

To drive home his point Paul contrasts those "who glory in Christ" with those who "put confidence in the flesh" (Phil. 3:3, 4, NIV). The apostle uses his own experience before he established a relationship with Christ to illustrate how futile it is to "put confidence in the flesh." A circumcised Jew and a Pharisee, he meticulously kept every detail of the law. "As for legalistic righteousness," he was "faultless" (verse 6).

But when he met Christ, Paul discovered the secret of becoming righteous experimentally "through faith in Christ" (verse 9). The apostle's righteousness now came from establishing a personal, day-by-day, moment-by-moment relationship with Jesus. Allowing Jesus to speak to him through His Word and keeping in constant contact with him through prayer transformed Paul's daily life.

Because of that same "surpassing greatness of knowing Christ," Jesus can do for us what He did for Paul.

DRG

THE MASTER ARTIST

For [God] chose us in [Christ] before the creation of the world to be holy and blameless in his sight. In love he predestined us to be adopted as his sons through Jesus Christ . . . to the praise of his glorious grace, which he has freely given us in the One he loves.
Eph. 1:4-6, NIV.

Driving through New England in early October, one finds that every hill, valley, and tree along the roads is alive with a riot of color. The maples, white birches, elms, and a dozen other trees and shrubs, and even the ground cover, are on fire. The leaves vary from bright yellow to deep amber and from bright orange to deep red. Some trees meld all these colors into a unique pattern. The variety of colors, their brilliance, and their abundance can lead to no other conclusion than that God is the Master Artist. Viewing them is truly a spiritual experience.

On Sabbath evening a fabulous sunset viewed from Cadillac Mountain, the highest point in Acadia National Park in Maine, led me again to conclude that God is the Master Artist. The Master Artist also paints portraits. As Christians we are portraits "to the praise of his glorious grace." All that the Master Artist does to transform a filthy sinner into a Christlike saint is a miracle of "his glorious grace."

What makes the portrait of a Christian possible? Jesus! God "chose us in [Christ] before the creation of the world to be holy and blameless in his sight. In love he predestined us to be adopted as his sons through Jesus Christ . . . to the praise of his glorious grace, which he has freely given us in the One he loves."

How much did creating Christian portraits cost Jesus? It demanded His very life blood. "In him we have redemption through his blood, the forgiveness of sins, in accordance with the riches of God's grace that he lavished on us" (Eph. 1:7, 8, NIV). Before He died, Jesus shouldered the sins of the world so "the forgiveness of sins" can be ours. The character of Jesus mirrored in the life of a Christian is a portrait that reveals "the praise of [God's] glorious grace."

Have you sat for the Master Artist? Is your life a portrait that depicts Jesus to those about you? He wants to paint your portrait in His image today.

DRG

OCTOBER 2

A CHRISTIAN'S PROFIT AND LOSS STATEMENT

But whatever was to my profit I now consider loss for the sake of Christ. What is more, I consider everything a loss compared to the surpassing greatness of knowing Christ Jesus my Lord, for whose sake I have lost all things. I consider them rubbish, that I may gain Christ and be found in him.

Phil. 3:7-9, NIV.

When Lillian and I reminisce about the tremendous people who have been our personal friends, we marvel at the opportunity God has given us to associate with some of the world's greats. During our many years at the Voice of Prophecy, H.M.S. Richards would come to my office and talk with me, or I would go to his study at the back of his home and drink in the marvelous insights and inspiration that flowed from his heart. When I told an international radio broadcaster, "I manage the Voice of Prophecy," he said, "Oh, that man Richards, he is the preacher's preacher!" Pastor Richards continually inspired me and warmed my soul by the way he uplifted Jesus, and for that I will be forever grateful. His power as a preacher and his charm as a person was that he, like Paul, considered "everything a loss compared to the surpassing greatness of knowing Christ Jesus." "Knowing Christ," being "found in him," meant everything to both Paul and Pastor Richards. It transformed the two men and made their lives fulfilling—and worth living.

In his message to the church at Philippi, Paul draws up a personal profit and loss statement. On the loss side he places his former self as a faultless Hebrew Pharisee with a "legalistic righteousness" (Phil. 3:5, 6, NIV). On the profit side he received "the righteousness that comes from God and is by faith" (verse 9, NIV). How did the books balance out? When Paul put the dust of his own righteousness on the scales, it did not make even a quiver, but the greatness of Jesus' righteousness on the profit side caused the scales to hit bottom.

The greatness of Jesus does not stop with our receiving righteousness from "knowing Christ" by faith. Those who "know Christ and the power of his resurrection" will also "attain to the resurrection from the dead"—will have eternal life (verses 10, 11, NIV). Talk about profit and loss—what a fantastic exchange!

DRG

THE POWER OF CHRIST'S RESURRECTION

I want to know Christ and the power of his resurrection and the fellowship of sharing in his sufferings, becoming like him in his death, and so, somehow, to attain to the resurrection from the dead.
Phil. 3:10, 11, NIV.

In the Voice of Prophecy Bible school we often witness the "power of [Christ's] resurrection" in letters like this one from Debby: "You've done the most fantastic job with people I would have written off as faithless losers (including myself). You helped one friend find the way out of drugs; you helped another friend find her way out of her seemingly useless existence (she was a self-made atheist and proud of it). Although I wasn't an atheist, I didn't know how to communicate with God, and I would have never guessed that it was through Jesus Christ. But I've found Him, and I've never been so happy in all of my 17 years. Thank you!"

Debby and her friends found the only solution for those helplessly trapped in sin: "to know Christ and the power of his resurrection."

Christians often wonder what is their part and what is God's part in the Christian walk. Jesus told us to "make every effort to enter through the narrow door," and if we stand "firm to the end [we] will be saved" (Luke 13:24; Matt. 24:13, NIV). The context of both passages reveals that we are to do these things by faith—by totally responding to Christ's power working in us as a result of our relationship with Him.

Because of Jesus' death and resurrection, He can clear the tally of our sins in heaven and replace it with the record of His righteous life. That is the objective side of righteousness by faith. Then, as we fellowship with Christ day by day, the risen Christ empowers us to live the Christian life. And that is the subjective side of righteousness by faith. Both justification and sanctification, the objective and subjective sides of a Christian's righteousness, are Jesus' doings, not ours. Not what we do, but what "the power of his resurrection" does in and through us is the motivating force behind all our activities.

Here is more good news: the same power Jesus used to conquer death and the grave is available to each of us today, assuring us of attaining "the resurrection from the dead."

DRG

OCTOBER 4

THE NEWS THAT TRANSFORMS US

Rejoice in the Lord always. I will say it again: Rejoice! Let your gentleness be evident to all. The Lord is near. Do not be anxious about anything, but in everything, by prayer and petition, with thanksgiving, present your requests to God. And the peace of God, which transcends all understanding, will guard your hearts and your minds in Christ Jesus.
Phil. 4:4-7, NIV.

Did Paul himself live up to his admonition that he sent to the church at Philippi? A prisoner in Rome, he served an undetermined sentence for a crime he didn't commit. He had every human reason to be down in the mouth. Yet he writes that we should rejoice, be gentle, not be anxious, be thankful, be at peace, and think only right thoughts (Phil. 4:8). It was a tall order to follow, even for those at Philippi who were not under arrest.

What was Paul's secret? He was living "in Christ Jesus." His relationship with Jesus was his secret weapon. "The peace of God, which transcends all understanding," guarded the avenues to and from his mind and heart. A relationship with Jesus kept him going despite extremely trying circumstances.

Only a stable relationship with Jesus can make possible such actions and attitudes. "Circumstances have but little to do with the experiences of the soul. It is the spirit cherished which gives coloring to all our actions. A man at peace with God and his fellow men cannot be made miserable. . . . The heart in harmony with God is lifted above the annoyances and trials of this life. But a heart where the peace of Christ is not, is unhappy, full of discontent; the person sees defects in everything, and he would bring discord into the most heavenly music" (*Testimonies for the Church,* vol. 5, p. 488).

If Paul has not described your present attitude toward life—if you are still struggling with yourself—do not feel downcast or discouraged. By improving your relationship with Jesus "the peace of God, which transcends all understanding, will guard your hearts and your minds in Christ Jesus."

DRG

PSYCHOLOGICAL NEUROLOGICAL IMMUNIZATION

And the peace of God, which surpasses all understanding, will guard your hearts and minds through Christ Jesus.
PHIL. 4:7, NKJV.

A medical intern said to a nurse, "I'm never sick, so I can't understand why I caught this cold." The nurse responded, "Are you kidding, with all the stress you have been under?"

That intern is now a practicing psychiatrist with many years of experience. He explains the meaning of the medical abbreviation PNI: psychological neurological immunization. The psychological (what we say and do) affects the neurological (the brain and nervous system) and can either strengthen or weaken our immune system.

Although it is a relatively new concept in modern medicine, the concept is as old as the Bible. Paul clearly points out that "the peace of God" received through a relationship with Jesus has a profound effect on the entire being—"your hearts and minds." The book of Proverbs defines precisely the connection between spiritual health and a healthy body: "Fear the Lord and depart from evil. It will be health to your flesh, and strength to your bones" (Prov. 3:7, 8, NKJV). "Listen, son of mine, to what I say. . . . Keep these thoughts ever in mind; let them penetrate deep within your heart, for they will mean real life for you, and radiant health" (Prov. 4:20-22, TLB). "A heart at peace gives life to the body, but envy rots the bones" (Prov. 14:30, NIV).

Ellen G. White endorsed the concept that emotional and spiritual health are powerful factors toward keeping us physically healthy: "The relation that exists between the mind and the body is very intimate. When one is affected, the other sympathizes. The condition of the mind affects the health to a far greater degree than many realize. Many of the diseases from which men suffer are the result of mental depression. Grief, anxiety, discontent, remorse, guilt, distrust, all tend to break down the life forces, and to invite decay and death" (*The Ministry of Healing,* p. 241).

"Through Christ Jesus" the promise is ours: "the peace of God, which surpasses all understanding, will guard your hearts and minds."

DRG

OCTOBER 6

HELP FOR EVERY TIME OF NEED—1

But my God shall supply all your need according to his riches in glory by Christ Jesus.

Phil. 4:19.

A friend lamented, "My life is so empty." She went on to tell her tale of woes: a job she didn't enjoy, an abusive husband, a battle with headaches, and . . . What my friend needed was Jesus. What Jesus has done and is doing for each person makes it possible for God to "supply all your need according to his riches in glory." Jesus will equip us with whatever it takes to enable us to cope with every problem we face.

J. L. Shuler, often spoken of as the man who organized Seventh-day Adventist evangelism, wrote a Good News tract entitled "Help for Every Time of Need." Though composed more than 50 years ago, its message is fresh and up-to-date today. Here are some excerpts:

"We bring you the good news that no matter what condition you are in, regardless of what situation you face, and despite the circumstances that surround you, there is a promise in God's Book to fit your case, and bring you just the help you need.

"Does life seem vain and empty? Does the evil one suggest that death ends everything forever? That is the time to let the voice of Jesus be heard in the most wondrous promise: 'For God so loved the world, that he gave his only begotten Son, that whosoever believeth in him should not perish, but have everlasting life' (John 3:16).

"Are you troubled over wrong things you have done? Does your conscience smite you with guilt? Here is God's promise for you: 'Come now, and let us reason together, saith the Lord: though your sins be as scarlet, they shall be as white as snow; though they be red like crimson, they shall be as wool' (Isa. 1:18).

"Are there times of perplexity in your life, when you are puzzled as to which course you should follow? Here is a promise from God's Book that exactly fits this condition:

" 'I will instruct thee and teach thee in the way which thou shalt go: I will guide thee with mine eye' (Ps. 32:8)." Whatever your need is today, Jesus will supply it.

DRG

HELP FOR EVERY TIME OF NEED—2

I can do all things through Christ which strengtheneth me.
PHIL. 4:13, KJV.

Yesterday we discovered that God supplies our every need through Jesus. Today's passage drives home the point that we can face trials and problems with assurance because Christ strengthens us. Here are more reassuring promises from J. L. Shuler's Good News tract:

"Do you feel lonely? Does it seem at times as though everybody has forsaken you? Does even God seem far away? This is the time you need to know and use Matthew 28:20 and Hebrews 13:5.

"The Lord Jesus says to you: 'Lo, I am with you alway, even unto the end of the world.' 'I will never leave thee, nor forsake thee.'

"Remember that in these promises, the Lord is speaking to you individually just as though you could hear His audible voice addressing you. It is your privilege to take these promises and put your name into the promise in place of the 'you' or 'thee.'

"Do you long for perfect peace, unruffled, and undisturbed by the vexations of life? Here is the way to secure it:

" 'Thou wilt keep him in perfect peace, whose mind is stayed on thee: because he trusteth in thee' (Isa. 26:3).

"Are you facing an unusually trying situation in the matter of physical impairment? Do your surroundings and the daily grind get on your nerves? There is help for you in this promise:

" 'He said unto me, My grace is sufficient for thee' (2 Cor. 12:9).

"Does some subtle temptation lie in your path? Are you encountering such severe temptations that you feel you cannot withstand them? Here is your special promise:

" 'There hath no temptation taken you but such as is common to man: but God is faithful, who will not suffer you to be tempted above that ye are able' (1 Cor. 10:13).

"Does everything seem to go against you, and you have so many troubles that you feel overwhelmed? Are you burdened with a load of care? . . .

" 'Cast thy burden upon the Lord, and he shall sustain thee: he shall never suffer the righteous to be moved' (Ps. 55:22)."

Jesus has a promise to meet our every need today, and He is with us to give us help and strength in time of need.

DRG

OCTOBER 8

THE SUPREMACY OF CHRIST—1

He is the image of the invisible God, the firstborn over all creation. For by him were all things created: things in heaven and on earth, visible and invisible, whether thrones or powers or rulers or authorities; all things were created by him and for him. He is before all things, and in him all things hold together.

Col. 1:15-17, NIV.

At the beginning of the twentieth century T. Dewitt Talmage was a popular preacher. During his last illness, his son asked, "Father, what do you believe in now?" He replied: "When I began to preach, I had many themes to preach. Now I am about to die, and I have just one: I am a great sinner, but Jesus is a great Saviour!"

Doctrines are important. Like beams of sunlight that radiate from the sun, each true doctrine is a beam of Sonlight that centers in Jesus, the Son of God. True doctrine reflects some vital aspect of the character of a God who comes into a personal relationship with us through Jesus, the living center of all doctrine.

Colossians 1:15-20 declares Jesus' superiority over all other beings in the universe. In the passage Paul points out great truths that establish Christ's supremacy.

1. "By him all things were created." Though a man, Christ participated with the Father and the Holy Spirit in the creation of our world (Gen. 1:1, 2; Heb. 1:1-3).

2. "He is the image of the invisible God." Writers have compared Jesus to a portrait or photograph of God. But Jesus is much more: He is God and equal with the Father. Yet He is also a human being. By becoming a man like us we can see in a real, living individual what God is like. Jesus is not a still photograph, but a warm, living, breathing person. Having experienced our hopes and longings, He understands and knows our needs.

DRG

THE SUPREMACY OF CHRIST—2

> *He is before all things, and in him all things hold together. . . . He is the beginning and the firstborn from among the dead, so that in everything he might have the supremacy.*
> COL. 1:17, 18, NIV.

Some time ago we received a flyer in the mail headed "Paid Advertisement." It headlined: "At least 513 eyewitnesses. A high-level government cover-up to hide the truth. Convincing documentation. And last, but most compelling, an empty tomb. Makes you wonder how anyone could not believe!"

These headlines caught my imagination, so I read on: "More than Easter bunnies and colored eggs, Easter is the celebration of two historical events, the death and the resurrection of Jesus of Nazareth. We believe Jesus died and rose again to enable us to have a restored relationship with God. Because of His resurrection He offers forgiveness, peace with God, and eternal life to those who accept this freely offered gift.

"If the resurrection of Jesus were a hoax, a myth or a hallucination, faith in Christ would be worthless and, as Paul the apostle said, Christians of all people would be most pitied. However, the resurrection of Jesus has been well documented historically, and provides strong reasons for each of us to consider the truth of His claims for our life."

Next to this declaration appear the names of 62 professionals—professors, physicians, scientists, engineers, secretaries, and others—who affirm: "We believe He is risen."

Paul also believed all this and more. In fact, the majesty of the Resurrection is Paul's next point in His declaration of the supremacy of Christ in Colossians 1:15-20.

3. "He is the beginning and the firstborn from among the dead, so that in everything he might have the supremacy."

4. "He is before all things." Jesus is the I Am who has existed as God from eternity (John 8:58).

5. "And in him all things hold together." Christ is the glue that holds the universe together.

DRG

THE SUPREMACY OF CHRIST—3

And he is the head of the body, the church; he is the beginning and the firstborn from among the dead, so that in everything he might have the supremacy. For God was pleased to have all his fullness dwell in him, and through him to reconcile to himself all things, whether things on earth or things in heaven, by making peace through his blood, shed on the cross.

Col. 1:18-20, NIV.

The six verses in Colossians 1:15-20 describing the supremacy of Christ focus on the incredible characteristics that set Jesus apart from any other human being who has ever lived on earth. Let's continue our look at the points that Paul makes in these verses.

6. "He is the head of the body, the church." Our head controls our circulatory, digestive, respiratory, and nervous systems. Without our head, we could not live. As its head, Christ is the life of the church. Thus without Jesus, the church would be dead or at best just another social club.

7. Jesus made "peace through his blood, shed on the cross." The fear that caused Adam and Eve to hide from God, the enmity that separated humanity from deity, melted at the cross. Murderers, thieves, adulterers, soldiers, and ordinary citizens who were far from God and fighting against allowing Him in their lives were drawn to him "through his blood, shed on the cross." Seeing such love come into focus on the cross also attracts us to Jesus.

8. Most important for us, because of Christ's supremacy, God can "reconcile to himself all things," including you and me. Jesus died and rose again to enable us to have a restored relationship with God, and He provides a strong reason for each of us to consider His claims on our life.

No wonder Paul exclaimed, "Christ is all" (Col. 3:11, NIV). Is He "all" in your life? Is He everything to you? Are you experiencing a close relationship with Christ? Is He supreme in your life?

DRG

JESUS OUR CREATOR

Christ himself is the Creator who made everything in heaven and earth, the things we can see and the things we can't; the spirit world with its kings and kingdoms, its rulers and authorities; all were made by Christ for His own use and glory.
Col. 1:16, TLB.

On a dark night the human eye can detect about 3,000 stars. We can see only a few planets, for nearly all of what we call stars are really giant suns. Beyond the stars looms the misty cloud of the Milky Way, the galaxy our world belongs to. Some telescopes can detect billions of galaxies, but only a few of them, including Andromeda, are barely visible to the naked eye. The vastness of the universe "made by Christ" is beyond understanding.

What is even more incomprehensible to us is that Jesus "became a human being and lived here on earth among us and was full of loving forgiveness and truth" (John 1:14, TLB). Our Creator became a human being—a mere atomic particle compared to the vastness of His creation.

Astronaut James B. Irwin went to the moon in 1971 and returned a changed person. Although he had grown up in a Christian environment and still prayed, he was not close to the Lord. As he contemplated the vast universe on his flight to the moon, it transformed his life. In his book *To Rule the Night* he says that he came "back to earth a different person, bound for a higher flight" (p. 185). He recounts: "As we reached out in a physical way to the heavens, we were moved spiritually. As we flew into space, we had a new sense of ourselves, of the earth, and of the nearness of God. We were outside of ordinary reality; I sensed the beginning of some sort of change taking place inside of me. . . . On the moon the total picture of the power of God and His son Jesus Christ became abundantly clear to me" (pp. 6, 7).

The Creator who made the starry heavens came to our world to make new hearts in people like James Irwin. Not only celebrities such as Irwin, but the people we eat with, the young people we meet on the street, the neighbor who lives next door—all feel God's ability to transform. Jesus exercises His creative power every day in our hearts, making life worth living by changing our lives.

DRG

OCTOBER 12

RECONCILED BY THE CROSS

For God was pleased to have all fullness dwell in [Christ], and through him to reconcile to himself all things, whether things on earth or things in heaven, by making peace through his blood, shed on the cross.

Col. 1:19, 20, NIV.

On His way to Calvary Jesus collapsed under the crushing weight of the cross. A stranger passing must have turned a sympathetic gaze toward the suffering Saviour. In any case, the soldiers quickly conscripted him. Simon the Cyrenian had heard the cry, "Make way for the King of the Jews." He had drawn near to see what was going on, and suddenly he found himself compelled to carry the cross.

Mark 15:21 speaks of Simon as the father of Alexander and Rufus, who evidently later became prominent figures in the apostolic church (see Rom. 16:13). It must be that Simon's carrying the cross that terrible day led to his conversion and changed his life. You might say that he was reconciled by the cross, just as Jesus reconciles us to God through the cross.

The cross Simon helped to carry did not belong to Jesus; it really belonged to Simon himself, and to you and me, and to every person who has ever lived on earth. We must never forget that Jesus trudged to Calvary to die for our sins. He took our evil, our pride—our sins—and asks us to take His holiness, His purity, His righteousness, as a blessed gift. "Without the shedding of blood there is no forgiveness" for our sins (Heb. 9:22, NIV). But thanks to the blood Jesus shed, the only sins for which we will ever have to suffer are those we refuse to let God pardon.

Almost 2,000 years ago the God of heaven called the universe to witness a strange yet wonderful act. In the midst of the jeering crowd and the agonies of Calvary and the mysterious darkness that covered Jerusalem, Jesus reconciled the entire universe to God by making "peace through his blood, shed on the cross." He took our sins and those of the whole world and consumed them in the fire of His love until not one trace of them remained. God's forgiveness and our salvation through a loving Saviour are free—but they cost all that Heaven could give.

HMSR

REFLECTING THE FULLNESS OF CHRIST

For in Christ all the fullness of the Deity lives in bodily form, and you have been given fullness in Christ, who is the head over every power and authority.

Col. 2:9, 10, NIV.

The Associated Press released this story about Ian O'Gorman's fifth-grade classmates in Vista, California. When Ian was diagnosed with cancer and began chemotherapy, he had his head shaved when his hair started to fall out. If you had gone to his school, you would have seen many of his classmates also running around with bald heads. When Ian became bald, the other boys went to a barber together and had their heads shaved. When asked why, one of them said, "We just wanted to make him feel better and not left out." Their teacher Jim Alter was so pleased that he had his own head shaved. "They're showing the world what kids can do," he commented. "People think kids are going downhill. Not these kids! They are the best."

What the kids did reminds us of something Jesus would do. He was "the fullness of the Deity," yet He came to our world "in bodily form," becoming like us. Christ wanted to reveal through a genuine, living person the love that motivated Him to redeem humanity. Jesus longed for us to see the extent to which He would go to supply everything necessary for us.

In the way Jesus treated people, we see the fullness of the Deity's empathizing love. By the way we live as Christians, we can reflect the "fullness" of Christ. How is this possible?

1. By "putting off of the sinful nature" (Col. 2:11, NIV), we experience the miracle of being dead *to* sin, rather than being dead *in* sin.

2. By being "raised with [Christ] through your faith in the power of God," you become alive (verse 12, NIV). "When you were dead in your sins . . . , God made you alive with Christ" (verse 13, NIV).

3. By delivering us from a legalistic way of thinking, Jesus enriches our lives and equips us to reflect His fullness (verse 14, NIV).

4. By disarming "the powers and authorities" through making "a public spectacle of them, triumphing over them by the cross" (verse 15, NIV), Jesus armed us for the lifelong battle of triumphing over the devil's attempt to mar our reflection of the "fullness" of Christ.

With Jesus in our hearts, how can we fail!

DRG

JESUS AND THE OCCULT EXPLOSION

Then, having drawn the sting of all the powers ranged against us, he exposed them, shattered, empty and defeated, in his own triumphant victory.
COL. 2:15, PHILLIPS.

Today we are witnessing an explosion of the occult. The term *occult* means something hidden, obscure, out of sight, mysterious. It includes what we call astrology, divination, magic, incantations, and all kinds of arcane speculation and theory. Occultism, therefore, refers to belief in hidden or mysterious powers and the possibility of human control of them or of being controlled by them.

On the radio, TV, and in books and magazines we see featured New Age channelers, astrology, tarot cards, and out-of-body experiences. Universities and hospitals across the country are studying psychic phenomena, astro-projection, and extrasensory perception. One modern seer has sold millions of copies of her books on esoteric prophecy. Concepts of self-realization such as scientology and nonverbal sensitivity groups are attracting growing interest. Yoga mysteries, macrobiotic diets, and spiritual fasts have extended the theologies and theogonies of the East into the West.

Even religious leaders, college professors, and scientific investigators are studying psychic phenomena. Where will it all lead? The Bible in many places condemns tampering with the occult. "Our fight is not against human foes, but against cosmic powers, against the authorities and potentates of this dark world, against the superhuman forces of evil" (Eph. 6:12, NEB). This great confederacy of evil but powerful beings bitterly opposes Christ.

The New Testament pictures Jesus in conflict with evil beings. At the cross He defeated Satan, his angels, and all others involved in occult phenomena: "Having drawn the sting of all the powers ranged against us, he exposed them, shattered, empty and defeated, in his own triumphant victory." The only defense against the occult explosion is not philosophy, science, or a new religion—but Jesus.

HMSR

CHRIST IS ALL

Christ is all and in all.
Col. 3:11, NKJV.

Polycarp, bishop of Smyrna who lived in the early part of the second century, was brought as an old man before the Roman governor.

"We will banish you," the governor threatened.

The old man replied, "Well, you cannot do that, for I am at home wherever Christ is.""Then I will take away your property."

"But I have none. And if I had, and you took it away, I would still be rich, for I have Christ," Polycarp said.

"Well, then, I will take away your good name," the governor roared.

"That is gone already," said the undisturbed old Christian, "for I have long since reckoned it a great joy to be counted as the offscouring of all things for Christ's sake."

"Then I will put you in prison."

"You may do as you please," Polycarp responded, "but I will always be free, for where Christ is there is perfect liberty."

Finally the governor proclaimed, "Then I will take away your life."

"Long ago I hid it with Christ in God, and when the glad resurrection morning dawns, I shall live forever with Him in glory."

The Roman governor kept this threat, sacrificing Polycarp's life because the bishop believed in Christ.

Polycarp's testimony mirrored his conviction that "Christ is all and in all." He believed in the reality of Jesus Christ and committed his entire life fully to Him. To Polycarp Jesus was everything, the all-sufficient Saviour.

Each one of us is privileged to make Christ real in our life. In fact, every activity of life can reflect the fact that Christ is present, that He walks by our side. That He is "all and in all," that He is everything to us. "All that can satisfy the needs and longings of the human soul, for this world and for the world to come, is found in Christ" (*Christ's Object Lessons,* p. 115). Putting Christ first in my life witnesses to others that I believe Him to be my constant companion, an indispensable necessity in my life.

HMSR

OCTOBER 16

JESUS CHANGED EVERYTHING

For if we believe that Jesus died and rose again, even so God will bring with Him those who sleep in Jesus.
1 Thess. 4:14, NKJV.

The catacombs—great rooms and passageways on up to six levels—under the city of Rome ran far beyond the ancient city limits. The citizens of Rome entombed multitudes there through the centuries. Thousands were buried in the catacombs long before Christ's birth. One can read the pagan epitaphs there, such as "Goodbye, Mother; goodbye forever." "Farewell, sweetheart; I'll never see you again."

But that changed after Christ came and Christians began burying their dead in the sides of those endless passageways. Then we find epitaphs that read something like this: "Goodbye, Mother; I'll see you when Jesus comes." "Farewell, friend, until the morning of the resurrection." "I'll see you again, sweetheart, and we will never part again."

Jesus changed everything. He gave us a divine hope. No wonder the apostle says we are not to "sorrow as others who have no hope" (1 Thess. 4:13, NKJV). Why not? "For if we believe that Jesus died and rose again, even so God will bring with Him those who sleep in Jesus."

Deep in the heart of every human being resides the conviction that death is not the end. And just as God the Father brought Jesus our Saviour back from the dead on the morning of His resurrection in the garden outside the wall of Jerusalem, so with Him He will bring our beloved dead to life again when He comes the second time. And those who are asleep and those who are awake alike "shall all be changed" (1 Cor. 15:51, NKJV). How? Gradually? No. "In a moment" (verse 52, NKJV). God will make our corruptible bodies incorruptible, and our mortal bodies will put on immortality (verse 53, NKJV).

When Jesus Christ rose from the dead long ago, He settled the death question forever. And He made our resurrection certain. In John 6 four times Christ promised, "I will raise him up at the last day." God accepted Christ's sacrifice on the cross, and His resurrection was God's amen to that mighty deed. Yes, Jesus changed everything. He altered the future from a dead-end street to a blessed promise, a divine hope.

HMSR

LORD OF SPACE

> *For the Lord Himself will descend from heaven with a shout. . . . And the dead in Christ will rise first. Then we who are alive and remain shall be caught up together with them in the clouds to meet the Lord in the air. And thus we shall always be with the Lord.*
>
> *1 Thess. 4:16, 17, NKJV.*

When we consider space travel, we think of speed. For example, let's take a jet flight from Los Angeles to Boston. Our flying speed will be about 600 miles per hour at an altitude of 33,000 feet. But if we are to get anywhere in outer space, we must be able to travel at least at the speed of light. Light hurtles at the rate of 186,282 miles per second. But even at that speed it would take us 4.3 years to travel to Alpha Centauri, the sun nearest to our sun. We would be journeying only through a minuscule part of our own galaxy, and literally billions of other galaxies exist beyond. Humanity has made strides toward exploring nearby space, but really our efforts are meaningless in comparison to the vast universe beyond.

When Christ descends from heaven and the angels catch us up to meet the Lord in the air, I wonder how fast we will travel when we start our space journey with Jesus. I have often thought about how it will feel to travel through space and see the planets and stars at close range. Of course, not everyone will be taking this trip, so it will be a real privilege, something extraordinary. It will not be anything we can achieve by rocket power, for only believers in Jesus will participate in the event. No dangers will befall us because of lack of oxygen or proper nutrition. Nor will we have to worry about our vital functions, because "we shall all be changed, in a moment, in the twinkling of an eye" (1 Cor. 15:51, 52).

How do we reserve a place on God's space flight to our heavenly home? "As many as received him, to them gave he power to become the sons of God, even to them that believe on his name" (John 1:12). That's the ticket that makes it possible for us to take this journey through space. So believe and receive the Lord of space as Saviour and King of your life.

HMSR

OCTOBER 18

CHRIST'S RELATIONSHIP TO HIS FATHER

Beyond all question, the mystery of godliness is great: He appeared in a body, was vindicated by the Spirit, was seen of angels, was preached among the nations, was believed on in the world, was taken up in glory.
1 TIM. 3:16, NIV.

The other day I read in Calvin's *Institutes of the Christian Religion* what he said about God and Christ and their relationship. The Reformation theologian considered it one of the great mysteries of Scripture and that we should be careful what we say about it. "On this, . . . we ought to philosophize with great sobriety and moderation; and also with extreme caution, lest either our ideas or our language should proceed beyond the limits of the Divine word. For how can the infinite essence of God be defined by the narrow capacity of the human mind?" I think that is a good rule for all of us to follow.

Of course, hundreds of passages of Scripture do reveal Christ's relationship to His Father. Let's look at a few. Christ affirmed that He is "the Son of the living God" (Matt. 16:16, NKJV). He declared that He raises the dead as does the Father (John 5:21). We are to honor the Son as we do the Father (verse 23). Jesus said that to know Him is to know the Father (John 14:7-9). Just as the Father has life in Himself so does Jesus (John 5:26). The personal name of God given in the Old Testament the New Testament applies to Christ. The word translated "Lord," Yahweh—sometimes pronounced Jehovah—and used in Psalm 102:22 Hebrews 1:10-12 employs of Jesus. Just as our text today says, Jesus is actually God revealed in human flesh: "Beyond all question, the mystery of godliness is great: He appeared in a body."

Understanding Jesus' relationship to His Father is important. Equally vital is understanding our relationship to Jesus. When Jesus "appeared in a body, [He] was vindicated by the Spirit, was seen of angels, was preached among the nations, was believed on in the world, was taken up in glory." And as believers in Jesus, we are "sons of God" and "joint heirs with Christ" (Rom. 8:14-17).

How essential it is to daily cultivate a relationship with our infinite God!

HMSR

MAKING JESUS ATTRACTIVE

Make the teaching about God our Savior attractive. For the grace of God that brings salvation has appeared to all men.
Titus 2:10, 11, NIV.

It never ceases to amaze me to see what people can become through God's grace. As director of the Voice of Prophecy Bible schools in Singapore and then in North America, I witnessed such miracles take place in the lives of many of the students.

An alcoholic took one of our Bible courses. Years later he wrote to us: "One time I was a drunkard. One day after leaving the saloon, I saw a card in the gutter. I picked it up, filled it out, and received my first true knowledge of Christ. This is when my life changed. Shortly after taking your course, I gave my heart to God, and I lost the taste of whiskey and joined the church." Such is the powerful transformation in the life of a despairing drunkard touched by the gracious gift of God's Son. A new life such as his is a miracle of grace.

In presenting Jesus to those who need Him, we must make "God our Savior attractive." What enables us to do this? "The grace of God that brings salvation . . . to all men."

What does God's grace do for us? "It teaches us to say 'No' to ungodliness and worldly passion, and to live self-controlled, upright and godly lives" (Titus 2:12, NIV).

Our crucified and risen Saviour does more than forgive our sins. Grace led Jesus to give "himself for us to redeem us from all wickedness and to purify for himself a people that are his very own" (verse 14, NIV). Jesus releases us from guilt, then plants His love in our hearts and transforms our life by making us "eager to do what is good" (verse 14, NIV). Being saved is not just a passing thing, because the good news changes the life. And that new life certainly makes "God our Savior attractive" to others.

Dwight L. Moody, a powerful evangelist at the end of the nineteenth century, once wrote: "Of one hundred men, one will read the Bible; the ninety-nine will read the Christian." Does my life make "God our Savior attractive"?

DRG

OCTOBER 20

THE GREATEST OF ALL MIRACLES

> *God, who at various times and in different ways spoke in time past to the fathers by the prophets, has in these last days spoken to us by His Son, whom He has appointed heir of all things.*
>
> *Heb. 1:1, 2, NKJV.*

I believe in miracles. I believe that Christ fed 5,000 persons from five loaves and two fish and that He actually walked on water. And I believe that He healed the paralytic. Yes, I believe in miracles, even though many people think the miracle stories in the Bible must be just quaint ways of conveying spiritual truth and that we should not take them literally. If we believe in God's existence, then we should have no problem with miracles, because He is by definition all-powerful.

It is a philosophical truth that unless God should choose to reveal Himself to us, we could never know about Him. He is far beyond our ability to perceive. I believe that He has historically revealed Himself to us through Jesus Christ, that God has "spoken to us by His Son." Many find it difficult to believe that a human being could become God. I agree—but I can believe that God became a human being instead.

As we study the life of Jesus, we find that He was different from anyone else who has ever existed. He is the only person known to history who presented Himself as divine and yet has been considered sane by much of the human race. The founders of other religious systems, such as Islam, Buddhism, or Hinduism, did not claim to be God in the flesh.

While Jesus lived on earth He convinced multitudes of all ages, races, and walks of life that His claims to divinity were genuine. The Bible records His miraculous works: the water turned into wine, the nobleman's son healed, the centurion's servant healed, devils cast out, Peter's mother-in-law healed, dropsy cured, Lazarus raised from the dead. Every miracle that Jesus performed indicated His divinity—God speaking to us through His Son. Jesus' life, God in human flesh living in us and transforming our lives, is the greatest of all miracles.

HMSR

JESUS TASTED DEATH FOR YOU

But we see Jesus, who was made a little lower than the angels, for the suffering of death crowned with glory and honor, that He, by the grace of God, might taste death for everyone.
HEB. 2:9, NKJV.

I watched 50 worshipers with two long ropes pull a float down the main street of Chiang Mai, Thailand. A money tree, surrounded by offerings of food in silver bowls, was the central feature of the float. Occasionally the procession stopped and a dozen girls formed in front of the float and danced a Thai finger dance. After the dance the girls took their place along each side of the street. Each girl held a silver bowl. To gain merit, devoted Buddhists dropped offerings into the silver bowls or walked out to the float and attached paper money to the money tree. Since Thailand's Buddhists believe in reincarnation—that each person must pay in the next life for the sins of the present one—they hope that by gaining merit each worshiper will be born into a higher form and more prosperous state in the next life.

They do not understand that God's grace saves us from our past. Christ's death annuls the sinner's guilt, cancels the record of past sins. Peace, assurance, and joy then follow (Rom. 5:1, 2).

God's grace saves us in the present. Christ not only puts us into a right relationship with God at our conversion, but keeps us in it from day to day. "There is therefore now no condemnation for those who are in Christ Jesus" (Rom. 8:1, RSV).

Also God's saving grace assures those of us who are in Christ of a bright future. Not only does Christ free us from sin's penalty and power, but someday God will remove us from its presence. God's "free gift is eternal life through Jesus Christ our Lord" (Rom. 6:23, Phillips).

How can we enter into a right relationship with God? Only one way. God's gift of grace is "to be received by faith" (Rom. 3:25, RSV). Faith is "looking unto Jesus" (Heb. 12:2), the simplest definition of faith in the entire Bible. If we will just look to Jesus we will be saved by God's gift of grace.

DRG

HOLD FAST TO JESUS

Seeing then that we have a great High Priest who has passed through the heavens, Jesus the Son of God. . . . Let us therefore come boldly to the throne of grace, that we may obtain mercy and find grace to help in time of need.

Heb. 4:14-16, NKJV.

S. D. Gordon tells about a college in the American Midwest having financial difficulty. A professor went to a distant city to request a donation from a wealthy man. As he entered the outer office a former student that he had once taken a special interest in now greeted the professor. The college teacher hadn't realized the wealthy businessman was the father of his former student.

After the young man greeted his professor, he immediately ushered him into his father's office. With all the assurance of a son who is on good terms with his father, he said, "Father, here is an old friend of mine. He's all right. Please give him whatever he wants."

The businessman hardly glanced up. Reaching for his checkbook, he mumbled, "How much do you want?" The professor managed to blurt out the needed amount. With check in hand he soon found himself out on the street with a spring in his step, praising God for His guiding hand.

Jesus, the eternal mediator, is always ready to usher us into His Father's presence. And because Jesus is "the Son of God," His Father responds, "You can 'come boldly to the throne . . . [and] obtain mercy and find grace to help in time of need.' "

When they were growing up, my children would "come boldly" to me. They would seek me out when they had fallen and hurt themselves, when they needed money, when they wanted permission to go someplace, or when they wanted me to fix something. It always thrilled me most when they came and climbed up on my lap for no other reason than that they loved me and wanted to be with me.

The Father and His Son invite us to come boldly to them. They are ready, willing, and able to supply "help in time of need." Each longs to help us in every difficulty, worry, or care. But I believe They experience Their greatest joy when we draw near for the sheer joy of reveling in Their eternal presence because we love Them and want to be with Them. Will you "come boldly" just now and bring joy to the divine heart?

DRG

JESUS MINISTERS TO OUR NEEDS

Because Jesus lives forever, he has a permanent priesthood. Therefore he is able to save completely those who come to God through him, because he always lives to intercede for them. Such a high priest meets our need—one who is holy, blameless, pure, set apart from sinners, exalted above the heavens.

HEB. 7:24-27, NIV.

Have you ever felt lonely, helpless, in need of a friend? Then you can sense the condition Jesus' followers must have been in when Jesus died. Their depression was short-lived, though, for Jesus came out of the tomb and spent 40 fulfilling days with them. Afterward, "while he was blessing them, he left them and was taken up into heaven. Then they worshiped him and returned to Jerusalem with great joy" (Luke 24:51, 52, NIV).

Why were they joyful? Because Jesus had assured them before His crucifixion that He would come again (John 14:1-3), and at His ascension two angels reaffirmed His promise (Acts 1:9-11). He had also declared, "I am with you always" (Matt. 28:20, NIV). If you are lonely, helpless, depressed, or in need of a friend, remember that these promises are also for you.

From the day Jesus returned to heaven He has been with His people. As our sympathetic High Priest, He "meets our need." "He always lives to intercede" for us. His whole purpose in coming, living, dying, rising, and ascending has been to make it possible for Him to mediate salvation to hurting people. "Therefore he is able to save completely those who come to God through him."

As our sympathetic intercessor, Jesus constantly waits to help us overcome sin when we face temptation. Although He is not visible to the physical eye, we can sense His presence by the spiritual eye. The same Jesus who showed compassion on the woman taken in adultery, who forgave the dying thief, and who helped so many find freedom from their lives of sin is an ever-present help to us today. He is with us as we encounter life's challenges, difficulties, and joys, for "such a high priest meets our need." So as you face today, tomorrow, and even the regrets of your yesterdays, look to Jesus, for He is an empathetic counselor who "lives to intercede" and meet "our needs."

DRG

OCTOBER 24

JESUS WRITES GOD'S LAW IN OUR HEARTS

I will put my laws into their minds, and write them on their hearts, and I will be their God, and they shall be my people.

Heb. 8:10, RSV.

I had always dreamed of climbing Mount Sinai. Now I was about to fulfill my ambition. As I stood at the foot of what many consider to be a sacred site, a sense of awe filled my whole being. For here God revealed Himself and His will to us. On its summit Israel received "the most wonderful revelation ever made by God to men. Here the Lord had gathered His people that He might impress upon them the sacredness of His requirements by declaring with His own voice His holy law. . . . God was working to lift them to a higher moral level by giving them a knowledge of Himself" (*Patriarchs and Prophets,* p. 302).

As the sun set behind the mount, our party retired for the night. The next morning all awakened early, eager to climb the steep ascent to where Moses had stood with God. We began by going up 4,000 steep steps. A monk had worked 70 years, a whole lifetime, to build this stairway to the Mount of God. Soon we found ourselves on a long, steep, winding pathway that eventually led to a rest point in the heart of a fertile, green valley where we found a well of cool water. Leaving the valley, we climbed the final steep ascent to Mount es-Safsafeh.

When I reached the top, although exhausted from the climb, I felt exhilarated. Looking out over the Wilderness of Sinai, I imagined row after row of tents and thousands upon thousands of Israelites bowing reverently as God's voice thundered forth His revelation of love. Then I visualized Moses, with white beard and flowing robe, being enveloped in the cloud of God's presence as His finger etched His commandments on tables of stone. After repeating aloud the Ten Commandments, I knelt and prayed that God would write them on the fleshly tables of my heart.

The message of Sinai is for all Christians today. A crucified and risen Saviour can and will write His commandments on your heart if you will give your life to Him in full surrender. Here is His promise to you and to me: "I will put my laws into their minds, and write them on their hearts, and I will be their God, and they shall be my people."

DRG

BECOMING LIKE JESUS

Christ was sacrificed once to take away the sins of many people; and he will appear a second time, not to bear sin, but to bring salvation to those who are waiting for him.

Heb. 9:28, NIV.

As Pastor and Mrs. Chamberlain camped near Ayers Rock in Australia, a dingo seized their infant from their tent and killed the child. The authorities did not believe the Chamberlains' story. A court convicted Mrs. Chamberlain of murder, and her husband of being an accessory to murder. Mrs. Chamberlain spent several years in prison. Her husband and many friends worked hard to establish her innocence and obtain her release. Finally, because new evidence made her guilt seem doubtful, the authorities pardoned her.

But a pardon is only being forgiven for a crime you have committed, not a declaration of innocence. A pardoned person is still a convicted felon. And the Chamberlains were not satisfied with that, even though the court did release Mrs. Chamberlain from prison. So they fought on until the authorities cleared their names and reversed their felony convictions. At first they were pardoned only for murdering their daughter, but their record of guilt remained. Later they were acquitted—declared not guilty of that crime. Their legal record was now clear.

Does an entirely new picture now flash into your mind when you read that "Christ was sacrificed to take away the sins of many people." When Jesus died on the cross, He made it possible not only to forgive us for our sins, but to "take away the sins," to totally expunge our record of them. So when Jesus comes for us a second time, it will be "without sin" (Heb. 9:28). It is as if we have never sinned.

Thus it is a fantastic experience to be forgiven and have our record cleared of every sin we ever committed. But even more wonderful, God credits Jesus' righteous life to us in place of our life of sin (Rom. 4:4, 5). Not only are we forgiven, not only is our record cleared of sin, but Jesus' perfect life appears in place of our sinfulness. Doesn't your entire being want to shout, "Thank You, Jesus!"

DRG

JESUS IS THE GOOD NEWS

> *Therefore, brethren, having boldness to enter the Holiest by the blood of Jesus.*
>
> *HEB. 10:19, NKJV.*

Gordon and I had been college classmates and pastors in the same conference. And I had always looked on him as a conservative but dedicated minister of Christ. So naturally I was surprised when he came rushing up to me with a gleam in his eyes and fairly shouted: "Dan, I've been converted."

He went on to explain that he had discovered the good news of the gospel: that Jesus saves us simply because by faith we believe in Him. We do not have to strive to earn salvation. When we come to Him, He takes away our old life of sin and replaces it with the record of His sinless life. Therefore, we have "boldness to enter the Holiest by the blood of Jesus."

Recently Gordon and his wife spent a couple days in our home. One evening he sat across from us and recited this verse:

I should have been crucified;
I should have suffered and died.
I should have hung on the cross in disgrace;
But Jesus, God's Son, took my place.

Then he solemnly continued: "On his deathbed John Wesley, the founder of the Methodist Church, exclaimed, 'I can remember only two things: I am a great sinner, but Jesus is a great Saviour.'

"Martin Luther, the founder of the Lutheran Church, said, 'When I look at myself, I don't see how I can be saved! But when I look at Jesus, I don't see how I can be lost!'

"John Calvin, the founder of the Presbyterian Church, said, 'Upon a life I did not live, upon a death I did not die, I hang my whole eternity.'

"John Bunyan, the author of *Pilgrim's Progress,* said, 'It is the greatest truth in the universe, that a righteousness that is in a Person in heaven should justify me a sinner on earth!' "

Now, isn't that good news! No wonder Gordon was so excited. The gospel is not only the good news about Jesus; He Himself is the good news. "Hanging upon the cross Christ was the gospel. . . . This is . . . the hope for every believer. If we can awaken an interest in men's minds that will cause them to fix their eyes on Christ, we may step aside, and ask them only to continue to fix their eyes upon the Lamb of God" (Ellen G. White, in *Questions on Doctrine,* p. 662).

DRG

OUR SINLESS RECORD

Having therefore, brethren, boldness to enter into the holiest by the blood of Jesus, by a new and living way; . . . let us draw near with a true heart in full assurance of faith. . . . For he is faithful that promised.
Heb. 10:19-23.

When we first lived in Singapore, I was the Southeast Asia Union evangelist and often had to be gone for six weeks while holding meetings. When our two little girls would plead, "Daddy, why do you hav'ta go away again?" I would mollify their apprehension by promising, "When I come back, I'll bring you both a present." On my return they would ask with delight, "Daddy, where is my present?" They didn't inquire, "Daddy, did you bring me a present?" They were sure I had presents. The only question was Where are they?

When God promised Adam and Eve He would someday send the Messiah to defeat the devil by dying for their sins (Gen. 3:15), they took God at His word. God promised it, so even though Christ did not come until thousands of years later, the people sacrificed lambs daily because they believed the Messiah would come to die for their sins. Isaiah 53 gives a moving picture of Christ's suffering and death for our sins as though it had already taken place. It was not, "Will the Messiah really die for me?" but rather "When?"

At the cross Jesus' blood forgave and cleansed our sins. Instead of asking, "When will You forgive and blot out our sins?" we should rejoice that Jesus has already done so (1 John 1:7-9).

His work as our mediator in the pre-Advent judgment that began in 1844 is to blot out with His own blood the record of our sins (Acts 3:19). Though Jesus' promise to erase our sins did not become effective until 1844, the book of Hebrews was so convinced of its certainty that its author wrote as if the promise were already fulfilled: We now have "boldness to enter into the holiest by the blood of Jesus, by a new and living way."

Since 1844 Jesus has been in the Most Holy Place blotting out our sins and placing His perfect record in their place. So "let us draw near" to Jesus "in full assurance of faith" and thank Him for our sinless record! "For he is faithful that promised."

DRG

OCTOBER 28

THE CERTAINTY OF OUR HOPE

Now faith is being sure of what we hope for and certain of what we do not see.

Heb. 11:1, NIV.

Archimedes once said, "Give me a lever long enough, and a place to put it on, and I will move the world." Such a lever does exist, and we call it faith. And there is a place to rest it on—God. The power that can swing that lever we refer to as human choice. Someone has correctly said, "Faith is to believe what we do not see, and the reward of faith is to see what we believe."

How is it possible to believe something that we cannot see—or even understand? Both Christians and non-Christians daily live a life of some type of faith. If you have an operation you have faith enough in the surgeons to permit them to render you unconscious while they make incisions on your body. Before that, when you were shown the X-rays, which didn't mean much to you, you had faith in the doctors' diagnosis that the dark spot was an obstruction, and you then placed your life in their hands. You took all this for granted because of your faith in the doctor's judgment and skill.

We don't even take a glass of water, go to bed at night, or drive an automobile without faith. You wouldn't accept a check without faith that you can cash it at the bank. So without faith, business—even life itself—would cease. If in our daily transactions we live by our faith in others, surely we should have faith in matters of our spiritual welfare.

Years ago when I visited Teheran, I witnessed the making of a beautiful Persian rug. A little woman who would take a year to complete the beautifully designed rug wove each thread in place. As I watched, I had faith that the thousands of threads she wove together would someday result in a beautiful carpet.

We are saved by our faith that God's plan will result in His taking us to a beautiful place called heaven. "Now faith" in our Father and in Jesus, our Saviour, compels us to be "sure of what we hope for and certain of what we do not see." This vibrant, living faith in Jesus is available to you just now.

HMSR

HOW NECESSARY IS FAITH?

Without faith it is impossible to please God, because anyone who comes to him must believe that he exists and that he rewards those who earnestly seek him.
Heb. 11:6, NIV.

It disturbed me greatly to read the response a senior in one of our large universities made to a question asked him about his faith in God. "The trouble with me," he said, "is that I can't believe in anything. On some days I can, but most of the time I'm smarter than that. I have been taught to question, not to believe, so I never know where to stop."

That's serious, for "without faith it is impossible to please God." We must have faith that He exists. Faith is more than mere intellectual assent, or we are no better than Satan or the fallen angels who believe and tremble (James 2:19).

Along with belief and faith comes trust. "Not because we see or feel that God hears us are we to believe. We are to trust in His promises. When we come to Him in faith, every petition enters the heart of God. When we have asked for His blessing, we should believe that we receive it, and thank Him that we have received it. Then we are to go about our duties, assured that the blessing will be realized when we need it most" (*The Desire of Ages,* p. 200).

No person is as blind as the one who will not see. Faith is ours if we want it, if we are willing to find it, if we are willing to "believe that [God] exists and that he rewards those who earnestly seek him."

Humanity cannot prove God by any hypothesis or test-tube method of investigation, but as Christians we can find sufficient evidence for our belief in God, as did the Roman officer who stood at the foot of Calvary's cross: "When the centurian, who stood there in front of Jesus, heard his cry and saw how he died, he said, 'Surely this man was the Son of God!' " (Mark 15:39, NIV).

Jesus makes God real and believable.

HMSR

OCTOBER 30

WILLING TO DIE FOR CHRIST

Looking unto Jesus, the author and finisher of our faith, who for the joy that was set before Him endured the cross, despising the shame, and has sat down at the right hand of the throne of God.

Heb. 12:2, NKJV.

Years ago Pastor A.V. Olson met with the committee overseeing the Adventist Church in Europe. Receiving word that the only pastor in a certain European country had been martyred, they pondered what to do. If they sent someone else, he might meet the same fate. Yet to fail to replace the person would mean that God's last message for a perishing world would probably die out in that particular country. The committee decided to ask Brother A to go, for he was the only one who knew the language.

Pastor Olson and another pastor went to see Brother A. They told him that if he agreed to go, he might in a few weeks be sleeping in a martyr's grave. His wife might become a widow, and his children fatherless. But they said, "The Lord has impressed us to come and ask you to go."

Brother A shook, tears came to his eyes, his mouth moved in prayer. Finally he lifted his head, rose to his feet, wiped away the tears, and said, "When I was lost, without hope in the world, Jesus found me. I wanted to be a minister. But I never expected a call like this." With quivering voice he continued, "Jesus died for me. If I can do more by death than by life, then I'll go."

He did go, and suffered beatings and imprisonment. While in prison he preached to the other prisoners, won many of them to Christ, and organized a church in the prison. When not in prison he was active in preaching the message of Jesus for the last days. After several months he had 500 ready to confess their faith in Jesus by baptism.

Because he believed in God's message for the last days, the young man was willing to suffer imprisonment and if need be even death itself to spread the good news about Jesus under even threatening circumstances. How like Jesus, "who for the joy that was set before Him endured the cross, despising the shame, and has sat down at the right hand of the throne of God."

DRG

PARTAKERS OF CHRIST

You were not redeemed with corruptible things, like silver or gold, . . . but with the precious blood of Christ, as of a lamb without blemish and without spot.
1 Peter 1:18, 19, NKJV.

A questionnaire went out to hundreds of listeners of a worldwide broadcast. One of the many questions asked was: "Do you smoke cigarettes, cigars, or a pipe?" A follow-up question asked: "If you do not smoke, would you care to tell us why not?"

A young queen in a country in Africa returned one of the questionnaires. Her answer was "I don't smoke because I am a Christian, saved by the blood of Jesus." In today's secular age it is refreshing to see a young person, and a queen at that, recognize the power of the "precious blood of Christ."

A minister in La Paz, Bolivia, training young people for Christian service, challenged them with these words: "On the steeple of almost every church in Latin America you will find the cross. That's the trouble. It's always on the steeple. Your job now is to put the cross into the hearts of people."

What takes place in the heart of a person who has the cross in his or her heart, who is "redeemed . . . with the precious blood of Christ," is far more than a blood transfusion that merely revives the body. It imparts to that individual a new kind of life, and an everlasting one as well. The Christian who aims for the highest and the best will find in these words a powerful challenge to godly living and an escape from merely living unhappily on spiritual lowlands only slightly above the level of the unregenerate world.

Those truly redeemed by the blood of Christ possess a saving faith based on participation in the life of Jesus Christ, "for we have become partakers of Christ" (Heb. 3:14, NKJV).

A person once commented, "It is such a thrilling experience that I have had practicing the presence of Jesus. When I get into my car, I open the door and step aside and ask the Lord to go first. And you know, that car does not go a lot of places it used to go." Yes, when we recognize that Jesus redeemed us with the costly price of His blood, it will mean a consecration, a setting apart of all that we have and are to our Saviour.

HMSR

NOVEMBER 1

JESUS OUR SINLESS LIFE-GIVER

> ***Christ suffered for you, leaving you an example, that you should follow in his steps.***
>
> *1 Peter 2:21, NIV.*

Many years ago my brother-in-law who is a contractor told me about a wonderful new invention. He explained that when you push a button in your car your garage door automatically opens. Having a hard time visualizing what he was describing, I asked him to draw a diagram, but it just didn't make sense. Later that day he took me to a house he was building, and for the first time I saw a garage door opener in action. I now knew what the opener looked like and how it worked.

During Old Testament times the prophets explained how to live a satisfying life with God. But only when Jesus came and demonstrated such an existence did people begin to comprehend how rich and full life can be when experienced as God suggests we live it.

Christ came to our world to live as "an example," and we are to "follow in his steps." He showed us how to cope with life's temptations and difficulties. Although He could have attempted through mere words to persuade us that a life free from sin is more satisfying, the life He lived is a far more effective persuader. God could have just told us that a better life is possible, but He was aware that demonstrating it would be far more powerful.

And Jesus left us a wonderful example! When things went wrong, instead of reacting negatively, "He entrusted himself" to His Father (1 Peter 2:23, NIV). All of our problems would be solved if we too would always trust God. Jesus is able "to sympathize with our weaknesses" because He "has been tempted in every way, just as we are—yet was without sin" (Heb. 4:15, NIV). Since Jesus experienced to the full the problems and temptations of life, He understands our problems, our temptations, and our needs.

Jesus did far more than leave us an example, however. He died on the cross as our substitute "so that we might die to sins and live for righteousness" (1 Peter 2:24, NIV). He lived a sinless life with the express objective of passing it on to us. For Jesus to exchange His sinless life for our scarred and battered sinful existence is almost beyond comprehension, but thank God "by his wounds you have been healed" (verse 24, NIV)!

DRG

THE SUPREME SACRIFICE

He himself bore our sins in his body on the tree, so that we might die to sins and live for righteousness; by his wounds you have been healed.
1 PETER 2:24, NIV.

In Denver, Colorado, a physician examined a man whose life was fading away with no apparent cause. Although financially secure, he had no friends or relatives and was drifting out of the world a bleak, desolate old man.

When the physician could find no organic disease, he questioned the patient, and the man admitted he was dying of a broken heart. He said, "I came out here to die in peace and alone. My past is sealed in the shadow of a terrible crime. I am already dead to all who ever knew me, and over my nameless grave not even a memory must hover."

"Are you a criminal?"

"No, but I assumed the stigma to shield an only son. He murdered a man, and I assumed the crime. Then I escaped, not to evade the law, but to spare my boy the disgrace of a felon's death."

"How long ago was that?" the physician continued.

"Twelve years."

"And you have been a wanderer ever since?"

"Ever since," the man answered, his feeble pulse fluttering as the shadows grew more gloomy.

"Tell me more," the doctor whispered.

"That's all I have to tell." The next instant he was dead. But he had kept his secret and sacrificed his life in doing so.

His was a great sacrifice, but in comparison to what Jesus has done for us, it was nothing. With an infinite price He paid for the world's salvation! "He himself bore our sins . . . so that we might die to sins and live for righteousness."

What that father did for his son, Jesus wants to do for each of us. No matter what we have done, or who we are, we can "live for righteousness" in a sin-drenched world of frustration and fear, suffering and sorrow, heartache and heaviness. Jesus releases us from the sin and guilt that destroy us, from the problems and troubles that hound us, from the depression and loneliness that creep in. "By his wounds you have been healed."

HMSR

NOVEMBER 3

MADE ALIVE IN THE SPIRIT

For Christ also died for sins once for all, the righteous for the unrighteous, that he might bring us to God, being put to death in the flesh but made alive in the spirit.

1 PETER 3:18, RSV.

Some time ago the press reported that a boy in Florida picked up an old Spanish coin bearing the date 1796 and the Latin words *Plus Ultra,* meaning "more beyond." Before the days of Columbus, Spanish coins bore the inscription *Ne Plus Ultra,* "no more beyond." Beyond the "Pillars of Hercules" separating the coasts of Spain and Africa the mysterious and dreadful ocean stretched away to the edge of the world. There was no more beyond—out there all was water, chaos, night, the unknown! But after the voyages of Columbus and other great navigators had pushed the empires of Spain and Portugal far over the Atlantic Ocean to the New World, Spain proudly changed the motto on its coins to *Plus ultra,* "more beyond."

Just so, on the morning of the Resurrection when Jesus was "made alive in the spirit," humanity could blot out the tear-stained words "no more beyond." For now the glad promise of eternal hope reads "more beyond!" Before Christ entered our world, graves bore an inscription of despair: "no more beyond." But then Jesus, our Redeemer, died for our sins "once for all." He did not die only as a good person to give us an example of how to cope with sin, but He died as our substitute. Jesus, the "righteous," died for you and me, the "unrighteous, that he might bring us to God."

Jesus was "put to death in the flesh," but we need not despair, for He was "made alive in the spirit." Divinity revived His dead body, and He triumphed over death. That's good news for those who respond to Jesus' magnanimous deed.

Plus Ultra—"more beyond." There is life in Christ, an entirely new life, and there is also life beyond the grave. The old world of hopelessness and despair and night is behind us. Ahead stretches a new realm of faith and delight to live in now, and immortality beyond the sleep of death, all because of what Jesus has done for us. What tremendous good news!

HMSR

FOR A LIMITED TIME ONLY

He isn't really being slow about his promised return, even though it sometimes seems that way. But he is waiting, for the good reason that he is not willing that any should perish, and he is giving more time for sinners to repent.

2 Peter 3:9, TLB.

In one of his sermons Dr. Clarence Macartney told of a Saxon king who went with his army to put down a rebellion in his kingdom. When he had defeated the rebels and quelled the insurrection, the king placed a candle in the archway of the headquarters' castle. Then, lighting the candle, he sent his herald to announce to the rebels that all who would surrender and take an oath of allegiance while the candle still burned would be saved. The king offered clemency and mercy, but limited the offer to the life of that candle.

We are all living on candle time. While the candle still burns, we have another opportunity to prepare ourselves for Jesus' coming. "The Lord is not slow in keeping his promise. . . . He is patient with you, not wanting anyone to perish" (2 Peter 3:9, NIV).

Many offers come to us for a limited time only. The summons to be ready when Jesus returns still lingers, but time is short. God's prophetic timetable has marked the mileposts of human history—Jesus' first coming, the gospel to the Gentiles, the apostasy of the Dark Ages, the Lisbon earthquake, the falling stars, and the increase of prophetic knowledge predicted by Daniel the prophet have all seen their fulfillment. Step by step the waymarks of prophecy have occurred just as God's timetable foretold, and in our day fulfilling prophecies describe our world politically, economically, morally, and spiritually. Time is running out. The candle is burning low. "He is waiting [to come again] for the good reason that he is not willing that any should perish."

Christ continues to allow the lost a little more time to repent. Christians still have time to prepare for His coming. Our Saviour wants you, and He wants me, to be ready. Life is short. We have just so many heartbeats. Our life is for a limited time only. Now is the time to be ready for Jesus' return.

HMSR

FREEDOM FROM GUILT, MISERY, AND DOUBT

If we walk in the light, as he is in the light, we have fellowship one with another, and the blood of Jesus Christ his Son cleanseth us from all sin.
1 John 1:7.

An old man in a caravan crossing to the north of India collapsed from the heat and hardship of the journey. Finally he could go no farther, and the others left him beside the road to die. Among the travelers was a missionary who knelt down beside the poor man and whispered into his ear, "Brother, what is your hope?" The dying man raised himself a little to reply and with great effort succeeded in saying, "The blood of Jesus Christ his Son cleanseth us from all sin." Then he gave his last gasp and died.

The Christian was surprised at the answer and at the calm and peaceful assurance of the dying man. At first he could not imagine how the man had obtained any knowledge of salvation. Then he noticed that the dead man tightly held a piece of paper in his hand. As he pried open the fingers, he found a single page of the Holy Scriptures containing 1 John 1. From that one page the old man had found eternal life.

In one of His parables Jesus told of a Pharisee who went up to the Temple and prayed, "God, I thank thee, that I am not as other men are, extortioners, unjust, adulterers, or even as this publican. I fast twice in the week, I give tithes of all that I possess." In contrast, Jesus then told of a publican who prayed, "God be merciful to me a sinner" (Luke 18:9-13). Both the old man who dropped out of the caravan in India and the publican were kindred spirits as both claimed the promise "The blood of Jesus Christ his Son cleanseth us from all sin."

Are we willing to bare our hearts to the all-seeing eye of God? Are we willing to search our lives today and ask forgiveness for sin through Jesus' blood—yes, even to go so far as to say, "God be merciful to me a sinner"? Millions struggling with guilt, doubt, misery, and self-recrimination need to respond to Jesus' offer and allow Him to apply His simple remedy—His cleansing blood. When we reach out by faith and accept what Jesus offers, we have the assurance of sins forgiven and the hope of eternal life.

HMSR

JESUS' GOOD MEMORY AND HIS GOOD FORGETTER

If we confess our sins, he is faithful and just and will forgive us our sins and purify us from all unrighteousness.
1 John 1:9, NIV.

One time when Lillian and I were out for our daily walk, I attempted to recall a name but couldn't. Of course, this is common for an older person. In frustration I said to my wife, "As you know, I have a photographic memory. My problem is that I have trouble developing the film when I want to remember something."

We have a Redeemer who never forgets. He reminds us, "I have engraved you on the palms of my hands" (Isa. 49:16, NIV). The names of the tribes of Israel were inscribed on semiprecious stones and fastened to the ephod on the priest's chest and on the priest's shoulders as a double memorial. In the same way, the hands of Jesus, our High Priest, have engraved on them the names of God's people as an indication that He never forgets us.

In the previous verse the Lord asks, "Can a mother forget the baby at her breast and have no compassion on the child she has borne?" (NIV). Then He answers His question: "Though she may forget, I will not forget you!" (NIV). Our Saviour has a good memory when it comes to our good points, but He has an equally wonderful forgetter when it involves our bad points. He not only forgives our sins, but also promises "to purify us from all unrighteousness." In the great judgment day He so thoroughly wipes out our sins, it is as if we have never sinned. Our record is clean.

Only a few days after Peter cursed and denied knowing Him, Jesus appointed him as a leader in the Christian church. Today Jesus is just as faithful about forgetting our sins. He hurls all our iniquities into "the depths of the sea" (Micah 7:19, NIV), removing them from us "as far as the east is from the west" (Ps. 103:12, NIV). Christ blots our sins out "as a thick cloud" that even heaven does not look through (Isa. 44:22). What a wonderful Saviour!

DRG

NOVEMBER 7

JESUS OUR DEFENDER

My dear children, I write this to you so that you will not sin. But if anybody does sin, we have one who speaks to the Father in our defense—Jesus Christ, the Righteous One.
1 John 2:1, NIV

A woman attending my evangelistic meetings said, "I know the Bible teaches I should keep the commandments, but I've tried my very best and just can't keep them. I'm beginning to believe no one else can." Have such thoughts ever crossed your mind?

Although Jesus taught a gospel of love, He told a large crowd not to even consider the possibility that He had sought to do away with the commandments or even change "the smallest letter" or "the least stroke of a pen" (Matt. 5:17, 18, NIV). Jesus came to do just the opposite—to give the commandments a deeper meaning (verses 19, 20). He emphasized their observance, yet "if anybody does sin, we have one who speaks to the Father in our defense—Jesus Christ, the Righteous One." Jesus is eminently qualified to be our defender, since the following verse tells us that "He is the atoning sacrifice for our sins" (1 John 2:2, NIV). He, "the Righteous One," kept the law for us, then died so He can forgive our lawbreaking. The KJV says: "If any man sin, we have an advocate with the Father, Jesus Christ the righteous." Confessing our guilt to Jesus, our advocate, is our only hope. Dewitt Talmage once said: "There is only one Advocate in all the universe that can plead our case in the last judgment. Sometimes in earthly courts attorneys have specialties, and one man succeeds better in patent cases, another in land cases, another in will cases; and his success generally depends upon his sticking to his specialty. I have to tell you that Christ can do many things; but it seems to me that His specialty is to take the sad case of the sinner, and plead it before God until He gets eternal acquittal."

The meaning of *advocate* is "one who stands alongside of." In ancient times the advocate was often a friend who stood by the accused in a court of law and interceded with the judge on the friend's behalf. Jesus' role in the judgment is to intercede in our behalf as our friend. That is good news! How thankful we can be that when we do sin, our Friend, Jesus, stands alongside us and comes to our defense!

DRG

A FATHER'S EXTRAVAGANT LOVE

Behold what manner of love the Father has bestowed on us, that we should be called the children of God!
1 John 3:1, NKJV.

In Luke 15 Jesus tells the story of a boy who got lost. Reared in a Christian home, he had a praying, kind, loving, and tenderhearted father. So it almost broke his father's heart when one day the son said, "Dad, I'm leaving home. I'm tired of all these foolish restrictions. I want to get out and enjoy life, so I'm going to the city."

The boy left home for the New York of his day. He was popular with the gang as long as his money held out. But he gambled with it, spent it on prostitutes, and wallowed in drink. "The treasure of his young manhood is wasted. The precious years of life, the strength of intellect, the bright visions of youth, the spiritual aspirations—all are consumed in the fires of lust" (*Christ's Object Lessons,* pp. 199, 200).

When his money disappeared, his friends vanished with it. He felt empty inside. Desperately lonely and starving, he envied what the pigs ate. Sensing his wasted life and facing what a terrible thing it is to be lost, "he came to himself" (Luke 15:17). "I'll go to my father," he decided, "and ask to be one of his hired servants."

His father had been praying and watching for him. When he saw his son "a great way off," he "had compassion, and ran" to meet him (Luke 15:20). Taking his wayward son in his arms, he smothered him with kisses. As the father said to his elder son, it is good "that we should make merry, and be glad: for this thy brother was dead, and is alive again; and was lost, and is found" (verse 32).

Jesus is that forgiving Father. We are the forgiven children. "Behold what manner of love the Father has bestowed on us, that we should be called the children of God!" Think of what it means to us as God's children to come home to our Father! It gives us the assurance of salvation that brings an entirely new life of happiness—and the hope of heaven.

DRG

NOVEMBER 9

JESUS' VICTORY OVER SATAN

He who does what is sinful is of the devil, because the devil has been sinning from the beginning. The reason the Son of God appeared was to destroy the devil's work.

1 John 3:8, NIV.

One night Thomas Carlyle took Ralph Waldo Emerson through some of the worst streets of London's East End. As they walked along silently, looking at the misery and evil everywhere, Carlyle finally inquired, "Do you believe in the devil now?" Whether people believe or don't believe a devil exists, they must pay taxes to support foster homes, hospitals, prisons, welfare, and war. They must suffer pain and die.

The Bible pictures the devil as intelligent, beautiful, and able to portray himself as exactly opposite to his real character. The apostle Paul wrote: "Satan himself masquerades as an angel of light" (2 Cor. 11:14, NIV). But he is the source and promoter of all evil. He wants us to worship him instead of Christ, being jealous of Christ and wanting to take His place in heaven (Isa. 14:13, 14). Now he is at war with Christ and His church in a last desperate effort to wrest our world from Jesus (Rev. 12). As "the god of this world," he has "blinded the minds of them which believe not, lest the light of the glorious gospel of Christ, . . . should shine unto them" (2 Cor. 4:4). However, Christ defeated this apostate rebel at the cross. There Jesus settled His victory over Satan in the great contest between good and evil and became the victor over Satan, sin, and death (John 12:31, 32).

Our world is a stage on which this mighty drama, the great struggle between good and evil, is playing itself out. We are near the end of the drama when at last the whole universe of unfallen worlds will see that love is stronger than sin and that God is just and true. Once the curtain falls, no more sin or sorrow will remain. Nothing will be wrong with the universe. Only eternal harmony will reign, because Jesus, the Son of God, has destroyed "the devil's work." It's that world we long to see! Nobody will be hungry, sick, or homeless. No murderous dictators will thirst for power. Hatred, pain, agony, disappointment, and heartbreak will have vanished forever. Old age and death will cease. May that day not be long delayed! I can hardly wait! And you?

HMSR

CAPTIVES OF JESUS' LOVE

Whoever does not love has never come to know God by experience, because God is love.
1 John 4:8, Williams.

The Bible tells us that "God is love." If you do not "know God by experience," then you are not really aware of what genuine love is. Some people feel that God does not love them, so they run away from Him, repeating the experience of Adam and Eve in the Garden of Eden. After they sinned, they hid from God. They were afraid of Him, because they had become separated from Him. But we cannot hide from God, nor can we ignore Him. We are either fugitives from God, or captives of His love.

Dwight L. Moody, the great Baptist lay evangelist, said concerning love: "If I could only make men understand the real meaning of the words of the apostle John—'God is love,' I would take that single text and go up and down the world proclaiming this glorious truth. If you can convince a man that you love him, you have won his heart. If you could really make people believe that God loves them, how we should find them crowding into the kingdom of heaven" *(The Way to God,* p. 7).

People prize nothing in this world so much as they do love. Show me a man or a woman who has no one to care for or love him or her, and I will show you one of the most lonely persons on earth. One reason people commit suicide is that they think no one loves them, and they would rather die than live without love. Ever since the Fall God has been trying to persuade human beings that He does love them. The devil has spent the same time sowing the seeds of doubt as to whether God actually does care.

Some parents make the great mistake of teaching their children that God does not love them when they do wrong—only when they do right. But wrongdoing does not change God's love for us. Even if we have fled God, He still loves us. He hates only sin. Sometimes we try to measure God by our own small rule, from our own standpoint. But the true measure of God's love is Calvary. The cross shouts to us that "God is love." Are you listening? Do you hear Him speaking to you today?

HMSR

YOUR LOVE RELATIONSHIP WITH JESUS

He who does not love does not know God, for God is love.
1 John 4:8, NKJV.

People often say to me, "Pastor Richards, how can I get acquainted with Jesus? Even though I have been a Christian for several years, I recognize a lack in my life, that something has gone wrong."

When people ask me this question, I like to remind them of the days of their courtship. I can remember mine very well. I did not court my wife by remote control or by proxy. I saw her as often as possible. We walked together, we talked together, and we prayed together. It is the very same experience that we must have with Jesus. We need to get acquainted with Him. Each of us needs to walk with Him and talk with Him through prayer and meditation, spending time with Him day by day and hour by hour. In other words, we must fall in love with Him, a fact made quite clear in today's text: "He who does not love does not know God, for God is love."

Love is life's highest and purest emotion, and only the individual who has it within his or her heart and mind can even begin to comprehend God—who is love divine. God loves us so much, even though we are undeserving of His love. Human love might lead one to die for some friend, but to die for an enemy or a rebel—who would do such a thing? Notice how Paul describes the unfathomable love of God and of Jesus Christ, His Son: "But God demonstrates His own love toward us, in that while we were still sinners, Christ died for us" (Rom. 5:8, NKJV).

God gave His Son. Jesus gave His life. And whether you think so or not, God loves you! The redeeming love of God, expressed by Jesus at Calvary, inspired Charles Wesley to write these beautiful lines:

O for a thousand tongues to sing
My great Redeemer's praise,
The glories of my God and King,
The triumphs of His grace!

This can be our experience if we are daily cultivating our love relationship with Jesus. We do this through listening and meditating as He speaks to us through His Word and as we talk with Him in prayer. Why not spend a little time with Him right now?

HMSR

LIVING LIFE THROUGH GOD'S SON

This is how God showed his love among us: He sent his one and only Son into the world that we might live through Him.

1 John 4:9, NIV.

One evening at dusk, when it was time for the streamliner, the railroad bridge-keeper went to his post to make sure the bridge was down so the train could pass over safely. It was his duty to raise the bridge so ships could pass through and to lower it for trains. To his amazement he found the lock that secured the bridge in the down position broken. As the train approached, he pulled with all his might on the bar that fastened the lock. He knew it was the only hope of preventing the train from plunging into the river below. The safety and lives of hundreds of people depended on his strength in those tense moments.

Just as the train whistle blew, he heard another sound that made his heart stand still with fear. It was the voice of his little 3-year-old son calling, "Daddy, where are you?" He glanced up and saw his only child toddling between the rails toward the bridge and the onrushing train. Should he leave his post of duty and save the son he loved with all his heart, or should he sacrifice his only child for the lives of hundreds of people who knew nothing of their danger? He had only one choice, and he made it. The train passed on its way without the passengers realizing the great sacrifice a loving father had made so they could live.

Our heavenly Father saw a world rushing on in sin to its eternal ruin. He knew He must either give His only Son to save billions from ruin or save His Son and let a lost world go down to destruction. What did He do? As a God of love He did the only thing He could do. "This is how God showed his love among us: He sent his one and only Son into the world that we might live through Him." Unlike the railroad bridge-keeper's son, Jesus willingly gave His life because of His love for us.

HMSR

THIS IS LOVE!

This is love: not that we loved God, but that he loved us and sent his Son as an atoning sacrifice for our sins.
1 JOHN 4:10, NIV.

In December of 1995 the news reported that a low-paid office worker left a fortune of $22,000,000. She had saved, scraped, and lived frugally her entire life. Investing wisely in stocks, she parlayed her $5,000 in savings into millions. Then she willed her millions to Yeshiva University for scholarships for young women. Because of prejudice against women, especially Jewish women, she felt that she had not been able to get ahead in life. As a result she wanted other women to have the opportunity she never had.

When students at the college heard about it, they thought someone had invented the story as a joke. They just couldn't believe it. It was too good to be true.

For God's Son to come to our world "as an atoning sacrifice for our sins" also seems too good to be true. But it is true!

Recently our pastor put a slant on this woman's story missing from the newscast I heard. When she died, she not only left a will, but also a letter to the college. It revealed her bitterness and pain because of the way she had been treated as a Jewish woman. She gave to others out of her pain, not out of love. Although she gave without loving, we cannot really love without giving.

When we see God giving us His Son, we observe what real love is. It's not our love for God, but God's love for us. Consider what it means to love a sinful human race. Think of loving a rapist who killed 23 of his victims, or a woman who drowned her two children so she could marry a man who didn't want children. Imagine loving a woman who paid $500 to have her husband killed so she could inherit the fortune he had won in the lottery and then marry her illicit boyfriend. Could you love such individuals? When we see God loving people like that and people like us, no wonder John exclaimed, "This is love!" It is incredible love. "This is love: not that we loved God." After all, God is easy to love. Real love is that God "loved us and sent his Son as an atoning sacrifice for our sins."

DRG

CONQUERING FEAR

There is no fear in love; but perfect love casts out fear, because fear involves torment. But he who fears has not been made perfect in love.
1 JOHN 4:18, NKJV.

An ancient legend from the East tells the story of Cholera riding high upon his camel. He met an inquiring nomad of a Bedouin tribe who asked where he was going. Cholera answered, "I am going to Baghdad to kill 20,000 people."

The legend says they met again later, and the Bedouin chided Cholera, saying, "You lied to me. Not 20,000 died in Baghdad, but 100,000."

Cholera replied, "I killed 20,000—fear killed the rest."

Fear, like a great octopus, wraps its slimy tentacles of despondency, nervousness, worry, anger, and hatred around the lives of nations and individuals today. No one is immune from it. It may be fear of darkness, fear of the streets, fear in the heart, fear of the unknown, fear of failure, fear of global warming, or fear of overpopulation, the future, pain, or death.

Such fears rob us of sleep, of joy, sometimes of life itself. We need to remember that God's message for our age is relevant. He speaks to our basic and deepest needs. When we recognize that we cannot trust in our own resources, like Abraham we will hear God's voice: "Do not fear, for I am with you" (Gen. 26:24, NKJV).

Hundreds of books come off the press today on the subject of fear and how to overcome it. They urge people to relax, to believe in themselves. But the real cure for fear is simple faith in the One who has come to cast out all fear—Jesus! When we fall in love with Jesus, our love for Him and His "perfect love" for us "casts out fear." Fellowship with Jesus each day—thinking about Him, meditating upon Him, receiving Him into our hearts—fills us with love for Him and builds faith that drives away all the fear in our hearts. Fear is the opposite of faith. Faith in Jesus is a means of victory over fear. "This is the victory that has overcome the world—our faith" (1 John 5:4, NIV). Doubt paralyzes while faith vitalizes. It brings reconciliation with God that leads to forgiveness, peace, and eternal life. You can reach out for life without fear! Then let fear be changed to faith . . . let doubt give place to hope . . . let weakness be turned to strength . . . and let sin be supplanted by obedience and righteousness and peace!

HMSR

NOVEMBER 15

EVERYTHING DEPENDS ON JESUS—1

What is it that God has said? That he has given us eternal life, and that this life is in his Son. So whoever has God's Son has life; whoever does not have his Son, does not have life.
1 John 5:11, 12, TLB.

Everything depends on Jesus. If we accept His offer of salvation, we have eternal life. But if we reject it, we do not receive eternal life. "But," some ask, "what about the millions who don't know about Jesus?" Don't worry about them. When those who have never heard the gospel and who "have not the law, do by nature the things contained in the law, these, having not the law, are a law unto themselves" (Rom. 2:14).

God doesn't hold people responsible for what they do not know and have never had the opportunity of learning. He does not deal with them on the same basis as He does with those acquainted with the gospel. Everyone born has some sense of responsibility, for Jesus is "the true Light, which lighteth every man that cometh into the world" (John 1:9). Every man and woman, and every boy and girl, has some light. Those who know God's will and yet do wrong have greater responsibility and will suffer more if they are lost. Those who have little understanding will suffer less (Luke 12:47, 48). God, who reads our hearts, knows all about us.

Those who existed before the cross are saved in the same way as those who lived afterward—by the grace of God. God has never had any different way of salvation. "Grace" is not exclusively a New Testament word. "Noah found grace in the eyes of the Lord" (Gen. 6:8). He was "heir of the righteousness which is by faith" (Heb. 11:7). Through the offering of an innocent lamb people in ancient times demonstrated their faith in a coming Redeemer. The bleeding lamb symbolized faith in Jesus, "the Lamb of God, which taketh away the sin of the world" (John 1:29).

We must never stop talking about Jesus on the cross. He opened heaven's door to us by His sacrifice there. By dying there for sinners, He brought peace to our hearts in a troubled world. "Whoever has God's Son has life; whoever does not have his Son, does not have life." Everything depends on Jesus!

HMSR

EVERYTHING DEPENDS ON JESUS—2

God has given us eternal life, and this life is in His Son. He who has the Son has life; he who does not have the Son of God does not have life.
1 John 5:11, 12, NKJV.

An old peasant on a cooperative farm in an Eastern country said, "We used to call the priests in to bless our fields in the spring when we planted the crops. But we don't need to do that anymore. Now we have commercial fertilizer and tractors to help us." If we went a little further with such reasoning, we could claim that if we have bulldozers to move mountains, we don't need faith; or if we have antibiotics, we don't need prayer. With positive thinking we don't need salvation, and with science we don't need God.

What is our basic problem? Ourselves! The existential philosophers have been speaking about it for years. Psychiatry, through psychoanalysis, has sought to adjust what is wrong with people. Sociology has attempted the same thing through environmental change. Yet the problem of our century—and it has been the problem of every century—remains unsolved by human efforts. The human heart continues in rebellion, because "the heart is deceitful above all things, and desperately wicked" (Jer. 17:9, NKJV). We bury our heads in the sand and do not admit our need of salvation. Looking at ourselves deflects our gaze from Christ.

Men and women—all of us—are lost and in need of a Saviour. The Lord begins the salvation process by providing us that Saviour. "God has given us eternal life, and this life is in His Son." The life, death, resurrection, and continual ministry of Jesus Christ, the divine Son of the living God, meets our deepest need today. A person "who has the Son has life," while a person "who does not have the Son of God does not have life."

Happiness in the present life and an eternal life of happiness depend on having Jesus at the very center of our life. Possessing eternal life now is no legal fiction, no dream, no figure of speech. Having eternal life when we know Jesus as our Saviour is the deepest reality in human experience. Eternal life begins for us the moment we accept Jesus. Through Christ dwelling in us by His Spirit, we have His kind of life.

HMSR

PRAYING WITH CONFIDENCE

And this is the confidence which we have in him, that if we ask anything according to his will he hears us. And if we know that he hears us in whatever we ask, we know that we have obtained the requests made of him.

1 John 5:14, 15, RSV.

When Henry M. Stanley, the noted explorer, emerged from the jungles and fever swamps of Africa, he said that prayer made him stronger morally and physically than his non-praying companions. "It did not blind my eyes or dull my mind or close my ears," he added. "On the contrary, it gave me confidence." Stanley's assurance was well placed, for today's text declares to those who believe in the Son of God: "This is the confidence which we have in him, that if we ask anything according to his will he hears us. And . . . we know that we have obtained the requests made of him."

Like Stanley and millions of other Christians, I believe in prayer. It is impossible for us to live a successful, complete life without communicating with Jesus, seeking His will for our lives each day. We certainly are not wise enough to know His plans for our lives without seeking His guidance in prayer. Many of the troubles that we struggle with in this life result from demanding our own way. It is time we let God guide our hearts. To pray "Thy will be done" is to place ourselves at God's disposal. It is really putting our lives in His hands.

Some things are especially "according to his will" for us, giving us "confidence" to "know that we have obtained the requests made of him." We can pray for forgiveness for all our sins (1 John 1:9), for increased faith (Mark 9:24), and for the gift of the Holy Spirit, and know for sure that God will hear all our prayers and answer them.

Jesus waits to hear our requests—and our gratefulness. As we come to Him in full assurance of faith, we will receive from His boundless supply all that we need. So "let us therefore come boldly unto the throne of grace, that we may obtain mercy, and find grace to help in time of need" (Heb. 4:16).

HMSR

THE UNVEILING OF JESUS CHRIST

The revelation of Jesus Christ, which God gave him to show his servants what must soon take place. He made it known by sending his angel to his servant John.
Rev. 1:1, 2, NIV.

The book of Revelation is "the revelation of Jesus Christ," a phrase that can mean either that the book is a revelation *from* Jesus or a revelation *to,* or *about,* Him. Since Christianity is a relationship with Jesus, discovering the good news about Jesus in Revelation is vital to us as Christians.

Revelation, from the term *apocalypse,* means "an unveiling." The book of Revelation gives picture after picture of Jesus in every aspect of His being and in every phase of His determined effort to save us. Since Jesus is not only the book's subject, but also its author, Revelation breathes His character. Christ breaks forth on every page with assuring messages that meet our every need.

As I've come into intimate contact with people, I've been impressed again and again that deep within every human heart resides a longing for God. Some people misinterpret the desire and seek to satisfy it with material things and pleasures. But we cannot satisfy such heart longings in our world, for they are in reality God-implanted desires to search for and find Him. Only a relationship with Jesus, a revelation of Him to our inner being, will fulfill them.

An alcoholic came to an evangelistic series we were helping with in the Olympic Stadium in Moscow. He often beat his wife and their son. After attending only five meetings, he had a TV reporter with little enthusiasm for the stadium meetings interview him on the street. The reporter asked, "Why do you go to these meetings? We don't need these foreigners here."

Millions heard this man's answer on TV: "All I know is I was an alcoholic. I have attended five meetings and haven't had a drink in 10 days. I haven't beaten my wife or hit my son. My life is changed. Our family is changed."

The Saviour he met is the Saviour John unveils in the Revelation. He transforms our lives and is the answer to our every longing, the fulfillment of our every need.

DRG

NOVEMBER 19

A RICH AND FULL LIFE FOR YOU

Grace and peace to you . . . from Jesus Christ, who is the faithful witness, the firstborn from the dead, and the ruler of the kings of the earth. To him who loves us and has freed us from our sins by his blood.

Rev. 1:4, 5, NIV.

A young man in Wichita, Kansas, heard the good news about Jesus on the Voice of Prophecy broadcast. As he listened, He experienced renewal in his life. The risen Christ, "who loves us and has freed us from our sins by his blood," miraculously changed his heart and life.

After the broadcast he wrote to H.M.S. Richards, Jr.: "I've been a Christian for only about 30 minutes, but I feel my life finally has meaning. I can't even begin to tell you the way I feel. God came into my heart like the sun rising in the morning. I couldn't believe it was happening to me, but I am so thankful. I feel God wants me to tell the whole world about my newfound life. A newfound Christian, Rob."

The wonder of what Jesus does for us and in us sets our hearts aflame. How John's heart must have glowed with thanksgiving as he wrote to the seven churches. His message of "grace and peace" from Jesus must have resonated in his transformed heart and life. Had not Jesus graciously taken him, a rough-and-ready fisher, and filled his life with peace? As John thought back on what he was and what he had now become in Christ, the wonder of it all must have touched him as he wrote about the crucified Christ, who had loved him and freed him from his "sins by his blood."

Jesus' life was a "faithful witness" to His fairness and His sterling character. He loved us so much that He died in our place. Then He broke out of the tomb and became "the firstborn from the dead," who is now rightfully "the ruler of the kings of the earth." And "he is coming with the clouds" to deliver us from our world of sin (Rev. 1:7, NIV). This vision of the living Christ must certainly have drawn John even nearer to the One whose life-changing presence means so much. The experience of the apostle John and that of the young man in Wichita is one that all who seek the personal presence of the living Christ may have. Do you have this personal relationship with Jesus?

DRG

JESUS THE LIVING CONQUEROR

Then I turned to see the voice that spoke with me. And having turned I saw seven golden lampstands, and in the midst of the seven lampstands One like the Son of Man.

Rev. 1:12, 13, NKJV.

A voice spoke to John, the last living disciple of Jesus, and instructed him to deliver a message to the churches of Asia. As John turned to see the source of the voice, he had a beautiful vision of the risen Christ; and then, wonder of wonders, the vision of Jesus became a living presence (Rev. 1:10-16).

As the only remaining founder of the Christian church, John felt the burden of the churches resting heavily upon him. For years he had been looking for the return of Jesus to bring triumph to the church. But now how dark the outlook! The early leaders were dead. The church slipped further and further into apostasy. The future kingdom of Christ seemed more remote than ever. And John, probably in his nineties, was in exile on the rocky Isle of Patmos (verse 9). No wonder Jesus came to encourage him.

"Richly favored was this beloved disciple. He had seen his Master in Gethsemane. . . . He had seen Him hanging on the cross of Calvary, the object of cruel mockery and abuse. Now John is once more permitted to behold his Lord. But how changed is His appearance! He is no longer a Man of Sorrows, despised and humiliated by men. He is clothed in a garment of heavenly brightness. . . . His voice is like the music of many waters. His countenance shines as the sun" *(The Acts of the Apostles,* p. 582). John emerged from his vision with firm faith in the final victory of the living Christ. The messages the apostle passed along to the churches from the living Christ must have given them similar assurance.

Jesus is with us today. The same Jesus who talked to the unhappy Samaritan woman at Jacob's well and by the drawing power of His presence opened to her a richer, more satisfying life. The Jesus who comforted the sick, the sorrowing, the lonely, and sent new life coursing through them as healing virtue flowed out from Him. The Jesus who bent low under the weight of our sins as He trudged to Calvary, there to die to free us from the sinner's lot of unhappiness, frustration, and guilt. The Jesus who died to point the way to real living. That Jesus lives! Is He alive in your heart? Then you'll have a wonderful day!

DRG

NOVEMBER 21

"THE MESSAGE OF THE CROSS"

The message of the cross is foolishness to those who are perishing, but to us who are being saved it is the power of God.
1 Cor. 1:18, NKJV.

John Johnson is not his real name, but the facts are real enough. His story is true.

"I started going out with the fellows. We'd stand on the corner and smoke marijuana.

"One night a man came by and said, 'I have something that will really turn you on.' He took us up to his room and let us sniff some powdered heroin. It made me sick, but after I left the room, I suddenly felt warm and good all over. For two or three months I came back for more. But I didn't miss work, and nobody knew about it.

"Finally I began increasing the doses. That's when I got into trouble. I began missing work and lost several jobs. I was a mainliner now, a slave to heroin. My habit was expensive. Needing money, I started to steal.

"My wife knew something was wrong and tried to help me. Finally she determined I was hopeless and left me. I began forging checks. The law caught me and time after time sent me to jail, where I'd stop cold turkey.

"Near Thanksgiving my brother and I were in New York's main drug area. We heard a sound truck. As it came near, we saw on it a man we knew as an addict. I touched my brother and said, 'Man, that's Bill! He looks clean. He's got a suit and tie on. What's he up to?'"

To make a long story short, the power of Jesus living in him broke John's slavery to drugs. Before John saw Bill on that truck, "the message of the cross [was] foolishness" to him. But when Jesus came into John's heart, he realized "it is the power of God."

The faith that looks at Jesus dying on the cross is not a mere poetic dream, a theory, or a philosophy—it is the power of God in the human heart that opens the door for Jesus to make changes in our daily life. We do not have to be a heroin addict to experience His transforming power. How thankful we can be for the good news that Jesus' power is available for every temptation that comes to us as Christians.

HMSR

JESUS IS ALIVE!

I am the First and the Last. I am the Living One; I was dead, and behold I am alive for ever and ever! And I hold the keys of death and Hades.

REV. 1:17, 18, NIV.

In India I saw the Taj Mahal in all its graceful splendor, shimmering in the reflecting pool in the soft light of a full moon. This monument to love, built by Shah Jahan as a burial crypt for the wife he loved, is without doubt the most beautiful tomb—in fact, probably the most beautiful building—in the world. Its graceful domes and spires of white marble are inlaid with semiprecious stones in delicate designs. As a tomb it is famous because of its beauty.

Visiting the Valley of the Kings, I went down into King Tut's tomb. There I saw the burial chamber and the stone sarcophagus in which his body once lay. The next day in Cairo I explored room after room containing the objects found in Tut's tomb. His is one of the few tombs of an Egyptian king not emptied by grave robbers before archaeologists discovered it. Tut's tomb is famous because it was full.

A few days later I visited Jerusalem and the Garden Tomb. Though it is probably not the actual tomb where Jesus was buried, to me it was the most inspiring place in old Jerusalem. The Garden Tomb is famous because it is empty.

Many years after leaving the tomb empty and ascending into heaven, Jesus announced to John, "I am the Living One." Jesus' world-shaking proclamation is a conqueror's ringing words of permanent victory over death. The triumph of the gospel came not through a dead man, but through the living God-man who is "alive for ever and ever."

The Saviour who announced after His death, "I am the Living One," is still alive. He holds "the keys of death and Hades [the grave]" and can give us eternal life. He declares: "Because I live, you also will live" (John 14:19, NIV). Christ is now here with us so we "may have life, and have it to the full" (John 10:10, NIV). We can come to Him at any time—morning, noon, or night—and in any place—whether it be at home, at work, or at play. Jesus wants to be involved and helpful in every aspect of our daily lives. Is He near you, with you, in you to guide and give you contentment today?

DRG

JESUS LIVES, SO "DON'T BE AFRAID!"

Though I am the First and Last, the Living One who died, who is now alive forevermore, who has the keys of hell and death—don't be afraid!
Rev. 1:17, 18, TLB.

As we traveled along the highway, my 5-year-old nephew sat meditating. Finally he looked at his mother and inquired, "Mama, is Jesus still on the cross?"

"Now, Kenny, you know better than that," his mother answered.

A brief silence followed; then Kenny said, "Yes, Jesus is in heaven, and He is coming again."

We do not serve a dead Saviour who is still on the cross. Jesus appeared to John with the pronouncement, "I am . . . the Living One who died, who is now alive forevermore." His words were like a flash of lightning that illuminated the world. The triumph of the risen Christ caught the imagination, the heart, the very life of people everywhere, and changed the face of the world as nothing else has ever done.

After seeing Jesus revealed in all His glory, John must have thrilled as Jesus announced, "John, I am alive! I am here with you to relieve you of your cares. I am bearing the burden of the churches on My heart. Rest in peace. I am alive—'alive forevermore.' 'Don't be afraid!' " The vision must have given John fantastic assurance and firm faith in the final victory of the living Christ. And the Jesus who on Patmos laid His hand of comfort on John's head is always near to bring help in every time of stress. No matter where we are or under what conditions we find ourselves, it is our privilege to feel that same hand comforting and strengthening us in trial, loneliness, sickness, or discouragement. Today we can hear that same voice saying, "Don't be afraid!"

"Through all our trials we have a never-failing Helper. He does not leave us alone to struggle with temptation, to battle with evil, and be finally crushed with burdens and sorrow. Though now He is hidden from mortal sight, the ear of faith can hear His voice saying, Fear not; I am with you. . . . The griefs that lie too deep to be breathed into any human ear, I know. . . . Though your pain touch no responsive chord in any heart on earth, look unto Me, and live" (*The Desire of Ages,* p. 483).

DRG

JESUS CARES ABOUT YOU

Do not be afraid. I am the first and the last, the living one. I am he who was dead, and now you see me alive for timeless ages! I hold in my hand the keys of death and the grave.

Rev. 1:17, 18, Phillips.

At one time Martin Luther became unbearably depressed as his reforms languished. His wife, knowing that she must do something about it, one day appeared before him dressed in black. "What is it? Who has died?" Luther questioned.

"Only think, my dear doctor, the Lord in heaven is dead! How could my lord be so discouraged if God were still living?"

Luther saw the point: Jesus lives! His face broke into an appreciative smile as he thanked his wife for the impressive lesson.

It must have lifted John's discouraged spirits on Patmos to see the divine glory of the risen Christ and hear His reassuring message, "I . . . was dead, and now you see me alive for timeless ages!" Jesus' message is also for us today. We need never face a single perplexity of life alone. Christ is vitally interested in us and concerned about our problems. We can bring to Him our every need, our every desire, our every joy. "Cast all your anxiety on him because he cares for you" (1 Peter 5:7, NIV). Then "mourn not as those who are hopeless and helpless. Jesus lives, and because He lives, we shall live also. From grateful hearts, from lips touched with holy fire, let the glad song ring out, Christ is risen! He lives to make intercession for us. Grasp this hope, and it will hold the soul like a sure, tried anchor. Believe, and thou shalt see the glory of God" (*The Desire of Ages,* p. 794).

Jesus also declares in His emancipation proclamation for the human race, "I hold in my hand the keys of death and the grave." His words have thundered through the ages. The message of the risen Christ burns brightly today with hope for dying people. When He comes again to release us and our loved ones from death and the grave, Jesus will use the same keys with which He unlocked His own tomb and released Himself. Because He lives, we too shall live!

DRG

NOVEMBER 25

JESUS, THE HOPE OF THE CHURCH

> *The mystery of the seven stars that you saw in my right hand and of the seven golden lampstands is this: The seven stars are the angels of the seven churches, and the seven lampstands are the seven churches.*
>
> REV. 1:20, NIV.

In the vision of Patmos, John saw the risen Christ walking "among the lampstands" (Rev. 1:13, NIV), holding the seven stars "in his right hand" (verse 16, NIV). The lampstands represent "the seven churches," while the seven stars are "the angels of the seven churches," a symbol of both heavenly and earthly messengers who guide the church. Jesus is in the midst of His church, holding its leadership in His right hand. The message given to encourage John also speaks to a languishing church: Christ is alive! John has seen Him! His presence is ever near, assuring our salvation. Despite trial, persecution, worldliness, or a forbidding future, Jesus stands in the center of His church, supporting its leaders in His hand.

Death and the grave still stalk the earth. The enemy continues to tempt God's people. The righteous may sigh and cry because of the lack of spiritual power among His people. But the message of Jesus to His church remains one of cheer: "I am in the midst of My church; I am holding its leadership in My right hand."

"But if men, looking upon the stricken human scene today, are fain to cry, 'Christ, Thou shouldst be living at this hour: the world hath need of Thee!'—back comes the answer with a thousand trumpets in it, 'Should be? He is!' 'I am He that liveth, and was dead; and, behold, I am alive for evermore.' And you, the commissioned servants of the Lord of the Resurrection, are to tell men that the same Jesus who was with Latimer and Ridley in the fire, . . . with Bunyan in prison, with Gordon in Khartoum, with Shackelton on the great ice-barrier, with Paul in the wilds of Asia, with John in the convict-mines of Patmos, with Peter in the Roman arena—that this same Jesus still travels through the world in the greatness of His strength, mighty to save, still meets the troubled heart with the divine promise, 'Lo, as I was with all those others, so will I be with thee!' " (James S. Stewart, *Heralds of God* [New York: Charles Scribner's Sons, 1946], p. 91).

DRG

JESUS MEETS OUR EVERY NEED

Write this letter to the messenger for the church in Ephesus. This is the message from the one who holds the seven stars in his right hand, the one who walks among the seven gold lampstands.

Rev. 2:1, margin, NLT.

In Revelation 2 and 3 John reviews the condition of the churches of Asia Minor. His thoughts begin with Ephesus, and then his mind goes in order around the circle of churches in Asia Minor and notes the major need of each of the seven local churches.

To each church Jesus introduces Himself with the words "These things saith he." Then follows a glimpse of some attribute of His character. Jesus presents Himself as the Saviour who can meet the specific need of each church. Each attribute appears in John's description of the living Christ recorded in Revelation 1:12-20. The introductions in Revelation 2 and 3 add to the description of Jesus in Revelation 1.

John is also looking down the stream of history from his day to ours. To each of the seven periods of the church John presents a character trait of Jesus tailored to the specific problem of that particular era of the church. As the need of each church unfolds, one fact becomes increasingly clear: Jesus is a Saviour who can help His church. The Saviour is "alive for evermore" (Rev. 1:18), walking among the people of each church, comforting, soothing, helping, drawing.

The church of Ephesus was noted for its purity. John records only one lament against it: "You don't love me or each other as you did at first" (Rev. 2:4, NLT). Although it remained faithful and true, it had lost the zeal and love that once fired its membership. So to Ephesus Jesus introduced Himself as "the one who holds the seven stars in his right hand, the one who walks among the seven gold lampstands." The picture here is one of vigorous activity to benefit the church. The church leadership and the church members, held securely by Jesus, have resulted in an apostolic church of purity. Wouldn't it be wonderful to belong to the Ephesus church?

DRG

JESUS, LIFE-GIVER TO THE MARTYR

Write this letter to the messenger for the church in Smyrna. This is the message from the one who is the First and the Last, who died and is alive.

REV. 2:8, MARGIN, NLT.

Poverty, tribulation, prison, and death characterize the church of Smyrna. Rome waged sporadic, localized, but severe persecutions against it. "The horrors of this persecution are vividly described by the church historian Theodoret, who describes the gathering of the bishops of the church to the Council of Nicaea some years after the end of the persecution (A.D. 325). Some came without eyes, some without arms, which had been pulled from their sockets, others with their bodies horribly maimed in different ways. Many, of course, did not survive this time of trouble" (*The Seventh-day Adventist Bible Commentary,* vol. 7, p. 748).

A young girl in the Roman arena who watched the soldiers throw her mother to the lions illustrates the spirit of the martyrs. As she saw her mother torn to bits, she could bear it no longer. Rising to her feet, she cried, "I too am a Christian." As a result the authorities hurled her to the lions.

To the Smyrna church Jesus introduced Himself as the life-giver, "the one who is the First and the Last, who died and is alive." He promised those suffering persecution and death, "Don't be afraid of what you are about to suffer. . . . Remain faithful even when facing death, and I will give you the crown of life" (Rev. 2:10, NLT). Jesus died at the hands of His persecutors, so His words of encouragement are particularly meaningful to those who suffer for their faith today.

You may be concerned about how to cope with persecution now and the threat of martyrdom in the end-time. Note these reassuring words from God's messenger to His church today: "Often your mind may be clouded because of pain [physical or emotional]. Then do not try to think. You know that Jesus loves you. He understands your weakness. You may do His will by simply resting in His arms" (*The Ministry of Healing,* p. 251).

DRG

WHAT ARE YOU THANKFUL FOR?

> *Give thanks to the Lord, for he is good; his love endures forever.*
> *Ps. 106:1, NIV.*

Ken was baptized as a result of the satellite evangelistic series our church sponsored. The next year the church decided not to participate. When Ken heard this, he persuaded the pastor to allow him to downlink the next satellite series in our church. Even with practically no advertising several nonmembers attended regularly.

Then one night at the meeting Ken told me that the editor of the church newsletter had asked him to write a Thanksgiving article. "What are you thankful for?" he questioned. Naturally I'm thankful for a new member like Ken who has a burden to win others to Jesus. Ken followed up with the question, What are you most thankful for? I'm thankful for a dedicated wife, for two loving daughters, for beautiful sunsets, and many other things, but I'm most thankful for the heart that bled. Jesus' blood washed away my sins, giving me a new and meaningful life and the assurance of eternal life with Jesus. In fact, I'm so thankful for Jesus' heart that bled that I feel like shouting "Praise the Lord!" "Give thanks to the Lord because He is good and His loving kindness endures forever. Who knows all the great things the Lord has done? Who can praise Him enough for His mighty acts?" (Ps. 106:1, 2, Clear Word).

When Matthew Henry—who wrote a popular Bible commentary—was mugged, he recorded in his diary: "Let me be thankful first because I had never been robbed before; second, although they took my purse, they did not take my life; third, because although they took my all, it was not much; and fourth, because it was I who was robbed, not I who robbed." Billy Graham asks: "I wonder if I could be that thankful. Could you?"

Daily Jesus' love that "endures forever" blesses each Christian. We just cannot "praise Him enough for His mighty acts." Have you responded to Jesus' unfailing love? What are you the most thankful for today? Why not lift up your heart in prayer just now and thank Jesus for His heart that bled, and for everything you can recall during the past year that you should be thankful for? Then share your thanks with others and make this a very special day.

DRG

JESUS, COMFORT TO THE BIBLE LOVER

Write this letter to the messenger for the church in Pergamum. This is the message from the one who has a sharp two-edged sword.

REV. 2:12, MARGIN, NLT.

The Pergamos church opened the door to pagan doctrine and practices. Christ condemned those who tolerated those "who are like Balaam. . . . He taught them to worship idols by eating food offered to idols and by committing sexual sin" (Rev. 2:14, NLT). A spirit of compromise led God's people to accept pagan ideas, dethroning the Bible as the standard of truth.

To Pergamos Jesus introduced Himself as "the one who has the sharp two-edged sword," a symbol of the Bible (Heb. 4:12). Jesus characterized Himself as the Saviour who reveals Himself through His Written Word. This striking revelation of Jesus must have been a great comfort to the believers in Pergamos who remained obedient to the Word.

A refugee from Russia with little English and thus with limited job opportunities told of being fired on Friday because he was not willing to work after sundown. His employer had given him a job as a favor and couldn't understand why he couldn't work Friday night to help get out the backlog of orders on the day before Christmas. The following week the employer called him back to work "because you are such a faithful worker." Standing firm for Jesus and His Word always pays. Remember, He stood firm for us at Calvary.

The church of Thyatira plunged into deep apostasy. Dark as the picture was, some did remain faithful and despite persecution clung to God's Word. Here is an item copied from a church register: "Indictments were found against Bible lovers as follows: 'Against John Barret, because he, John Barret, was heard in his own house, before his wife and maid there present, to recite the epistle of St. James, which epistle, with many other things, he had perfectly without book.'"

To a church suffering such indignities Jesus referred to Himself as "the Son of God, whose eyes are bright like flames of fire, whose feet are like polished bronze" (Rev. 2:18, NLT). The portrait of Jesus is primarily a message of assurance to those who stand true to God's Word.

DRG

JESUS, LIGHTER OF REVIVAL FIRES

Write this letter to the messenger for the church in Sardis. This is the message from the one who has the sevenfold Spirit of God and the seven stars.

Rev. 3:1, first part, margin, NLT.

To the church of Sardis, Jesus said, "You have a reputation for being alive—but you are dead" (Rev. 3:1, last part, NLT). Sardis had the reputation of being dynamically Christian, but formalism ate away the vitals of her experience. People considered Sardis as alive, but it had the smell of death about it. Jesus revealed Himself to Sardis as "the one who has the sevenfold Spirit of God." As Sardis came close to Jesus through the Holy Spirit's power, formalism received a deathblow. God's church today needs the sevenfold outpouring of the Spirit!

The Philadelphia church, the church of "brotherly love," was experiencing a great religious awakening. As revival fires burned, people searched diligently for a vital connection with Jesus and a deep personal experience. To this church Jesus described Himself as "the one who has the key of David" (Rev. 3:7, NLT). Holder of this key, He opens the door to the treasures of heaven for those who seek Him.

During the era of the historical Philadelphian church, Jesus inspired men, women, and children to light the fires of revival. He inflamed individuals such as James White. One night while White was preaching in a schoolhouse, a disorderly mob circulated outside. He laid aside his Bible and began to speak in a compelling way about the coming judgment day. Holding up a nail, he said, "Some poor sinner cast this spike at me last evening. God pity him! The worst wish I have for him is that he is at this moment as happy as I am. Why should I resent this insult when my Master had them driven through His hands?" White backed up against the wall with outstretched hands, dramatizing human cruelty to our crucified Saviour. He then made a fervent appeal, and more than 100 gave their hearts to Jesus. After White's stirring message, others escorted him through the dangerous crowd outside the building. He turned to thank the escort who had assured his safety, but, finding no one, concluded that his escort must have been an angel. Such was the spirit of the men and women in Philadelphia whom Jesus set on fire. How we need Jesus to set our hearts on fire today!

DRG

DECEMBER 1

JESUS, ADVOCATE IN TIME OF JUDGMENT

Write this letter to the messenger for the church in Laodicea. This is the message from the one who is the Amen—the faithful and true witness, the source of God's creation.

REV. 3:14, MARGIN, NLT.

The historical Laodicean church covers the years from 1844 to Christ's second coming. To the church of the judgment hour, a body suffering from a lack of spiritual power, Jesus presents Himself as the "Amen," meaning that no appeal exists above or beyond Him. Jesus is "the source of God's creation" and as Creator offers to renew the hearts of "lukewarm" Laodiceans who lack spiritual power (Rev. 3:16, NLT).

Also the "faithful and true witness," He does not gloss over a person's need and flatter the individual into thinking his or her condition is satisfactory when it really requires attention, for the judgment is in progress. Some think the straight testimony of the True Witness is to condemn a sinner. But the Laodicean is sick—sin-sick—and Jesus came not to condemn but to save (John 3:17). The "lukewarm" lack certainty and security. Jesus invites such downcast ones to grasp His hand in full assurance. The remedy for Laodicea is not condemnation, but Jesus—Jesus cures and saves.

In *How Can I Find God?* Dr. Leslie Weatherhead tells of a woman who in her dream stood before a plate-glass window, pounding on it, attempting to attract the attention of Jesus whom she saw standing on the other side. After she quit pounding and screaming, Jesus touched her on the shoulder and said quietly, "Why are you making so much noise? There is nothing between us."

It is a message Laodiceans need to hear! How many of us today are seeking to attract the attention of a Saviour whom we believe is far off in heaven, when He is by our side, offering to supply our every need. He wants to transform our lives. Through His Holy Spirit He seeks to be our personal Companion at work, at school, at play, around the home, in every aspect of life. He longs to give us guidance and comfort. Such a friendship with Jesus fills the life with peace, happiness, victory, and assurance. I know this is true, for many Christians are experiencing the satisfaction of a daily friendship with Jesus. Are you?

DRG

JESUS, MIRACLE DOCTOR FOR LAODICEA

My advice to you is to buy pure gold from me, gold purified by fire—only then will you truly be rich. And to purchase from me white garments, clean and pure, so you won't be naked and ashamed; and to get medicine from me to heal your eyes and give you back your sight.
Rev. 3:18, TLB.

A Sabbath school teacher lamented about the disciples going to sleep in Gethsemane when Jesus desperately needed comfort, then raised the pointed question: "What would you have done if you had been in their place?" He obviously didn't expect an answer. But a woman who possibly was suffering from spiritual blindness spoke up: "If I had been there, I wouldn't have slept." She echoed the self-righteous Laodicean cry, " 'I am rich, with everything I want; I don't need a thing!' And you don't realize that spiritually you are wretched and miserable and poor and blind and naked" (Rev. 3:17, TLB). Laodicea thinks it is spiritually rich, but it is blind to its need of Jesus, the all-sufficient panacea, the answer to our deepest longings. So Jesus prescribes three miracle medicines for Laodicea in verse 18:

1. "Buy pure gold from me," gold purified by fire, for "only then will you truly be rich." Those in Christ are "rich in faith" (James 2:5, TLB) and "rich in good works" (1 Tim. 6:18, TLB). They are consumed by a "faith working through love" (Gal. 5:6, TLB). Some say, "I don't want to be lukewarm. I want to love people with a zeal set on fire by genuine faith, but how?" Jesus gives us His faith to live by (Rev. 14:12) and His love to love with (Rom. 5:5).

2. "Purchase from me white garments, clean and pure" that represent "the righteousness of saints" (Rev. 19:8). Not the shameful rags of our own righteousness that make us "naked and ashamed," but the robe of Christ's righteousness that, because of His atoning death, He can pass on to us.

3. "Get medicine from me to heal your eyes and give you back your sight." Jesus anoints us with the Spirit to empower us to make giant strides in Christian living. The eyesalve of the Spirit heals our spiritual blindness, and we discern our need of Jesus.

Christ gives the most valuable and appropriate gifts in the world: riches for our poverty, white raiment for our nakedness, healing for our blindness. He is the sure cure for the Laodicean.

DRG

DECEMBER 3

JESUS IS AT THE DOOR KNOCKING

Behold, I stand at the door and knock. If anyone hears My voice and opens the door, I will come in to him and dine with him, and he with Me.

Rev. 3:20, NKJV.

A small boy and his father visited an art gallery at which the father, a minister, sought inspiration for his sermon. As they stood before Hunt's great painting of Jesus standing at the door, His "head . . . covered with dew" and His "locks with the drops of the night" (S. of Sol. 5:2, NKJV), a tear came to the father's eyes. The son looked up into the emotional face of his father and said, "Oh, Daddy, did that Man get in? Did He get in?" It is the question of the ages.

"Jesus stands knocking—knocking at the door of your hearts—and yet, for all this, some say continually, 'I cannot find Him.' Why not? He says, 'I stand here knocking. Why do you not open the door, and say, Come in, dear Lord?' I am so glad for these simple directions as to the way to find Jesus. If it were not for them, I should not know how to find Him whose presence I desire so much. Open the door now, and empty the soul-temple of the buyers and sellers, and invite the Lord to come in. Say to Him, 'I will love thee with all my soul. I will work the works of righteousness. I will obey the law of God.' Then you will feel the peaceful presence of Jesus" (Ellen G. White, in *Review and Herald,* Aug. 28, 1888).

The righteousness of Christ was at the heart of the 1888 message. According to some, we become righteous through meritorious works. But the Reformers recognized that we are declared righteous, not by works or merit, but by asking Jesus to bear our sins and clothe us with His righteousness. Jesus brought this message to Laodicea in 1888, and He desires to give it to the church today. He now stands knocking at the door of the church and of each heart in each congregation—your heart and mine.

DRG

JESUS IS AT THE DOOR WAITING

Look! I have been standing at the door and I am constantly knocking. If anyone hears me calling him and opens the door, I will come in and fellowship with him and he with me.

Rev. 3:20, TLB.

If a billionaire knocked at your door offering you riches, you would instantly invite him in. Should the president of the United States appear at your door to offer you honor, you would allow him in. Or if the queen of England stood at your door with an invitation to visit Buckingham Palace, you would usher her in. Jesus is knocking at your heart's door and mine. How foolish we would be not to open our lives to the One who owns all the wealth of the ages, the King of kings who wants to give us eternal riches and eternal life. When Jesus enters a person's heart, He becomes real in the life.

Jesus tells the one who opens the door, "I will come in and fellowship with him and he with me." He wants to form a personal union with each of us. True, He knocks at the door of the church and at the door of the world through the church, but He also stands at the door of every person's heart. He wants to "fellowship" with us—live in our hearts every moment of every day. Such a union is to be a heart union. Our spiritual nature controls the will, the reasoning powers, and the affections. Jesus wants to save the whole person, to satisfy every facet of our entire being. An eternal union, we will sit with Jesus and the Father on the thrones in heaven (Rev. 3: 21).

Jesus stands at your heart's door laden with heaven's riches—gold, white raiment, eyesalve. He freely offers the healing balm to satisfy our every need and longing, to ultimately save us from every trial, sorrow, sin, and woe, and even from eternal death.

DRG

DECEMBER 5

JESUS THE SLAIN LAMB

> *Then I saw a Lamb, looking as if it had been slain, standing in the center of the throne.*
> REV. 5:6, NIV.

Martin Luther, at one time in great distress, asked scholar and friend Johannes von Staupitz for advice. Staupitz declared, "Look to the wounds of Christ." Jesus, the wounded Lamb, has brought hope and courage to thousands of distressed sufferers. Like Staupitz to a distressed Luther, John invites every distressed sufferer to look to the wounded Lamb for hope and courage in suffering.

The suffering Lamb is the central figure in the sacrificial system. The Old Testament mentions the sacrificial lamb more than 100 times. The New Testament speaks of Jesus as the Lamb only four times outside the book of Revelation. Revelation refers to Him as the Lamb 27 times, and He is the central figure of the book. John first introduces Jesus as the Lamb in chapter 5: "Then I saw a Lamb, looking as if it had been slain, standing in the center of the throne." The "slain" Lamb has conquered death and the grave and sits on the throne in heaven.

The book of Revelation presents "Worthy is the Lamb, who was slain" as the theme of heaven's song (Rev. 5:12, NIV). The blood of the Lamb washes away the sins of the redeemed and clothes them with the white robes of Christ's righteousness (Rev. 7:9, 14). Through the blood of the Lamb the redeemed are victorious over Satan (Rev. 12:11). The church is the Lamb's wife (Rev. 21:9-10), and a marriage supper celebrates our marriage to the Lamb (Rev. 19:7, 9). We take up residence in the Holy City, where "the Lord God Almighty and the Lamb are its temple" and its source of light (Rev. 21:22, 23, NIV). From the throne of God and of the Lamb flows the water of life to the tree of life that produces leaves to heal us and fruit to give us life (Rev. 22:1, 2). The Lamb ministers to us, and we serve Him (verses 3, 4). As the saved we will see the Lamb's face and will reign with Him forever and ever (verse 5).

DRG

WORTHY IS THE LAMB

> ***Worthy is the Lamb that was slain to receive power, and riches, and wisdom, and strength, honour, and glory, and blessing.***
>
> *Rev. 5:12.*

Revelation 4:1 reveals that "a door was opened in heaven" and a trumpet-like voice invited John to behold a vision of Jesus, the Lamb of God. The vision focused on the crucifixion and its relationship to the conflict between Christ and Satan. All the inhabitants of the universe have their eyes fixed on a great drama playing out before the throne. As the vision opens, John sees the Father on His throne holding a book "sealed with seven seals" (Rev. 5:1). The prophet's attention then rivets on an "angel proclaiming with a loud voice, Who is worthy to open the book, and to loose the seals thereof?" (verse 2). No human being, no angel, no being in the entire universe offers to open the book (verse 3). All remain silent as John "wept much" because no one was qualified to unseal the book (verse 4).

At this dramatic moment the slain Lamb steps forward and takes "the book out of the right hand of him that sat upon the throne" (verses 6, 7). Then the heavenly choir of 24 elders, the angels around the throne, and every created being in the universe unite in singing, "Worthy is the Lamb that was slain. . . . Blessing, and honour, and glory, and power, be unto him that sitteth upon the throne, and unto the Lamb for ever and ever" (verses 8-13).

What is in the book to cause this ovation? Of the Judean leaders who rejected Jesus, *Christ's Object Lessons* states: "Their decision was registered in the book which John saw in the hand of Him that sat upon the throne, the book which no man could open. In all its vindictiveness this decision will appear before them in the day when this book is unsealed" (p. 294). In the final judgment when the Lamb opens the book, every being in the universe will see the part that each, both the righteous and the wicked, have played in the struggle between good and evil (see Mal. 3:16; Matt. 12:36; and *The Great Controversy,* pp. 666, 667). When these scenes pass before the inhabitants of the entire universe, everyone will be satisfied that the Lamb has dealt faithfully with saved people, lost people, fallen angels, and even Satan himself (Rom. 14:10-12). Worthy is the Lamb!

DRG

DECEMBER 7

DELIVERANCE FROM ABOVE

I watched as he opened the sixth seal. There was a great earthquake. The sun turned black like sackcloth made of goat hair, the whole moon turned blood red, and the stars in the sky fell to earth, as late figs drop from a fig tree when shaken by a strong wind. The sky receded like a scroll, rolling up, and every mountain and island was removed from its place.

REV. 6:12-14, NIV.

During the January 1995 floods in California, the Ventura River, not far from where we live, became a torrent rushing into the sea at 40 miles per hour. Some people found themselves marooned on higher ground when the river reached flood stage. As the river continued to rise, the water began to cover even those refuges. The rushing water drowned one person and swept toward the sea. Helicopter crews rescued 17 people, saving them from a similar fate. As the helicopter hovered overhead, the pilot lowered a rope and lifted them each to safety. Note that their deliverance came from above.

When Jesus opened the sixth seal, John witnessed three dramatic signs that Christ's coming is near. Jesus earlier had predicted the same three events (Luke 21:11, 25) and added a fourth: "And upon the earth distress of nations, . . . men's hearts failing them for fear, and for looking after those things which are coming on the earth" (verse 25, 26). The first three signs are now history, and the world today is in the throes of the fourth great sign. Fear and distress over what is coming dominates society everywhere.

Deliverance could come only from above for those surrounded by the treacherous Ventura River. And our rescue from a world filled with "distress" and "fear" must also have its source from above. Jesus promises to deliver those who are ready: "Then they will see the Son of Man coming in a cloud with power and great glory. Now when these things begin to happen, look up and lift up your heads, because your redemption draws near" (verses 27, 28, NKJV). It's time to "look up"! Jesus is returning to deliver us from a fear-filled world.

DRG

GOD'S MARK OF DISTINCTION

Then I saw another angel coming up from the east, having the seal of the living God. He called out in a loud voice to the four angels . . . : "Do not harm the land or the sea or the trees until we put a seal on the foreheads of the servants of our God."

REV. 7:2, 3, NIV.

Throughout the Far East married Hindu women identify themselves with a blood-red spot about half the size of a dime on the center of their foreheads. Girls eligible for marriage may also display such a spot, but society strictly forbids a widow to do so. The mark distinguishes the married and the marriageable woman from those who are widows.

Upon His followers God also places a symbol—not a red spot, but a seal on the forehead that will protect them at Jesus' second coming. The forehead represents our spiritual nature. The seal is a mark of spiritual distinction, not an arbitrary symbol of approval, but a result of daily uniting our life with Jesus. The sealed ones are "wearing white robes" made "white in the blood of the Lamb" (Rev. 5:9, 14, NIV). They are clothed with Jesus' garments of righteousness (Rev. 19:8).

The seal symbolizes what Jesus does through His personal presence in our lives. By placing God's seal upon those wearing the white robes of His righteousness, Jesus prepares them to stand unharmed and unafraid at His second coming. As four angels hold back a whirlwind of international strife and destruction (Rev. 7:1), a fifth angel (probably Jesus) calls out "in a loud voice" to the four angels and asks them to hold on until the faithful are sealed with God's saving mark of distinction.

Jesus does more than simply look for people fit to receive the seal of God: He prepares them for it. Longing for us to be ready when He comes a second time, He knows our sinful condition and that our only hope is receiving the gift of His righteousness. As our living Saviour, He daily works to woo and win us through the drawing power of Calvary. When we are receptive to His gift of righteousness, He covers the record of our sinful past life and our bungling present existence with His perfect life of righteousness. Are you thankful for heaven's gift to you? Then thank Jesus and the Father.

DRG

DECEMBER 9

JESUS' COMING SILENCES HEAVEN

> ***When the Lamb opened the seventh seal, there was silence in heaven for about half an hour.***
> *Rev. 8:1, RSV.*

The Reformation sparked by Martin Luther vindicated the martyrs who had died in centuries past. When the prelates at Worms asked Luther to recant because his teachings conflicted with the medieval church, he lifted one hand toward heaven and placed the other firmly on the Bible, declaring, "Here I stand; I cannot do otherwise; God help me!" Truly the Bible is a firm foundation on which to stand.

The firm biblical position the Reformers took, and the Protestant renewal that followed, prepared the way for the great advent awakening. The fulfilling signs of Christ's soon coming during the sixth seal have inspired the advent movement. People everywhere are preparing for the second coming of Jesus. The seventh seal will soon open.

"When the Lamb opened the seventh seal, there was silence in heaven for about half an hour." Heaven stands emptied of its multitudes of angels. They have come to earth with Jesus to gather the redeemed, who wear the white robes of Jesus' righteousness. That will be a wonderful day when Jesus puts an end to suffering, sorrowing, and death. Pain and hunger will vanish. Immorality and evil habits will disappear. Strife and threatened world destruction will cease. Jesus will satisfy to the fullest the wholesome desires of every heart. Happiness, a beautiful home, communion with congenial friends and loved ones, useful work to do and to enjoy—all await the redeemed.

Think of seeing Jesus the Lamb smiling down upon the redeemed. Imagine watching the graves open and seeing families long separated by death reunited. Deformed bodies will straighten, and the aged will take on the vigor of eternal youth. Then angels will carry the saved in all their radiant beauty to Jesus. The redeemed will ascend to heaven with Jesus to dwell with Him throughout all eternity. We all must be there!

DRG

JESUS OUR ETERNAL MEDIATOR

Another angel, who had a golden censer, came and stood at the altar. He was given much incense to offer, with the prayers of all the saints, on the golden altar before the throne. The smoke of the incense, together with the prayers of the saints, went up before God from the angel's hand.

Rev. 8:3, 4, NIV.

When our oldest daughter was 6, she and her sister who was two years younger had been having numerous quarrels. I felt it was time for a fatherly chat. So I called her aside and commended her for going into her bedroom to have her personal worship each morning and for asking Jesus to be with her. After I told her how much I appreciated how good she usually was, I cautiously suggested that it would be gratifying if she would not quarrel with her sister. "But, Daddy," she countered, "I try not to, and I ask Jesus to forgive me when I do."

"Yes, I know," I replied, "but I was just thinking how nice it would be if you didn't do these things."

"Well, Daddy," she responded, "everybody makes mistakes."

Yes, everybody makes mistakes. But Jesus, our eternal mediator, is near to rectify our errors and restore our union with God that sin has short-circuited.

In vision John saw Jesus' activity as our mediator before God's throne. "The prayers of all the saints" ascend to God and affirm Jesus' connection with us. He reaches up with His divine arm and encircles the throne of God, then with His human arm hugs lost people. Jesus is continually mediating, coming close to people, influencing their hearts, attempting to draw and to win.

"The golden altar before the throne" on which the incense burned perpetually is a type of Jesus' continual intercession. "As our Mediator, Christ works incessantly. Whether men receive or reject Him, He works earnestly for them. He grants them life and light, striving by His Spirit to win them from Satan's service" (Ellen G. White, in *Review and Herald,* Mar. 12, 1901). So if today you have made mistakes, if you need comfort, if you lack joy, if you need power to live a better life, then look toward the golden altar—to Jesus' continual activity in your behalf before God's throne. And if things seem rosy today, approach Jesus and tell Him that you love Him.

DRG

DECEMBER 11

JESUS, THE HOPE OF THE WORLD

I saw another mighty angel come down from heaven, clothed with a cloud: and a rainbow was upon his head, and his face was as it were the sun, and his feet as pillars of fire; and he had in his hand a little book open: and he set his right foot upon the sea, and his left foot on the earth.
REV. *10:1, 2.*

After a minister preached in a Southern city, a Black church member said to him, "You've got white skin, but you have a black heart." What did he mean? "You understand the needs and longings of the African-American soul."

Jesus has the heart of people from all races—an African heart, an Asian heart, a French heart, a Russian heart, an American heart, a Spanish heart—a world heart. Jesus' human heart senses the needs of all people. John testified about Christ that "he knew what was in man" (John 2:25). Issuing as it does from the heart of Jesus, Christianity has a universal appeal. It is the only religion that reaches the masses of both the Orient and the Occident. Jesus is the hope of the world.

In Revelation 10 John sees a vision of the global Christ with His feet stretching across the world, transcending the bounds of nationality and race. Jesus stands with an open book in His hand, making His plea felt in every human heart. John's description of Jesus in chapter 10 is similar to the picture of Jesus in Revelation 1:15, 16.

The vision in Revelation characterizes Jesus as a "mighty angel." Though He does not have the finite nature of an angel, as a messenger of good news He is director of the angels (1 Thess. 4:16). Holding the little book in His hand, Jesus announces that the seventh trumpet is about to sound and the "mystery of God," the gospel good news, is soon to "be finished" (Rev. 10:7). Jesus reaches into the hearts of people around the world, inspiring them to preach the everlasting gospel and prepare the way for His coming.

When Adventist preachers misunderstood the message, the bitter disappointment of 1844 followed. Then Jesus instructed us, "Thou must prophesy [witness] again before many peoples, and nations" (verse 11). You may ask, "How am I to witness?" Remember, Jesus knows what is in us, so ask Him for your instructions. He may say, "Witness daily by your godly life, or be a pastor, or give out literature, or . . ."

DRG

WASHED WHITE

These are they who have come out of the great tribulation; they have washed their robes and made them white in the blood of the Lamb.
Rev. 7:14, RSV.

The seal Jesus places upon His followers is not a visible mark on the forehead that protects them in the day of His coming. The forehead symbolizes our spiritual nature. When Jesus comes, the sealed ones are "clothed in white robes" (Rev. 7:9, RSV). "They have washed their robes and made them white in the blood of the Lamb." Having committed a personal, active, absolute surrender to Jesus, they bear His likeness in character.

Those God has sealed wear Jesus' garments of righteousness (Rev. 19:8). "All who cherish the Lord as their portion in this life will be under His control, and will receive the sign, the mark of God, which shows them to be God's special possession. Christ's righteousness will go before them" (*The Seventh-day Adventist Bible Commentary,* Ellen G. White Comments, vol. 7, p. 969).

He causes us to grow from day to day into His likeness. Upon His responsive followers who have won distinction in outstanding Christian living, Jesus places His seal. Are you thankful for heaven's gift to you? Then why not thank Jesus and the Father?

DRG

DECEMBER 13

JESUS, THE PRINCE OF PROVIDENCE

The kingdom of the world has become the kingdom of our Lord and of his Christ, and he will reign for ever and ever.
Rev. 11:15, NIV.

Mustering 129 vessels and a combined army and navy of 27,000 men, Philip II of Spain sent his seemingly invincible Armada across the English Channel in 1588. He intended to destroy Protestantism in England and restore Catholic rule. By all human standards he possessed the means to accomplish his purpose.

The British could oppose the invincible Armada with only 80 small, poorly fitted vessels. Victory for Spain appeared certain. But a mighty storm arose and left the British the victors. The failure of the Armada ended Spain's naval power. When Philip received word of the Armada's defeat, he exclaimed, "God's will be done; I sent my fleet to fight with the English, not with the elements." God shapes the destiny of the nations.

In the prophecy of the seven trumpets recorded in Revelation 8 to 11 John sees Jesus guiding in the affairs of the nations. Symbolized by an angel standing before the throne of God (Rev. 8:3-5), Jesus sent six angels with trumpets to accomplish the fall of Rome (Rev. 8:2-9:18). Jesus, as the voice from the horns of the golden altar, guided in events that saved Protestantism in Western Europe during the Reformation (Rev. 9:13-18).

The drama climaxes under the seventh trumpet when "the kingdom of the world has become the kingdom of our Lord and of his Christ." Heaven crowns Jesus, the Prince of providence, as King of kings, "and he will reign for ever and ever." Overjoyed that God's great purpose for our world is at last fulfilled, a heavenly chorus worships God, singing, "We give You thanks, O Lord God Almighty, the One who is and who was and who is to come, because You have taken Your great power and reigned" (Rev. 11:16, 17, NKJV). Jesus not only directs the nations; He continually guides our lives.

DRG

JESUS, BULWARK TO THE REMNANT

And the dragon was wroth with the woman, and went to make war with the remnant of her seed, which keep the commandments of God, and have the testimony of Jesus Christ.

Rev. 12:17.

Prominent in many homes in Singapore is a Buddhist altar. On it smoking incense and burning joss sticks surround food offerings. Fong Lee, who lived in such a home, came to evangelistic meetings I was holding. Convicted by what he heard, he surrendered his heart to Jesus, but he had great problems. His school held classes on Sabbath, and his Buddhist mother said no to his becoming a Christian. When I went to see the school principal, he gave permission for Fong Lee to miss Sabbath classes. The visit with his mother was not as successful. She pleaded, "He is my only son. I dedicated him to my god when he was only a baby. If he becomes a Christian, there will be no one to pray to my ancestors when I die. Please! Please! Don't allow my boy to become a Christian."

Fong Lee decided that he must give his heart to Jesus and follow God's commandments. He explained to his mother that he would become a much better son as a Christian. When she threatened to expel him from home, he stood firm, and later his mother gave in. He and a classmate he won to Christ became faithful members of the Seventh-day Adventist Church.

Because the devil could not destroy the incarnate Christ (Rev. 12:4-6) and could not eradicate the Christian church during the Dark Ages (verses 14-16), he is now angrily attempting to destroy the remnant church of our day (verse 17). But since the remnant church keeps God's commandments and has the testimony of Jesus, in them Satan has met his match.

Jesus is calling us, as His remnant, to fulfill a mission that knows no failure. He promises more than the external advantages of people skills—He is a bulwark to the remnant. Lives washed in the blood of the Lamb, hearts impregnated with the law of God, and minds saturated with the testimony of Jesus assure the remnant of victory. In this hour of destiny for His remnant God challenges us to be power-packed men and women in Christ.

DRG

DECEMBER 15

"I'D RATHER DIE THAN DO WRONG"

Then I looked, and there the Lamb was standing on Mount Zion, and with Him one hundred and forty-four thousand people who had His name and the name of His Father written on their foreheads. . . . These have been redeemed from among men as the first fruits for God and the Lamb, and they have never been known to tell a lie with their lips; they are blameless.

Rev. 14:1-5, Williams.

When he was only 7 years old, Ee Wow Fukazowa lay in his home dying of meningitis. Someone suggested that turtle soup would cure his disease. Ee Wow knew that turtle soup is unclean for food. So when someone brought the soup to him, he sealed his lips and would not eat it. Pleading with him to take it, his loved ones said, "You will die if you don't."

He responded firmly, "I would rather die than do wrong!"

Ee Wow remained faithful like the 144,000. With their Saviour's "name and the name of His Father" fixed firmly in their hearts, they would rather die than do wrong. Their strong, stable inner conviction of being in Christ distinguishes this very select group.

I once said to a fellow Christian, "When the gospel changes a person, the desire for sinful pleasure fades away."

"Yes," he replied, "as Christians we have many other things that make our lives rich and full." Genuine Christianity changes lives from within outward. Christianity is not just a set of propositions—it is a relationship with Christ.

The 144,000 "have been redeemed from among men as the first fruits for God and the Lamb." What could be more thrilling than being translated without tasting death! To all of us living in the last days of earth's history, here is a mighty incentive to aim high. What could be more of a dream than a trip through the star-studded universe with Jesus and the redeemed? An experience awaits the 144,000 that causes the imaginary, legendary tales of the Arabian knights and their flying golden carpets to pale into insignificance. The thought of being translated with the 144,000 challenges us to be among them, for they will have an incomparable experience that none of us will want to miss.

DRG

THE EVERLASTING GOOD NEWS TO THE WORLD

And I saw another angel flying through the heavens, carrying the everlasting Good News to preach to the people who belong to this world—to every nation, tribe, language, and people.

Rev. 14:6, NLT.

In the last generation "every nation, tribe, language, and people" will hear this message. And just as predicted, people around the world are responding to it. The result has been a modern hall of fame filled with outstanding Christians. They are a practical demonstration of outstanding achievement in everyday Christian living through obedient faith—spiritual giants through the indwelling Christ, "on whom our faith depends from start to finish" (Heb. 12:2, NLT).

What enables them to live such outstanding Christian lives? These spiritual giants in Christ have responded to the message of the three angels, "the everlasting Good News to preach to the people who belong to this world." It is not a new gospel, but the "everlasting Good News"—"Christ lives in you, and this is your assurance that you will share in his glory" (Col. 1:27, NLT). The gospel is "the everlasting Good News" about Jesus being carried to all the world.

It sounds the call to "fear God" and "give glory to him"—to reflect His character (Rev. 14:7, NLT). Through their lives of dynamic personal witness all who respond to this message will proclaim the character of God in Christ to the whole world, both in deed and in doctrine.

After the book of Revelation gives the details of the three angels, Jesus cautions: "I will come as unexpectedly as a thief! Blessed are those who are watching for me, who keep their robes ready" (Rev. 16:15, NLT). It is the first time in the book of Revelation that Jesus has spoken since His personal messages to the seven churches in chapters 1 to 3. He doesn't speak again until chapter 22, where He speaks four more times: 1. "Look, I am coming soon! Blessed are those who obey the prophecy (verse 7, NLT). 2. "See, I am coming soon and my reward is with me" (verse 12, NLT). 3. "I, Jesus, have sent my angel to give you this message for the churches" (verse 16, NLT). 4. "Yes, I am coming soon!" (verse 20, NLT). Jesus is at the door. Let's live out the good news about Jesus in our lives and be ready!

DRG

DECEMBER 17

REFLECTING JESUS

"Fear God," he shouted. "Give glory to him. For the time has come when he will sit as judge. Worship him who made heaven and earth, the sea, and all the springs of water."

Rev. 14:7, NLT.

A young boy wandered down the bombed-out main street of his hometown shortly after World War II. Some of the merchants had managed to repair their buildings. The ragged boy felt the attraction of a most delightful smell and headed across the street in its direction. His hungry stomach anticipated what he soon saw as he pressed his nose against the restored window.

A soldier driving by in a Jeep saw the lad. On impulse he pulled to an abrupt stop, walked over, and stood next to the boy. Looking in the window he saw the bakery full of goodies and the baker making doughnuts. Going inside, he bought a dozen doughnuts. As he walked past the boy, he asked, "Would you like to have these?"

"Oh, yes!" was the boy's grateful response.

After handing the boy the sack of doughnuts, the soldier turned and headed for his car. Then he felt a tug on his coat, and looking down, he heard the boy inquire, "Sir, are you God?"

That is just the reaction from us that God expects in these last days of the judgment hour in which we live. It is in our day that the angel shouts to us, "Fear God. . . . Give glory to him." What does the angel mean? How can we reverence God and give glory to Him? A very careful study of the word "glory" throughout the Bible indicates that the nearest equivalent to "glory" in English is "character." The angel is saying, "Reverence God and reveal His character." How do we do this? Like the soldier we display God's character by becoming like Jesus. We resemble the One we glorify.

A missionary described the life and teachings of Jesus to a village deep in the jungle. As he told the people about Jesus, someone spoke up excitedly and said, "Oh, we know him. For a short time he lived here with us." Whoever that Christian was, he gave "glory to God;" he reflected the character of Jesus. Have you responded to the angel's excited shout, "Fear God. . . . Give glory to him"? When people see us, do they see Jesus reflected in our demeanor, our words, our life?

DRG

THE FAITH OF JESUS

Here is the patience of the saints; here are those who keep the commandments of God and the faith of Jesus.

Rev. 14:12, NKJV.

Have you ever admired a strong, stable Christian, marveled at his or her devotion, patience, and faith, and then longed for a similar experience? God has given a special message capable of producing just such a character in modern men and women. Found in Revelation 14:6-20, it addresses people living just before the coming of Jesus. Those who respond to the message, the book of Revelation describes as patient "saints . . . who keep the commandments of God and the faith of Jesus."

Possessed with a deep integrity, they desire above all else to obey God's every wish and command and thus "keep the commandments of God." They "keep . . . the faith of Jesus," the faith Jesus taught, lived, and exemplifies. Such faith controls the hearts of those who seek Jesus during the last days. When Christ ascended into heaven, He promised to be even closer to people through His indwelling presence than when He lived with them. Now through the Holy Spirit, Christ lives continually in the hearts of His children by faith. The love and power of the indwelling Christ shines out to the world through them, and people take "knowledge of them, that they" have "been with Jesus" (Acts 4:13).

Theirs is not a superficial faith in Jesus—they actually possess "the faith of Jesus." It is a faith not of their own making, but a gift of God (Eph. 2:8). Having received and absorbed Christ's faith, they become Christlike. Seeing Christ in His true character and receiving Him into their hearts, they become monuments to the power of an indwelling Christ.

Those who respond to the message of Revelation 14 not only possess "the faith of Jesus," but "keep . . . the faith of Jesus." They not only have the truth, but their belief is correlated with practice. Obedience accompanies their faith. Through Christ's dwelling in them, taking full possession of their lives, flooding their hearts with "the faith of Jesus," they live a life of obedience to God's commandments. Theirs is an experience of obedient living through faith, what victorious Christians designate as righteousness by faith.

DRG

BLESSED ARE THOSE WHO DIE IN JESUS

Then I heard a voice from heaven say, "Write: Blessed are the dead who die in the Lord. . . ." "Yes," says the Spirit, "They will rest from their labor, for their deeds will follow them."

REV. 14:13, NIV.

Robert G. Ingersoll and his brother agreed that on the death of one, the other would deliver the funeral oration. The great agnostic was the survivor. Torn with grief, he stood by his brother's silent form and said: "Life is a narrow vale between the cold and barren peaks of two eternities. We strive in vain to look beyond the heights. We cry aloud—and the only answer is the echo of our wailing cry. From the voiceless lips of the unreplying dead there comes no word. But in the night of Death Hope sees a star and listening Love can hear the rustling of a wing." In his sorrow even the great doubter found light in the Star of Bethlehem and sought refuge under the shadow of His wings.

It is the glory of the Christian faith that Jesus answers the universal questions: Is there anything on the other side of death? Is there life beyond? Will we meet each other again? As Christians we have the promise: "Blessed are the dead who die in the Lord." Nowhere do we find the statement that the living are blessed merely because they are living, but "blessed are the dead who die in the Lord. . . . They will rest from their labor, for their deeds will follow them."

All who have suffered the loss of a loved one can find refuge in this promise. In the hour of sorrow when our heart is desolate, we long with Tennyson "for the touch of a vanished hand, and the sound of a voice that is still!"

When we ourselves face death, these words come with new force: the dead are blessed. That's what it means to have faith in Jesus. We are under His care and blessing throughout life, and at death we are with the blessed dead—if we die in the Lord. As Christians, even in death we have a bright future to look forward to because of what Jesus did for us at the cross and at His empty tomb.

HMSR

THE SONG OF JESUS, THE LAMB

"And they [the redeemed] sing the song of Moses, the servant of God, and the song of the Lamb, saying: "Great and marvelous are Your works, Lord God Almighty!"
Rev. 15:3, NKJV.

Our group had flown from Cairo, Egypt, 450 miles up the River Nile and landed near the little town of Luxor. We crossed the Nile by boat to the west bank and made our way to the lonely Valley of the Kings. Rocky hills surround the valley, their dramatic shapes looming up against the blue sky. No river runs through this valley. Without trees or bushes, its stiflingly hot landscape is as barren as a crater on the moon.

I had read about the Valley of the Kings, where the great pharaohs were buried. Now I would see the tombs of pharaohs from the time of Moses. The entrances to the many tombs hollowed out of the mountain pockmark the valley. Some are at the end of galleries hundreds of feet long, hewn out of the rock, that lead past chamber after chamber. The last chamber opens onto the "golden hall" where the body of the pharaoh once lay, enclosed in a golden coffin.

The story of Moses and the deliverance of Israel under his leadership filled my thoughts. God called Moses to rescue His people from slavery in the land of the pharaohs and lead them into the Promised Land (Ex.3:5-10). Years later, in the final months of his life just before Israel crossed over Jordan into Canaan, Moses informed Israel: "The Lord your God will raise up for you a Prophet like me from your midst" (Deut. 18:15, NKJV). In rescuing Israel from Egypt, Moses became a type of Christ.

Salvation is really a rescue operation, isn't it? The Holy Scriptures paint a thrilling picture of dramatic rescue, with a conquering Hero coming in at the right time to save the hopeless prisoners. Moses devoted 40 years to delivering Israel from slavery in Egypt and leading them into the presence of God. Jesus, the Lamb of God, gave His life to redeem us from slavery in the Egypt of sin and usher us into God's presence. Let us respond and be among the redeemed who "sing the song of Moses . . . and the song of the Lamb."

HMSR

DECEMBER 21

JESUS, THE VICTORIOUS LAMB-KING

They will make war against the Lamb, but the Lamb will overcome them because he is Lord of lords and King of kings—and with him will be his called, chosen and faithful followers.

Rev. 17:14, NIV.

Satan began his war against the coming Lamb of God in the Garden of Eden. He vowed to stop the coming Messiah by destroying Eve's offspring. Finally he sought to overcome Jesus, the Seed of the woman, by attempting to persuade Jesus to sin in the wilderness. When that failed, Satan incited the religious leaders of His day to crucify Him at Calvary.

The devil aims not only to eradicate Jesus, but also His faithful followers. Generally Satan works through human powers. But in the last days just before Jesus comes, we will experience Satan's greatest delusion. "Satan himself masquerades as an angel of light" (2 Cor. 11:14, NIV). He will make war on the Lamb of God by appearing as Jesus who has returned to earth a second time. To counterfeit the coming of Christ, Satan will make himself into a being of dazzling glory, surpassing anything that mortal eyes have ever seen.

Imagine the effect of this on the world! Skeptics, atheists, people of all religions and no religion, will surrender to his delusion. Speaking softly, the devil will lift up his hands in blessing as Jesus did and repeat truths that Christ presented when He was on earth. "This is the strong, almost overmastering delusion. . . . But the people of God will not be misled" (*The Great Controversy,* pp. 624, 625). But those who at this time trust in Jesus will be victorious. "The Lamb will overcome" Satan and his angels, "because he is Lord of lords and King of kings—and with him will be his called, chosen and faithful followers."

Are you among the "chosen and faithful followers" of the Lamb who are anticipating the return of Jesus, the Lamb who will be crowned King of kings?

HMSR

MY GROWN-UP CHRISTMAS LIST

Surely I come quickly. Amen. Even so, come, Lord Jesus.

Rev. 22:20.

When I was 10, an electric train headed my Christmas list. (Now, more than 60 years later, I still have the engine on the top shelf of my closet.) Another year an erector set stood at the top of the list. (When I tried to purchase one as a Christmas gift for a nephew, I found to my surprise that they don't make them anymore.)

My grown-up Christmas list is more like the one in the song of that name. I ask (1) that no more lives be torn apart; (2) that wars will never start; (3) that time will heal hearts; (4) that all will have a friend; (5) that right will always win; and (6) that love will never end.

The birth of Jesus in a stable in Bethlehem has made it possible for my grown-up Christmas list to become a reality. Jesus was a gift that changed our world. When Cain, the first child, was born, Eve exclaimed, "I have gotten a man from the Lord" (Gen. 4:1). She hoped her son would be the Child God had promised who would eliminate Satan and sin from our world—and the universe (Gen. 3:15). I'm sure that at the top of every wish list by every dedicated Jewish mother was the hope that her newborn would be the Messiah—Immanuel, God with us!

God came to our world as a baby. He lived a matchless life among us, and finally died for your sins and my sins and the sins of the entire world. Jesus made possible the transformation of our world and our lives. Now as I reflect on how this once helpless Babe has changed the world, my Christmas list is more mature, more in tune with the needs of today's world.

The grown-up list of every Christian should include the six items in the song "My Grown-up Christmas List." But at the top of that list I would add a seventh item: Jesus' return to transform us and the world about us permanently. So let us give thanks for Jesus' promise "Surely I come quickly."

Is the fulfillment of that promise at the top of your Christmas list this year? It is? Then shout and sing: "Amen. Even so, come, Lord Jesus."

DRG

JESUS BECAME ONE OF US

> *The Word became flesh and made his dwelling among us. We have seen his glory, the glory of the One and Only, who came from the Father, full of grace and truth.*
>
> *John 1:14, NIV.*

The most impressive card we received one Christmas had no picture on the front, but it did have this message in decorative lettering: "The Word did not become a philosophy, a theory, or a concept to be discussed, debated, or pondered. But the Word became a person to be followed, enjoyed, and loved." John, who lived with Jesus, "the Word," for three years, concurs: "The Word was with God, and the Word was God. . . . The Word became flesh and made his dwelling among us" (John 1:1-14, NIV).

In "the Word" we discover the true meaning of Christmas: giving! God gave Himself to us by becoming "flesh," a person like us. Jesus left heaven to join our corrupt world and rescue us from sin, degradation, and eternal death. God became flesh! Mary conceived and "gave birth to a son" (Matt. 1:25, NIV). He was no ordinary son. He is "Immanuel," God with us! (Isa. 7:14, NIV), "a Savior . . . ; he is Christ the Lord" (Luke 2:11, NIV).

Jesus, the eternal God, lived with us as a human being. He experienced the very things we go through. As a boy He had siblings to contend with. Then as a man He worked as a carpenter with sweat pouring from His forehead and knots in His aching muscles. After His call to the ministry, He returned to His hometown because He had a burden for His neighbors and friends. But they didn't appreciate His message, dragged Him to a cliff outside Nazareth, and attempted to throw Him over it and kill Him.

Jesus met the same temptations we struggle with, only with far more intensity. He was hungry, thirsty, and tempted by Satan to be somebody, to get ahead in life. Christ went through the trauma of having one of His best friends die. At the graveside "Jesus wept" (John 11:35, NIV). Suffering moved Him deeply, just as it does us.

But we must never forget that the human Christ was God with us, "a Savior." That is the "good tidings of great joy" message of Christmas (Luke 2:10). Immanuel is born! He can change people's hearts, raise the dead, and save us from eternal destruction. But to do so cost Him His life. We must always look at Bethlehem in the light of Calvary, and the hope that both the manger and the cross give us.

DRG

OUR GREATEST GIFT TO JESUS

Now when Jesus was born in Bethlehem . . . there came wise men from the east. . . . And when they were come into the house, they saw the young child with Mary his mother, and fell down, and worshipped him: and when they had opened their treasures, they presented unto him gifts; gold, and frankincense, and myrrh.
Matt. 2:1, 11.

On the day before Christmas a father baby-sat his four children. To him baby-sitting meant reading the paper while his children cluttered up the house. He was in his study reading the Christmas ads when a tap on the door brought an invitation to see a play. He followed his 10-year-old into the living room.

At the foot of the piano stool a lighted flashlight wrapped in swaddling clothes lay in a shoe box. The father recognized Joseph, who, dressed in his bathrobe and carrying a mop handle, took his place with Mary by the shoe box. Next his smallest daughter came in at a full run. She had pillowcases draped over both her arms. Spreading them wide, she announced, "I am an angel."

Then little Ann entered. The father knew she was a wise man, for she moved in her mother's high heels as though she were riding a camel. On a pillow she carried three items. Undoubtedly they represented gold, frankincense, and myrrh. Undulating majestically across the room, she bowed to the flashlight and then to Mary, to Joseph, to the angel, and last to her father. Then she said, "I'm all three Wise Men. I bring gold, circumstance, and mud." And that was the play.

Let us today bring our offering to Jesus—our love, our faith, our obedience. Not gold, circumstance, and mud, but a yielding heart. During this season the greatest gift we can present Jesus is ourselves. No matter how insignificant our lives, it's the pure intention and the act of faith that please Him.

But greater than any gift that we can bring to God is the one He has presented to us—His righteous life and His death for our sins. In His sight we are exceedingly valuable. In fact, by giving us His righteousness, He makes us "more precious than fine gold" (Isa. 13:12). He made this gift when He left the matchless splendor of heaven and was born that day in Bethlehem. So let us bow down on this eve of Christmas and worship Him!

HMSR

GOD'S GREATEST GIFT

The angel reassured [the shepherds]. "Don't be afraid!" he said. "I bring you the most joyful news ever announced, and it is for everyone! The Savior—yes, the Messiah, the Lord—has been born tonight in Bethlehem."

LUKE 2:10, 11, TLB.

Jesus came to our world not to bring evergreen trees or mistletoe or strings of colored lights, but salvation to sinners, healing for the distressed, and life for the dead. At Jesus' birth an angel announced: "The Savior . . . has been born tonight in Bethlehem." Many witnesses validated His first advent. To the shepherds of Bethlehem the angel proclaimed "the most joyful news ever announced." The Wise Men of the East were there, and Mary and Joseph, and Anna and Simeon, who miraculously learned of Jesus' arrival. Christ proclaimed to all that He is heaven's gift to our world. It was a gift wrapped not in silver or gold paper, but "in swaddling clothes, lying in a manger" (Luke 2:12).

The magnitude of the meaning and the glory of Bethlehem escapes words. It involved the whole universe, yet its events took place in a lowly cattle shed on our planet—just a speck in the great universe. The wonder was not so much that a child was born of a virgin—though that was humanly impossible—but that a human being gave birth to God. Through Mary, God's quickening Spirit became flesh; the One whom the heaven of heavens could not contain was imprisoned in a body of clay. Jesus was "the seed of the woman" for whom Eve had so hopefully looked. He was the fulfillment of prophecies proclaimed by holy people since the entrance of sin at Eden. The "seed of Abraham," He would bless all families of the earth. The royal "seed of David," He would sit on David's throne forever.

Because of God's great love, He gave us Jesus. Ours forever, He came as a Child born to us, as a Son given to us, and yet His name is "the mighty God, the everlasting Father, the Prince of Peace" (Isa. 9:6). Who can deny that this was the most wonderful event in the world's history—God's greatest gift to humanity? He entered the world to get near to us and to show us God's love and to give us eternal life.

HMSR

THE WEDDING SUPPER OF THE LAMB

Blessed are those who are invited to the wedding supper of the Lamb!
REV. 19:9, NIV.

God invites not only His friends but His enemies, those who have been in rebellion against Him. But no sooner does the invitation go out than the excuses begin to pour in.

Jesus, the greatest storyteller who ever lived, told of an invitation to a great supper. Those invited "all alike began to make excuses" for not accepting the invitation (Luke 14:18, NIV). The first man said that he had purchased a piece of land and wanted to see it (verse 18). Since he had already bought the land, he couldn't change that by looking at it now. Because he didn't want to go to the feast, he made up an excuse. The second man had bought a yoke of oxen and decided to test them (verse 19). Why hadn't he done so before he purchased them? The third man gave the excuse that he had married a wife (verse 20). But who likes to go to a feast or banquet more than a young bride with her new husband?

Jesus the Lamb—God's only Son—has invited all of us to a royal wedding feast, "the wedding supper of the Lamb!" The gospel invitation is good news for all the world, but millions, incredibly, have rejected it just as did the three men in Jesus' story. If the invitation had involved a funeral or even a lecture, we might understand their excuses. But they were to go to a feast. God repeatedly extends the gospel invitation, but if there is no response, He must finally say, "Yes, you may be excused. You need not attend the marriage supper." How tragic!

Christians sometimes become absorbed in material things, even good things such as marriage and a home. As a result we neglect to get ready for the wedding supper of the Lamb. Blessed, happy is the Christian who accepts Jesus' white robe of righteousness and attends the wedding supper as the bride of the Lamb.

Is being at that wedding supper a priority in your life?

HMSR

DECEMBER 27

JESUS' WONDER WORLD OF TOMORROW

And God shall wipe away all tears from their eyes; and there shall be no more death, neither sorrow, nor crying, neither shall there be any more pain: for the former things are passed away.
REV. 21:4.

Years ago at a prayer meeting Henry de Fluiter, the author and composer of many beautiful gospel songs, described the glories of heaven. After his talk a woman whose baby had died a few weeks previous said, "Oh, Uncle Henry, tonight you have made me homesick for heaven!"

Into de Fluiter's mind flashed the inspiration for a song. We were holding evangelistic meetings together at the time. I remember well the night he introduced the song for the first time. Its heartfelt appeal made it an immediate success. After hearing the story that inspired the song, the congregation sang with fervor:

So dear to my heart is the promise of God,
A home with the pure and blest;
Where earth-weary pilgrims, strangers here below,
Will find their eternal rest.
I'm homesick for heaven, seems I cannot wait,
Yearning to enter Zion's pearly gate;
There never a heartache, never a care,
I long for my home over there.

Are you longing to live forever in that heavenly home with Jesus? "The Spirit and the bride say, Come. And let him that heareth say, Come. And let him that is athirst come. And whosoever will, let him take of the water of life freely" (Rev. 22:17). That "whosoever" includes you and me! Since Jesus loved us enough to prepare a home for us in the new earth, the very least we can do is love Him enough to accept a place there. It seems unthinkable that anyone would ever reject the offer of a place in Jesus' wonder world of tomorrow. Suppose such a place existed in our present world. We would make a dash to get there. Make a rush for heaven—do it now!

DRG

CITY OF DREAMS

> *Come hither, I will shew thee the bride, the Lamb's wife. And he . . . shewed me that great city, the holy Jerusalem, descending out of heaven from God.*
>
> *Rev. 21:9, 10.*

On my first visit to Siem Reap in Cambodia I hired a cyclo, a two-wheeled open-air conveyance pulled by a motorcycle, and traveled through the dense jungle. Suddenly, emerging from the jungle, I saw before me the ruins of ancient Angkor Wat, cradle of Cambodian civilization 1,000 years ago. Awestruck by the massive temple, its towers reflected in the moat surrounding it, I crossed the causeway leading to the ruins. As I walked through the temple, bas-reliefs depicting ancient subjects of the Khmer Empire stared at me from all directions.

Climbing to the highest possible point and looking out over the grounds below, I imagined the scenes taking place pictured in the bas-reliefs: King Suryavarman II, the god-king, sitting on his portable throne shaded by ruffled umbrellas, being entertained by a harem of dancing maidens; or sitting on his royal white elephant, parading with troops ready to go forth to battle on elephant back or horse-drawn chariots. As I scanned the landscape surrounding the temple, my mind's eye pictured a royal city of a million inhabitants with houses for kings and nobles, sumptuous furnishings, and richly woven textiles. But the glory of this empire has faded. The Khmer race mysteriously disappeared and with it its proud civilization. Only the sandstone temples remain.

While standing there I thought of another empire whose glories will never fade and of a Lamb-King who will reign throughout eternity. Soon "shall the God of heaven set up a kingdom, which shall never be destroyed" (Dan. 2:44). This empire will have the New Jerusalem as its capital. John saw the "great city, the holy Jerusalem, descending out of heaven." Within it will be the "throne of God and of the Lamb" (Rev. 22:1). It will have no need of a temple, "for the Lord God Almighty and the Lamb are the temple of it" (Rev. 21:22). As for the subjects of that empire, "God shall wipe away all tears from their eyes; and there shall be no more death, neither sorrow, nor crying, neither shall there be any more pain" (verse 4). What a place to be! Are you looking forward to being there?

DRG

DECEMBER 29

ONE GLIMPSE OF JESUS' FACE

Then the angel showed me the river of the water of life, as clear as crystal, flowing from the throne of God and of the Lamb down the middle of the great street of the city. On each side of the river stood the tree of life, bearing twelve crops of fruit, yielding its fruit every month. And the leaves of the tree are for the healing of the nations. No longer will there be any curse. The throne of God and of the Lamb shall be in the city, and his servants will serve him. They will see his face, and his name will be on their foreheads.

REV. 22:1-4, NIV.

On the TV news program *Prime Time Live,* host Diane Sawyer, during an interview with Julia Roberts, asked her: "If you were designing heaven, what would you put in it?"

Roberts responded, "What a great question!" Then she described the kind of heaven she visualized—a place of all fun and games. What kind of heaven would you design? The breathtaking wonders that await us infinitely surpass fun and games.

Think of standing before the very throne of the Most High. Imagine drinking crystal-clear water from the river of life or each month eating one of the 12 kinds of fruit from the tree of life. The thought of heavenly music stirs us. Forever and ever we would serve the God of the universe. Home at last, we would sit at the feet of Jesus!

Loving ecstasy will fill the souls of the saved as they view the Lamb and look into His face. Words can never describe, human hands can never portray, the matchless qualities of Jesus' face. To behold Him will be an experience of breath-taking wonder. D. L. Moody, sensing this high privilege, said, "I am going to spend the first one thousand years in heaven looking at the face of Jesus."

Face to face with Christ my Saviour,
Face to face, what will it be,
When with rapture I behold Him,
Jesus Christ, who died for me?
–Mrs. Frank A. Breck

The treasures of earth will grow dim with just one glimpse at Jesus' face. What fantastic good news! I want to be there with Him, and I'm sure that you do too.

DRG

MUCH MORE GOOD NEWS!

The mighty oceans thunder your praise. You are mightier than all the breakers pounding on the seashores of the world!

Ps. 93:3, 4, TLB.

We have only skirted the edges of the good news about Jesus. It is as inexhaustible as the ocean waves that thunder out His praise. Because His character is love, He is "mightier than all the breakers pounding on the seashores of the world!" We will be thrilled with new insights about God's good news throughout eternity.

But think of sitting down with the Son of man in heaven and having Him unfold to you salvation's deeper meanings.

Consider, for example, Jesus' atoning death on the cross. "The revelation of God's love to men centers in the cross. Its full significance tongue cannot utter; pen cannot portray; the mind of man cannot comprehend" (*Testimonies for the Church,* vol. 8, p. 287). "We must look in living faith upon the cross, and thus begin the study which shall be the science and the song of the redeemed through all eternity" (*Messages to Young People,* p. 115).

What about God's plan for saving the people He created? "The plan of redemption will not be fully understood, even when the ransomed see as they are seen and know as they are known; but through the eternal ages new truth will continually unfold to the wondering and delighted mind" (*The Great Controversy,* p. 651).

Or turn to the mystery of "Christ in you" (Col. 1:27, NIV). "In the plan of redemption there are heights and depths that eternity itself can never exhaust, marvels into which the angels desire to look" (*Education,* p. 308).

These and hundreds of other questions about Jesus will receive satisfying answers as we delve into the meaning of life, sin, salvation, and the gift of eternal life. What could be more thrilling than looking into the mind and heart of God to find revelations of a love that motivated God to leave heaven and come to our world to die for us? Incredible as it may seem, we have only scratched the surface of the good news about Jesus. Its echoes will fill our hearts throughout eternity. So thunder "mighty oceans, thunder [out His] praise"!

DRG

NEW BEGINNINGS

> *If anyone is in Christ, he is a new creation; old things have passed away; behold, all things have become new.*
> 2 COR. 5:17, NKJV.

Beginning tomorrow, we will once more be saying, "Happy New Year!" Is it possible to have a happy new year? Can we really have a new 2003, or will it merely be the old year with a different number? Will it be a carbon copy of the past year and the year before that and the year even before that? Really, what's new? We still have the same old debts, the same problems, the same job, the same world, the same people, and the same old me! What can make this new year any different from the last? By having Jesus displace you as the Master of your life! "In Christ . . . old things have passed away; . . . all things have become new."

Let me share four new beginnings with you. First, Christ makes religion new because He makes people new. When we come to Jesus in full surrender, the eternally "new" pervades our being and remakes our spirit. As we live with Christ every day, we receive new understandings of His goodness and love, new insights into what He means to us and what it means to live for Him.

Second, Christ makes our social relationships new. When Jesus transforms us into new creatures, we see the people about us in a different way. We regard them not as competitors whom we must conquer, but sons and daughters of God whom we can love and win to Christ.

Third, Christ transforms our family relationships. It's utterly fantastic what Jesus can do in a home when Mom and Dad give Jesus first place in their hearts. The children can certainly see the difference when Jesus leads the family.

Fourth, Christ alters our business relationships. He enables us to be open and honest in all our transactions.

I can remember in the fifth grade having a difficult time seeing the blackboard. It affected not only my grades but also my relationships with other students. Then I was fitted for glasses. Everything looked so clear, so distinct. I didn't know the world was so beautiful, that people looked so nice. The only difference was that I was wearing lenses that brought things into focus. This is how Christ makes things new—He helps us see things in proper focus. So with confidence in Christ let's make 2003 a year of new beginnings!

HMSR